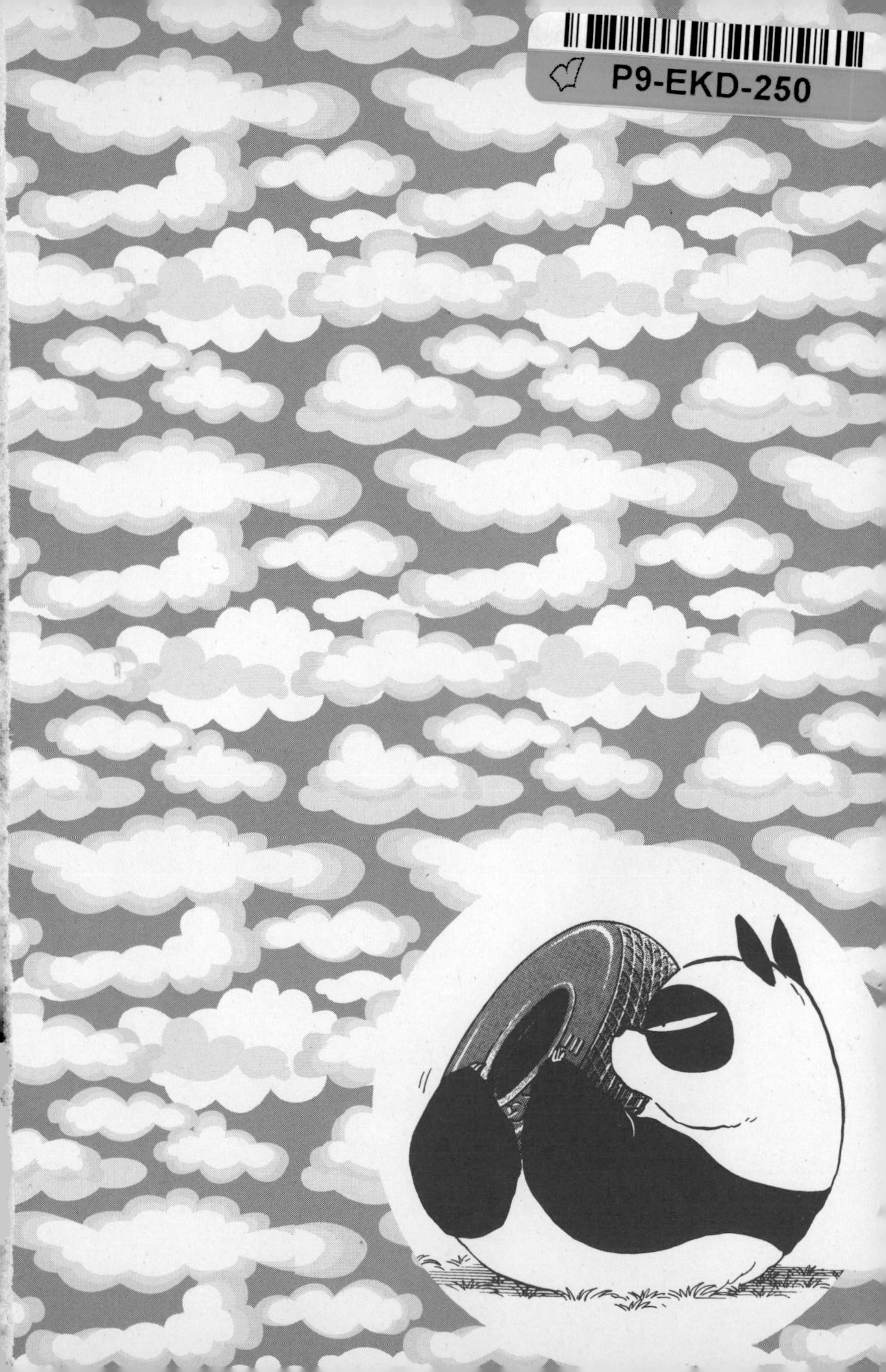

Ranma 1/2™

VOL. 4

Action Edition

STORY & ART BY

RUMIKO TAKAHASHI

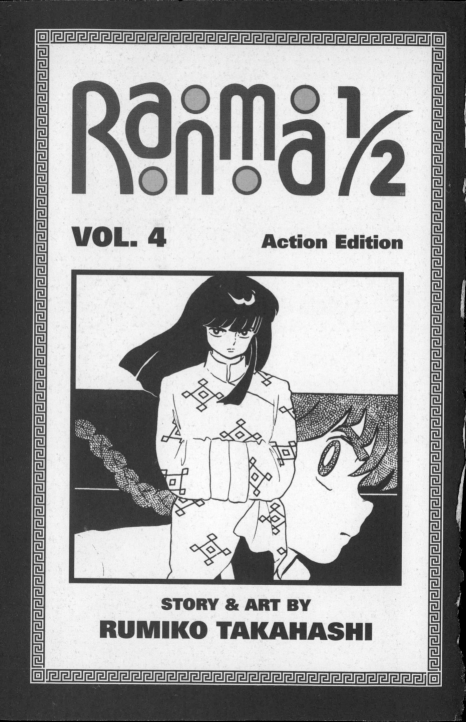

RANMA 1/2

VOL. 4
Action Edition

Story and Art by
RUMIKO TAKAHASHI

English Adaptation/Gerard Jones and Matt Thorn
Touch-Up Art & Lettering/Wayne Truman
Cover Design/Hidemi Sahara
Graphics & Design/Sean Lee
Editors (1st Edition)/Satoru Fujii and Trish Ledoux
Editor (Action Edition)/Julie Davis

Managing Editor/Annette Roman
Dir. of Licensing & Acquisitions/Rika Inouye
VP of Sales & Marketing/Liza Coppola
Sr. VP of Editorial/Hyoe Narita
Publisher/Seiji Horibuchi

RANMA 1/2 is rated "T+" for Older Teens. It may contain violence, language, alcohol or tobacco use, or suggestive situations.

Printed in Canada.

Published by VIZ, LLC
P.O. Box 77010
San Francisco, CA 94107

1st Edition published 1995

Action Edition
10 9 8 7 6 5 4 3 2
First printing, August 2003
Second printing, July 2004

VIZ

www.viz.com

store.viz.com

STORY THUS FAR

The Tendos are an average, run-of-the-mill Japanese family—at least on the surface, that is. Soun Tendo is the owner and proprietor of the Tendo Dojo, where "Anything-Goes Martial Arts" is practiced. Like the name says, anything goes, and usually does.

When Soun's old friend Genma Saotome comes to visit, Soun's three lovely young daughters—Akane, Nabiki, and Kasumi—are told that it's time for one of them to become the fiancée of Genma's teenage son, as per an agreement made between the two fathers years ago. Youngest daughter Akane—who says she hates boys—is quickly nominated for bridal duty by her sisters.

Unfortunately, Ranma and his father have suffered a strange accident. While training in China, both plunged into one of many "accursed" springs at the legendary martial arts training ground of Jusenkyo. These springs transform the unlucky dunkee into whoever—or whatever—drowned there hundreds of years ago.

From now on, a splash of cold water turns Ranma's father into a giant panda, and Ranma becomes a beautiful, busty young woman. Hot water reverses the effect...but only until next time.

Ranma and Genma weren't the only ones to take the Jusenkyo plunge—it isn't long before they meet several other members of the "cursed." And although their parents are still determined to see Ranma and Akane marry and carry on the training hall, Ranma seems to have a strange talent for accumulating extra fiancées, and Akane has a few suitors of her own. Will the two ever work out their differences, get rid of all these extra people, or just call the whole thing off? And will Ranma ever get rid of his curse?

CAST OF CHARACTERS

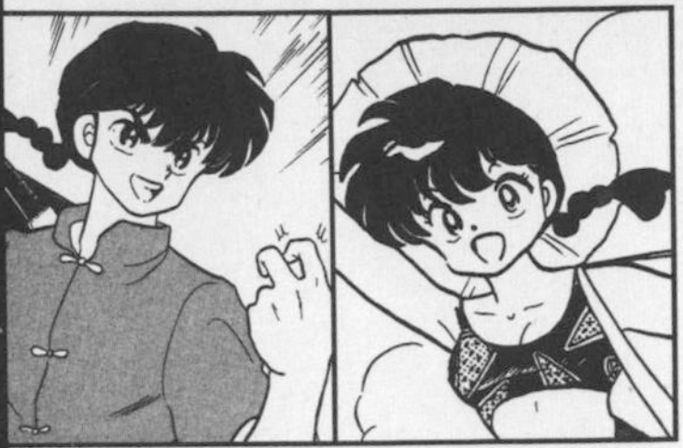

RANMA SAOTOME
Martial artist with far too many finacées, and an ego that won't let him take defeat easily. He changes into a girl when splashed with cold water.

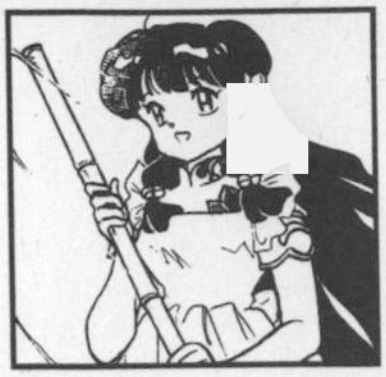

SHAMPOO
A Chinese Amazon warrior who has changed her mind from wanting to kill Ranma to wanting to marry him.

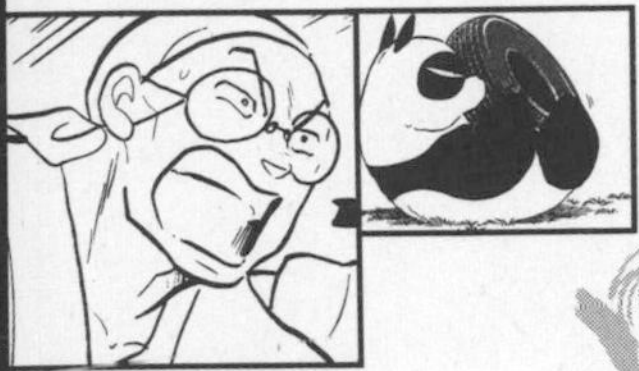

GENMA SAOTOME
Ranma's lazy father, who left his home and wife years ago with his young son to train in the martial arts. He changes into a panda.

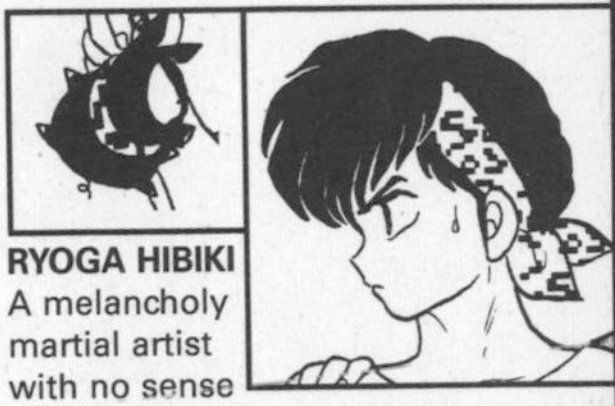

RYOGA HIBIKI
A melancholy martial artist with no sense of direction, a crush on Akane, and a grudge against Ranma. He changes into a small, black pig Akane calls "P-chan."

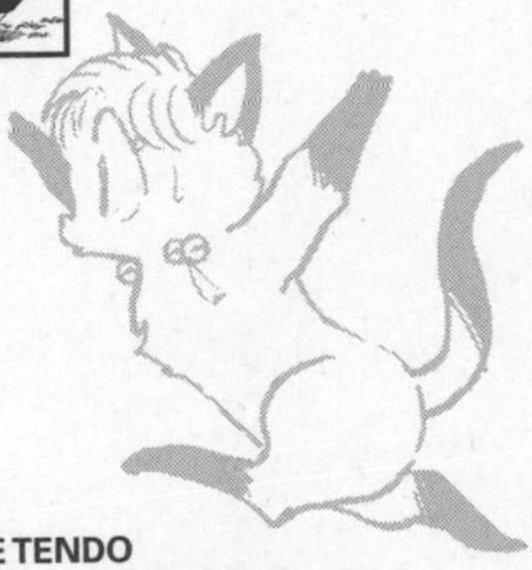

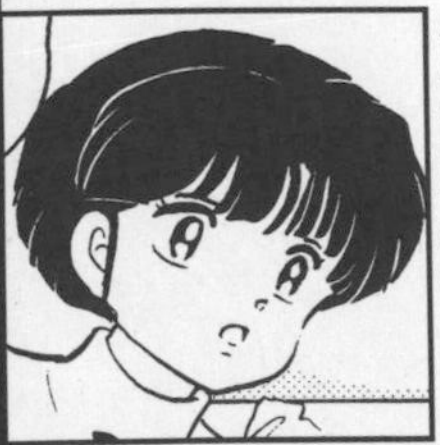

AKANE TENDO
A martial artist, tomboy, and Ranma's fiancée by parental arrangement. She has no clue how much Ryoga likes her, or what relation he has to her pet black pig, P-chan.

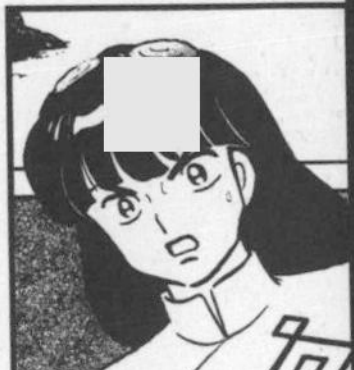

MOUSSE
A nearsighted martial artist and Shampoo's childhood suitor, Mousse's specialty is the art of hidden weapons.

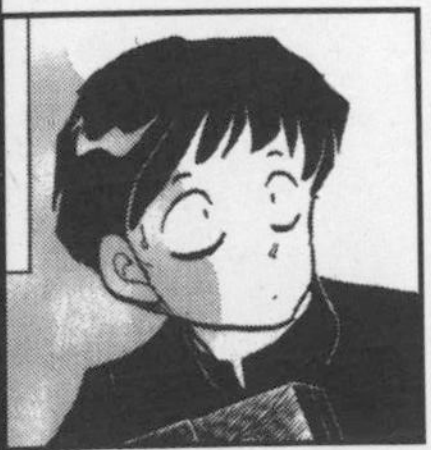

GOSUNKGUI
A spooky young man with a crush on Akane...and who hates Ranma.

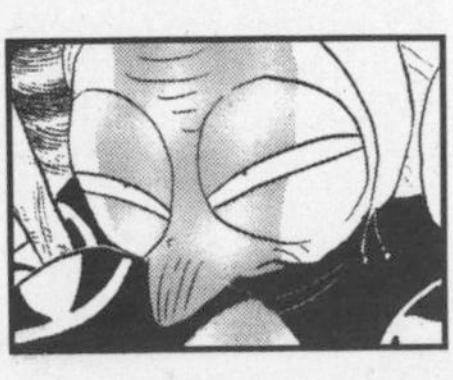

COLOGNE
Shampoo's great-grandmother, a martial artist and matchmaker.

CONTENTS

Part 1

LOOKING FOR A WEAK SPOT

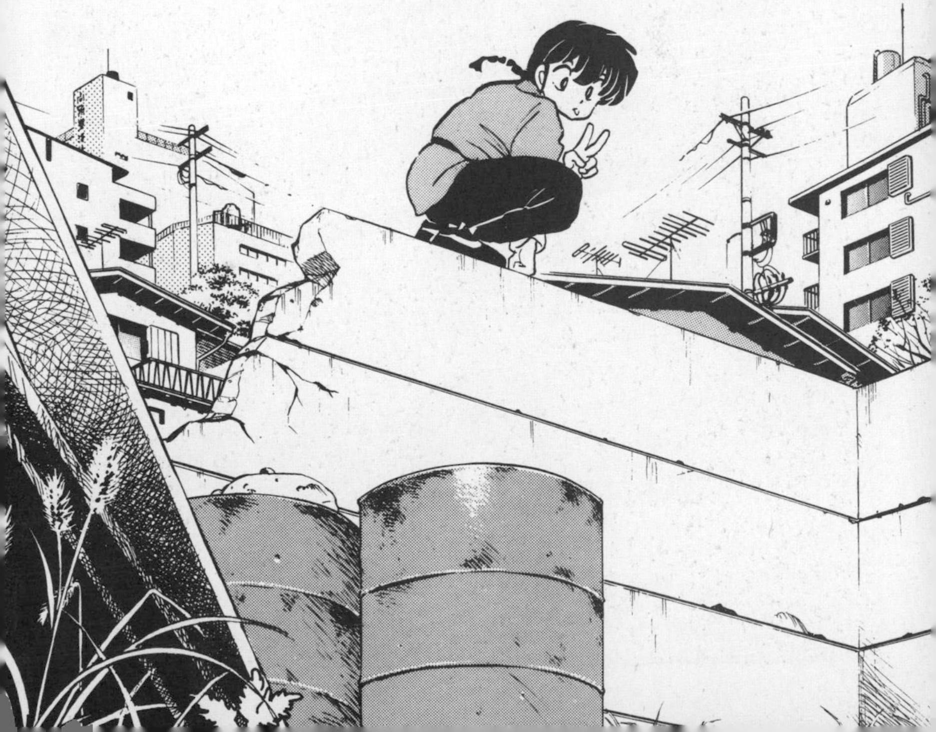

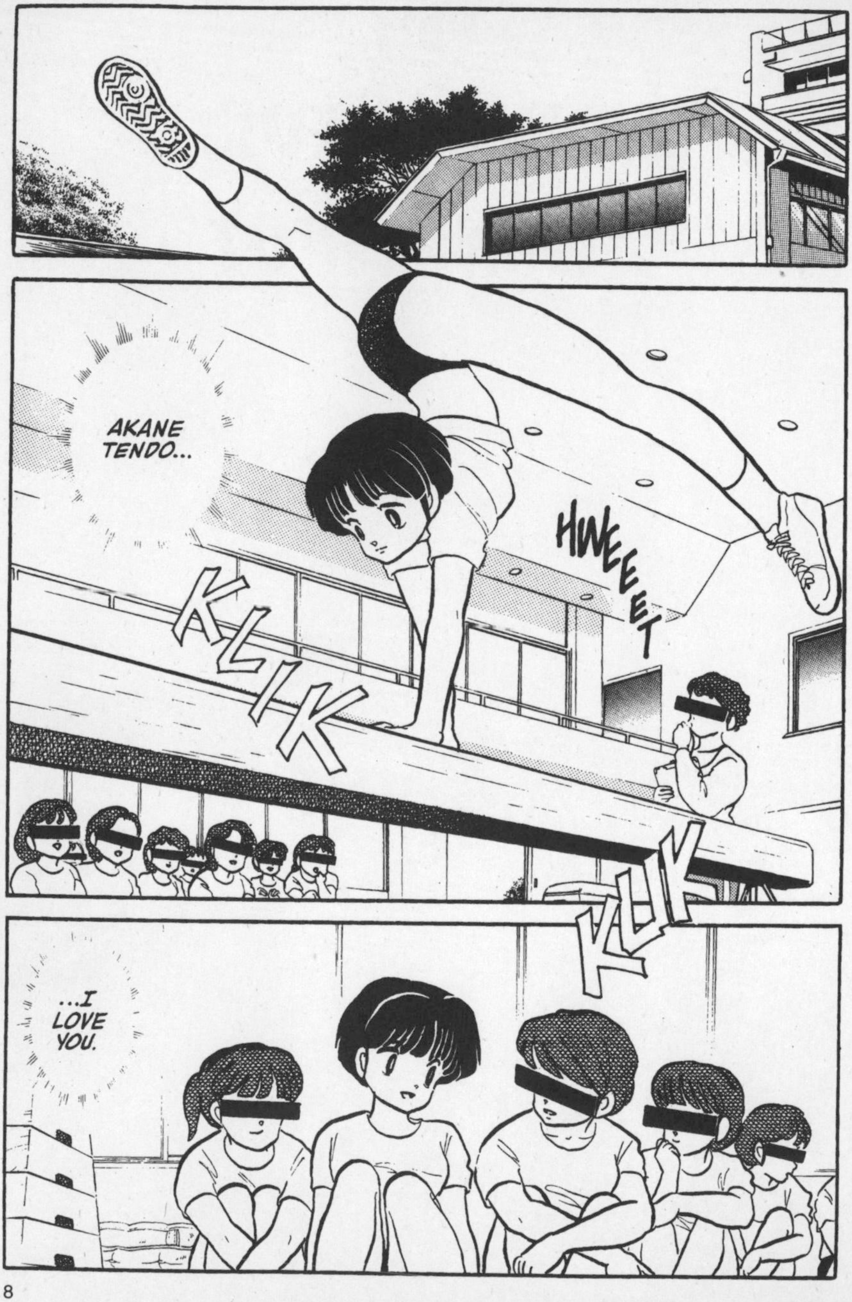
AKANE TENDO...
KLIK
HWEEEET
KLIK
...I LOVE YOU.

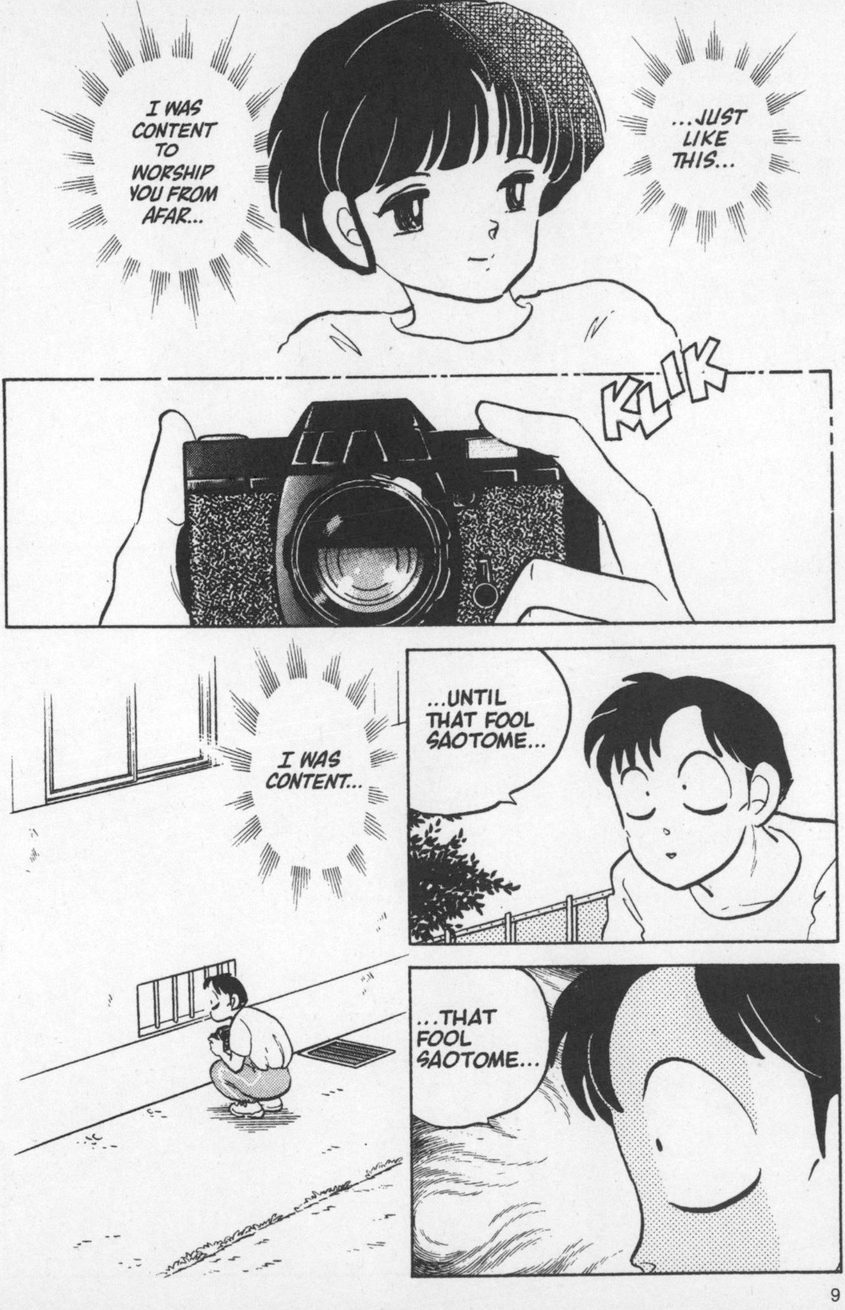
I WAS CONTENT TO WORSHIP YOU FROM AFAR...
...JUST LIKE THIS...
KLIK
I WAS CONTENT...
...UNTIL THAT FOOL SAOTOME...
...THAT FOOL SAOTOME...

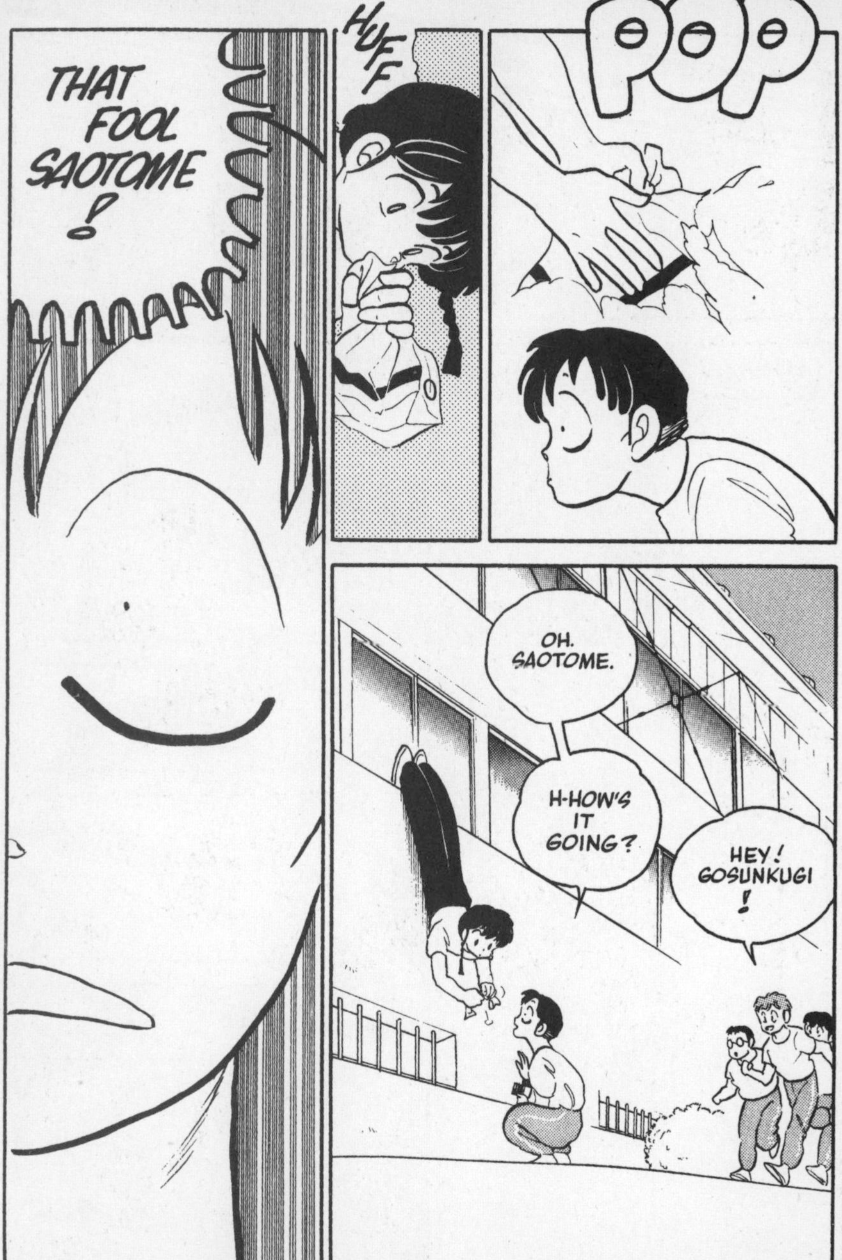
THAT FOOL SAOTOME!
HUFF
POP
OH. SAOTOME.
H-HOW'S IT GOING?
HEY! GOSUNKUGI!

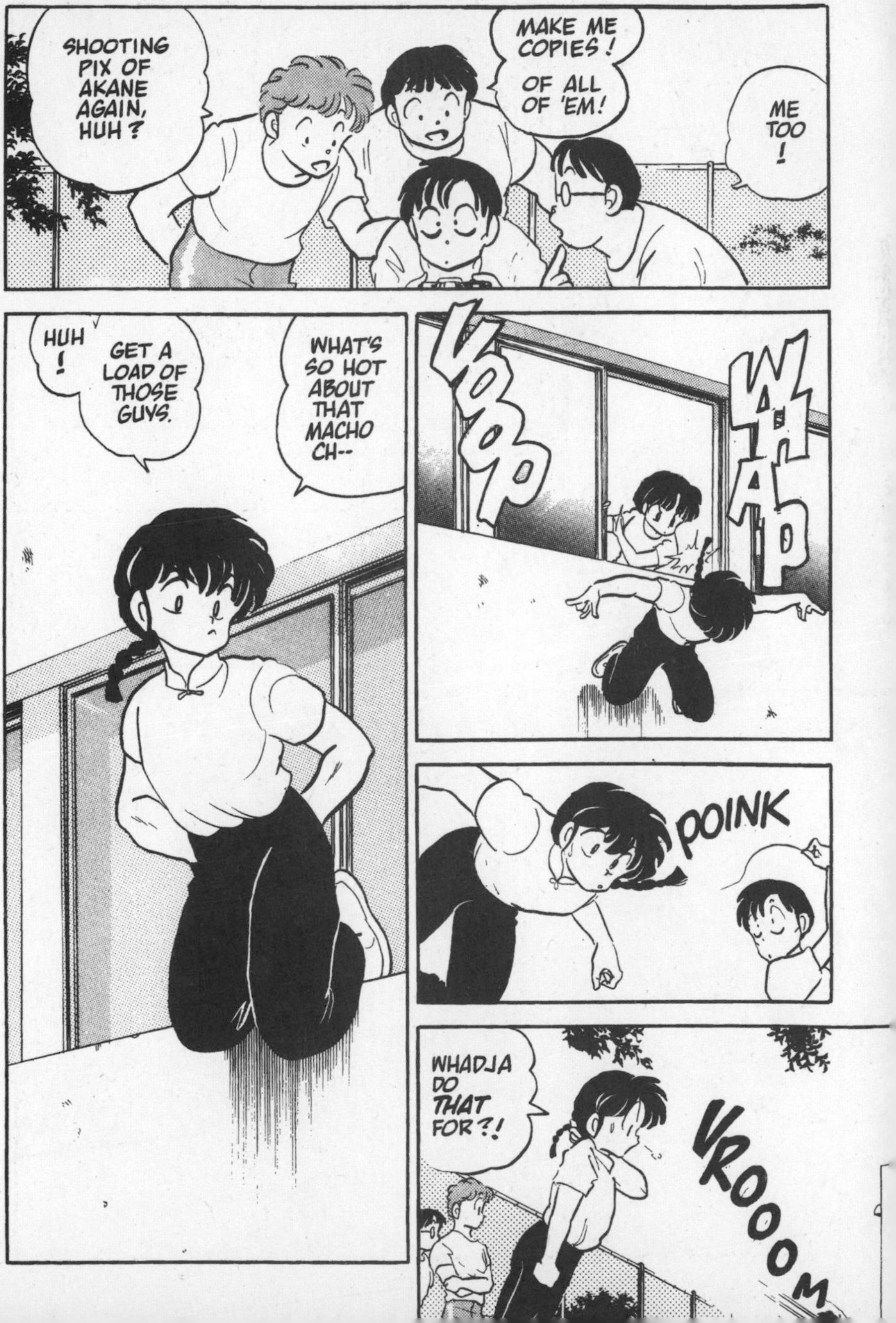
SHOOTING PIX OF AKANE AGAIN, HUH ?
MAKE ME COPIES ! OF ALL OF 'EM!
ME TOO !
HUH !
GET A LOAD OF THOSE GUYS.
WHAT'S SO HOT ABOUT THAT MACHO CH--
VOOOP
WAP
POINK
WHADJA DO THAT FOR ?!
VROOOOM

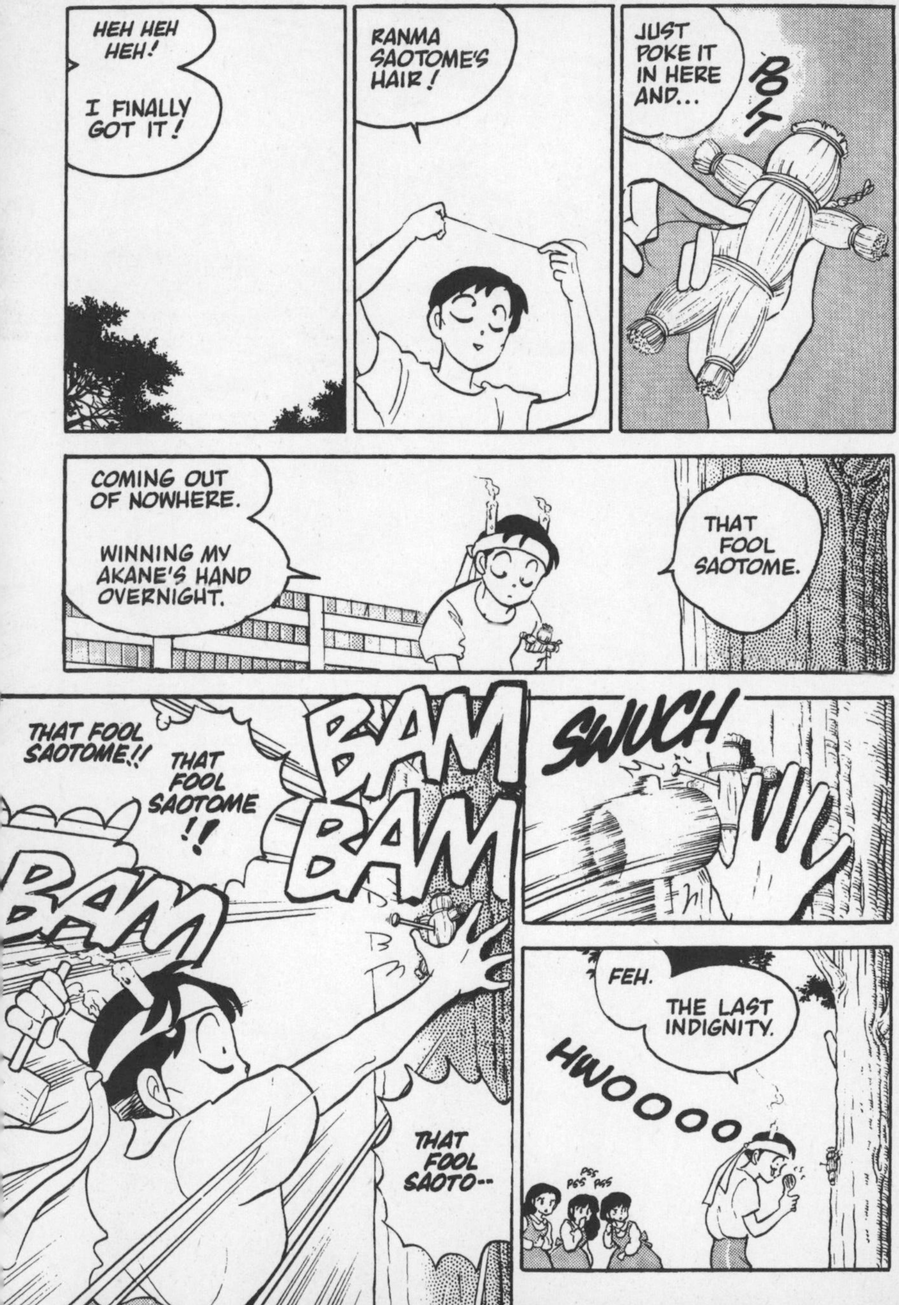
HEH HEH HEH!
I FINALLY GOT IT!
RANMA SAOTOME'S HAIR!
JUST POKE IT IN HERE AND...
POIT
COMING OUT OF NOWHERE.
WINNING MY AKANE'S HAND OVERNIGHT.
THAT FOOL SAOTOME.
THAT FOOL SAOTOME!!
THAT FOOL SAOTOME !!
BAM BAM
BAM
THAT FOOL SAOTO--
SWUCH
FEH.
THE LAST INDIGNITY.
HWOOOOO
PSS PSS PSS

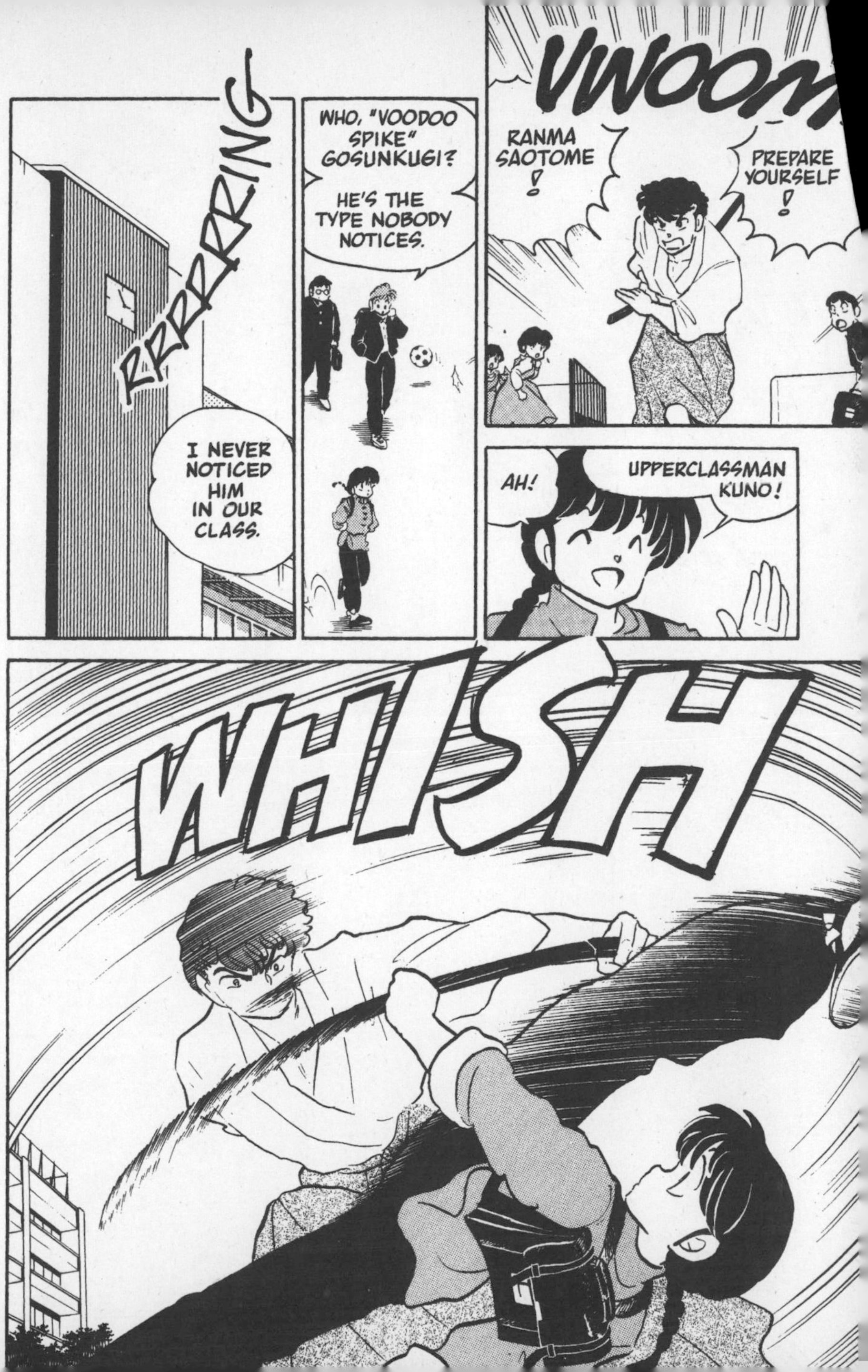
RRRRRRING
I NEVER NOTICED HIM IN OUR CLASS.
WHO, "VOODOO SPIKE" GOSUNKUGI?
HE'S THE TYPE NOBODY NOTICES.
VWOOM
RANMA SAOTOME!
PREPARE YOURSELF!
AH!
UPPERCLASSMAN KUNO!
WHISH

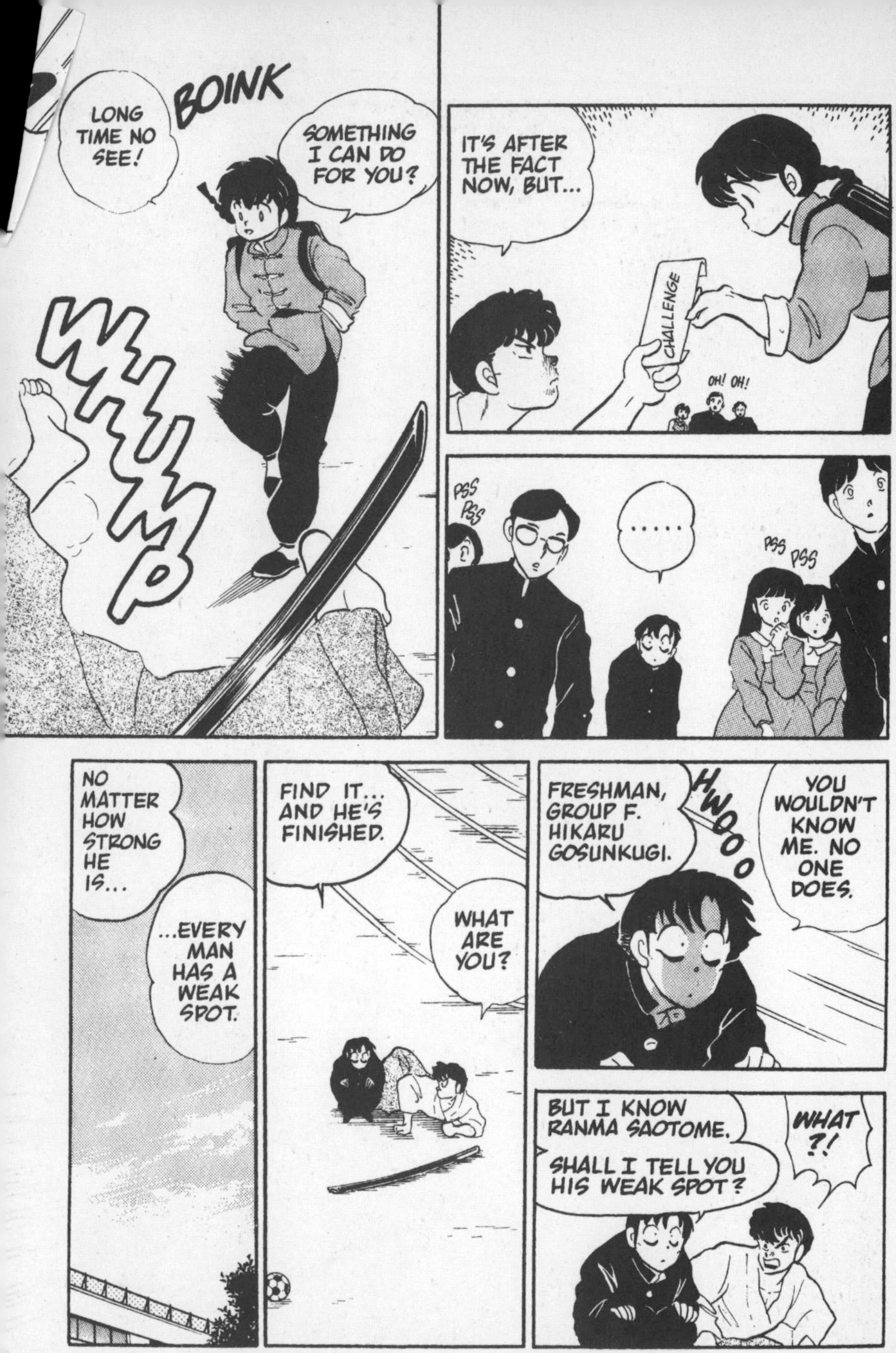
LONG TIME NO SEE!
BOINK
SOMETHING I CAN DO FOR YOU?
WHUMP
IT'S AFTER THE FACT NOW, BUT...
CHALLENGE
OH! OH!
PSS PSS
......
PSS PSS
NO MATTER HOW STRONG HE IS...
...EVERY MAN HAS A WEAK SPOT.
FIND IT... AND HE'S FINISHED.
WHAT ARE YOU?
FRESHMAN, GROUP F. HIKARU GOSUNKUGI.
HWOOO
YOU WOULDN'T KNOW ME. NO ONE DOES.
BUT I KNOW RANMA SAOTOME.
SHALL I TELL YOU HIS WEAK SPOT?
WHAT ?!

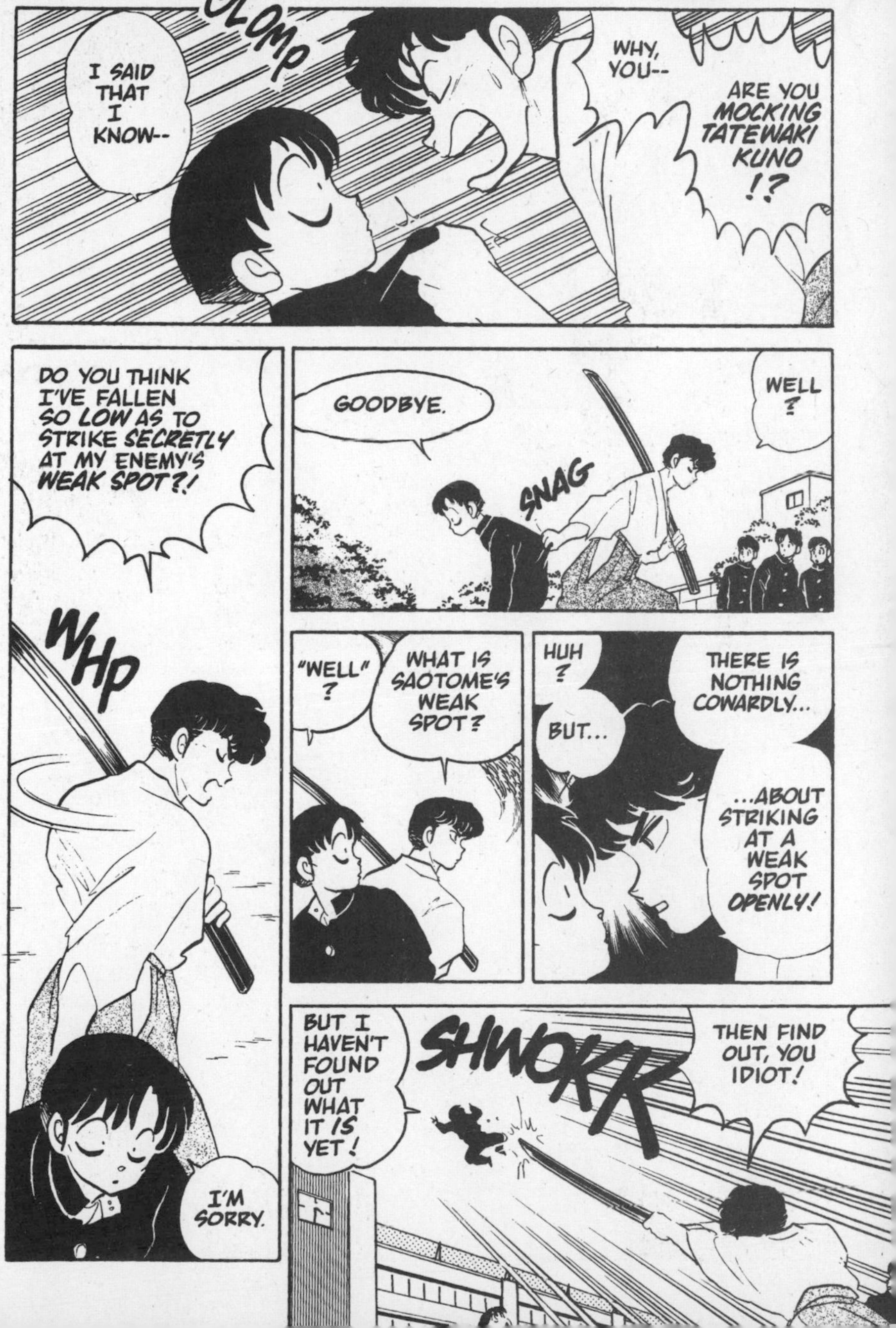
GLOMP
I SAID THAT I KNOW--
WHY, YOU--
ARE YOU MOCKING TATEWAKI KUNO !?
DO YOU THINK I'VE FALLEN SO LOW AS TO STRIKE SECRETLY AT MY ENEMY'S WEAK SPOT?!
GOODBYE.
WELL ?
SNAG
WHP
I'M SORRY.
"WELL" ?
WHAT IS SAOTOME'S WEAK SPOT?
HUH ?
BUT...
THERE IS NOTHING COWARDLY...
...ABOUT STRIKING AT A WEAK SPOT OPENLY!
BUT I HAVEN'T FOUND OUT WHAT IT IS YET!
SHWOKK
THEN FIND OUT, YOU IDIOT!

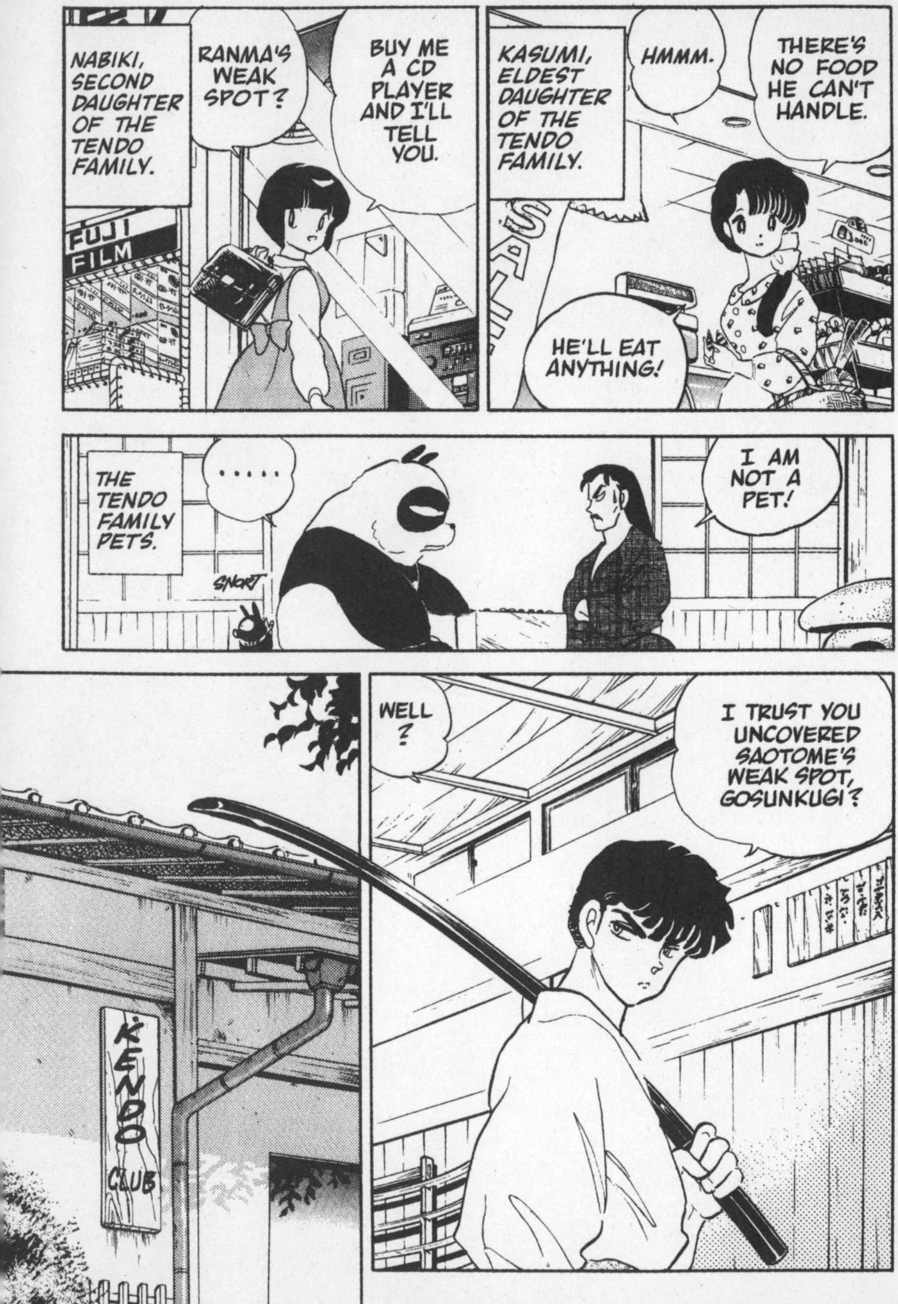
NABIKI, SECOND DAUGHTER OF THE TENDO FAMILY.
RANMA'S WEAK SPOT?
BUY ME A CD PLAYER AND I'LL TELL YOU.
FUJI FILM
KASUMI, ELDEST DAUGHTER OF THE TENDO FAMILY.
HMMM.
THERE'S NO FOOD HE CAN'T HANDLE.
HE'LL EAT ANYTHING!
THE TENDO FAMILY PETS.
.....
SNORT
I AM NOT A PET!
KENDO CLUB
WELL?
I TRUST YOU UNCOVERED SAOTOME'S WEAK SPOT, GOSUNKUGI?

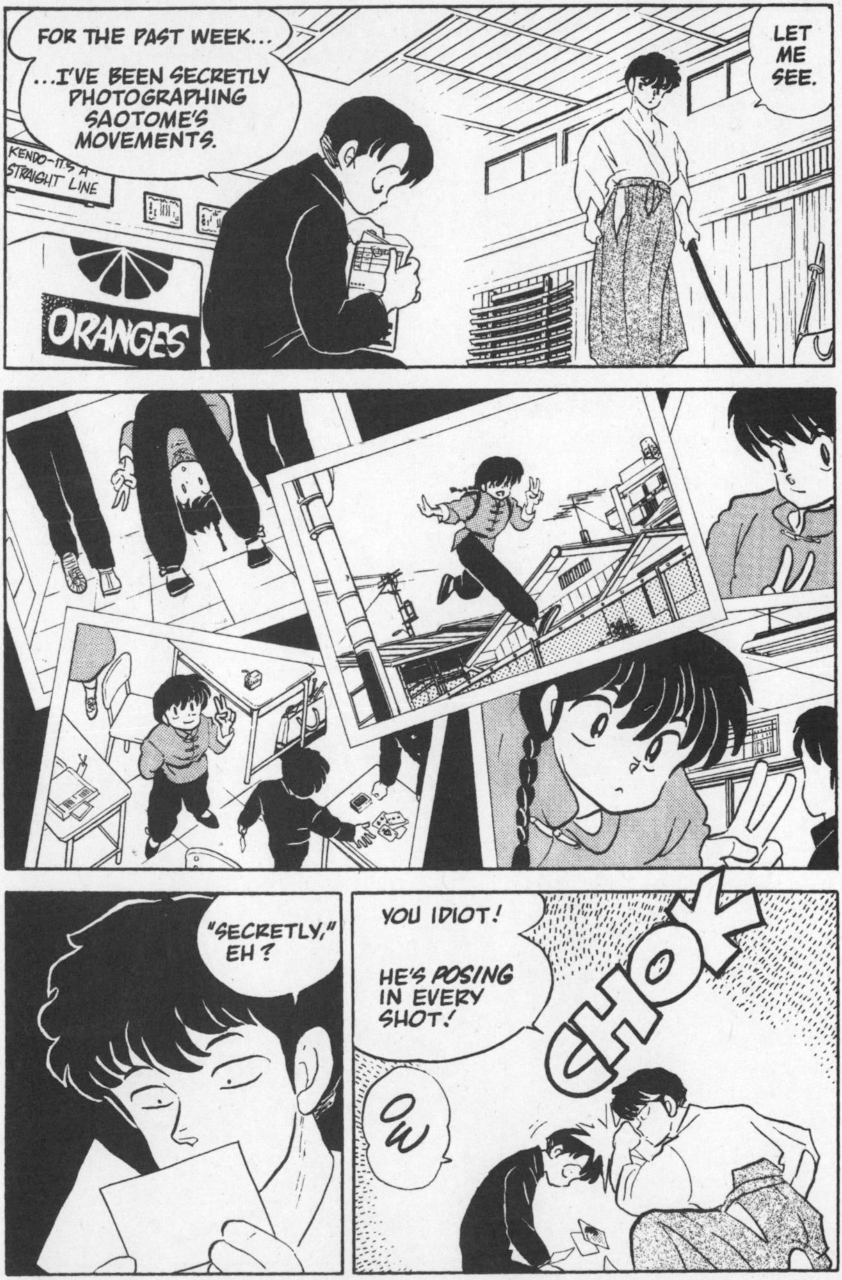
FOR THE PAST WEEK...
...I'VE BEEN SECRETLY PHOTOGRAPHING SAOTOME'S MOVEMENTS.
KENDO—IT'S A STRAIGHT LINE
ORANGES
LET ME SEE.
"SECRETLY," EH?
YOU IDIOT!
HE'S POSING IN EVERY SHOT!
CHOK
OW

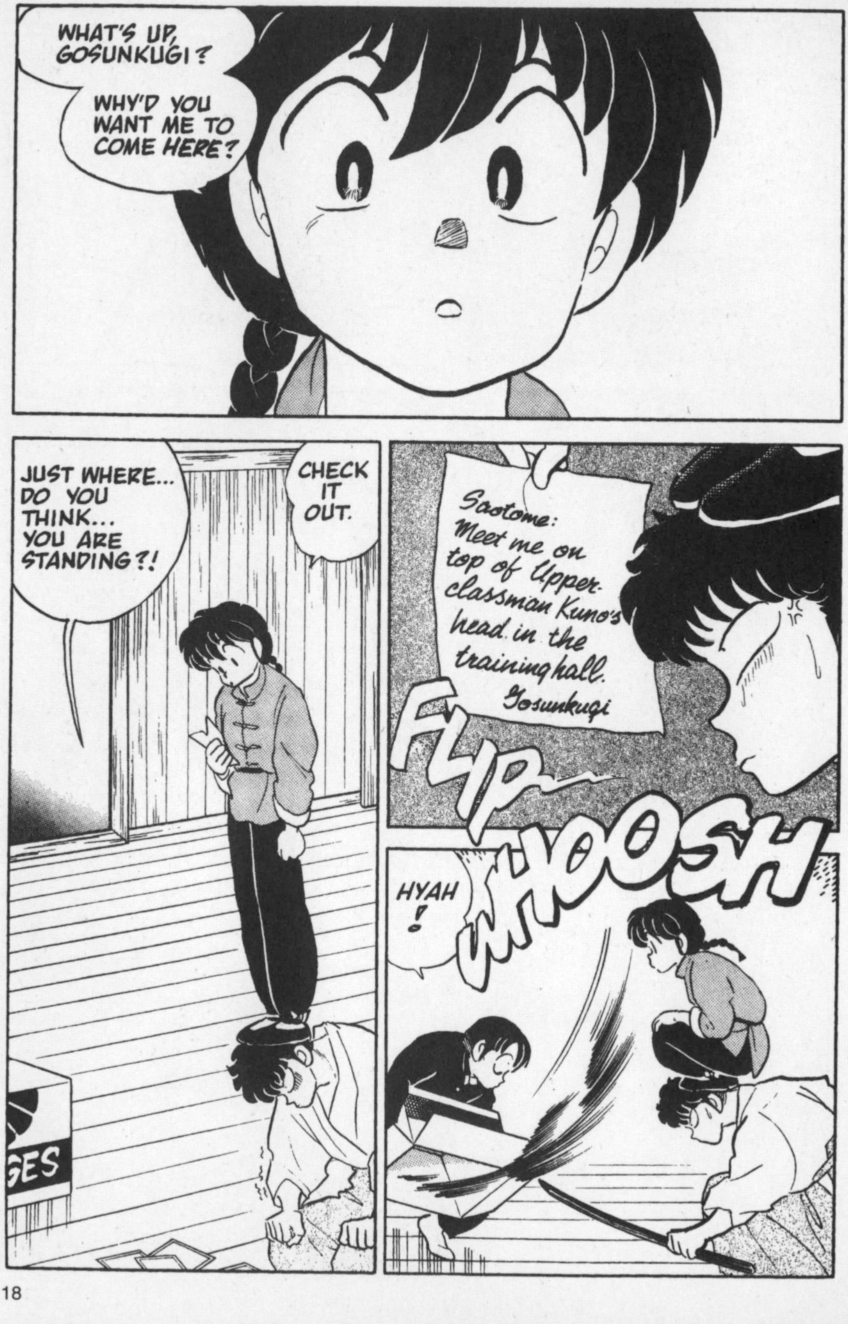
WHAT'S UP, GOSUNKUGI?
WHY'D YOU WANT ME TO COME HERE?
JUST WHERE... DO YOU THINK... YOU ARE STANDING?!
CHECK IT OUT.
Saotome: Meet me on top of Upper-classman Kuno's head in the training hall. Gosunkugi
FLIP
HYAH!
WHOOSH

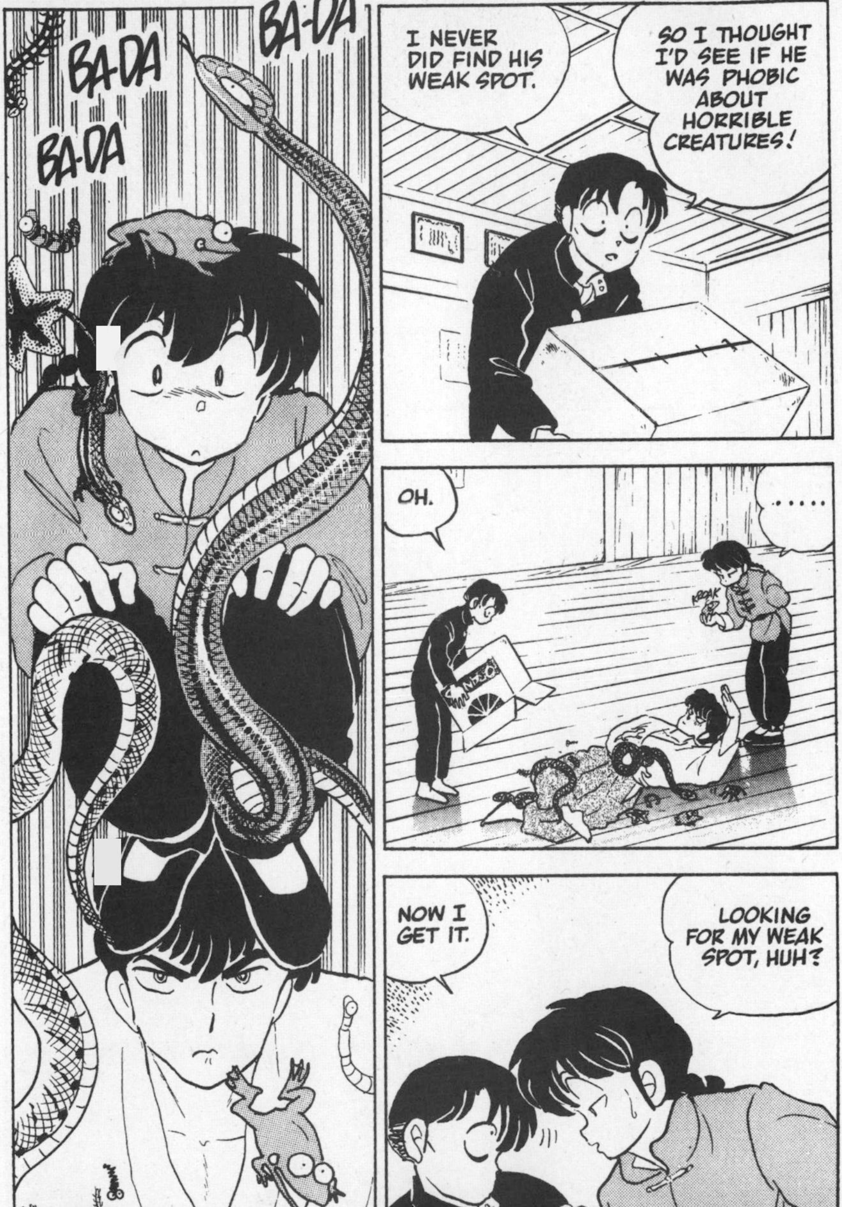
BA-DA
BA-DA
BA-DA
I NEVER DID FIND HIS WEAK SPOT.
SO I THOUGHT I'D SEE IF HE WAS PHOBIC ABOUT HORRIBLE CREATURES!
OH.
.....
NOW I GET IT.
LOOKING FOR MY WEAK SPOT, HUH?

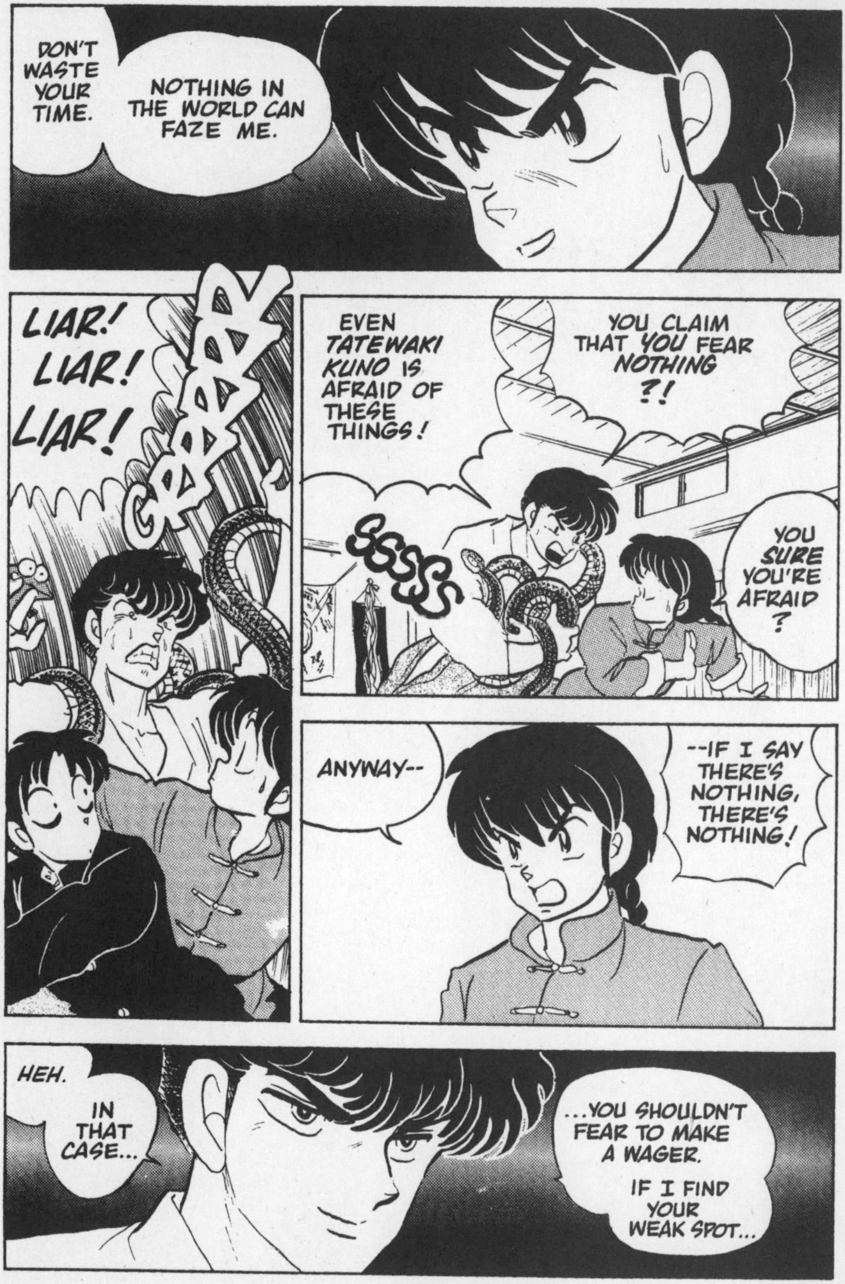
DON'T WASTE YOUR TIME.
NOTHING IN THE WORLD CAN FAZE ME.
LIAR! LIAR! LIAR!
CRAAAK
EVEN TATEWAKI KUNO IS AFRAID OF THESE THINGS!
YOU CLAIM THAT YOU FEAR NOTHING ?!
SSSSS
YOU SURE YOU'RE AFRAID ?
ANYWAY--
--IF I SAY THERE'S NOTHING, THERE'S NOTHING!
HEH.
IN THAT CASE...
...YOU SHOULDN'T FEAR TO MAKE A WAGER.
IF I FIND YOUR WEAK SPOT...

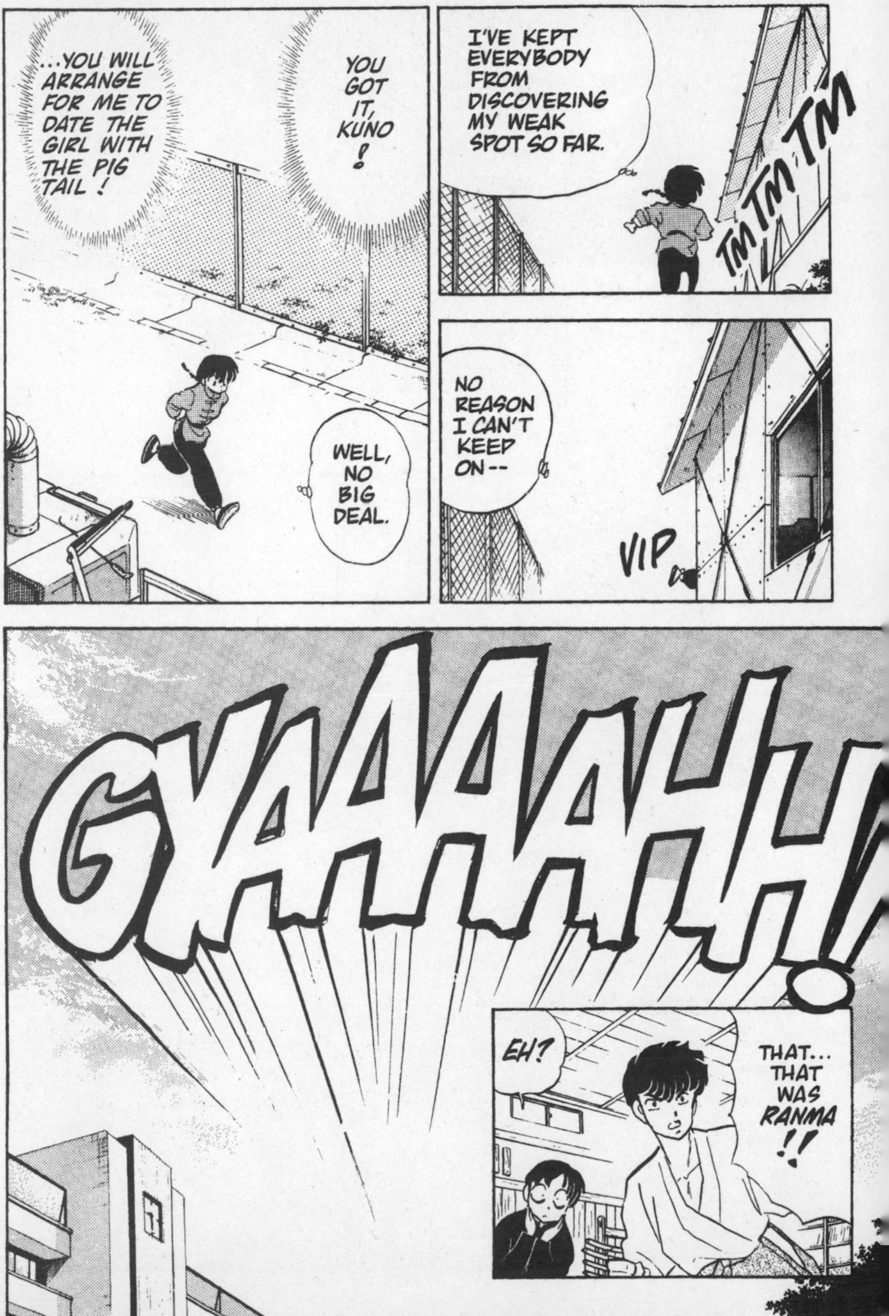
...YOU WILL ARRANGE FOR ME TO DATE THE GIRL WITH THE PIG TAIL!
YOU GOT IT, KUNO!
WELL, NO BIG DEAL.
I'VE KEPT EVERYBODY FROM DISCOVERING MY WEAK SPOT SO FAR.
TM TM TM
NO REASON I CAN'T KEEP ON--
VIP
GYAAAAH!!
EH?
THAT... THAT WAS RANMA!!

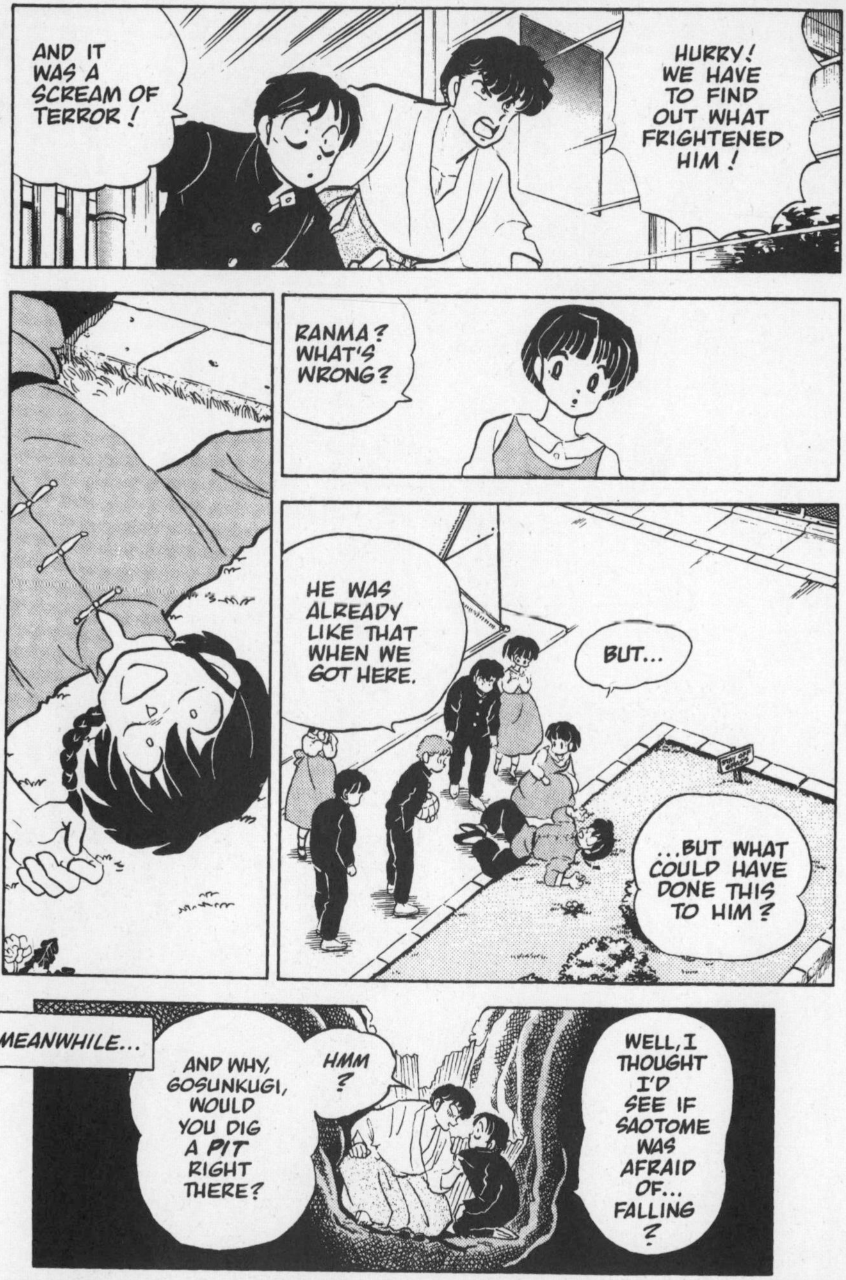
AND IT WAS A SCREAM OF TERROR!
HURRY! WE HAVE TO FIND OUT WHAT FRIGHTENED HIM!
RANMA? WHAT'S WRONG?
HE WAS ALREADY LIKE THAT WHEN WE GOT HERE.
BUT...
...BUT WHAT COULD HAVE DONE THIS TO HIM?
MEANWHILE...
AND WHY, GOSUNKUGI, WOULD YOU DIG A PIT RIGHT THERE?
HMM?
WELL, I THOUGHT I'D SEE IF SAOTOME WAS AFRAID OF... FALLING?

Part 2

WEAK SPOT–FOUND!

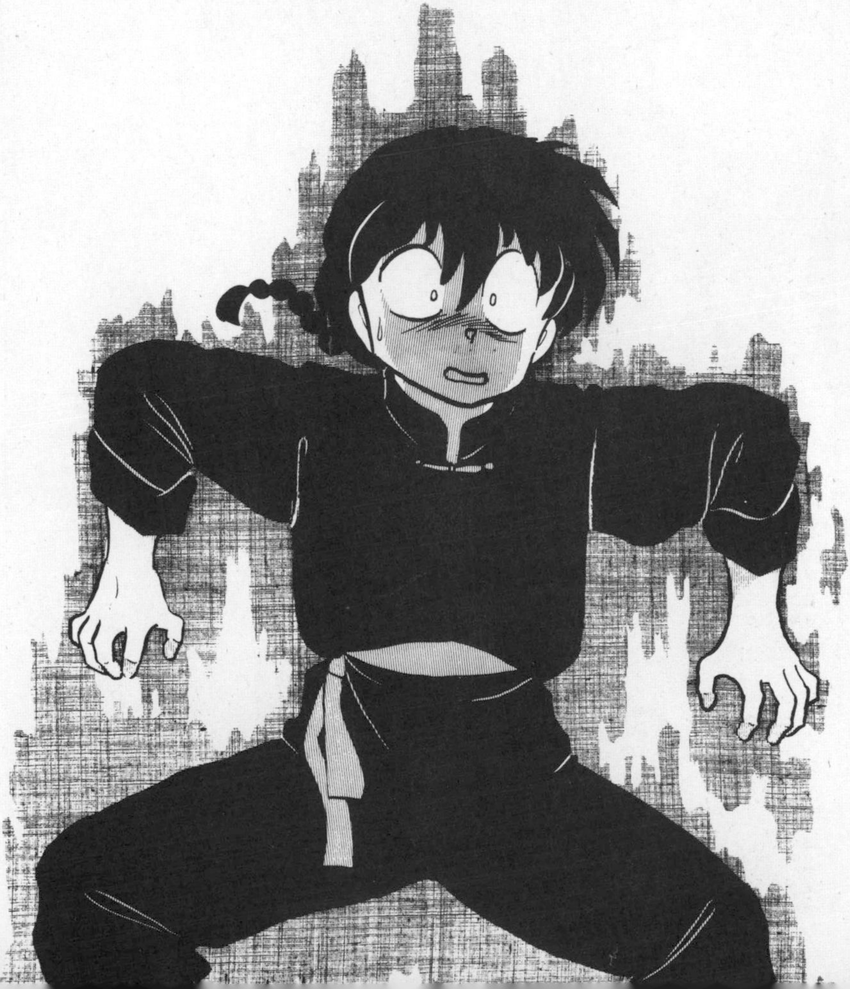

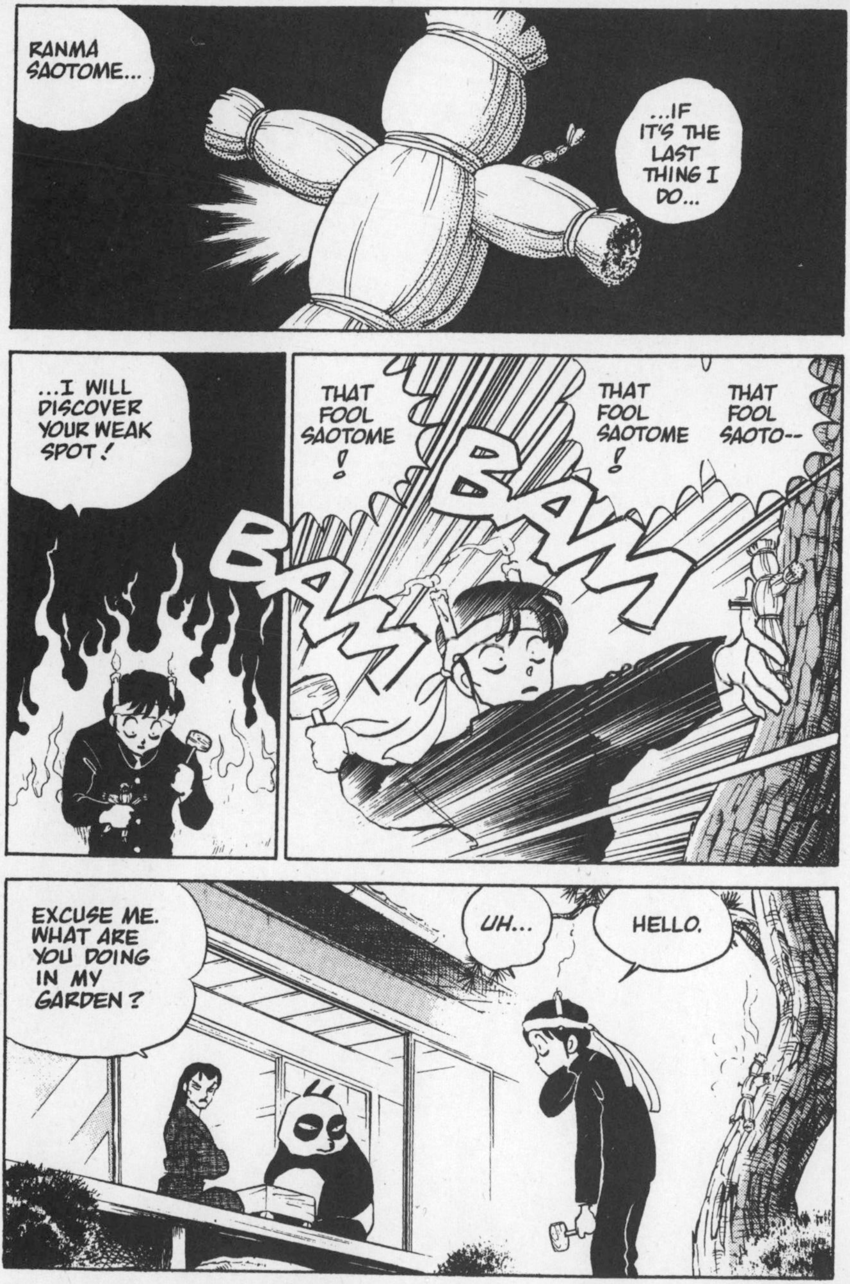
RANMA SAOTOME...
...IF IT'S THE LAST THING I DO...
...I WILL DISCOVER YOUR WEAK SPOT!
THAT FOOL SAOTOME!
BAM
BAM
THAT FOOL SAOTOME!
THAT FOOL SAOTO--
EXCUSE ME. WHAT ARE YOU DOING IN MY GARDEN?
UH...
HELLO.

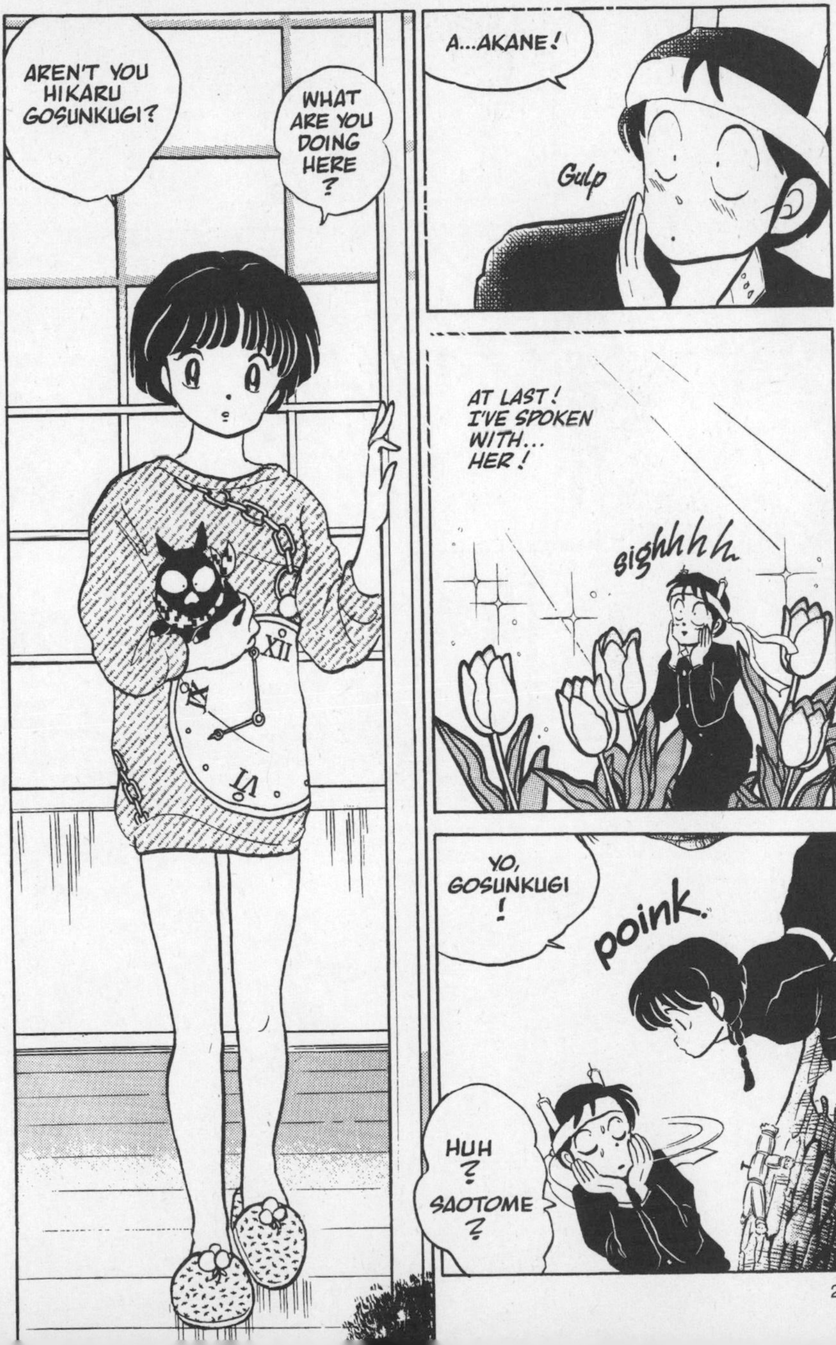
AREN'T YOU HIKARU GOSUNKUGI?
WHAT ARE YOU DOING HERE?
A...AKANE!
Gulp
AT LAST! I'VE SPOKEN WITH... HER!
sighhhh
YO, GOSUNKUGI!
poink
HUH? SAOTOME?

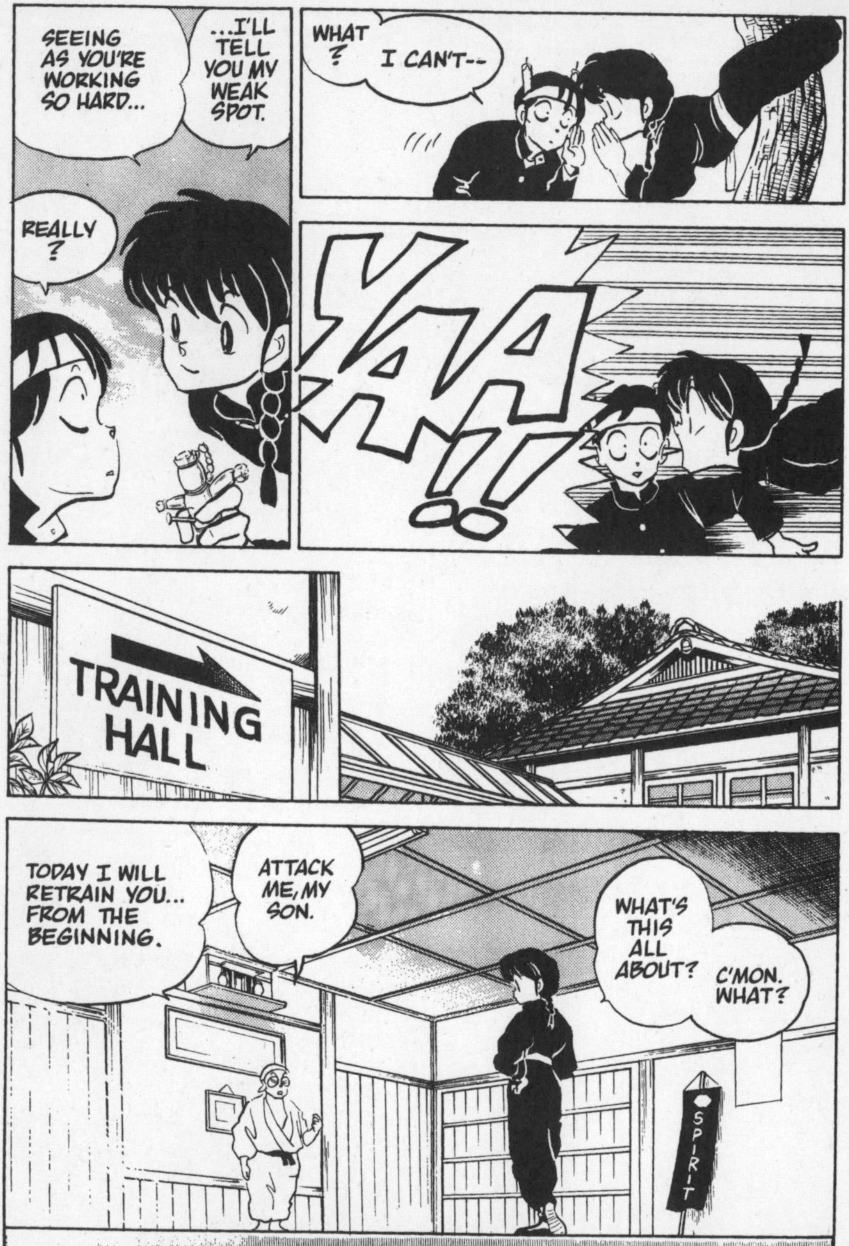
SEEING AS YOU'RE WORKING SO HARD...
...I'LL TELL YOU MY WEAK SPOT.
WHAT ?
I CAN'T--
REALLY ?
YAA!!
TRAINING HALL
TODAY I WILL RETRAIN YOU... FROM THE BEGINNING.
ATTACK ME, MY SON.
WHAT'S THIS ALL ABOUT?
C'MON. WHAT?
SPIRIT

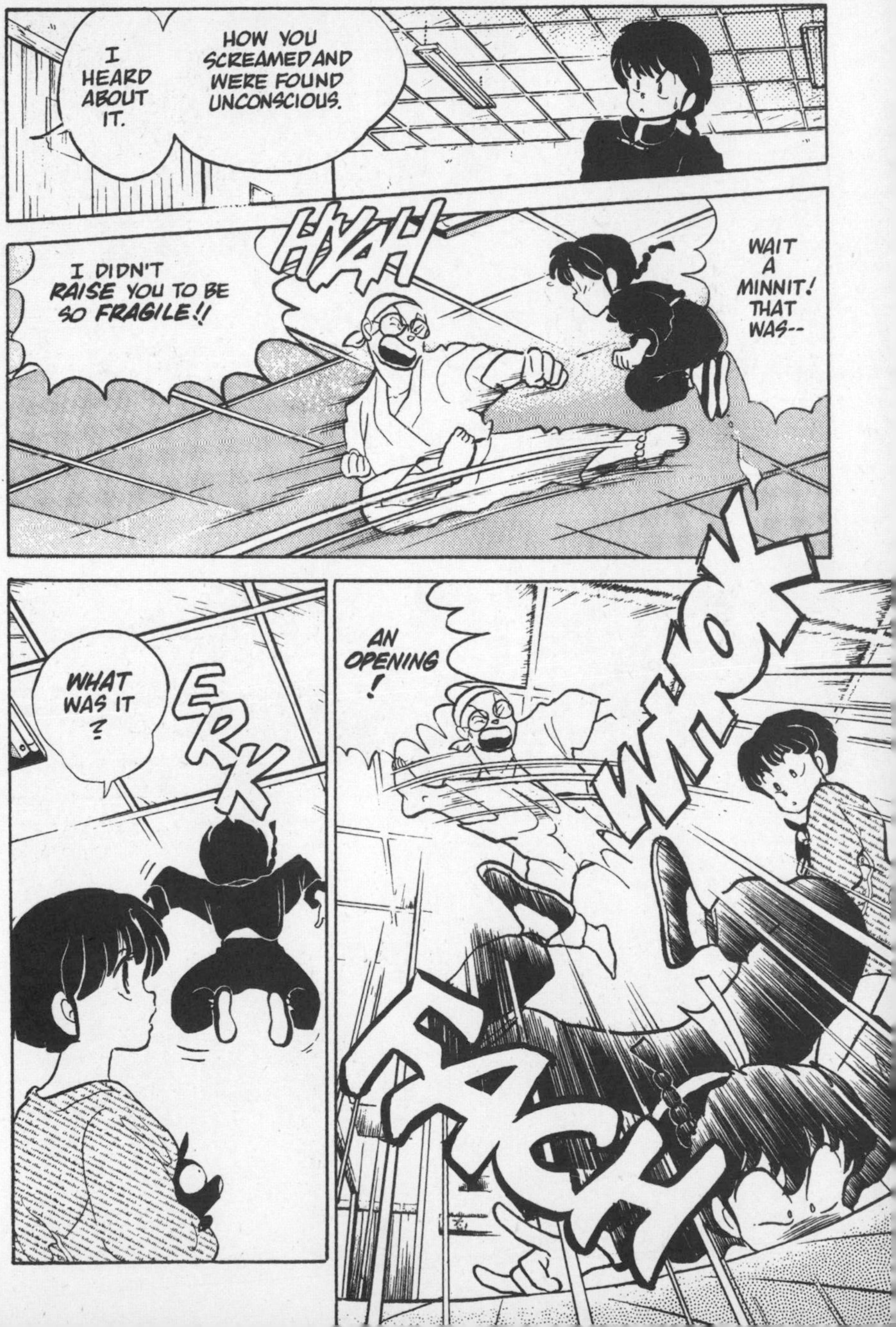
I HEARD ABOUT IT.
HOW YOU SCREAMED AND WERE FOUND UNCONSCIOUS.
HYAH
I DIDN'T RAISE YOU TO BE SO FRAGILE!!
WAIT A MINNIT! THAT WAS--
WHAT WAS IT?
ERK
AN OPENING!
WHOK
BOCH

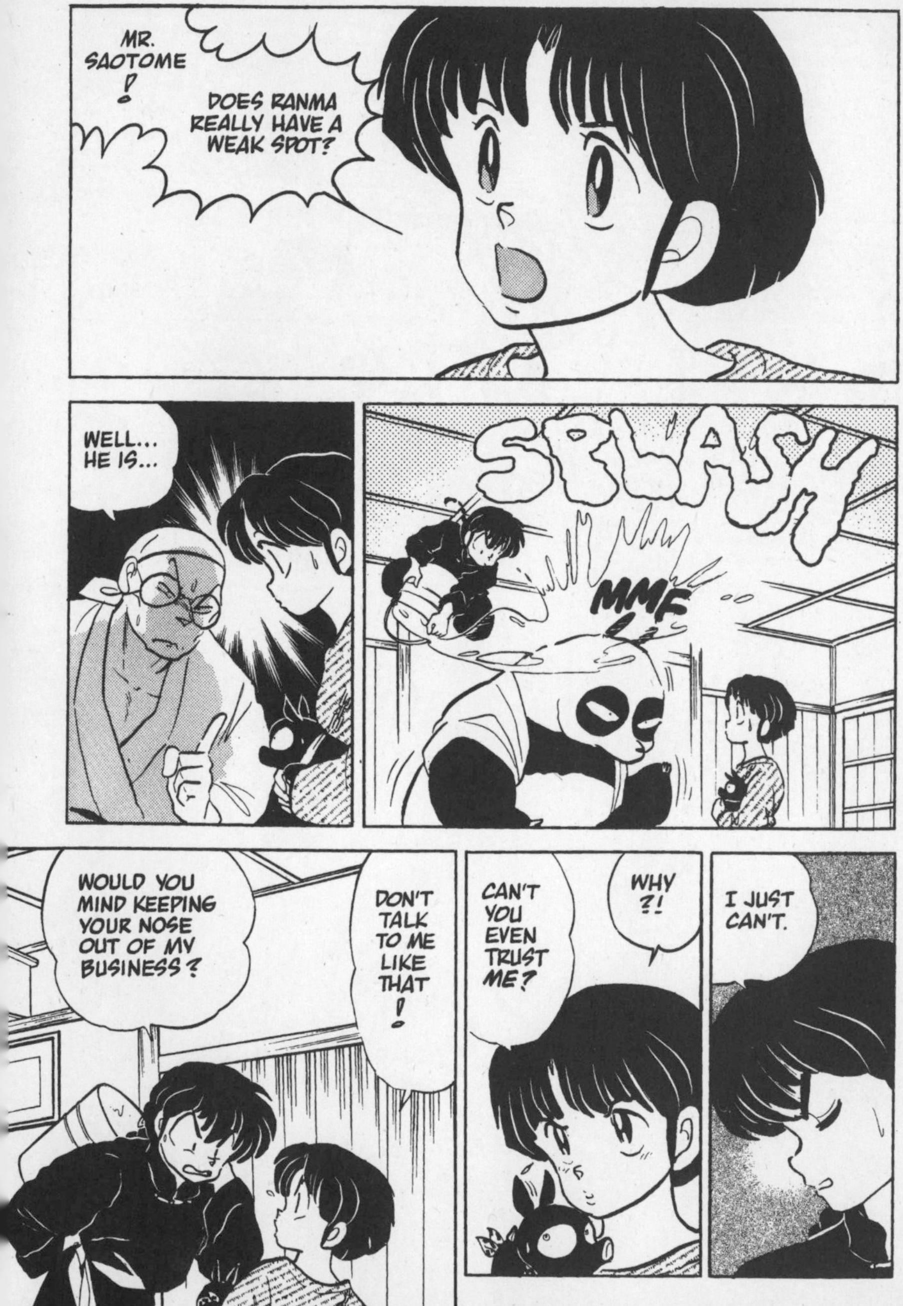
MR. SAOTOME !
DOES RANMA REALLY HAVE A WEAK SPOT?
WELL... HE IS...
SPLASH
MMF
WOULD YOU MIND KEEPING YOUR NOSE OUT OF MY BUSINESS?
DON'T TALK TO ME LIKE THAT !
CAN'T YOU EVEN TRUST ME?
WHY ?!
I JUST CAN'T.

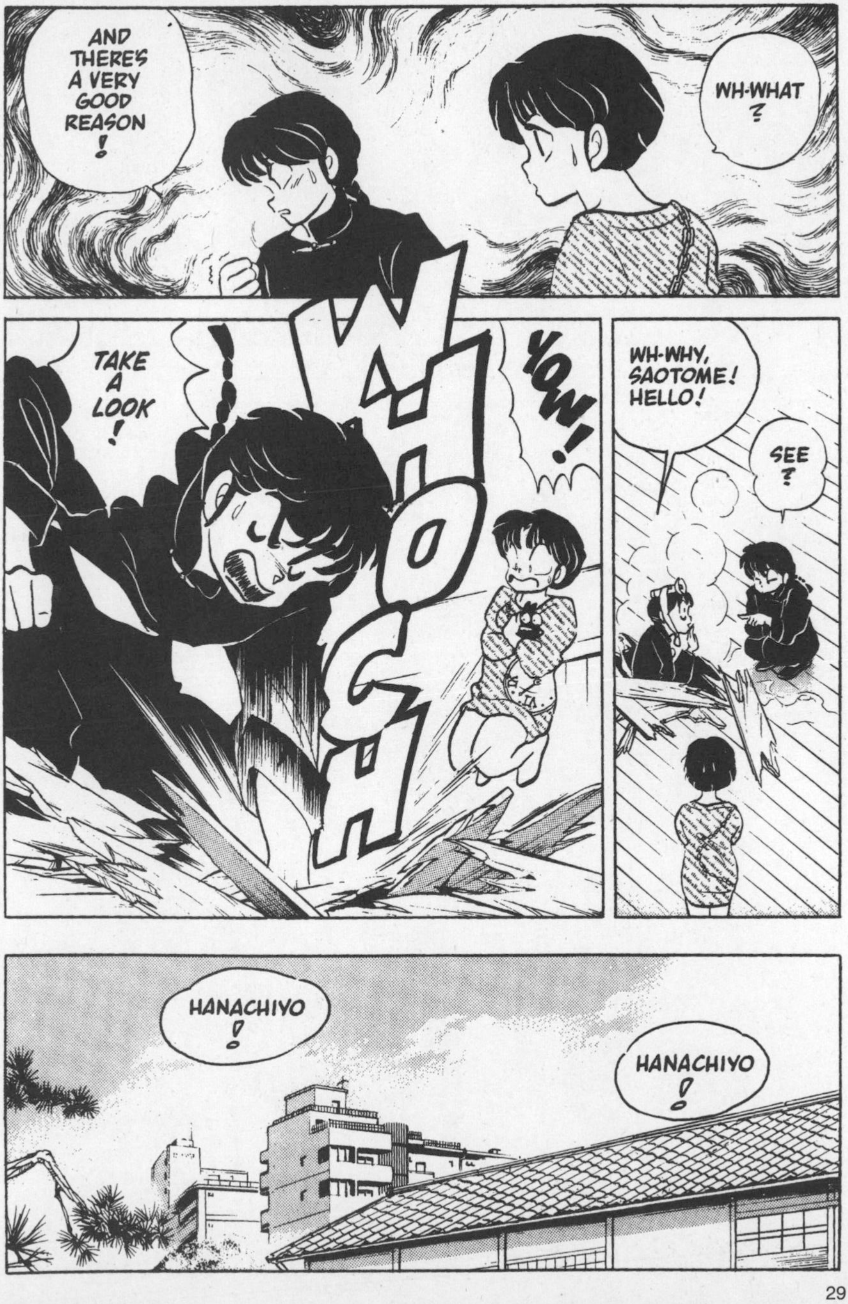
AND THERE'S A VERY GOOD REASON!
WH-WHAT?
TAKE A LOOK!
WHOOSH
YOW!
WH-WHY, SAOTOME! HELLO!
SEE?
HANACHIYO!
HANACHIYO!

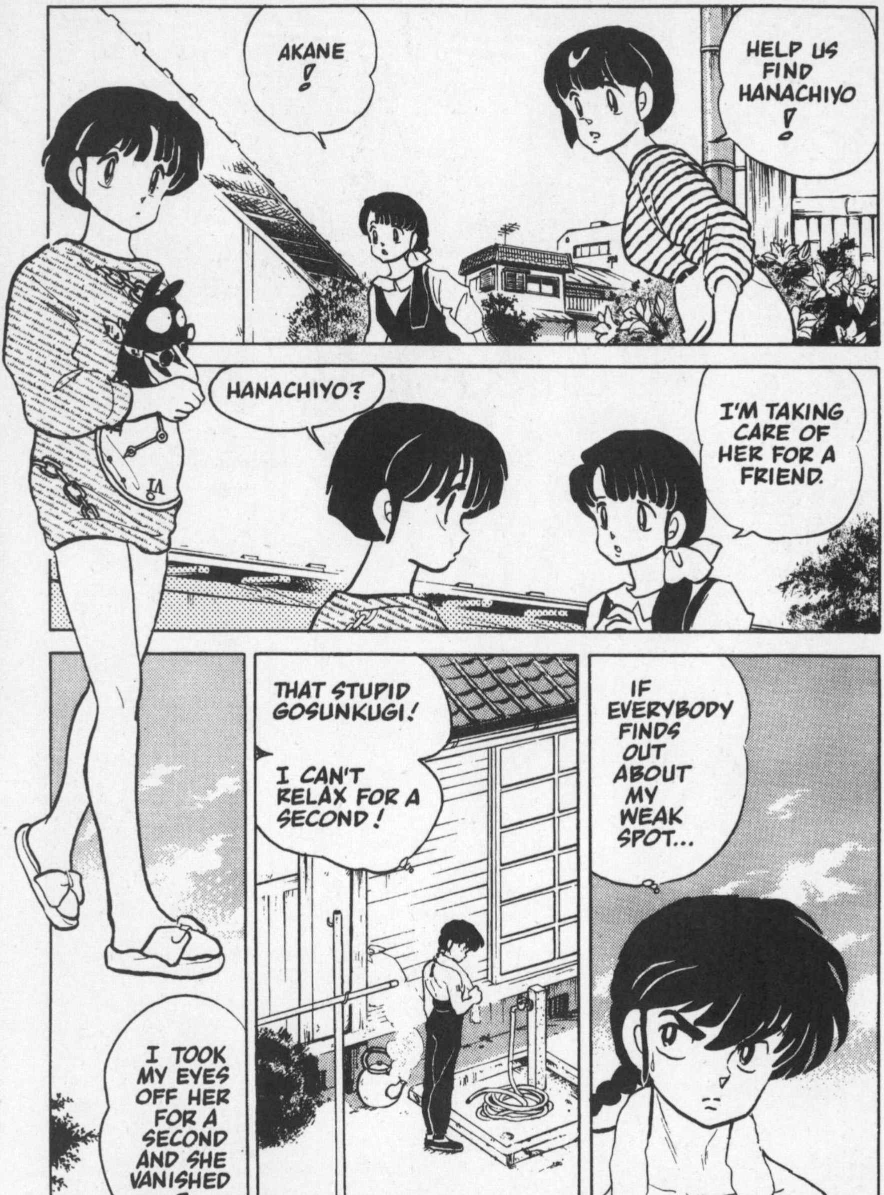
AKANE!
HELP US FIND HANACHIYO!
HANACHIYO?
I'M TAKING CARE OF HER FOR A FRIEND.
I TOOK MY EYES OFF HER FOR A SECOND AND SHE VANISHED!
THAT STUPID GOSUNKUGI!
I CAN'T RELAX FOR A SECOND!
IF EVERYBODY FINDS OUT ABOUT MY WEAK SPOT...

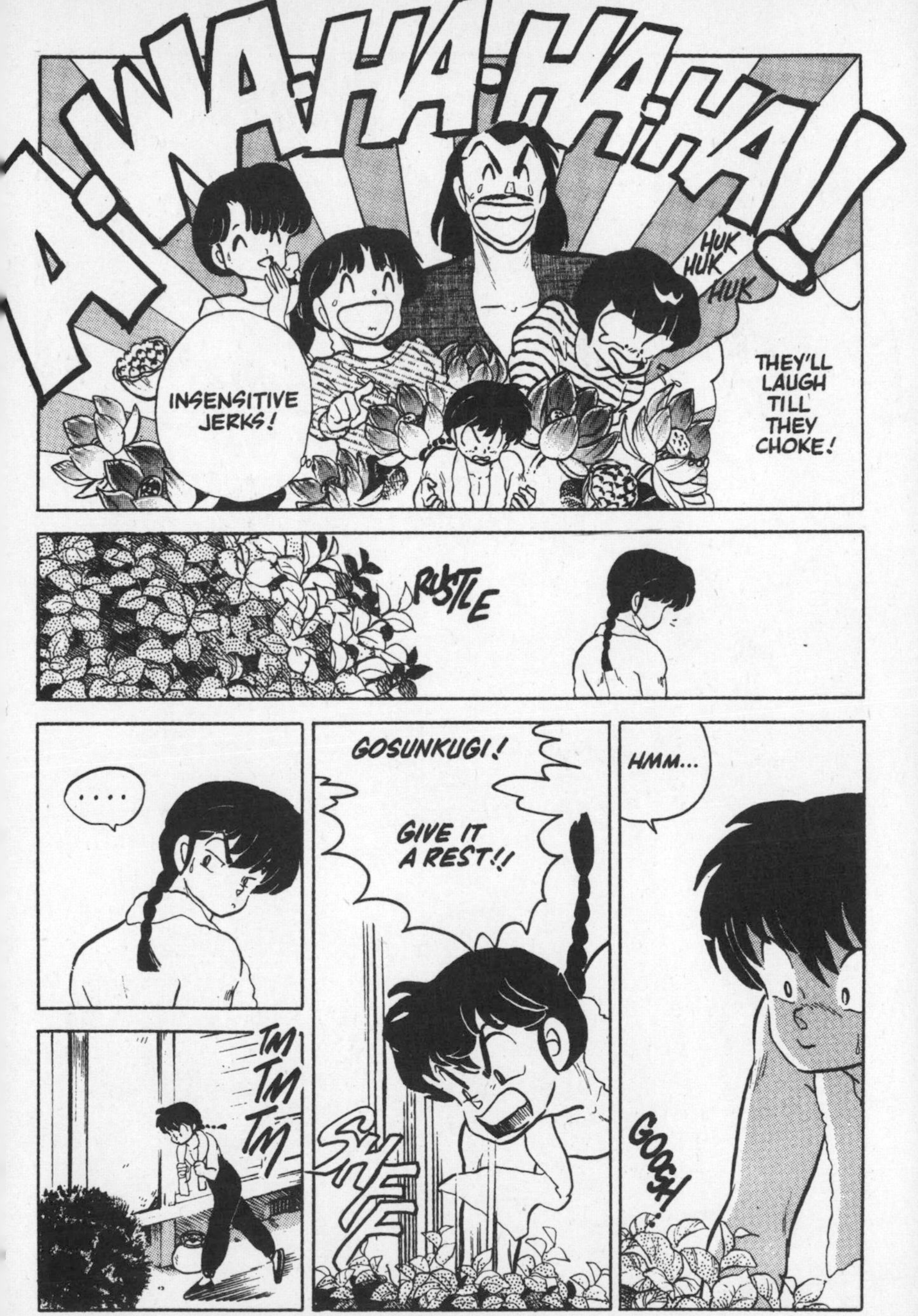
WA-HA-HA-HA-HA!!
HUK HUK HUK
INSENSITIVE JERKS!
THEY'LL LAUGH TILL THEY CHOKE!
RUSTLE
. . . .
TM TM TM
GOSUNKUGI!
GIVE IT A REST!!
SHF
HMM...
GOOSH!

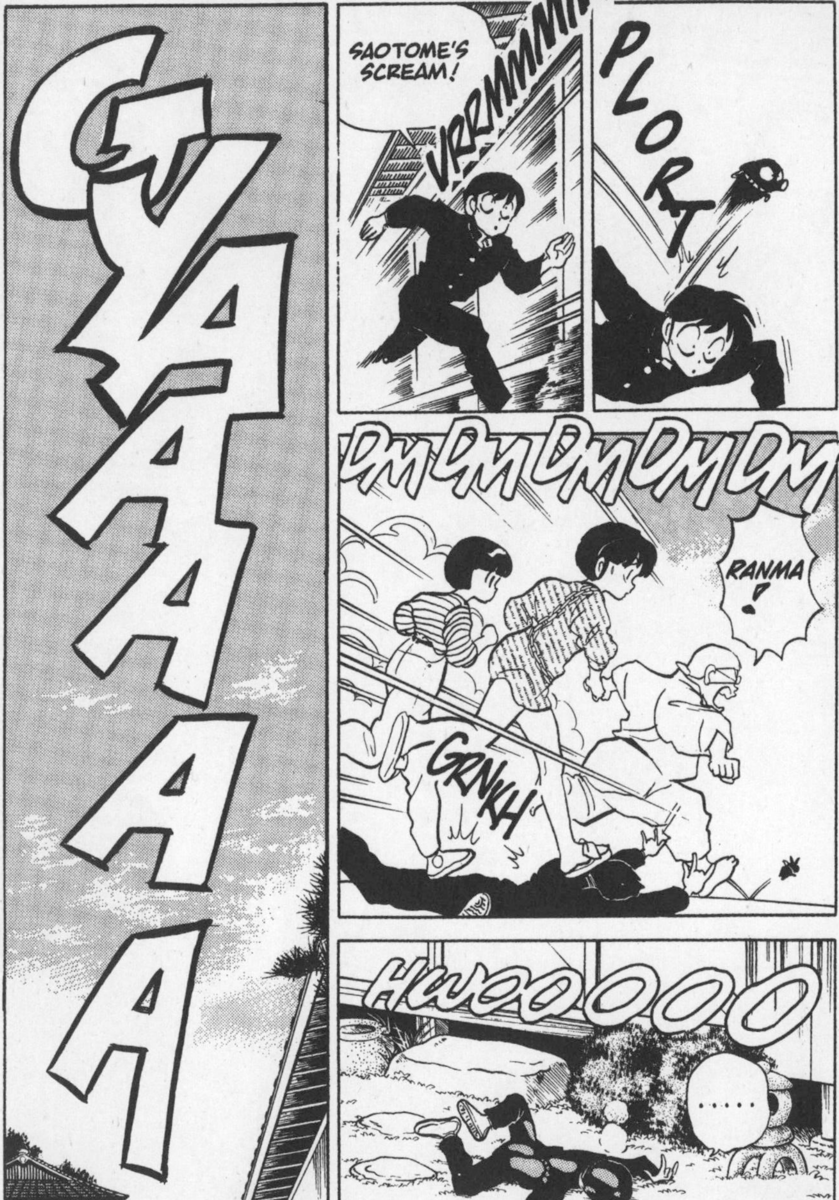
GYAAAAA
SAOTOME'S SCREAM!
VRRMMMMM
PLORT
DMDMDMDMDM
RANMA!
GRNKH
HWOOOOOO
.....

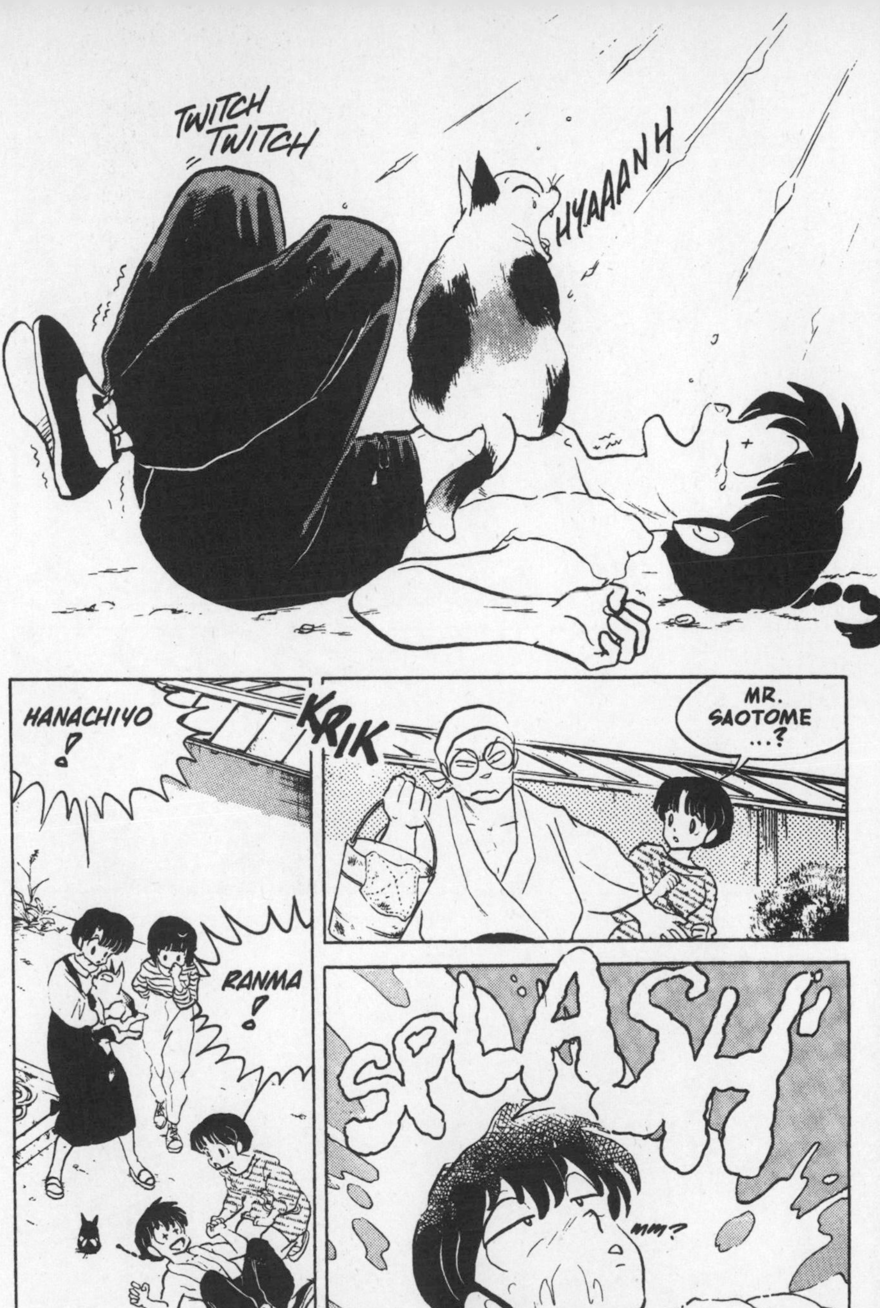
TWITCH TWITCH
HYAAANH
HANACHIYO!
RANMA!
KRIK
MR. SAOTOME ...?
SPLASH
MM?

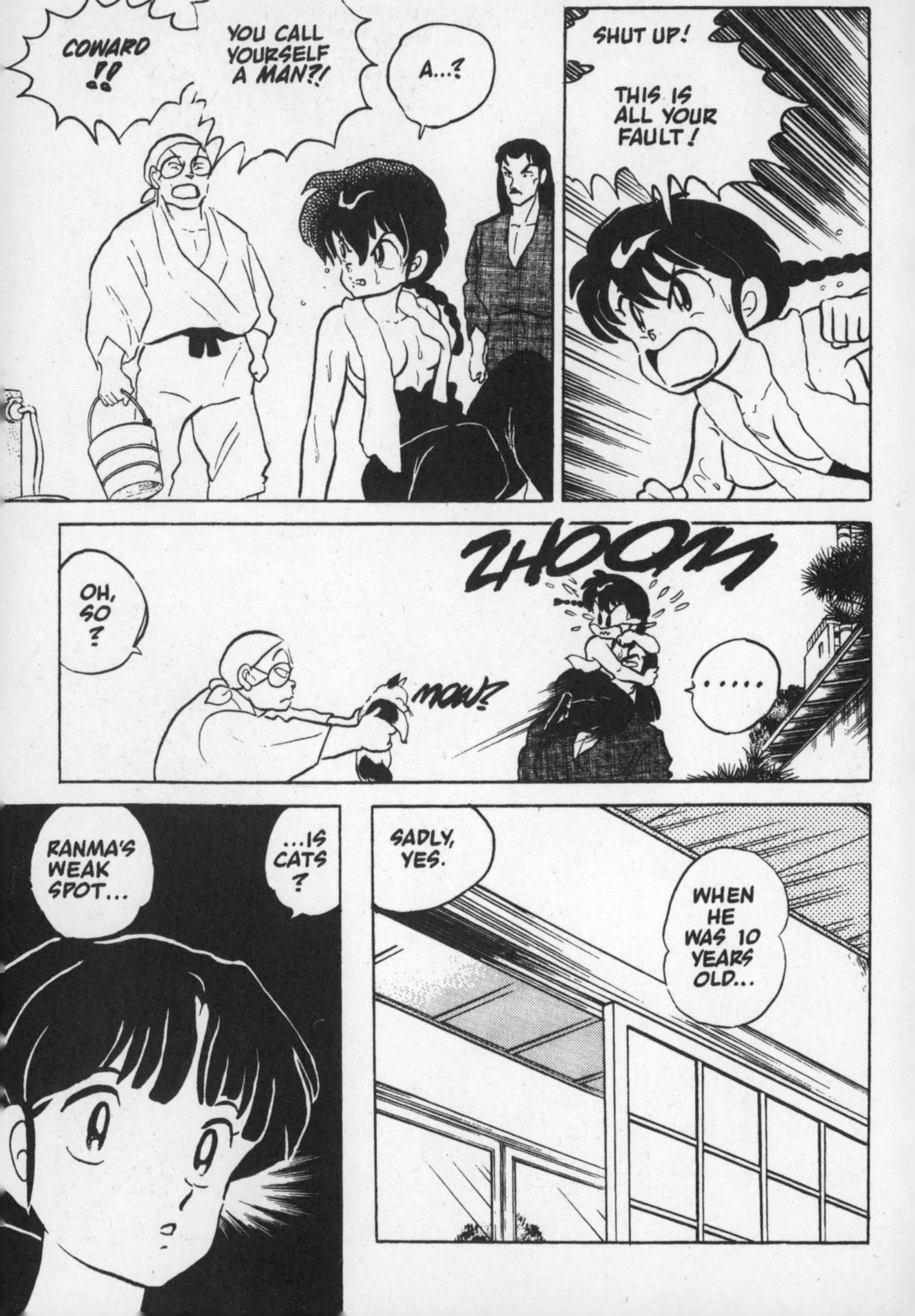
COWARD !!
YOU CALL YOURSELF A MAN?!
A...?
SHUT UP!
THIS IS ALL YOUR FAULT!
OH, SO?
ZHOOM
MOW?
.....
RANMA'S WEAK SPOT...
...IS CATS?
SADLY, YES.
WHEN HE WAS 10 YEARS OLD...

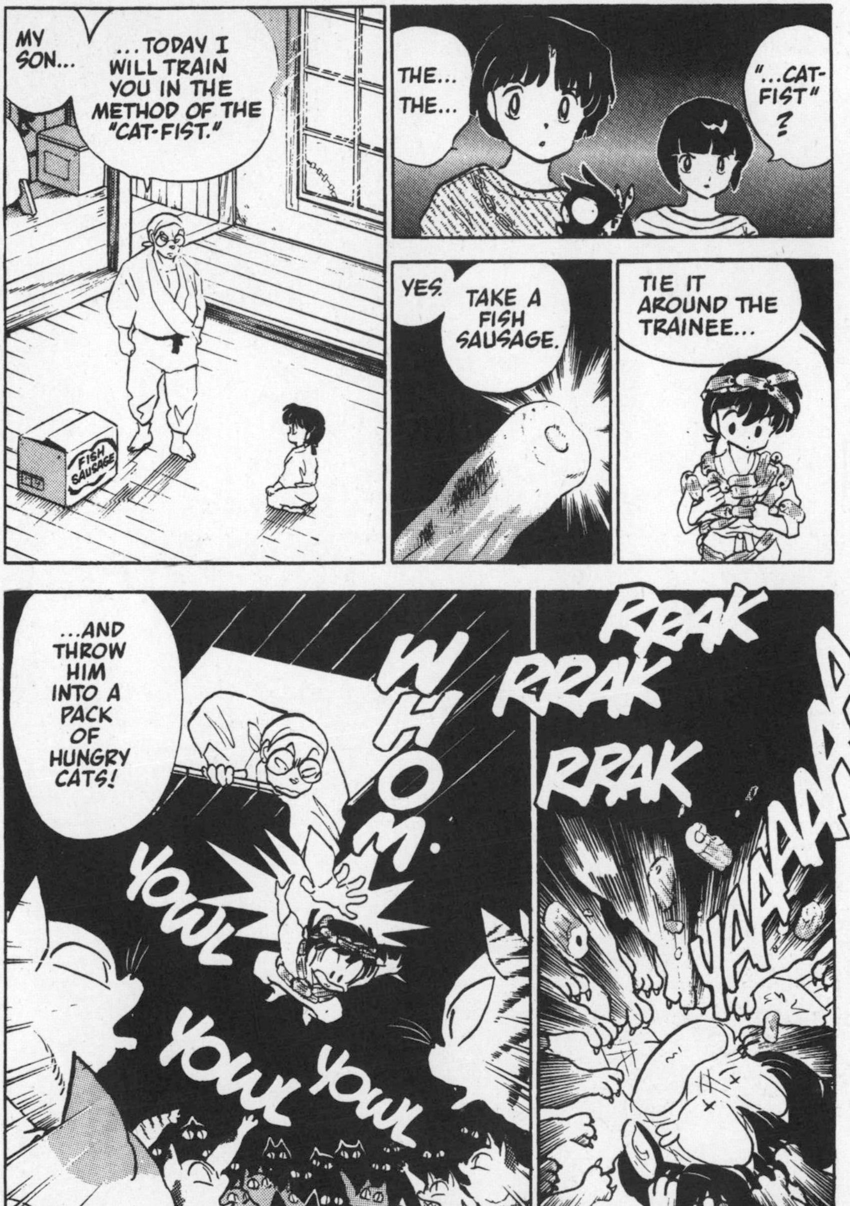
MY SON...
...TODAY I WILL TRAIN YOU IN THE METHOD OF THE "CAT-FIST."
FISH SAUSAGE
THE... THE...
"...CAT-FIST"?
YES.
TAKE A FISH SAUSAGE.
TIE IT AROUND THE TRAINEE...
...AND THROW HIM INTO A PACK OF HUNGRY CATS!
WHOOM.
YOWL
YOWL
YOWL
RRAK
RRAK
RRAK
YAAAAAAA

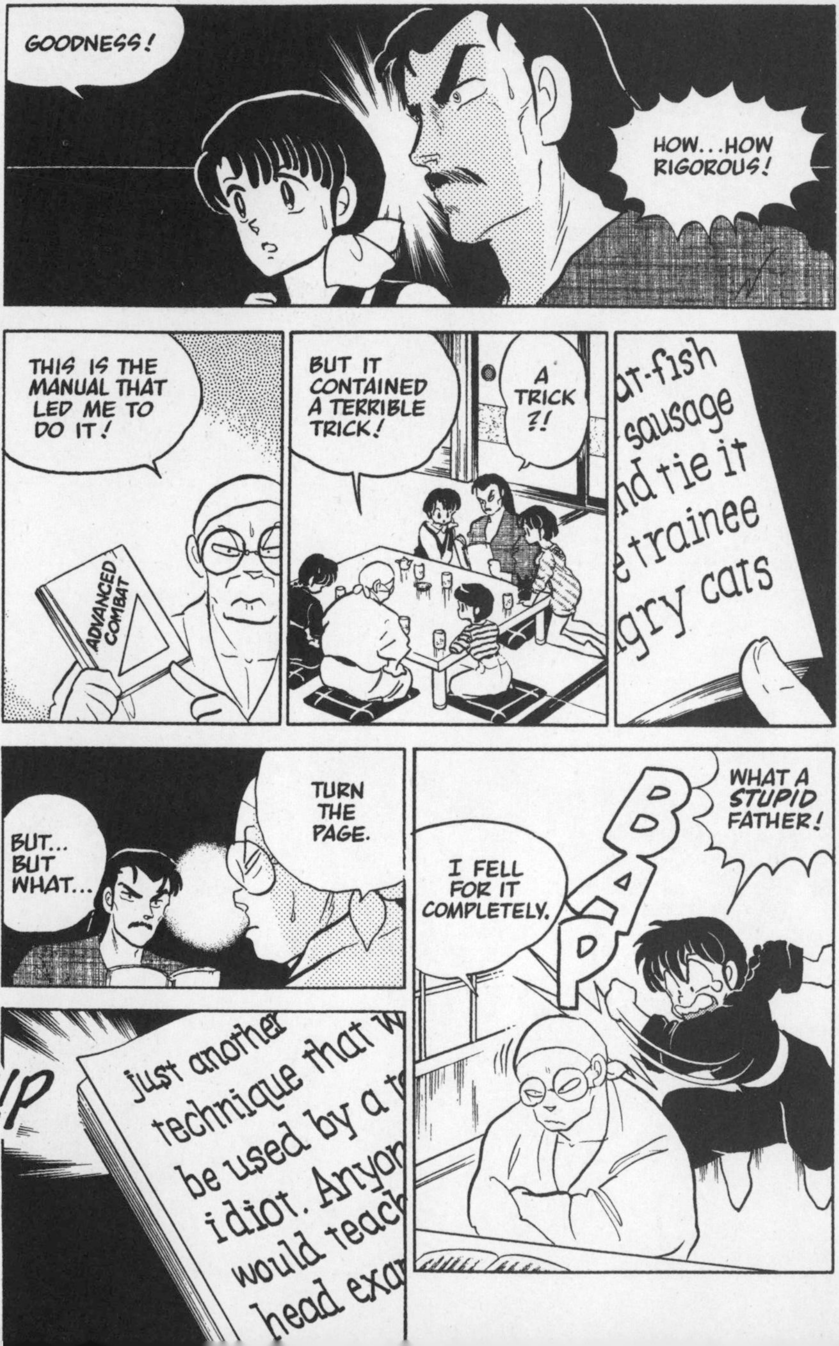
GOODNESS!
HOW...HOW RIGOROUS!
THIS IS THE MANUAL THAT LED ME TO DO IT!
ADVANCED COMBAT
BUT IT CONTAINED A TERRIBLE TRICK!
A TRICK ?!
at-fish
sausage
nd tie it
e trainee
gry cats
BUT... BUT WHAT...
TURN THE PAGE.
FLIP
just another
technique that w
be used by a t
idiot. Anyon
would teach
head exa
BAP
I FELL FOR IT COMPLETELY.
WHAT A STUPID FATHER!

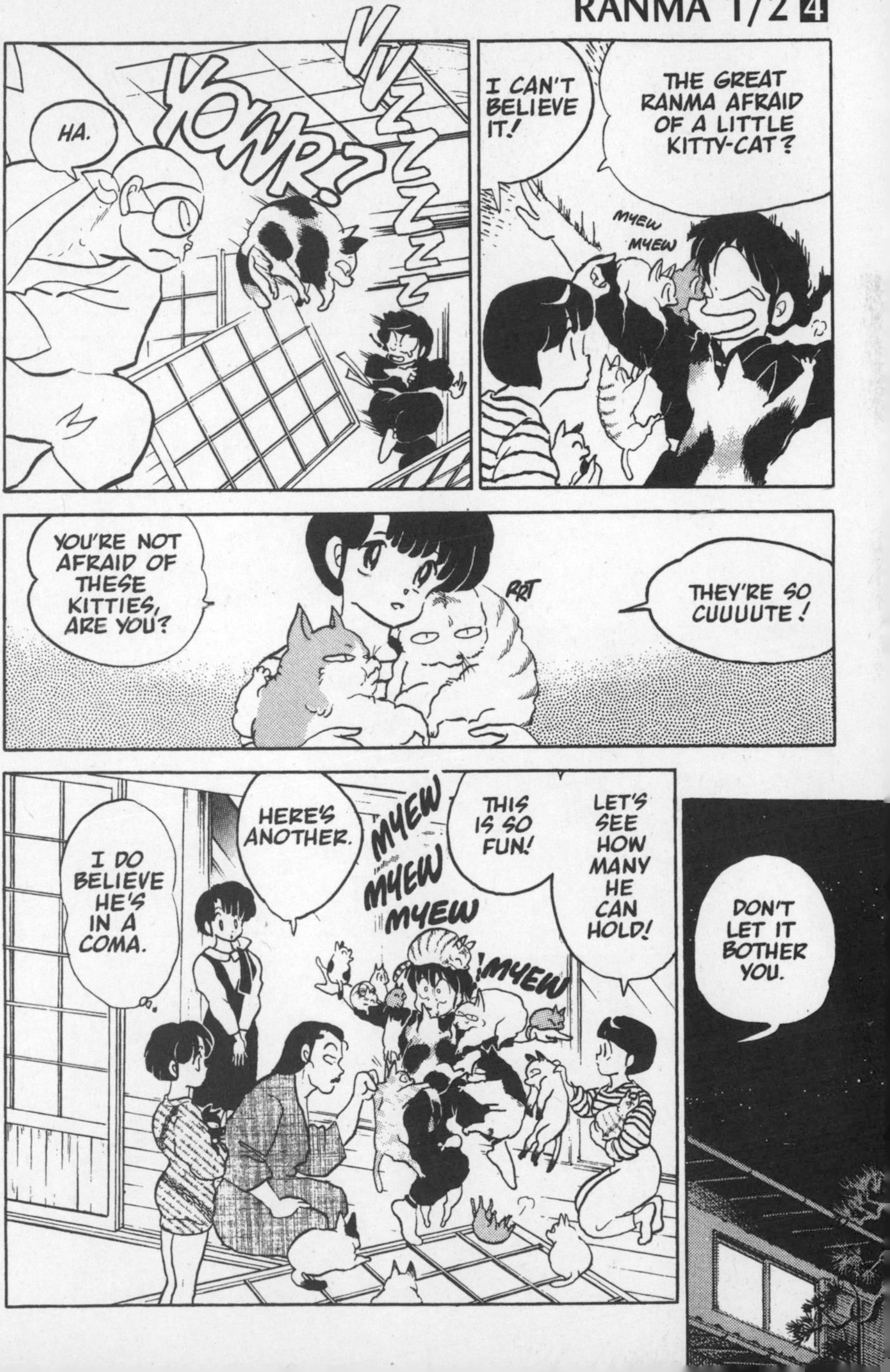
HA.
YOWR?!
I CAN'T BELIEVE IT!
THE GREAT RANMA AFRAID OF A LITTLE KITTY-CAT?
MYEW
MYEW
YOU'RE NOT AFRAID OF THESE KITTIES, ARE YOU?
RRT
THEY'RE SO CUUUUTE!
I DO BELIEVE HE'S IN A COMA.
HERE'S ANOTHER.
MYEW
MYEW
MYEW
THIS IS SO FUN!
LET'S SEE HOW MANY HE CAN HOLD!
MYEW
DON'T LET IT BOTHER YOU.

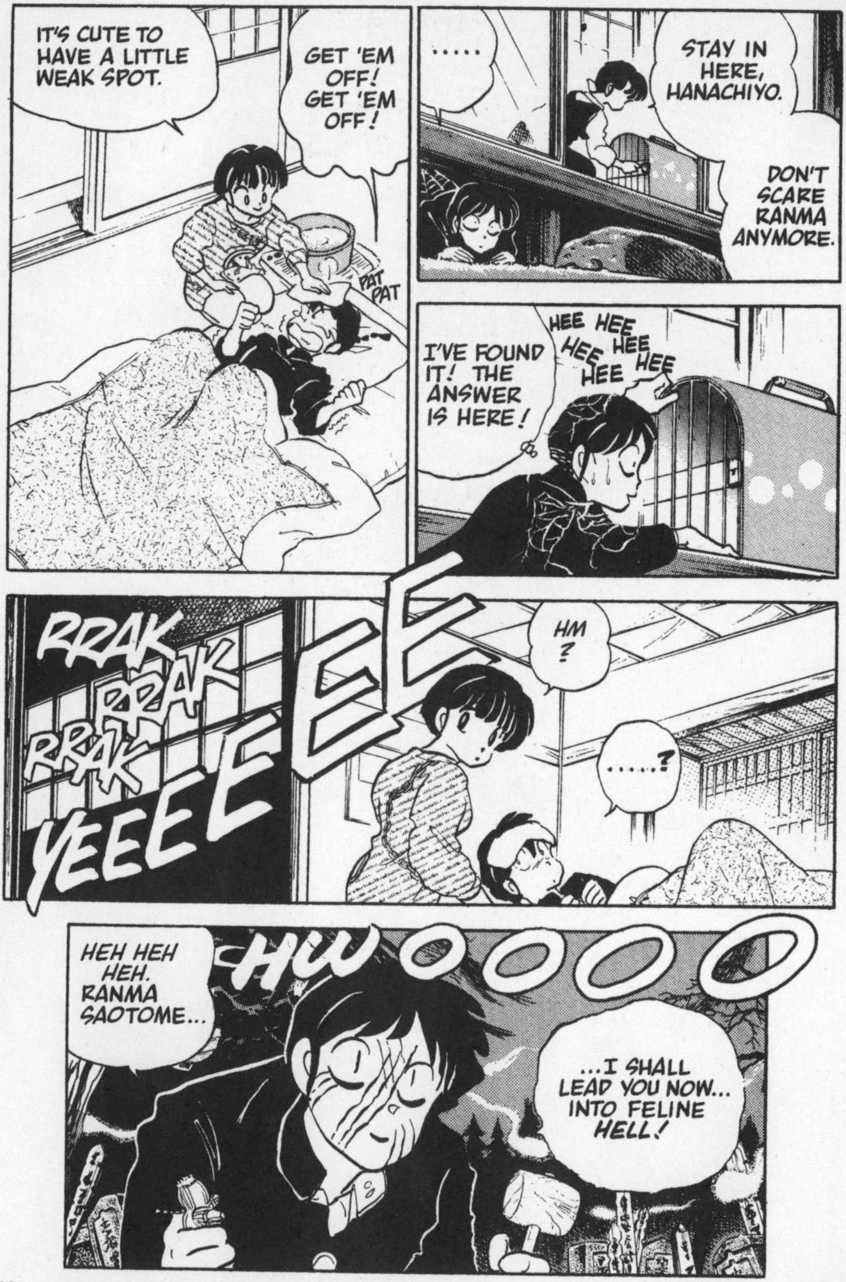

IT'S CUTE TO HAVE A LITTLE WEAK SPOT.
GET 'EM OFF! GET 'EM OFF!
PAT PAT
.....
STAY IN HERE, HANACHIYO.
DON'T SCARE RANMA ANYMORE.
I'VE FOUND IT! THE ANSWER IS HERE!
HEE HEE HEE HEE HEE HEE
RRAK RRAK RRAK
YEEEEEE
HM ?
......?
HEH HEH HEH. RANMA SAOTOME...
CHWOOOOO
...I SHALL LEAD YOU NOW... INTO FELINE HELL!

Part 3

CAT HELL

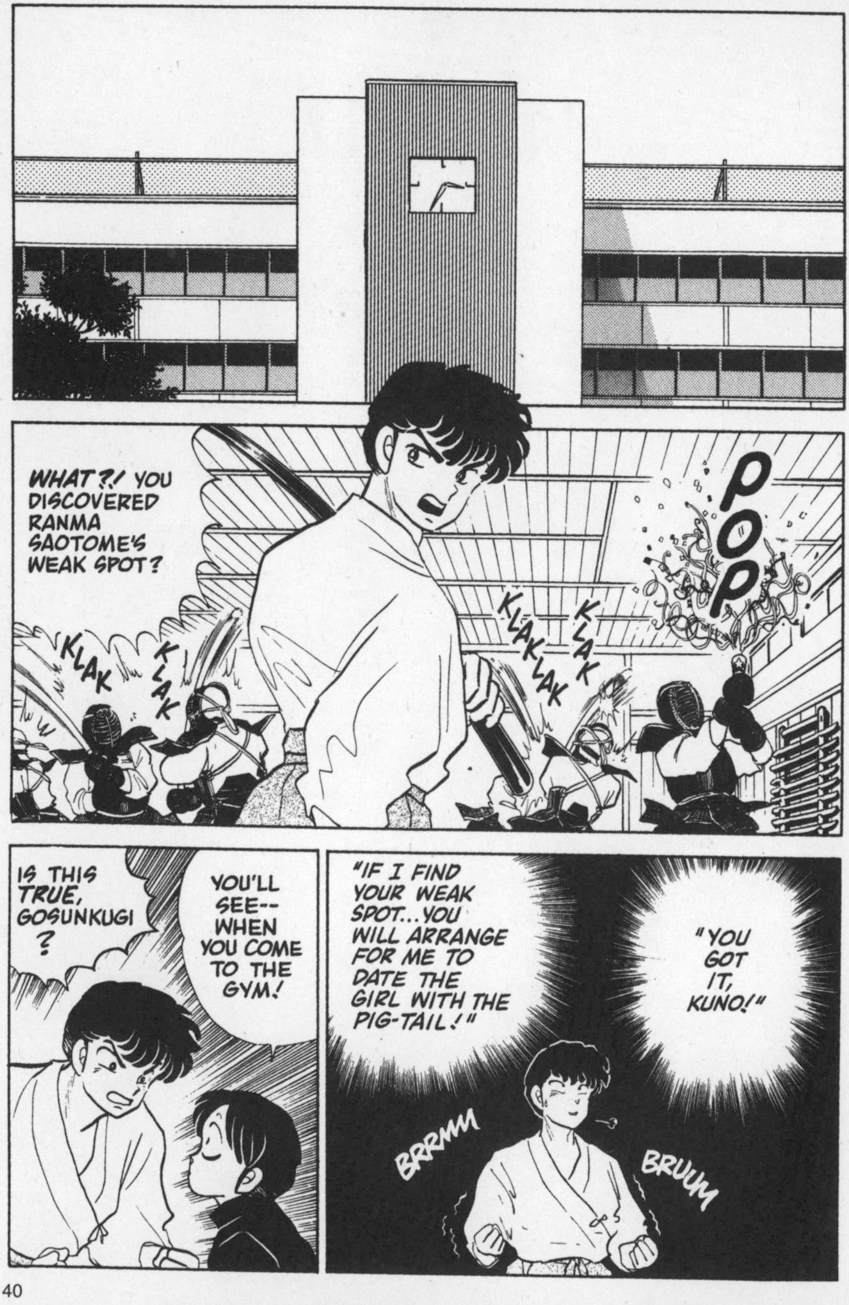
WHAT?! YOU DISCOVERED RANMA SAOTOME'S WEAK SPOT?
KLAK
KLAK
KLAKLAK
KLAK
POP
IS THIS TRUE, GOSUNKUGI?
YOU'LL SEE-- WHEN YOU COME TO THE GYM!
"IF I FIND YOUR WEAK SPOT...YOU WILL ARRANGE FOR ME TO DATE THE GIRL WITH THE PIG-TAIL!"
"YOU GOT IT, KUNO!"
BRRMM
BRUUM

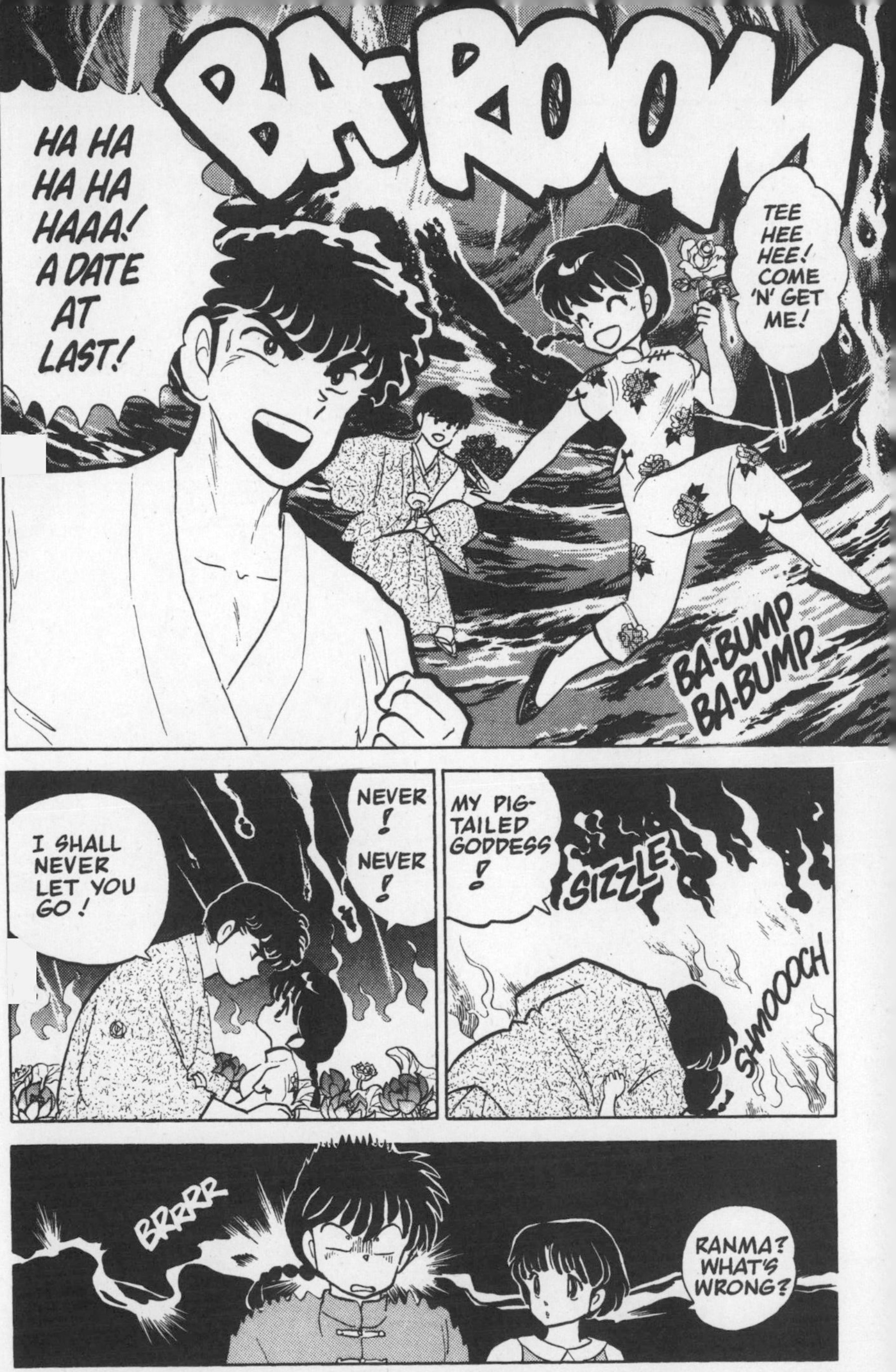
BA-ROOM
HA HA HA HA HAAA! A DATE AT LAST!
TEE HEE HEE! COME 'N' GET ME!
BA-BUMP BA-BUMP
I SHALL NEVER LET YOU GO!
NEVER! NEVER!
MY PIG-TAILED GODDESS!
SIZZLE!
SHMOOOCH
BRRRR
RANMA? WHAT'S WRONG?

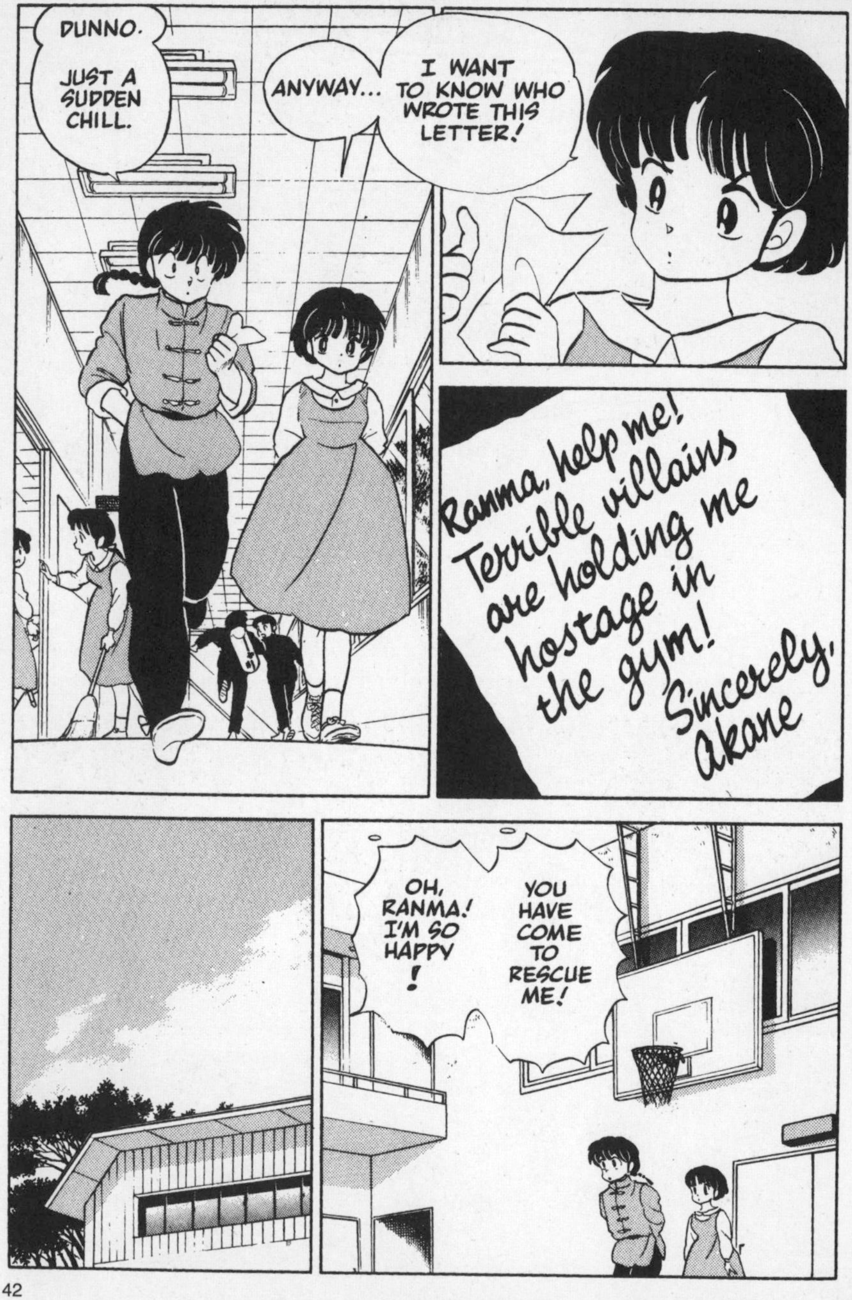
DUNNO.
JUST A SUDDEN CHILL.
ANYWAY...
I WANT TO KNOW WHO WROTE THIS LETTER!
Ranma, help me! Terrible villains are holding me hostage in the gym! Sincerely, Akane
OH, RANMA! I'M SO HAPPY!
YOU HAVE COME TO RESCUE ME!

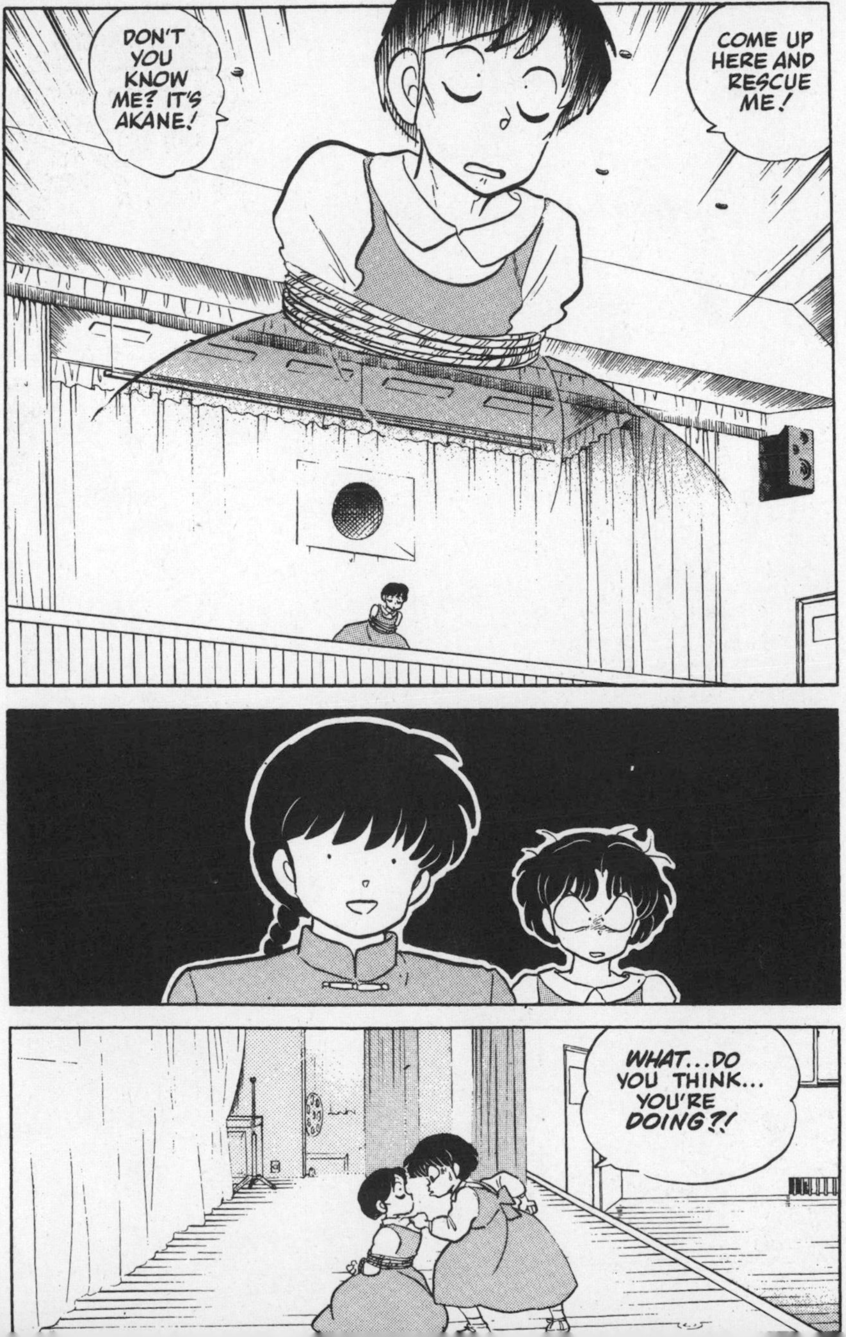
DON'T YOU KNOW ME? IT'S AKANE!
COME UP HERE AND RESCUE ME!
WHAT...DO YOU THINK... YOU'RE DOING?!

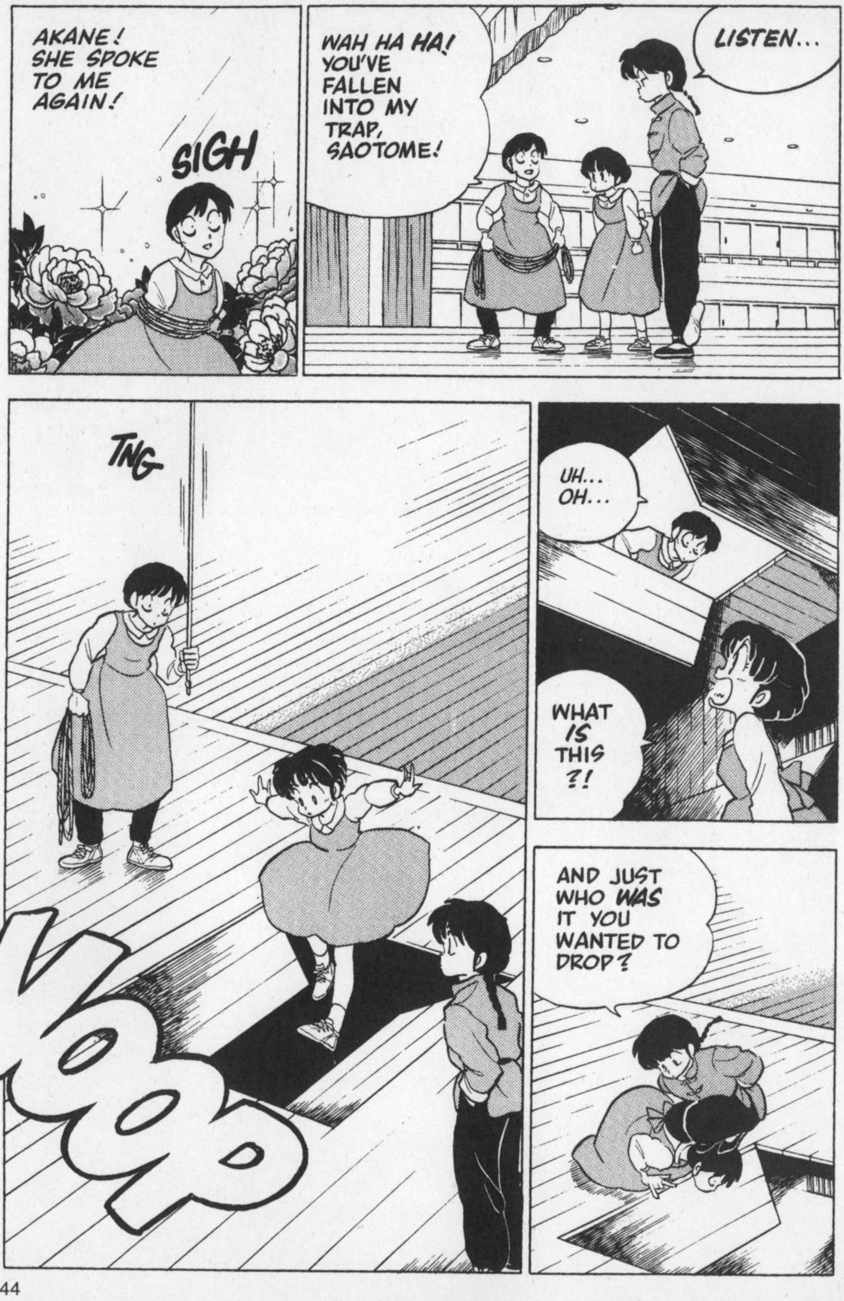
AKANE! SHE SPOKE TO ME AGAIN!
SIGH
WAH HA HA! YOU'VE FALLEN INTO MY TRAP, SAOTOME!
LISTEN...
TNG
VOOP
UH... OH...
WHAT IS THIS ?!
AND JUST WHO WAS IT YOU WANTED TO DROP?

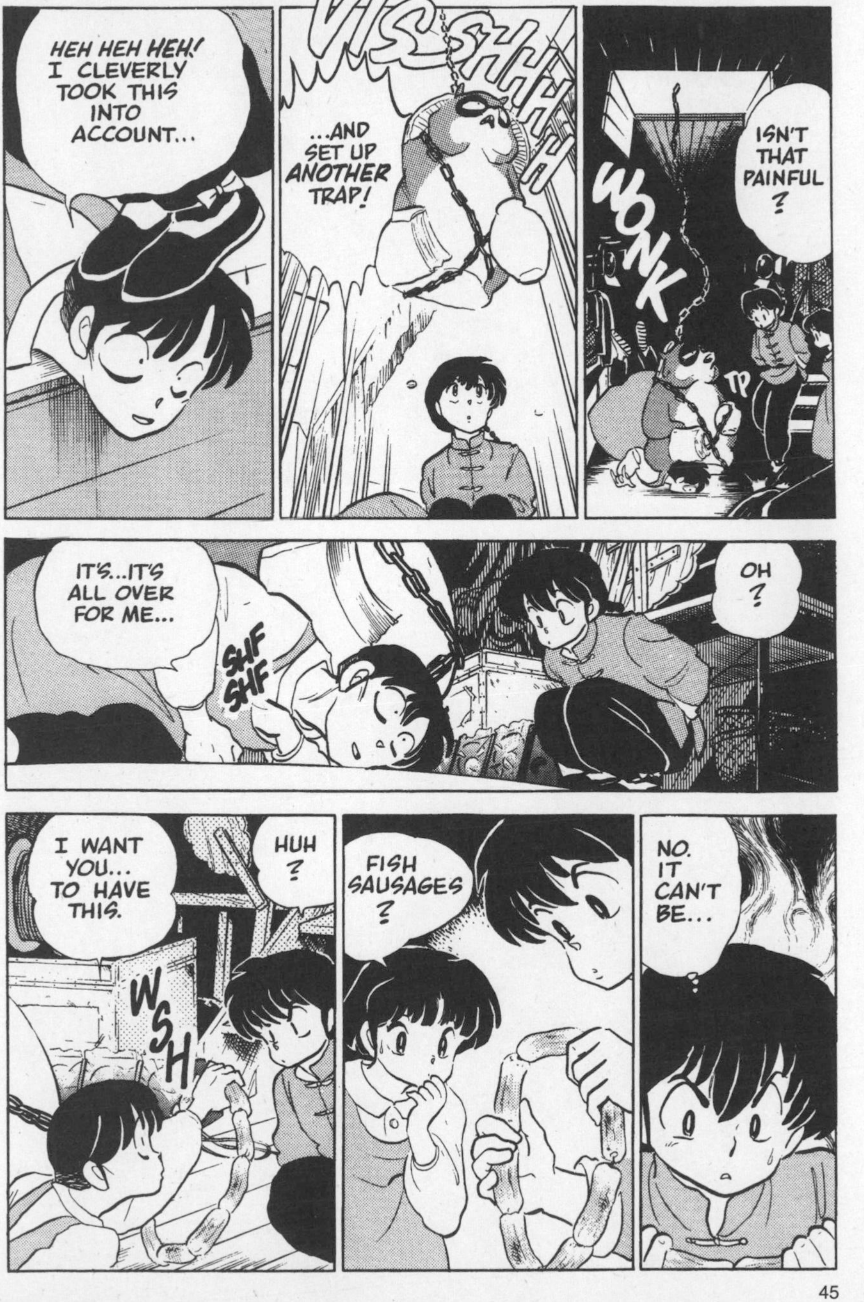
HEH HEH HEH! I CLEVERLY TOOK THIS INTO ACCOUNT...
VISSHHH
...AND SET UP ANOTHER TRAP!
WONK
ISN'T THAT PAINFUL ?
TP
IT'S...IT'S ALL OVER FOR ME...
SHF SHF
OH ?
I WANT YOU... TO HAVE THIS.
HUH ?
WSH
FISH SAUSAGES ?
NO. IT CAN'T BE...

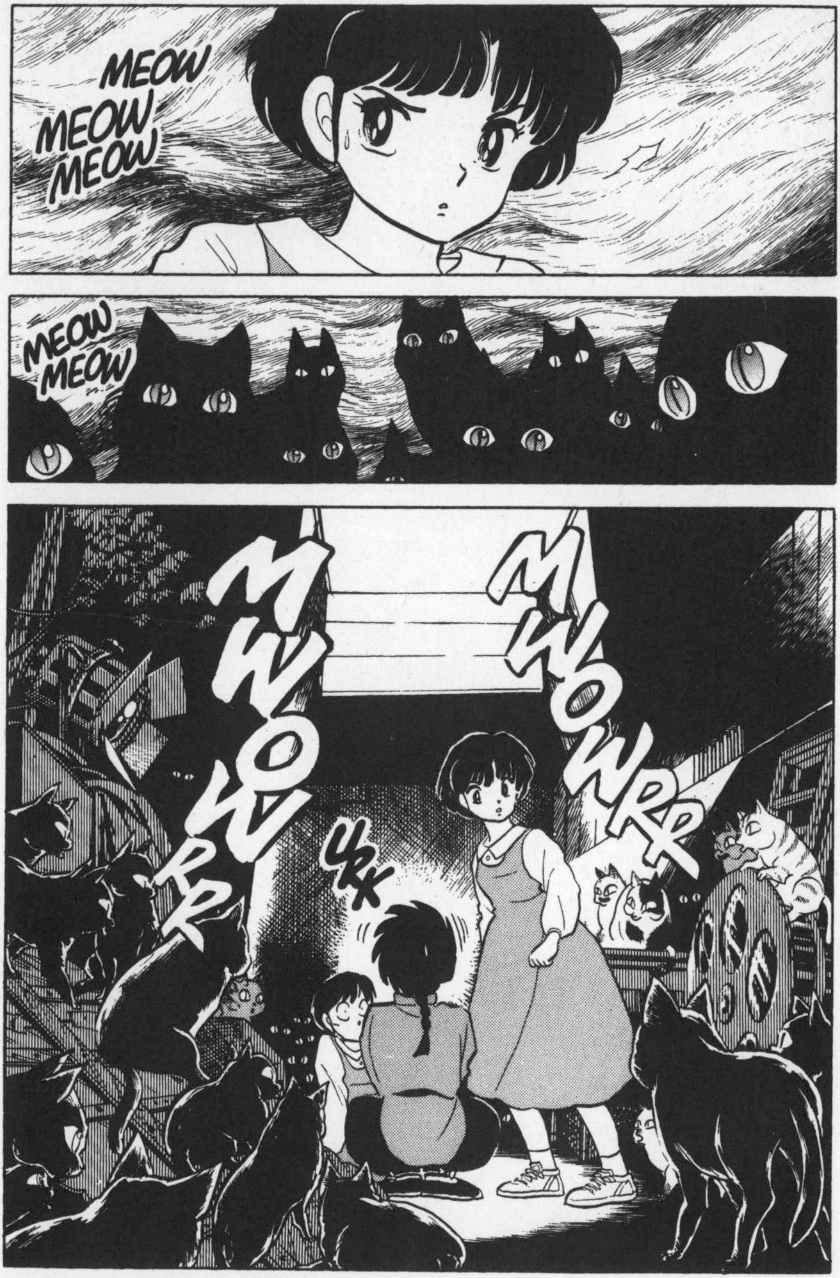
MEOW
MEOW MEOW
MEOW
MEOW MEOW
MWOWRR
MWOWRR
UKK

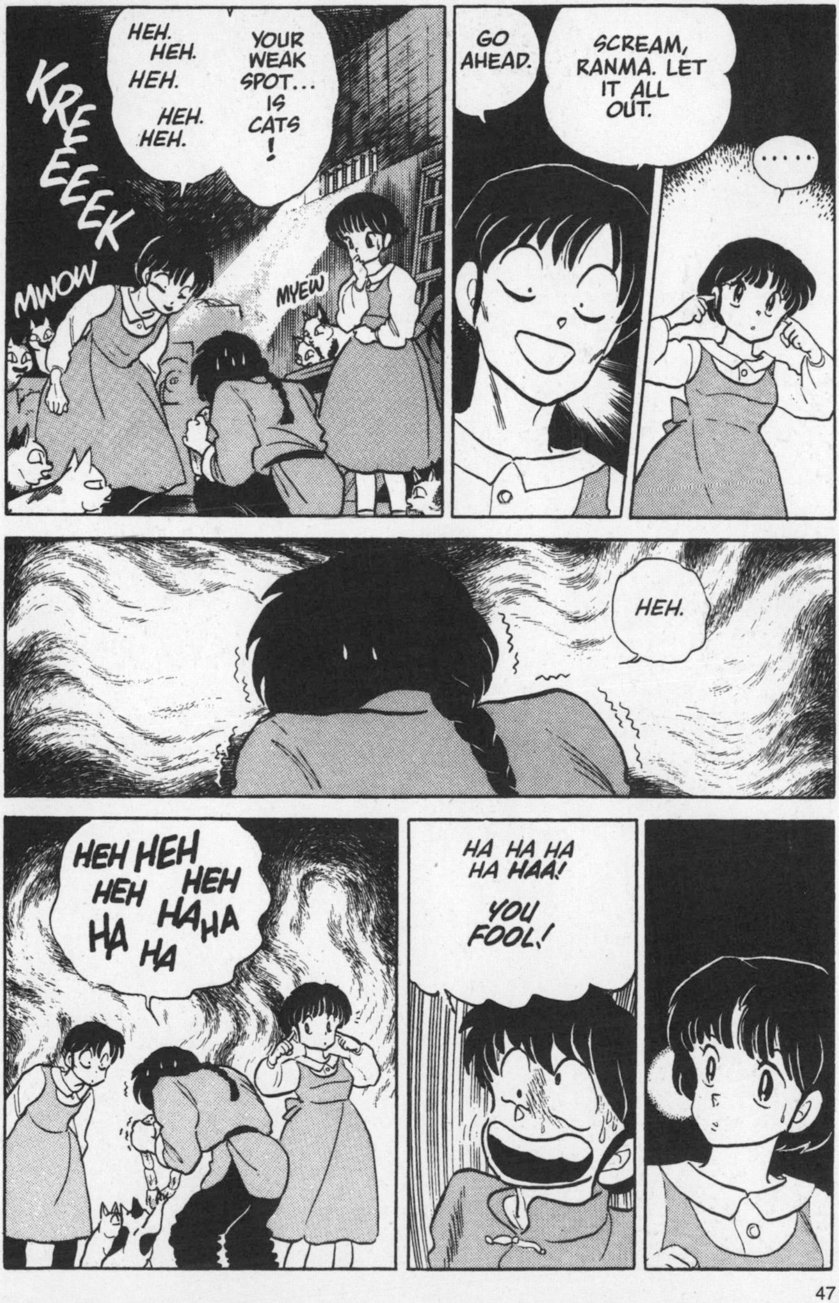
HEH. HEH. HEH. HEH. HEH.
YOUR WEAK SPOT... IS CATS!
KREEEEEK
MWOW
MYEW
GO AHEAD.
SCREAM, RANMA. LET IT ALL OUT.
......
HEH.
HEH HEH HEH HEH HA HA HA HA
HA HA HA HA HAA!
YOU FOOL!

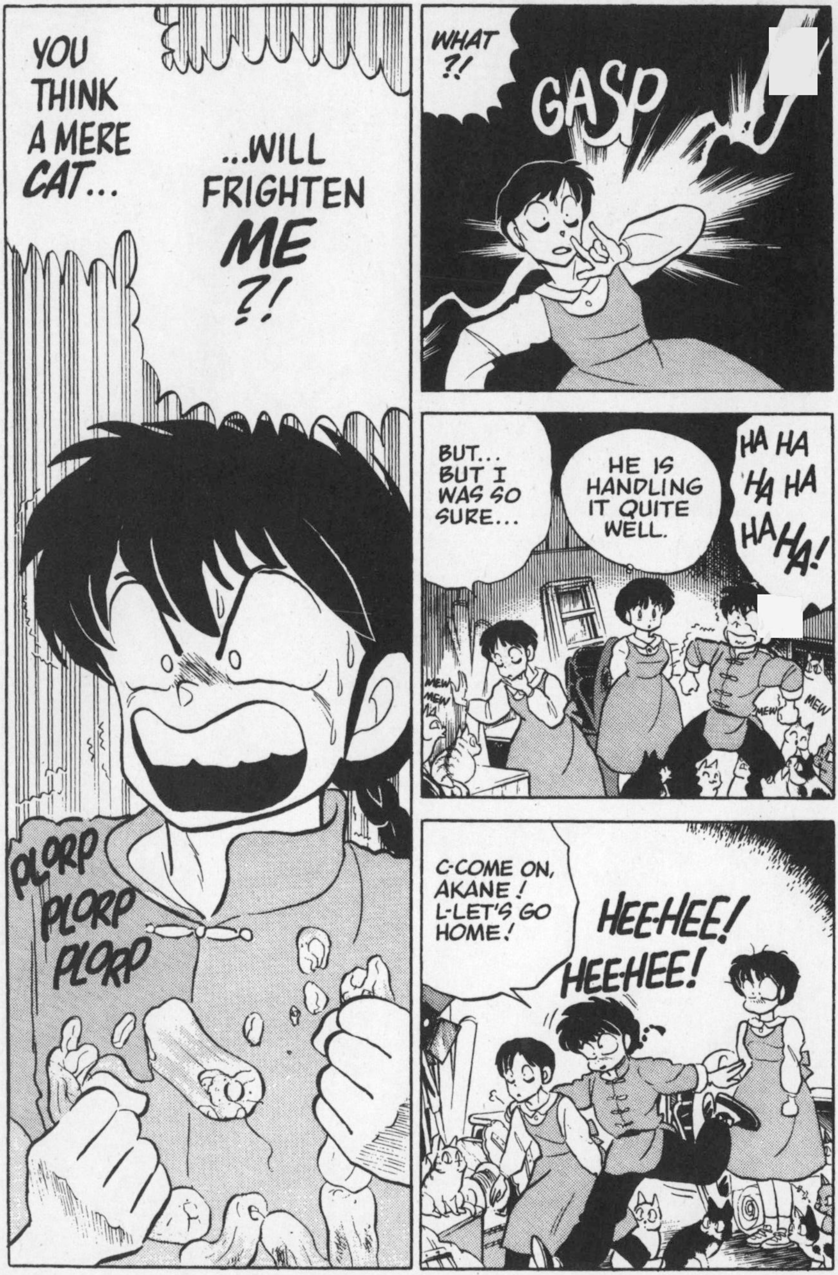
YOU THINK A MERE CAT...
...WILL FRIGHTEN ME ?!
PLORP PLORP PLORP
WHAT ?!
GASP
BUT... BUT I WAS SO SURE...
HE IS HANDLING IT QUITE WELL.
HA HA HA HA HA HA!
MEW MEW
MEW
MEW
C-COME ON, AKANE! L-LET'S GO HOME!
HEE-HEE! HEE-HEE!

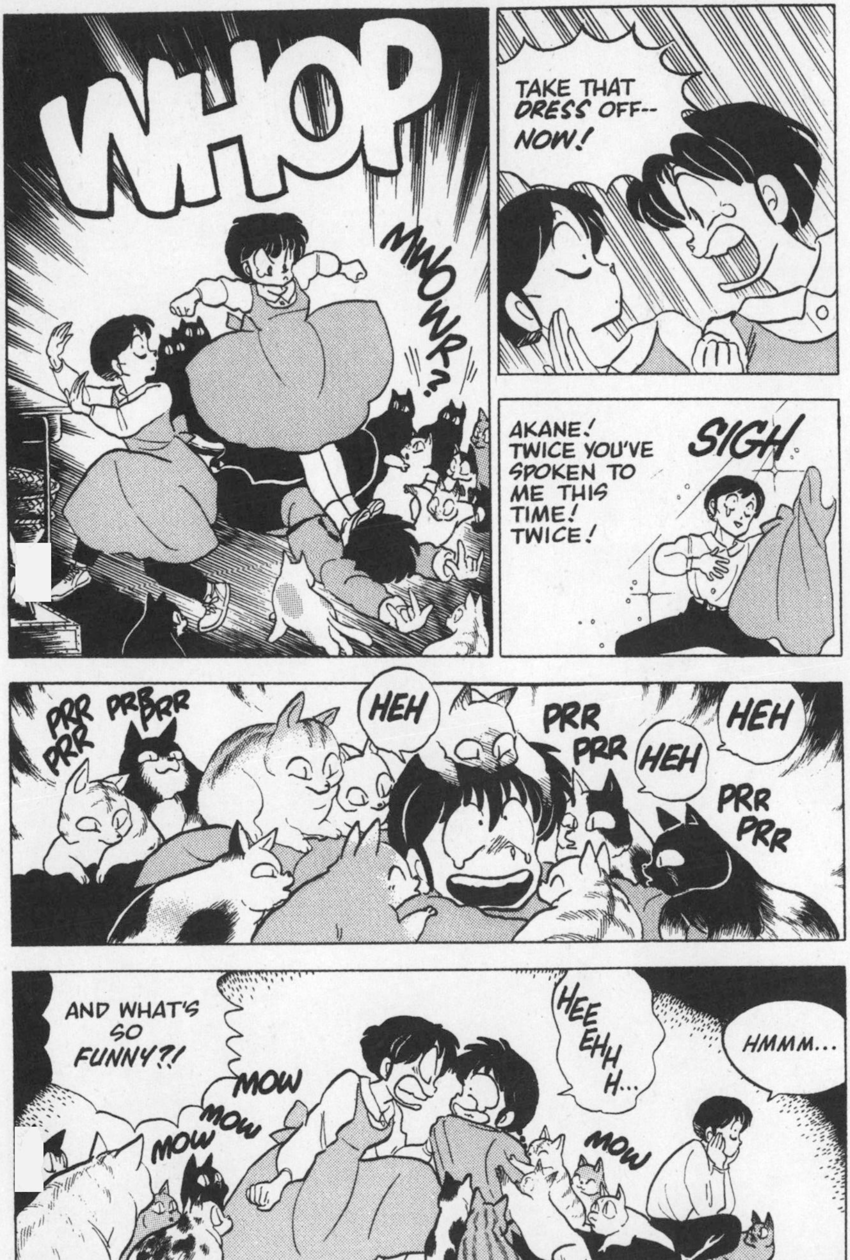
WHOP
MWOWR?
TAKE THAT DRESS OFF-- NOW!
AKANE! TWICE YOU'VE SPOKEN TO ME THIS TIME! TWICE!
SIGH
PRR PRR
PRR PRR
HEH
PRR PRR
HEH
HEH
PRR PRR
AND WHAT'S SO FUNNY?!
MOW
MOW
MOW
HEEEHHH...
MOW
HMMM...

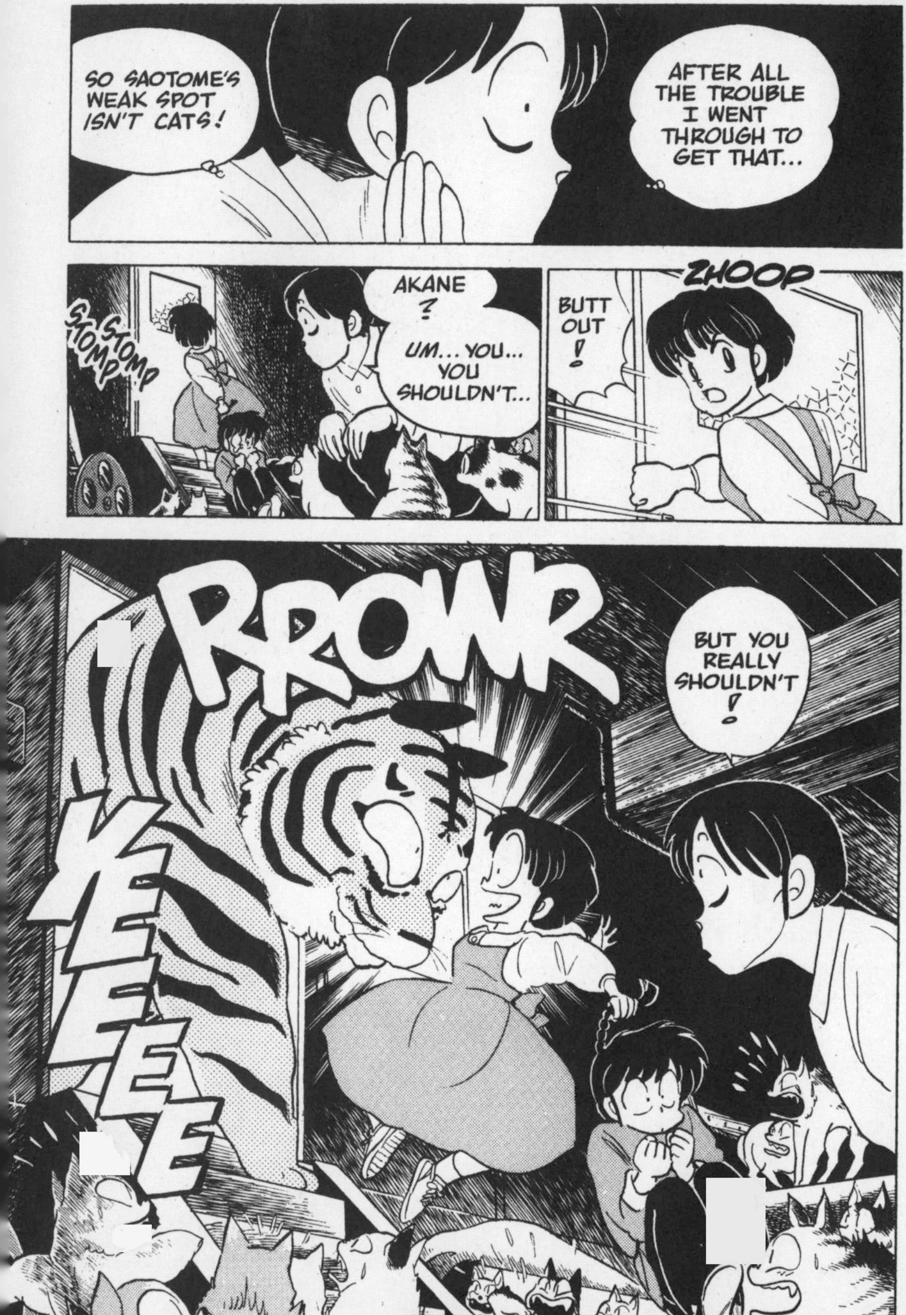
SO SAOTOME'S WEAK SPOT ISN'T CATS!
AFTER ALL THE TROUBLE I WENT THROUGH TO GET THAT...
STOMP STOMP
AKANE?
UM... YOU... YOU SHOULDN'T...
ZHOOP
BUTT OUT!
RROWR
BUT YOU REALLY SHOULDN'T!
YEEEEE

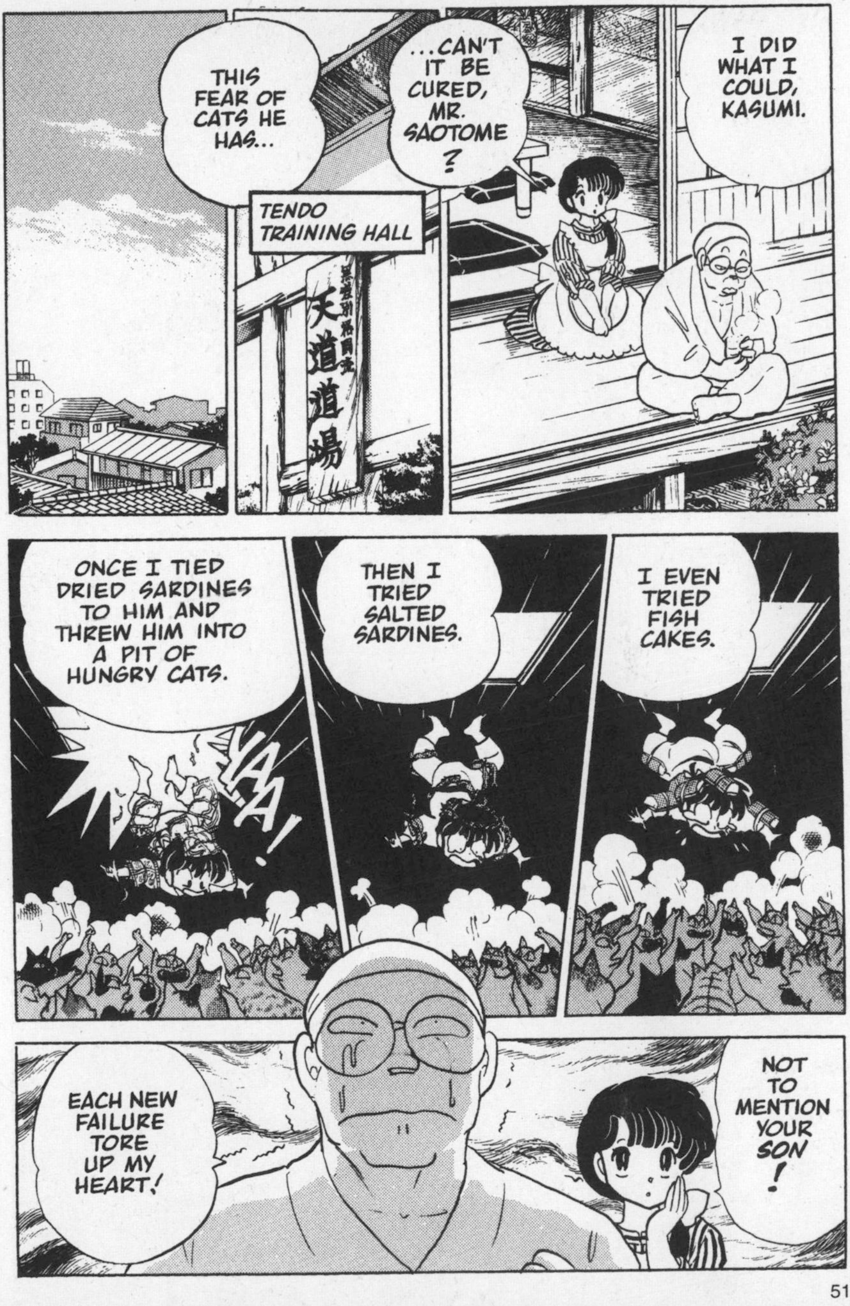
THIS FEAR OF CATS HE HAS...
...CAN'T IT BE CURED, MR. SAOTOME?
TENDO TRAINING HALL
天道道場
I DID WHAT I COULD, KASUMI.
ONCE I TIED DRIED SARDINES TO HIM AND THREW HIM INTO A PIT OF HUNGRY CATS.
YAAA!
THEN I TRIED SALTED SARDINES.
I EVEN TRIED FISH CAKES.
EACH NEW FAILURE TORE UP MY HEART!
NOT TO MENTION YOUR SON!

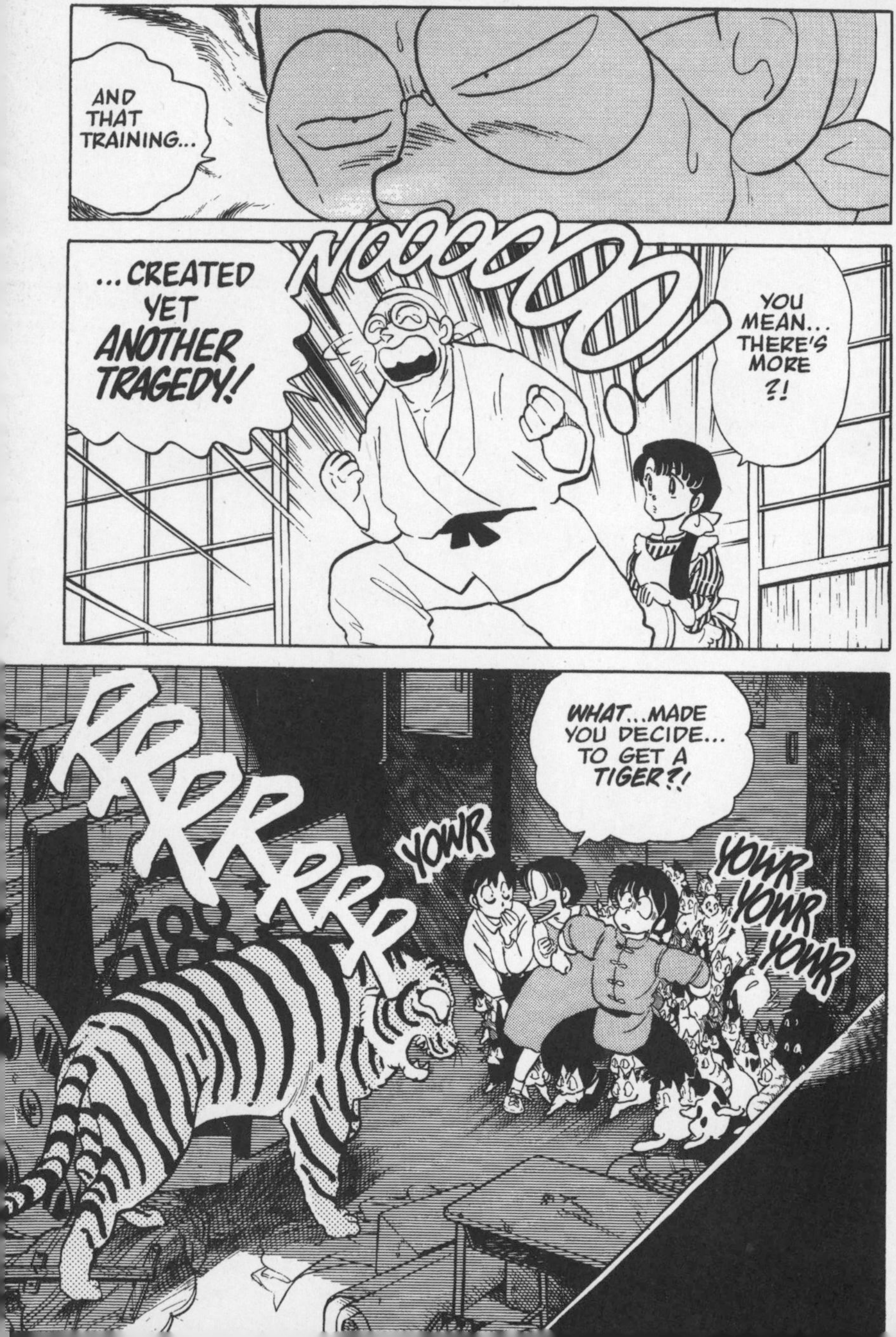

AND THAT TRAINING...
...CREATED YET ANOTHER TRAGEDY!
NOOOOOO!
YOU MEAN... THERE'S MORE ?!
RRRRRRR
WHAT...MADE YOU DECIDE... TO GET A TIGER?!
YOWR
YOWR YOWR YOWR

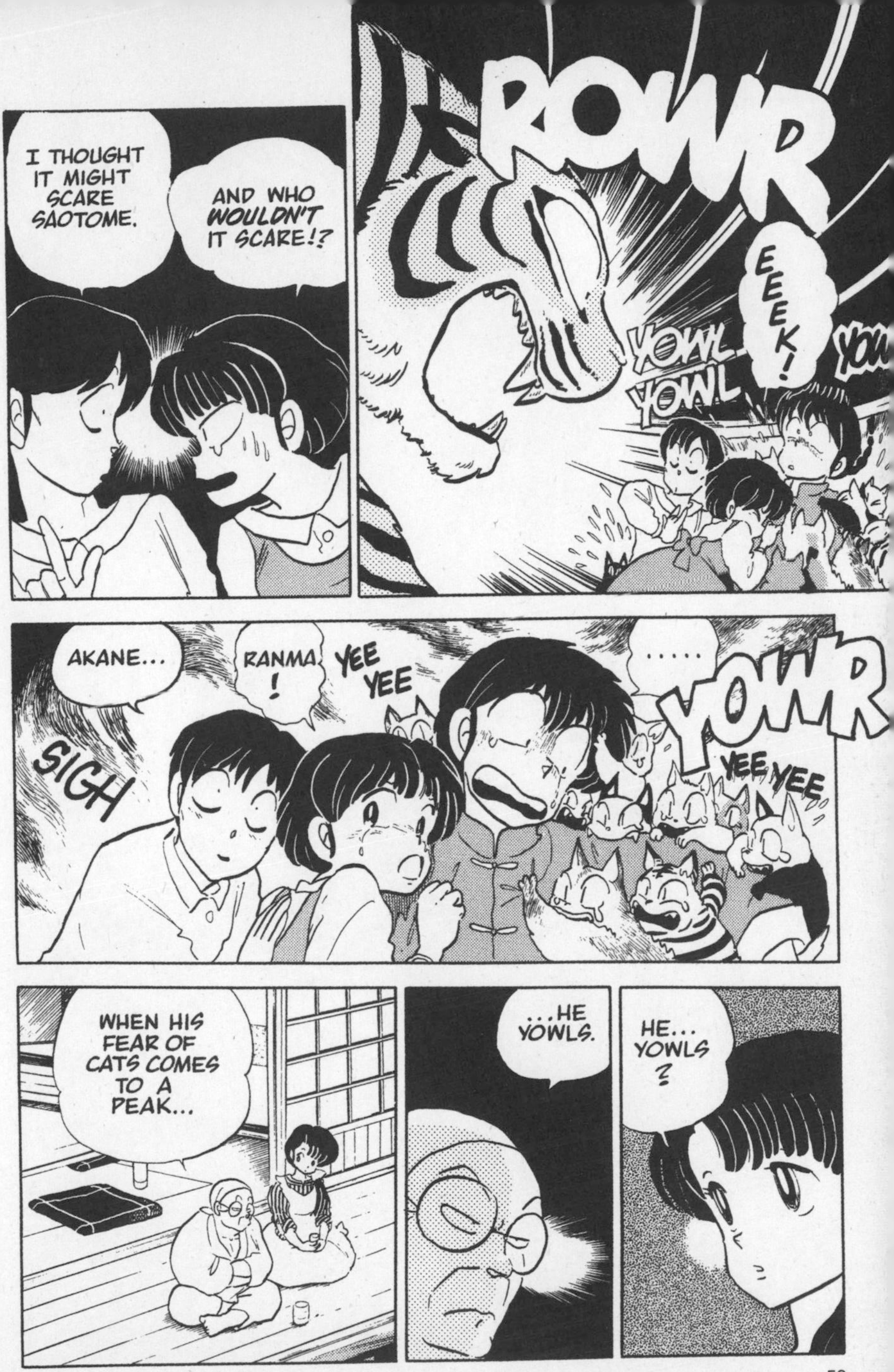
I THOUGHT IT MIGHT SCARE SAOTOME.
AND WHO WOULDN'T IT SCARE!?
ROWR
EEEK!
YOWL
YOWL
AKANE...
RANMA!
YEE YEE
SIGH
.....
YOWR
YEE YEE
WHEN HIS FEAR OF CATS COMES TO A PEAK...
...HE YOWLS.
HE... YOWLS?

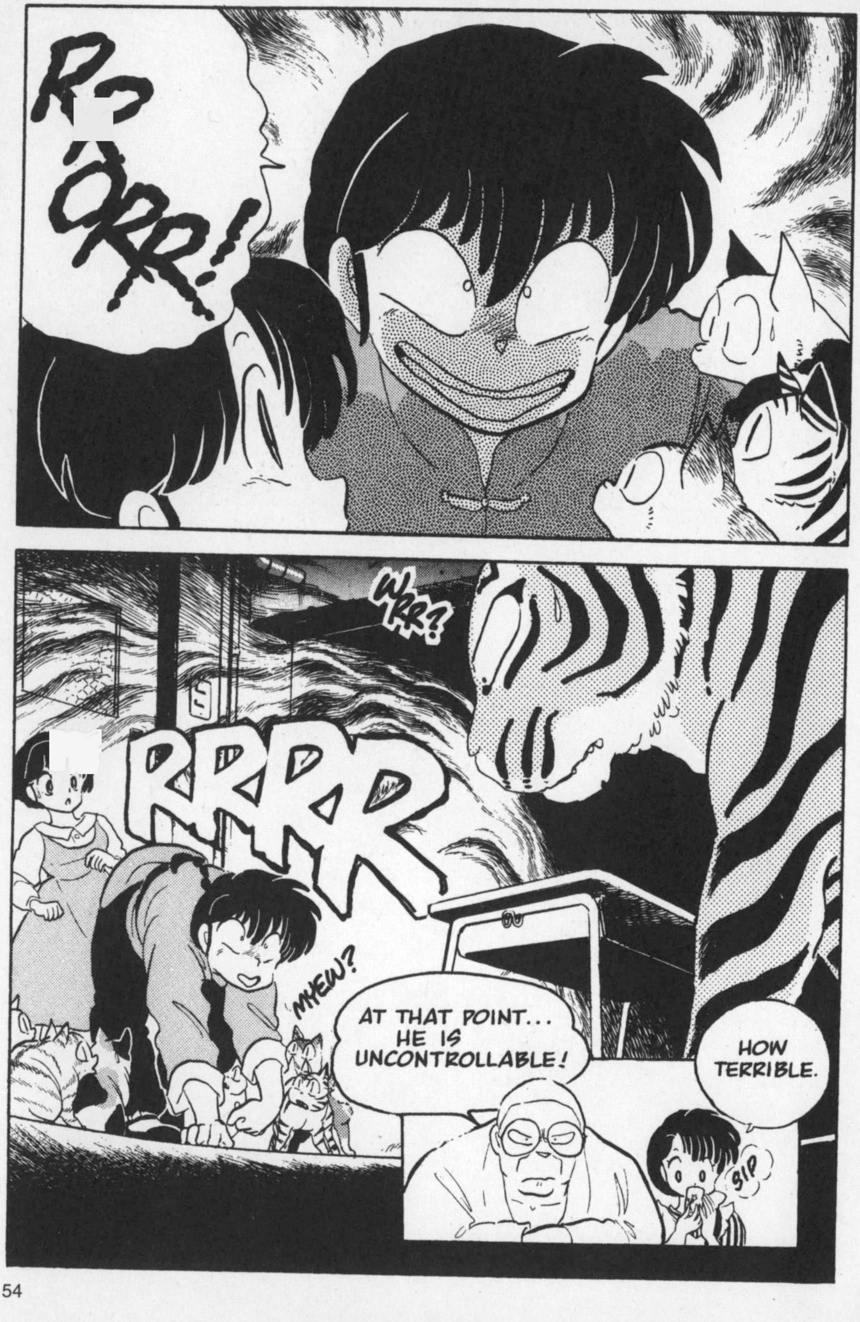
ROAORR!
WRR?
RRRR
MYEW?
AT THAT POINT... HE IS UNCONTROLLABLE!
HOW TERRIBLE.
SIP

Part 4

CAT-FU

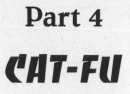

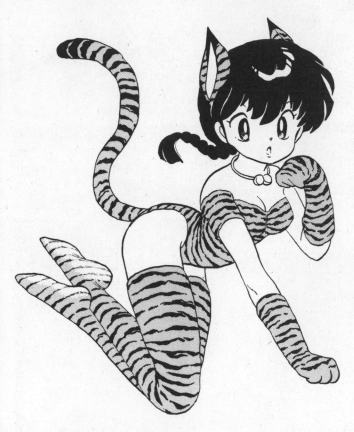

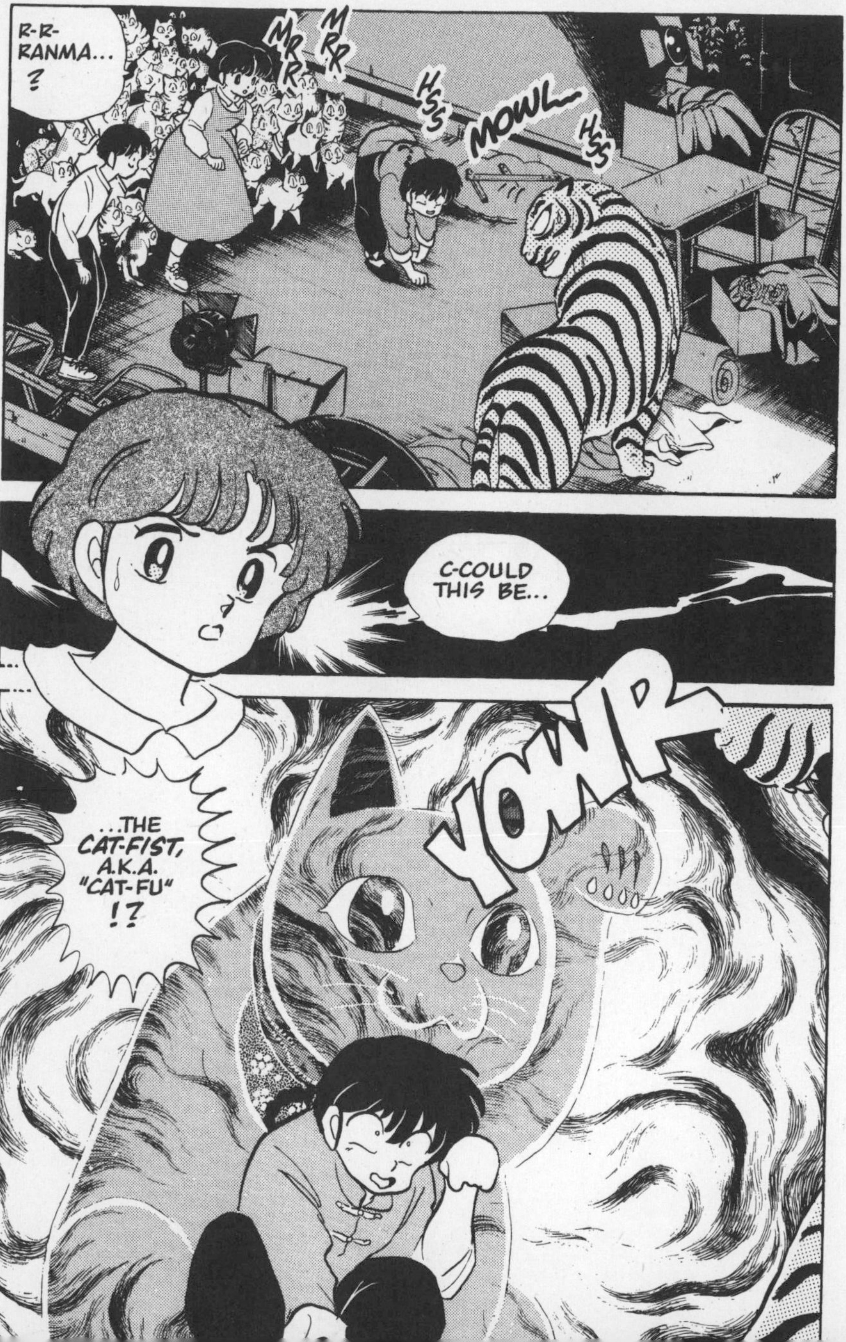
R-R-RANMA... ?
MRR
MRR
HSS
MOWL...
HSS
C-COULD THIS BE...
...THE CAT-FIST, A.K.A. "CAT-FU" !?
YOWR

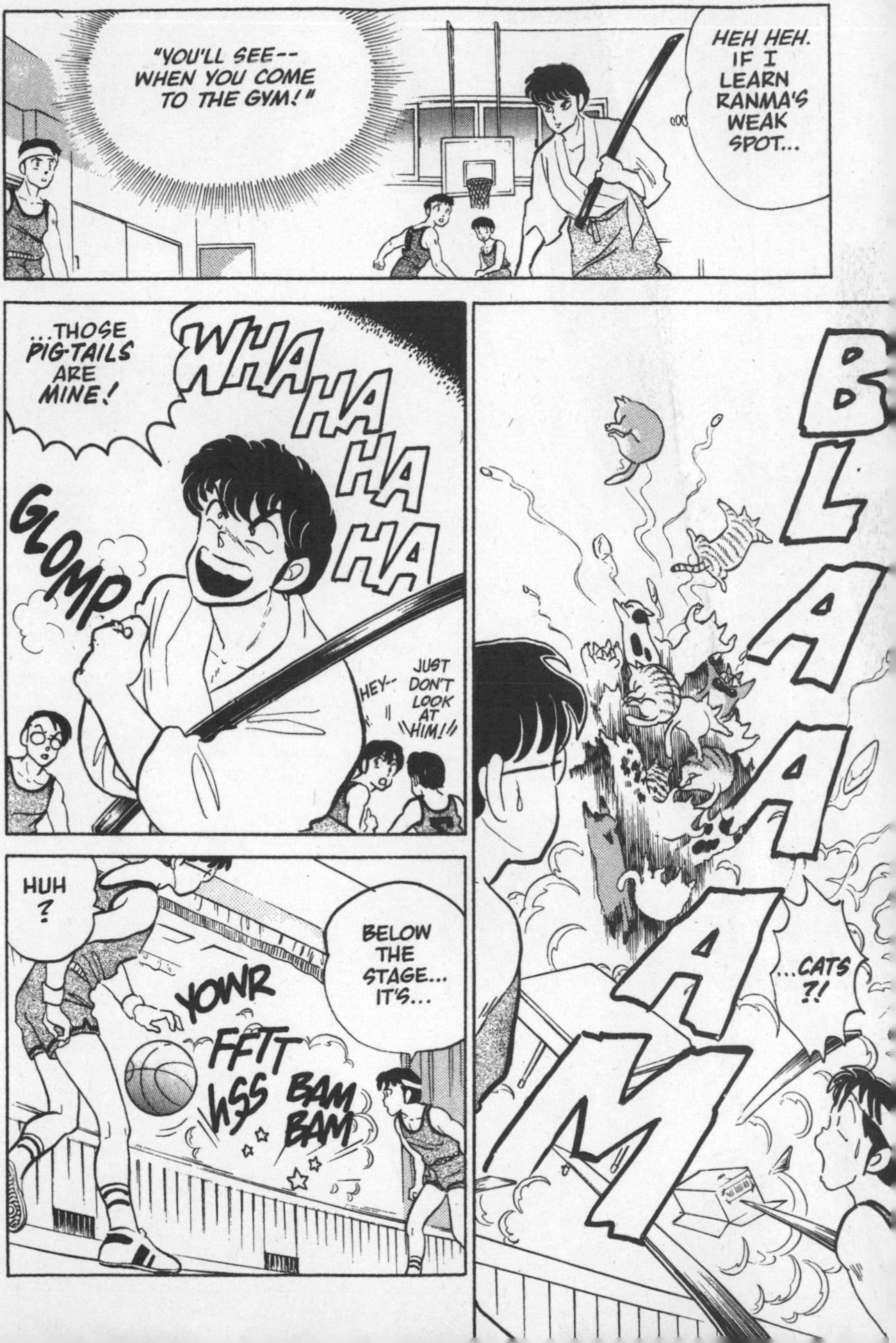
"YOU'LL SEE--
WHEN YOU COME
TO THE GYM!"
HEH HEH.
IF I
LEARN
RANMA'S
WEAK
SPOT...
...THOSE
PIG-TAILS
ARE
MINE!
WHA HA HA HA HA
GLOMP
HEY--
JUST
DON'T
LOOK
AT
HIM!
HUH
?
BELOW
THE
STAGE...
IT'S...
YOWR
FFTT
HSS
BAM
BAM
BLAAAAM
...CATS
?!

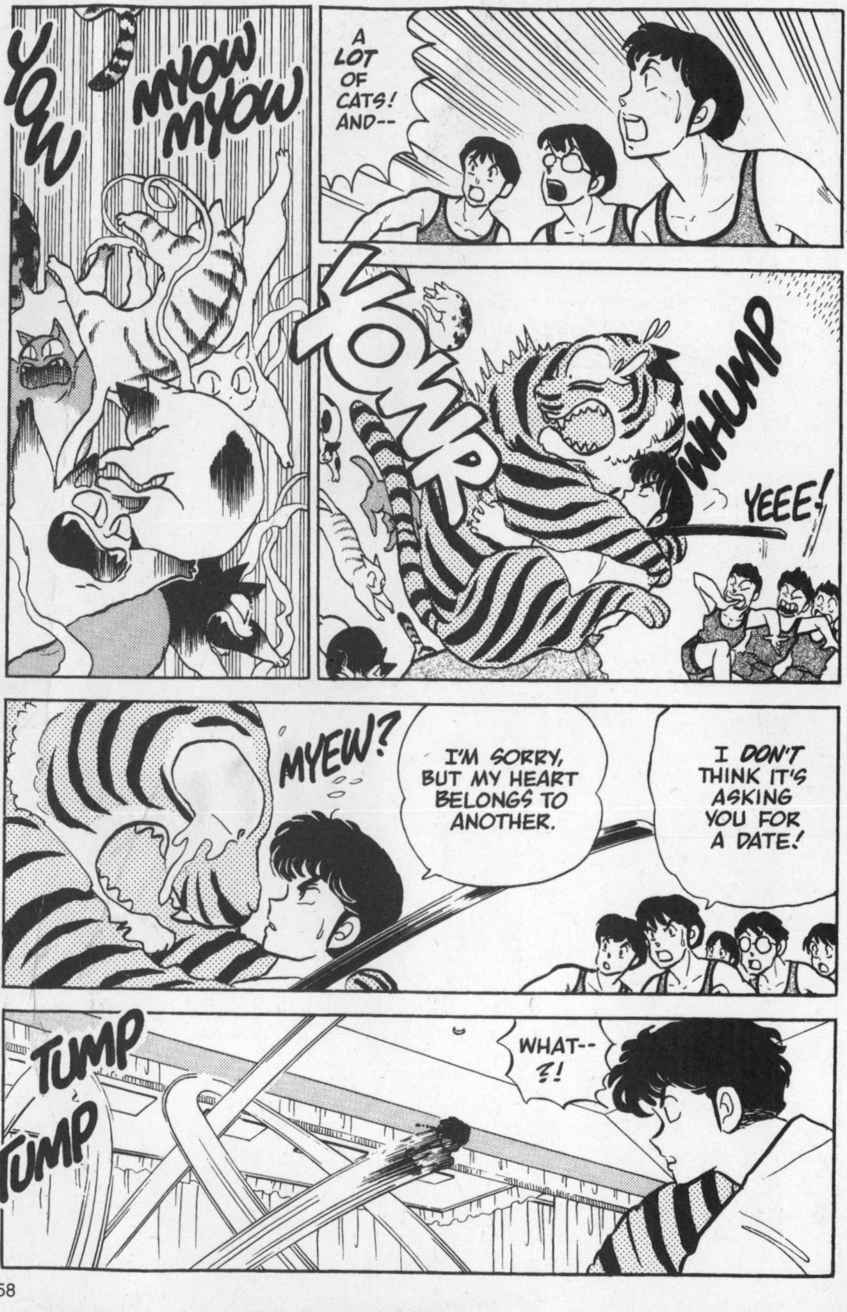
YOW
MYOW MYOW
A LOT OF CATS! AND--
YOWR
WHUMP
YEEE!
MYEW?
I'M SORRY, BUT MY HEART BELONGS TO ANOTHER.
I DON'T THINK IT'S ASKING YOU FOR A DATE!
TUMP TUMP
WHAT-- ?!

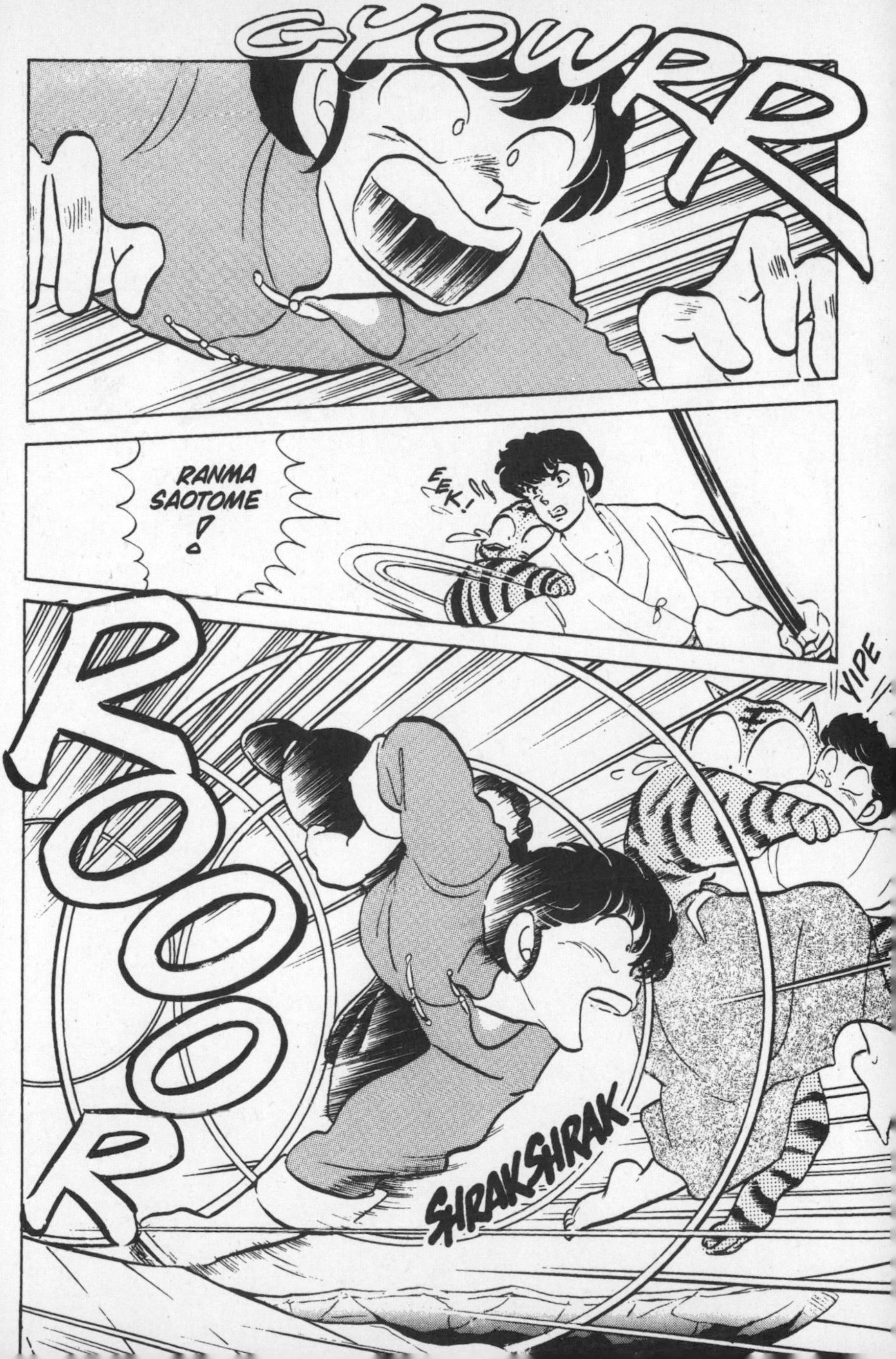
GYOWRR
RANMA SAOTOME !
EEK!
YIPE
ROOOOR
SHRAKSHRAK

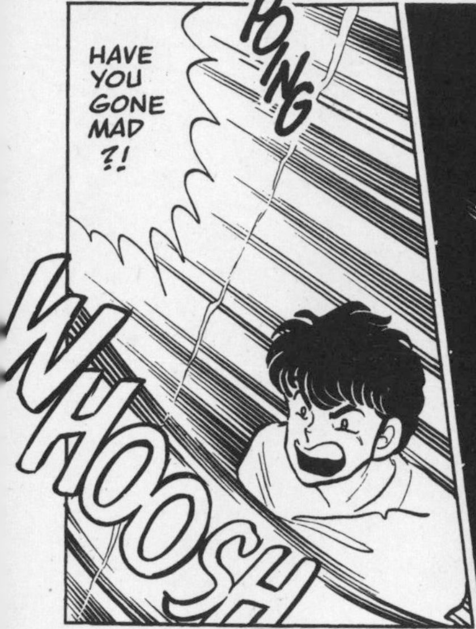
HAVE YOU GONE MAD ?!
POING
WHOOSH
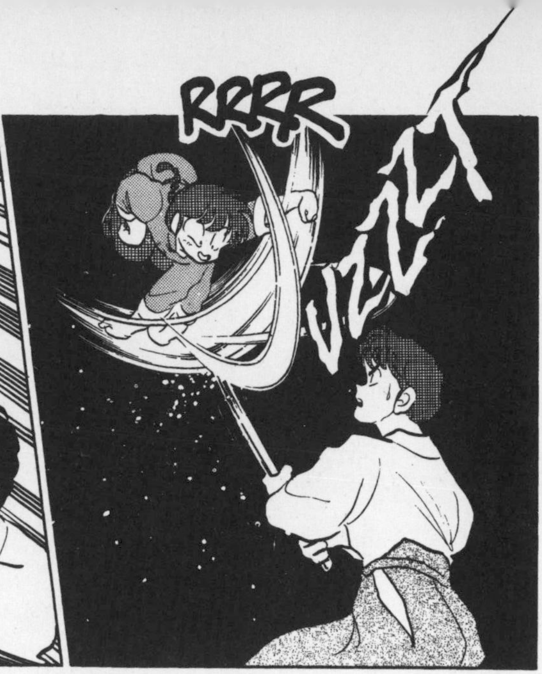
RRRR
VZZZT
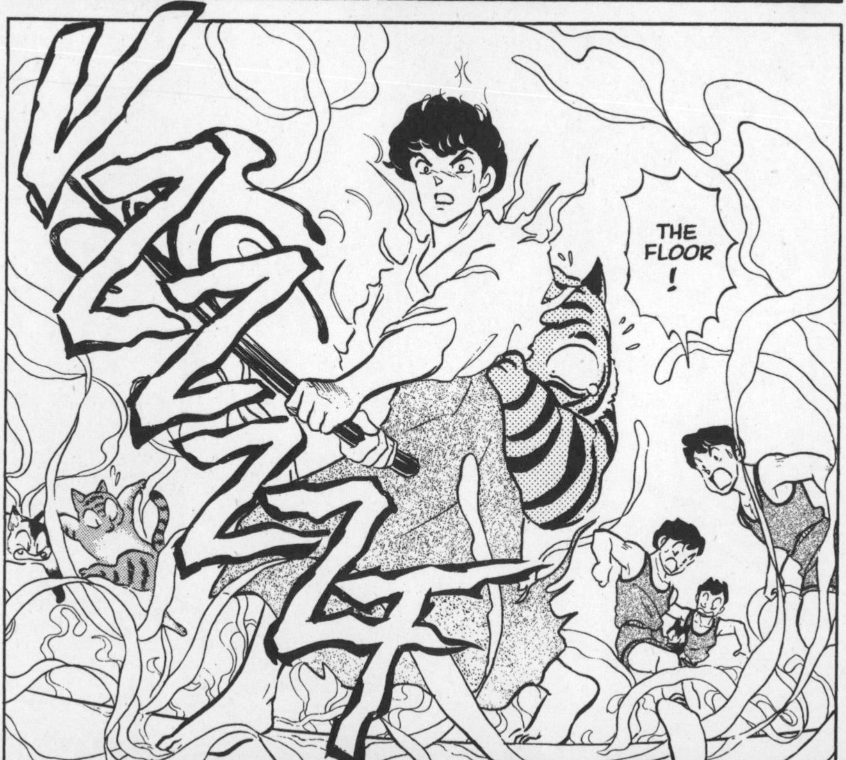
VZZZZ
THE FLOOR !

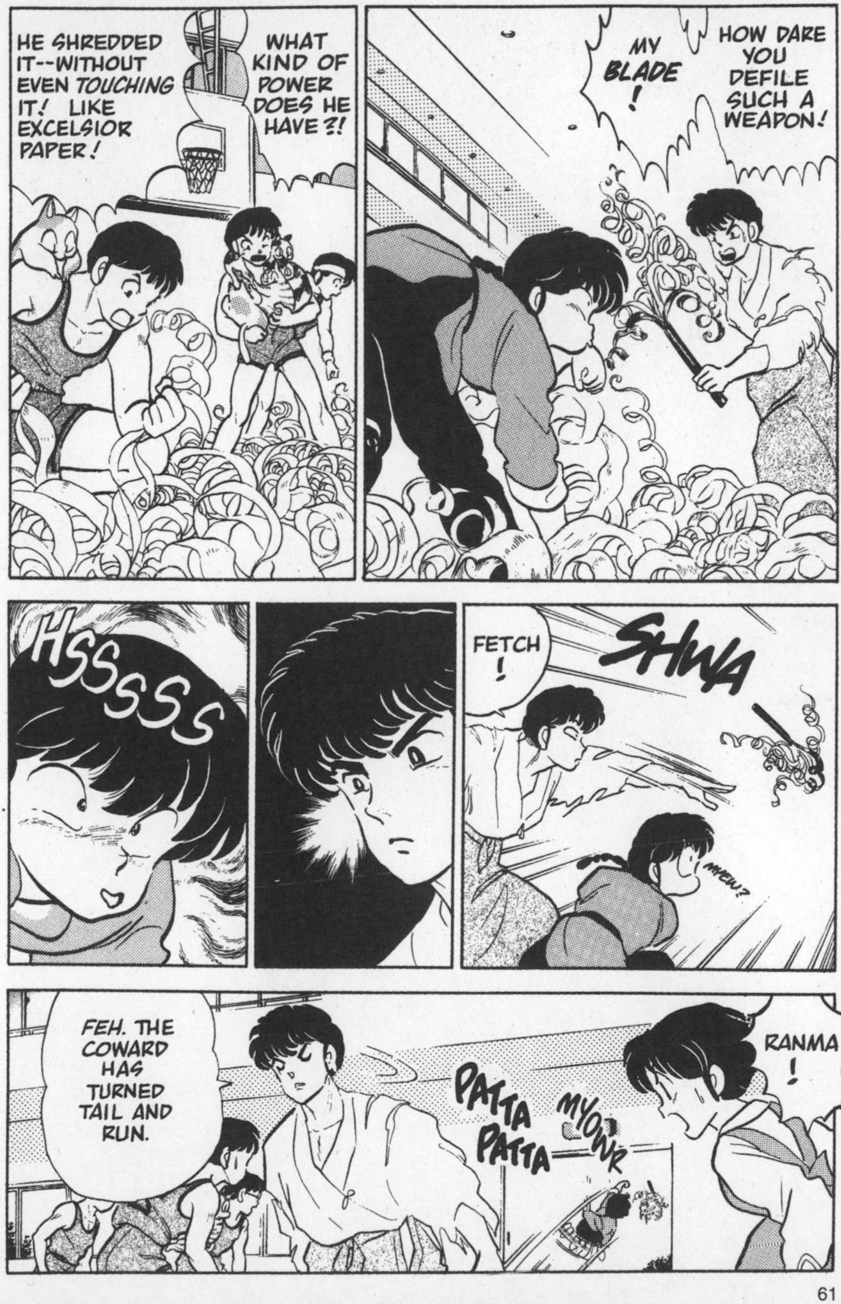
HE SHREDDED IT--WITHOUT EVEN TOUCHING IT! LIKE EXCELSIOR PAPER!
WHAT KIND OF POWER DOES HE HAVE?!
MY BLADE!
HOW DARE YOU DEFILE SUCH A WEAPON!
HSSSSSS
FETCH!
SHWA
MYEW?
FEH. THE COWARD HAS TURNED TAIL AND RUN.
PATTA PATTA
MYOWR
RANMA!

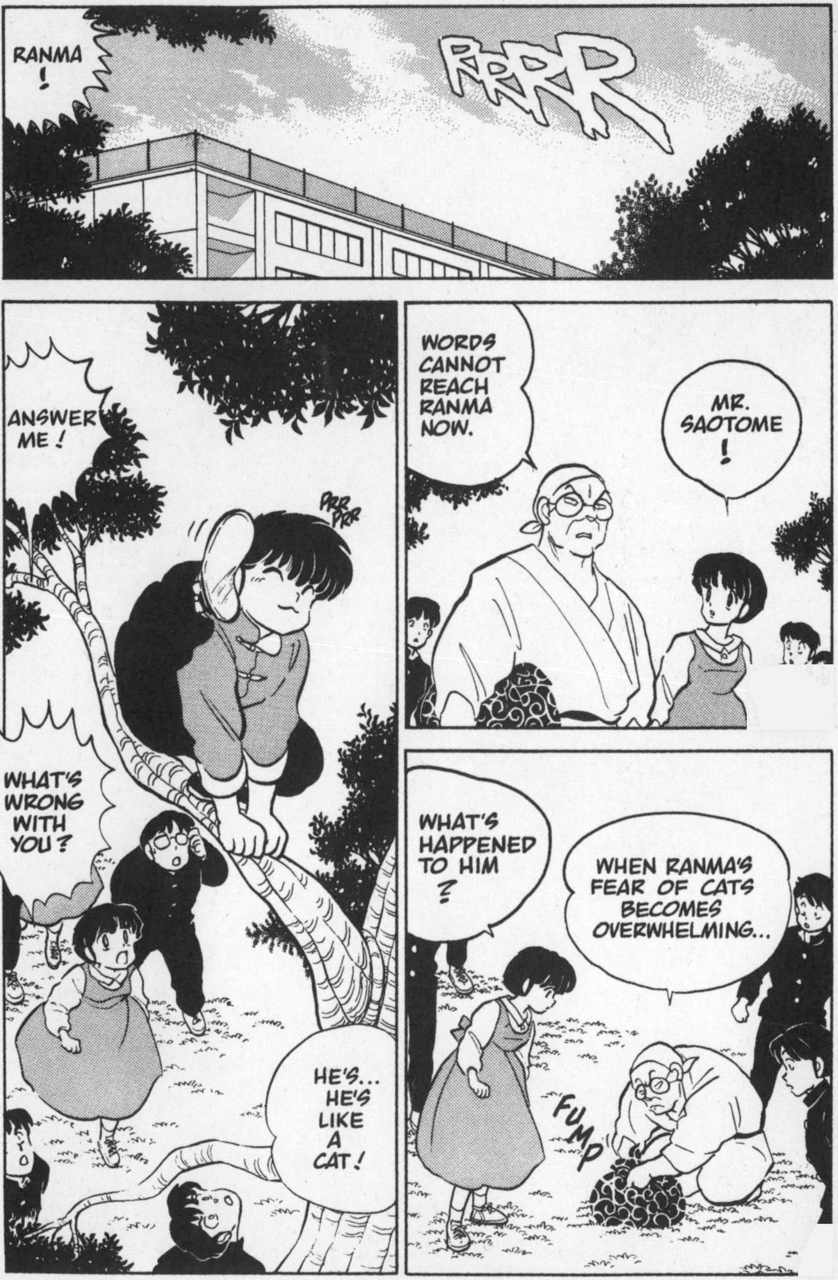
RANMA!
RRRR
ANSWER ME!
PRR PRR
WHAT'S WRONG WITH YOU?
HE'S... HE'S LIKE A CAT!
WORDS CANNOT REACH RANMA NOW.
MR. SAOTOME!
WHAT'S HAPPENED TO HIM?
WHEN RANMA'S FEAR OF CATS BECOMES OVERWHELMING...
FUMP

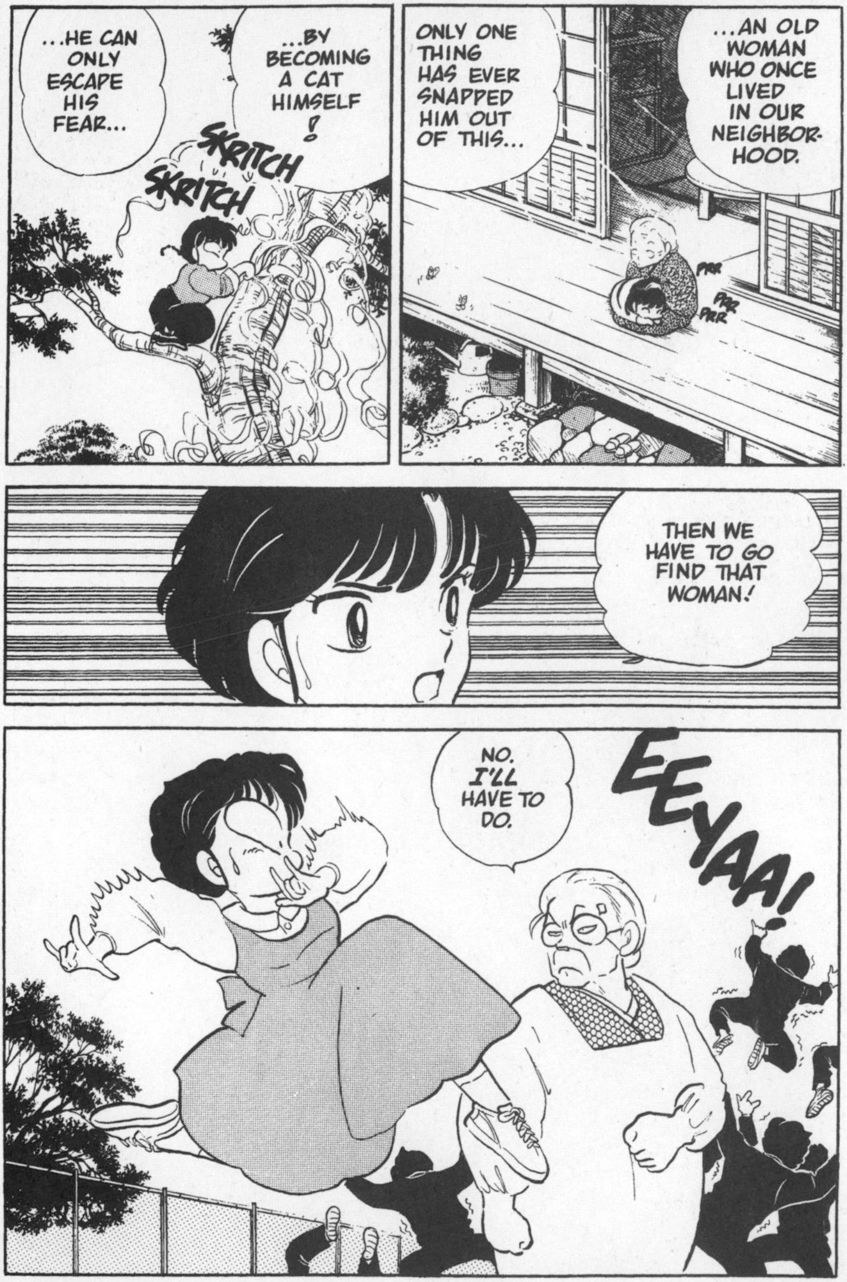
...HE CAN ONLY ESCAPE HIS FEAR...
...BY BECOMING A CAT HIMSELF!
SKRITCH SKRITCH
ONLY ONE THING HAS EVER SNAPPED HIM OUT OF THIS...
...AN OLD WOMAN WHO ONCE LIVED IN OUR NEIGHBOR-HOOD.
PRR
PRR PRR
THEN WE HAVE TO GO FIND THAT WOMAN!
NO. I'LL HAVE TO DO.
EEYAAA!

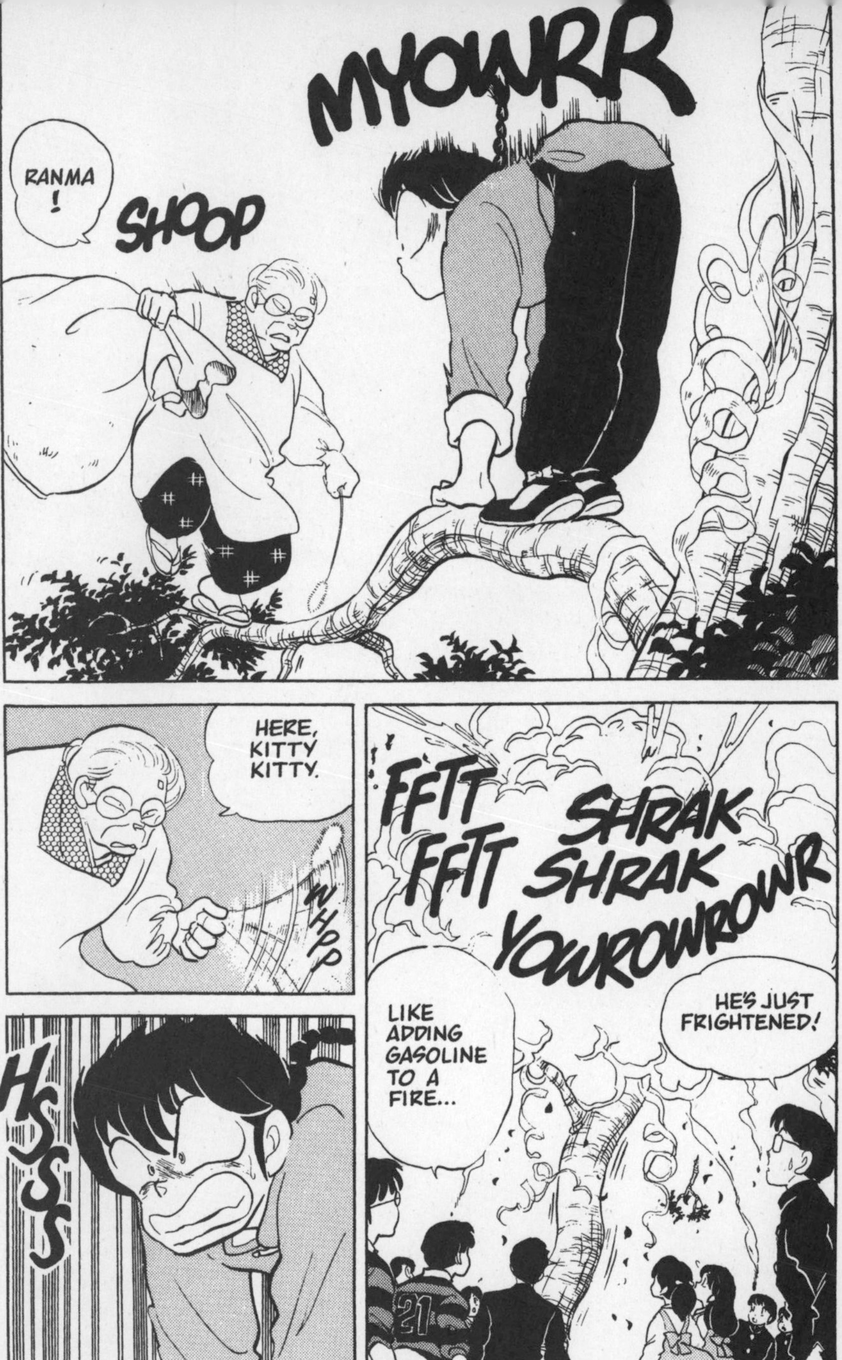
RANMA !
SHOOP
MYOWRR
HERE, KITTY KITTY.
WHPP
HSSS
FFTT FFTT
SHRAK SHRAK
YOWROWROWR
LIKE ADDING GASOLINE TO A FIRE...
HE'S JUST FRIGHTENED!

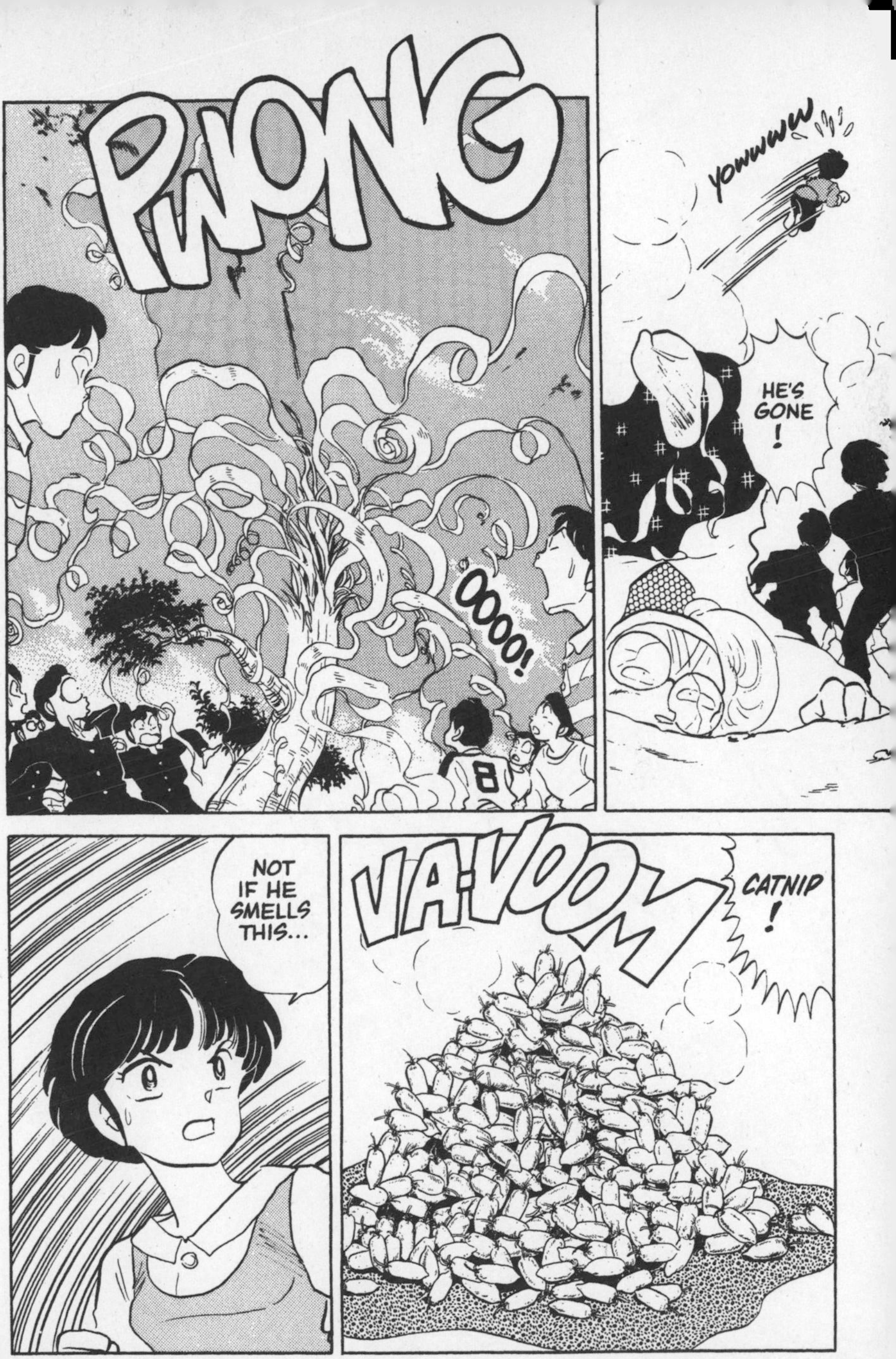
PWONG
OOOO!
YOWWWW
HE'S GONE!
NOT IF HE SMELLS THIS...
VA-VOOM
CATNIP!

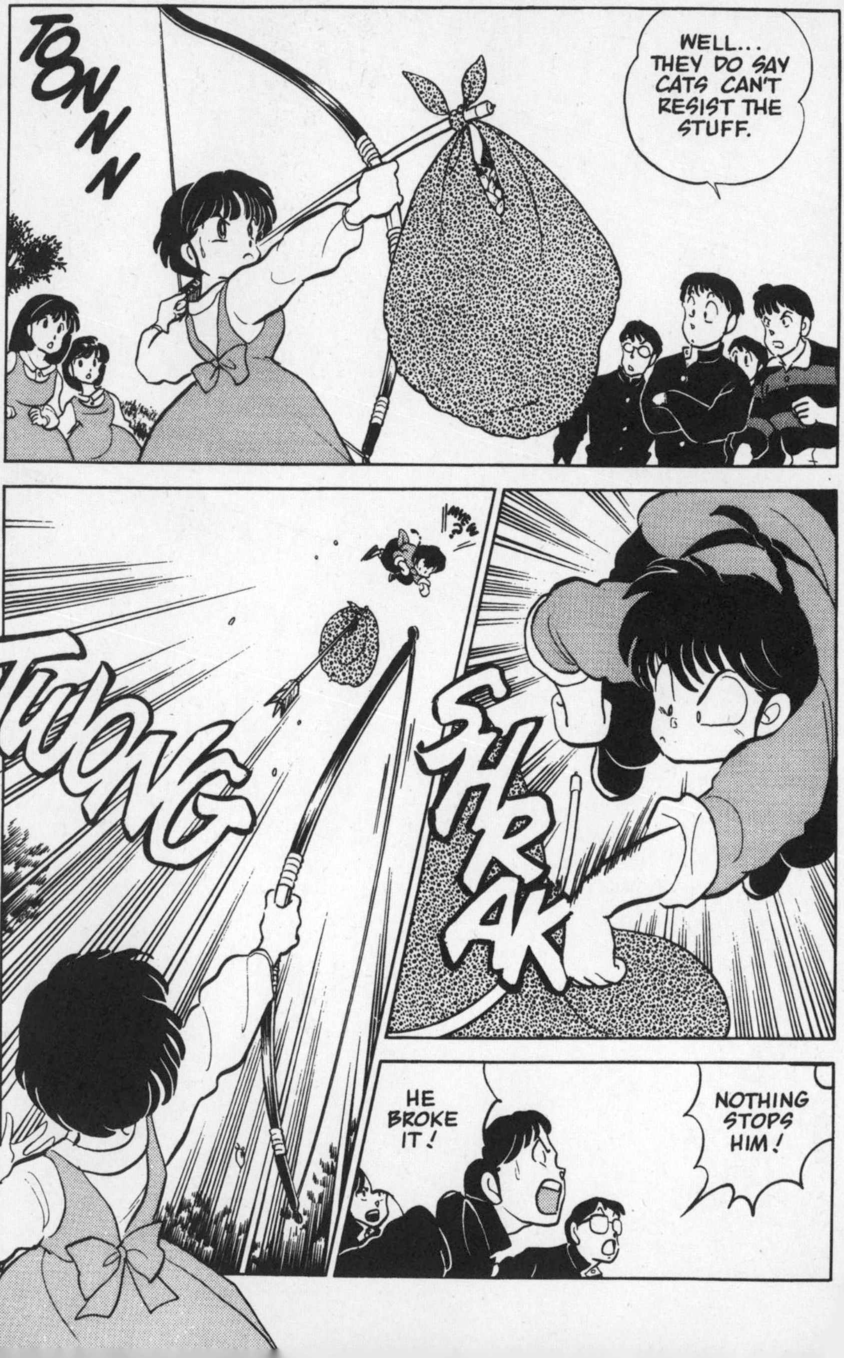
TOONNN
WELL... THEY DO SAY CATS CAN'T RESIST THE STUFF.
MEW?
TWUNG
SHRAK
HE BROKE IT!
NOTHING STOPS HIM!

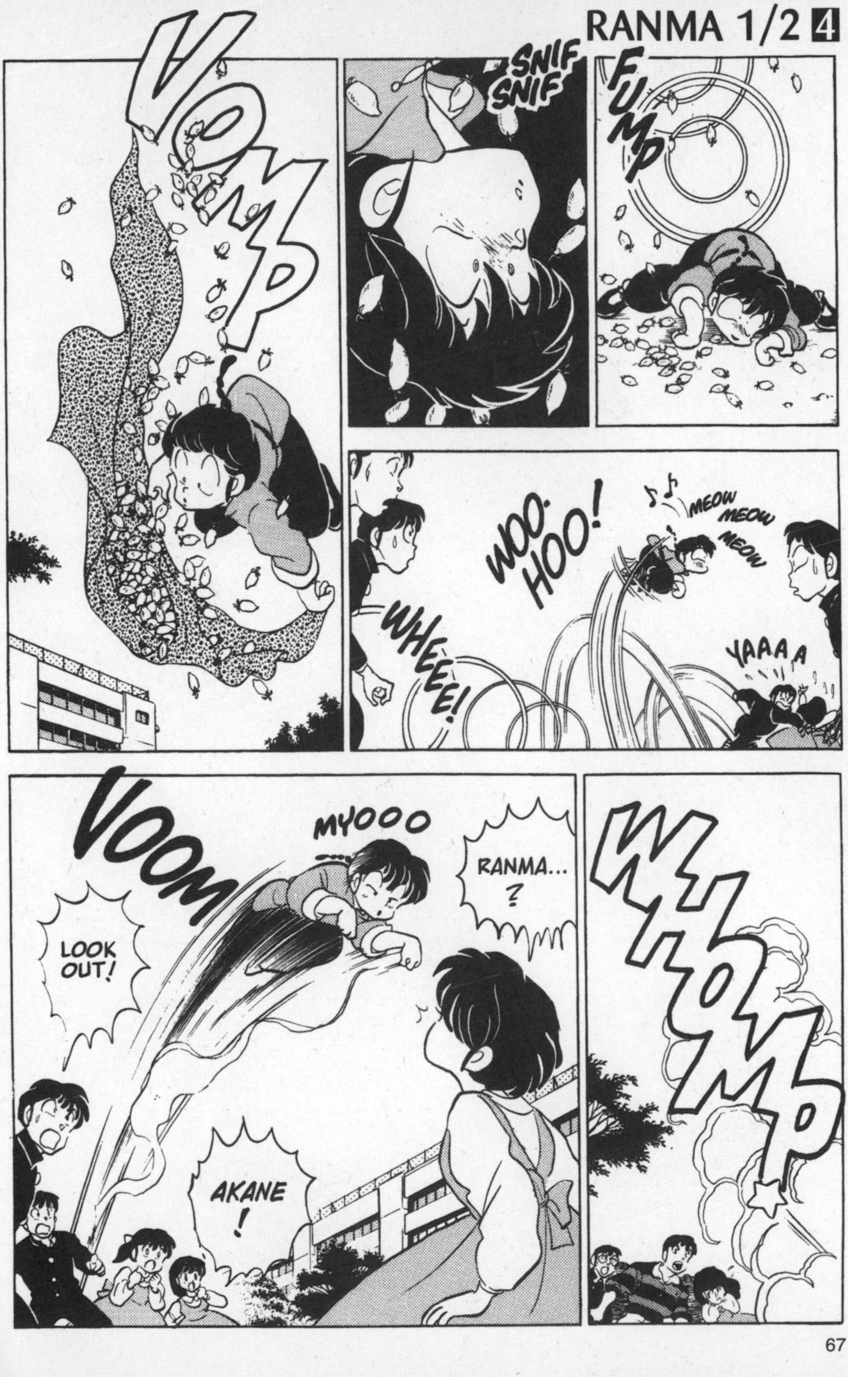
VOMP
SNIF SNIF
FUMP
WOO-HOO!
MEOW MEOW MEOW
WHEEEE!
YAAAA
VOOM
MYOOO
LOOK OUT!
RANMA...?
AKANE!
WHOMP

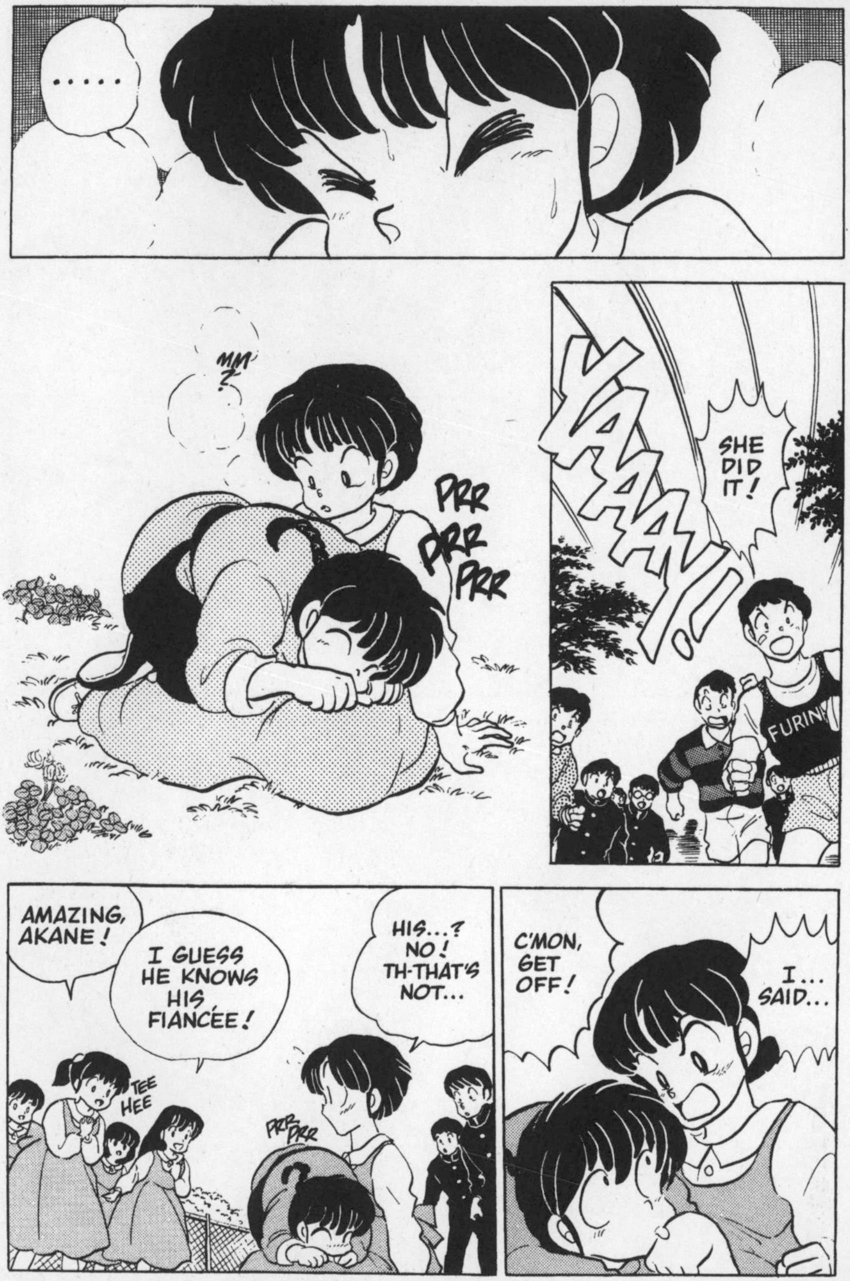
.....
MM ?
PRR PRR PRR
YAAAN!!
SHE DID IT!
AMAZING, AKANE!
I GUESS HE KNOWS HIS FIANCÉE!
TEE HEE
PRR PRR
HIS...? NO! TH-THAT'S NOT...
C'MON, GET OFF!
I... SAID...

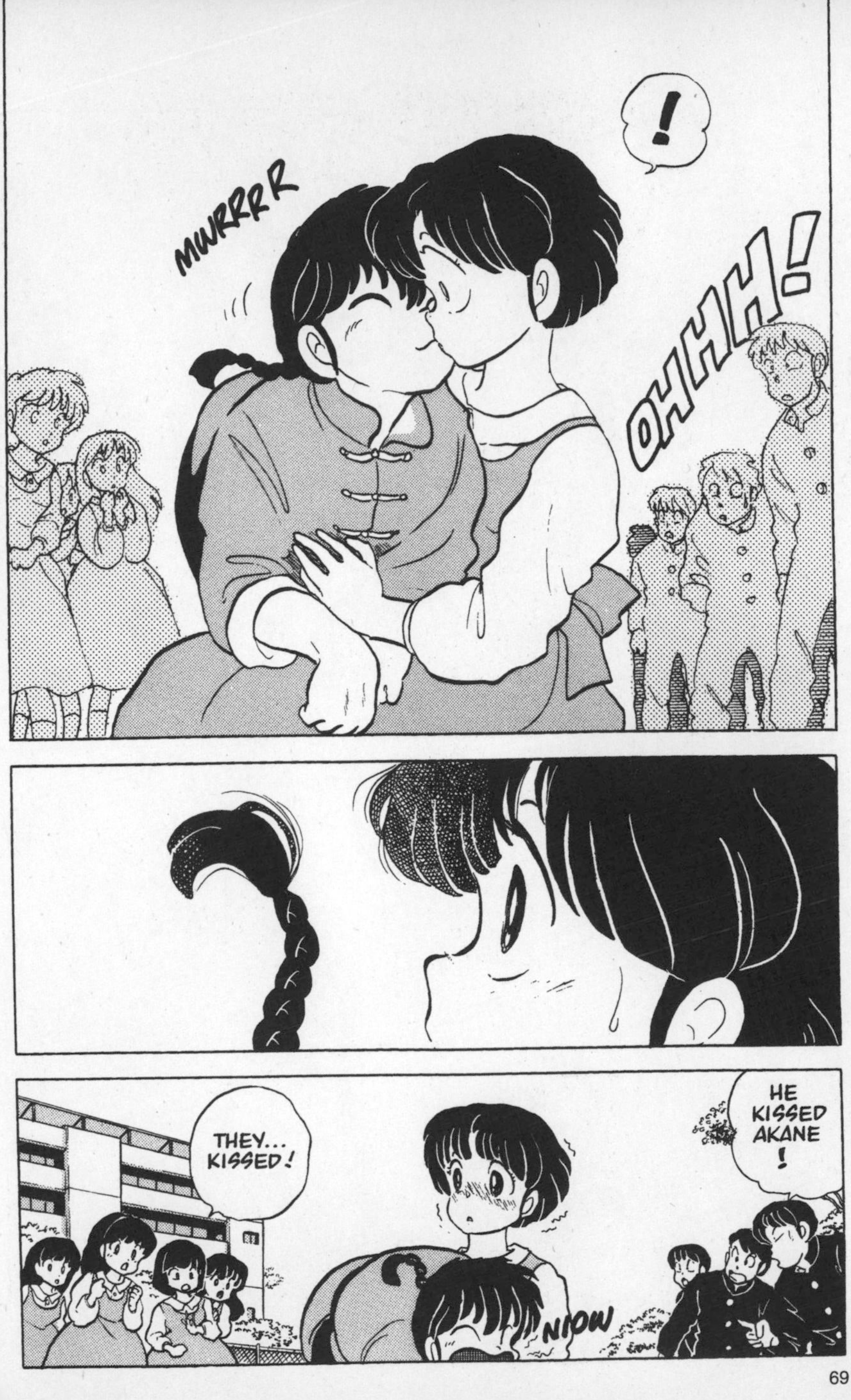
!
MWRRRR
OHHH!
THEY... KISSED!
HE KISSED AKANE !
NIOW

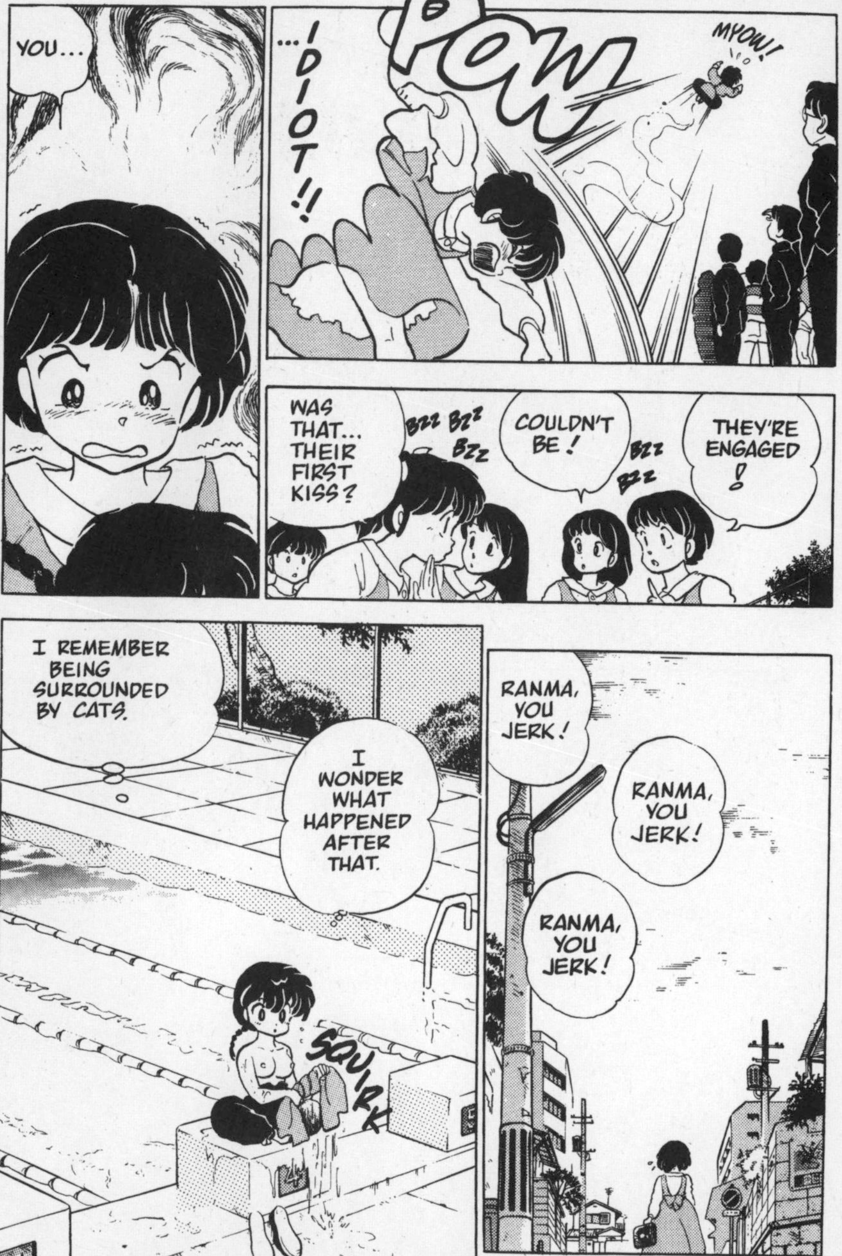
YOU...
...IDIOT!!
POW
MYOW!
WAS THAT... THEIR FIRST KISS?
BZZ BZZ BZZ
COULDN'T BE!
BZZ BZZ
THEY'RE ENGAGED!
I REMEMBER BEING SURROUNDED BY CATS.
I WONDER WHAT HAPPENED AFTER THAT.
SQUIRK
RANMA, YOU JERK!
RANMA, YOU JERK!
RANMA, YOU JERK!

Part 5

YOU'D HAVE KISSED ANYBODY?

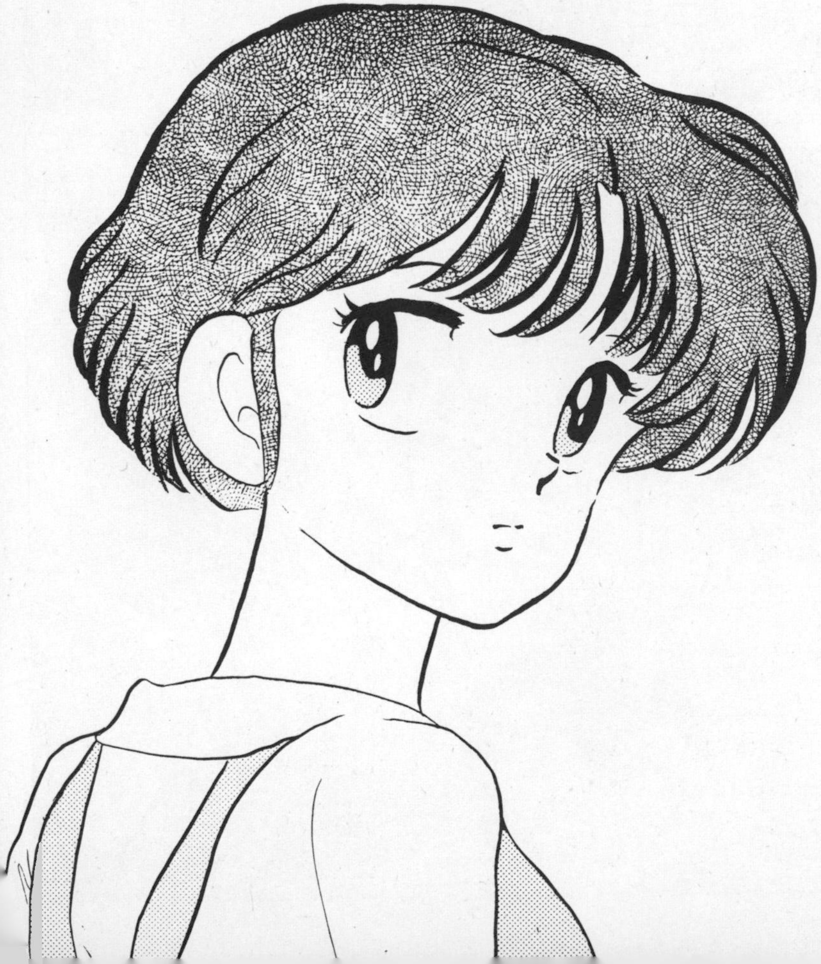

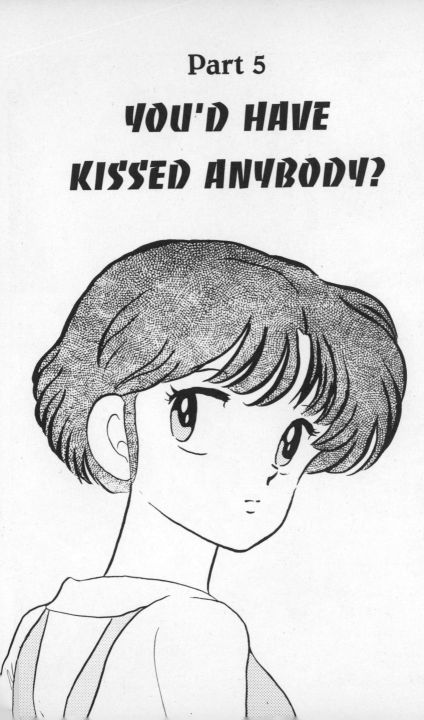

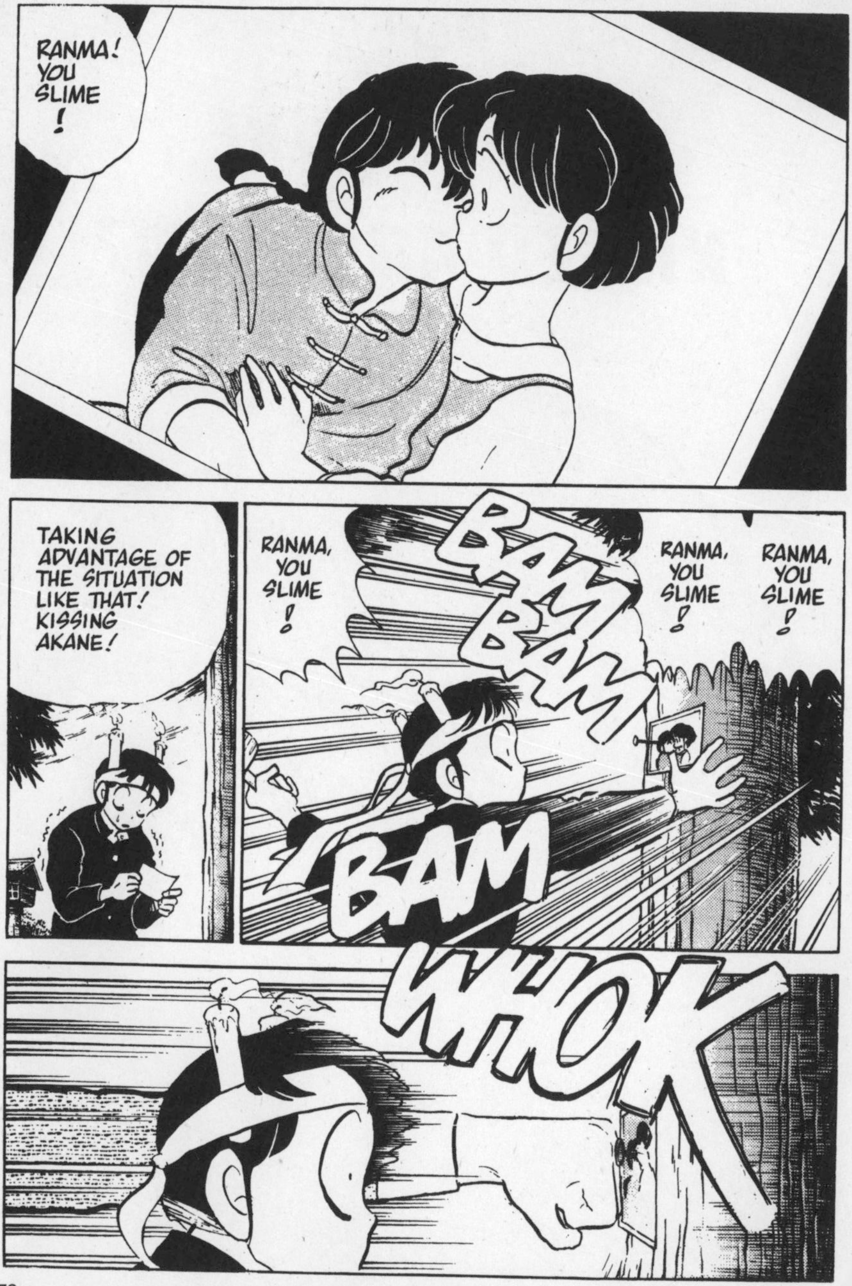
RANMA! YOU SLIME!
TAKING ADVANTAGE OF THE SITUATION LIKE THAT! KISSING AKANE!
RANMA, YOU SLIME!
BAM BAM
RANMA, YOU SLIME!
RANMA, YOU SLIME!
BAM
WHOK

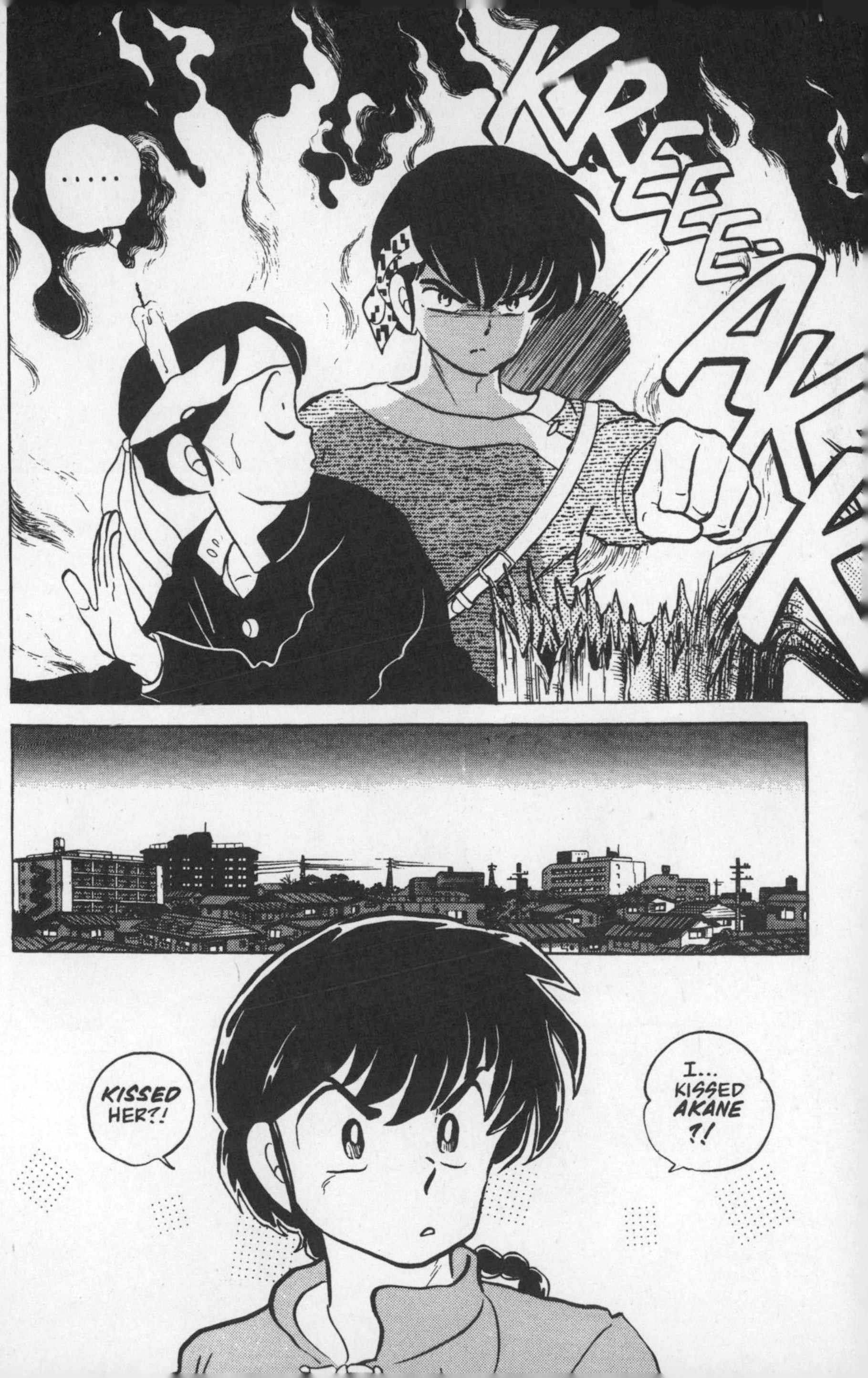
......
KREEE-AK
KISSED HER?!
I... KISSED AKANE ?!

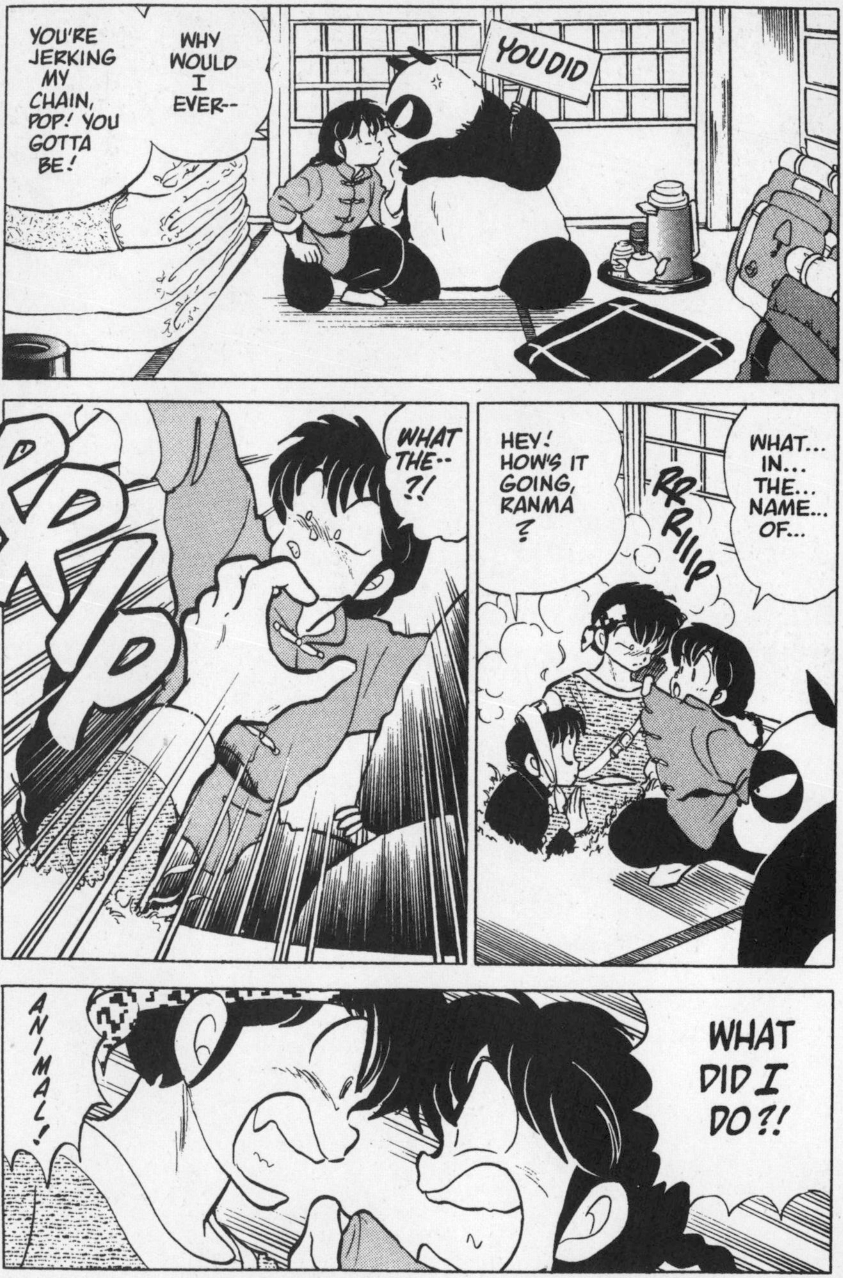
YOU'RE JERKING MY CHAIN, POP! YOU GOTTA BE!
WHY WOULD I EVER--
YOU DID
RRIP
WHAT THE-- ?!
HEY! HOW'S IT GOING, RANMA?
RRRIIIP
WHAT... IN... THE... NAME... OF...
ANIMAL!
WHAT DID I DO?!

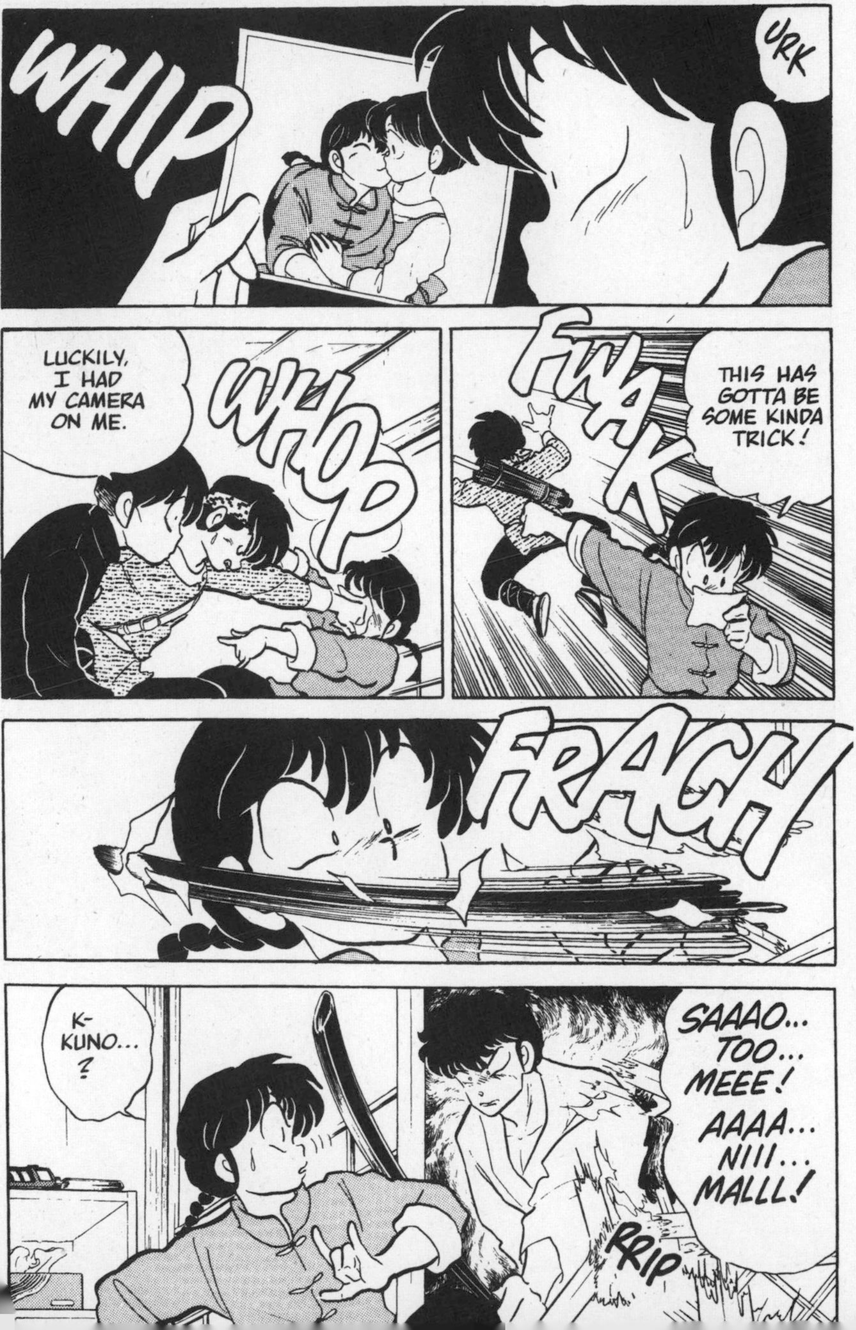
WHIP
URK
LUCKILY, I HAD MY CAMERA ON ME.
WHOP
FWAK
THIS HAS GOTTA BE SOME KINDA TRICK!
FRACH
K-KUNO...?
SAAAO... TOO... MEEE!
AAAA... NIII... MALLL!
RRIP

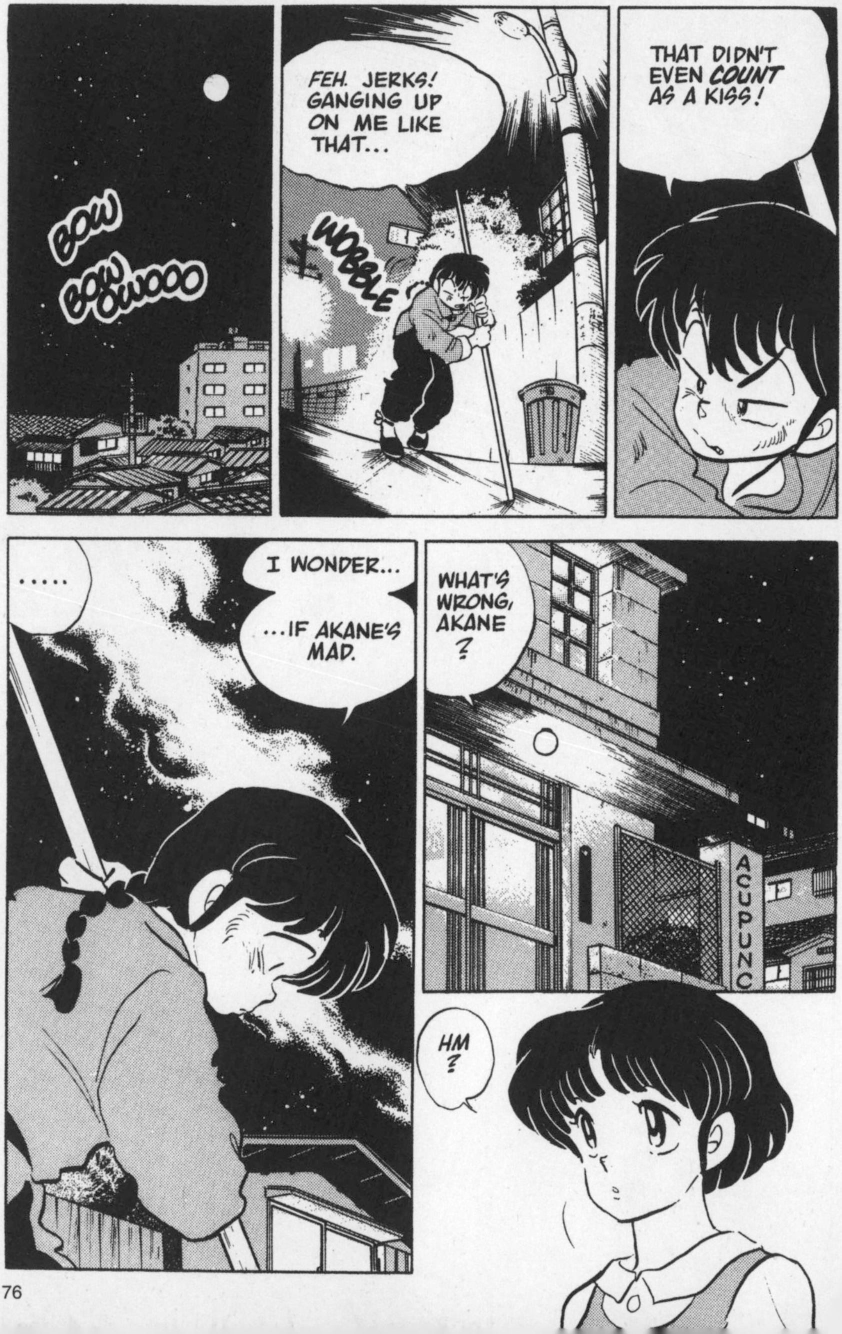
BOW
BOW OWOOO
FEH. JERKS! GANGING UP ON ME LIKE THAT...
WOBBLE
THAT DIDN'T EVEN COUNT AS A KISS!
.....
I WONDER...
...IF AKANE'S MAD.
WHAT'S WRONG, AKANE ?
ACUPUNC
HM ?

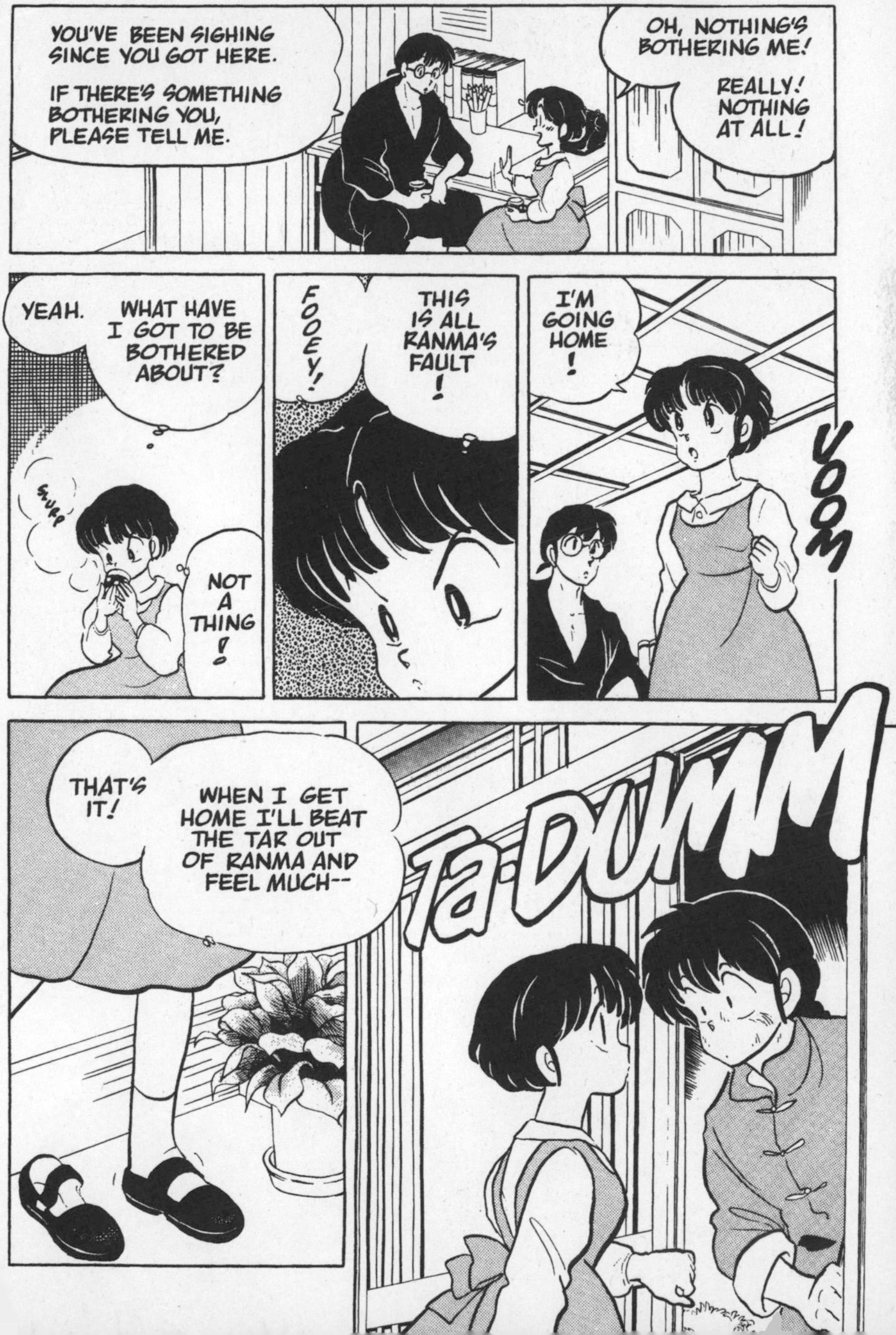
YOU'VE BEEN SIGHING SINCE YOU GOT HERE.
IF THERE'S SOMETHING BOTHERING YOU, PLEASE TELL ME.
OH, NOTHING'S BOTHERING ME!
REALLY! NOTHING AT ALL!
YEAH.
WHAT HAVE I GOT TO BE BOTHERED ABOUT?
SLURP
NOT A THING!
FOOEY!
THIS IS ALL RANMA'S FAULT!
I'M GOING HOME!
VOOM
THAT'S IT!
WHEN I GET HOME I'LL BEAT THE TAR OUT OF RANMA AND FEEL MUCH--
TA-DUMM

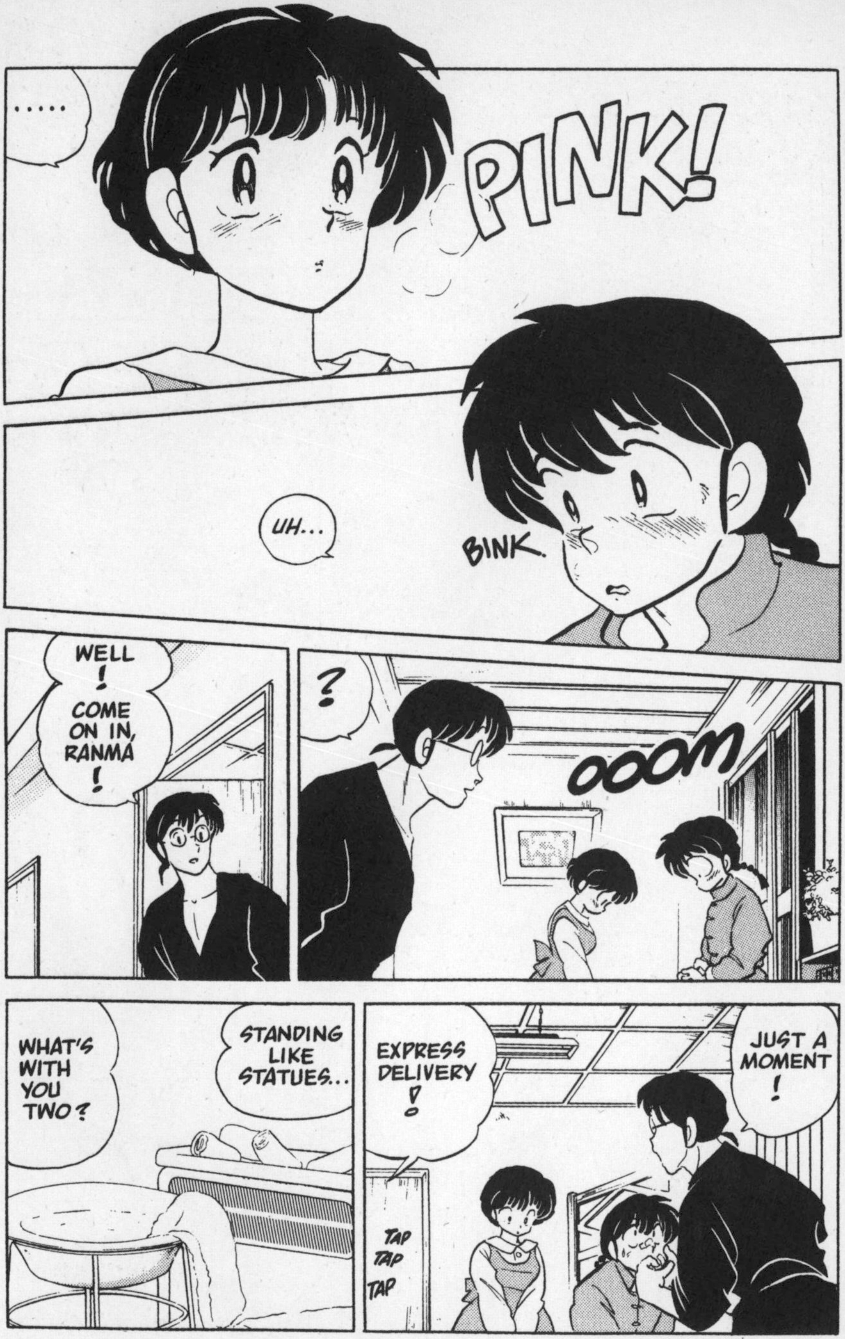
......
PINK!
UH...
BINK.
WELL! COME ON IN, RANMA!
?
OOOM
WHAT'S WITH YOU TWO?
STANDING LIKE STATUES...
EXPRESS DELIVERY!
TAP TAP TAP
JUST A MOMENT!

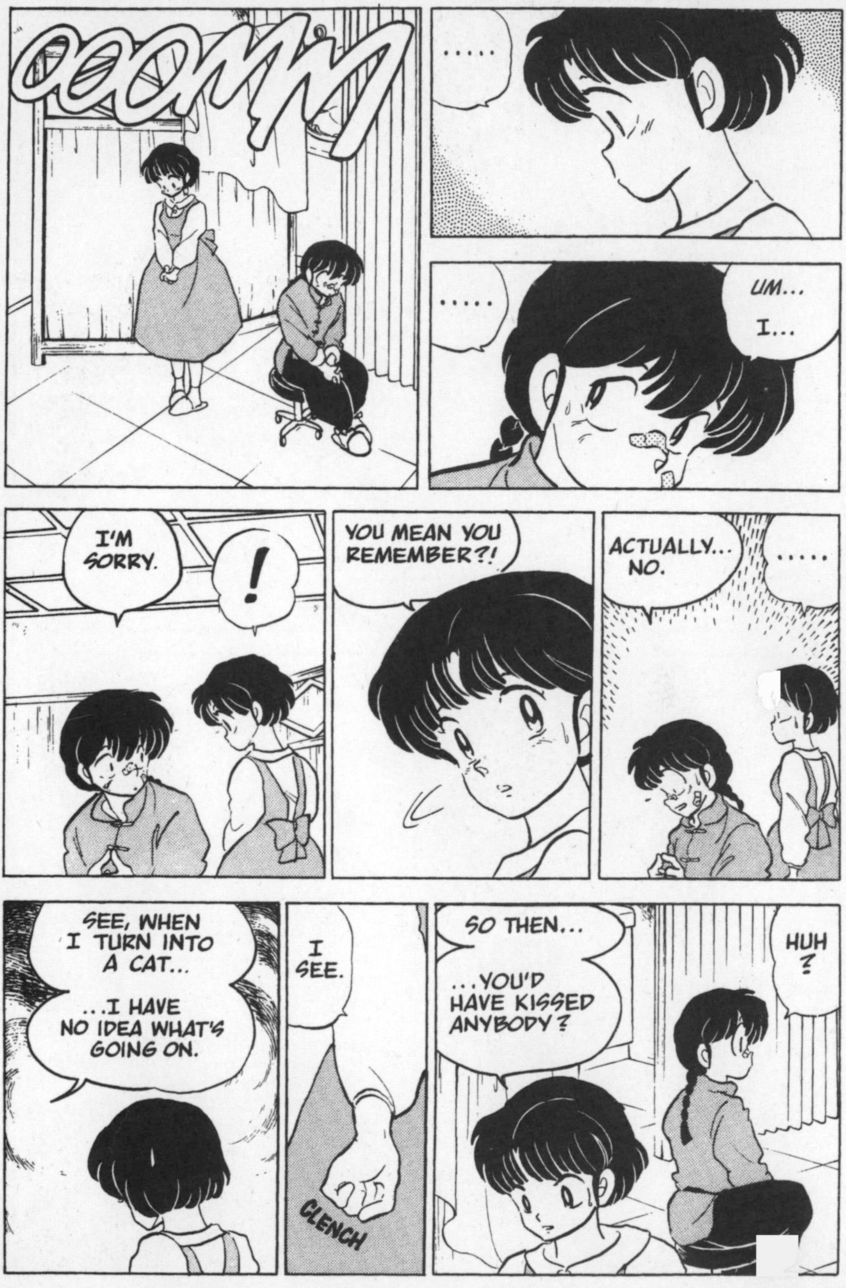
OOOMM
.....
.....
UM...
I...
I'M SORRY.
!
YOU MEAN YOU REMEMBER?!
ACTUALLY... NO.
.....
SEE, WHEN I TURN INTO A CAT...
...I HAVE NO IDEA WHAT'S GOING ON.
I SEE.
CLENCH
SO THEN...
...YOU'D HAVE KISSED ANYBODY?
HUH?

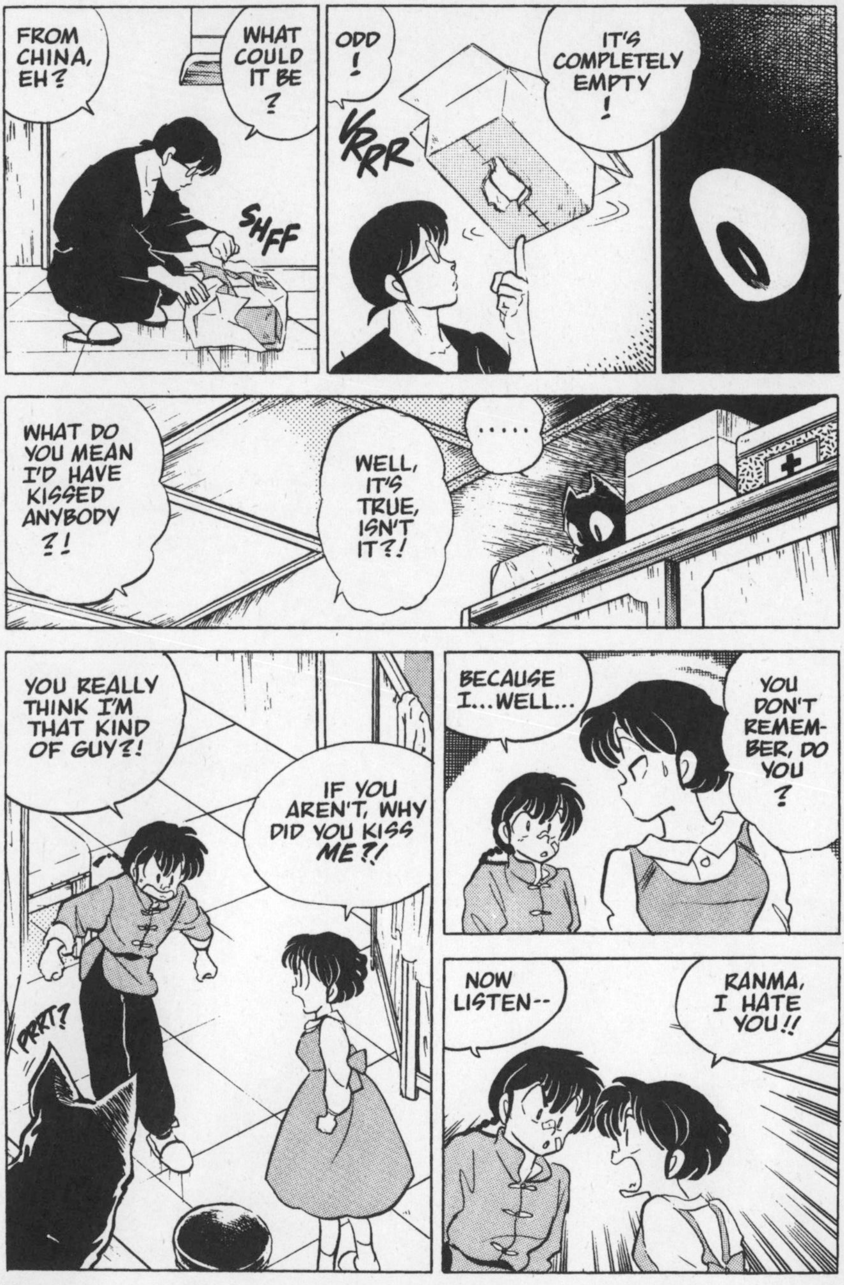

FROM CHINA, EH?
WHAT COULD IT BE?
SHFF
ODD!
VRRR
IT'S COMPLETELY EMPTY!
WHAT DO YOU MEAN I'D HAVE KISSED ANYBODY?!
WELL, IT'S TRUE, ISN'T IT?!
.....
YOU REALLY THINK I'M THAT KIND OF GUY?!
IF YOU AREN'T, WHY DID YOU KISS ME?!
PRRT?
BECAUSE I...WELL...
YOU DON'T REMEMBER, DO YOU?
NOW LISTEN--
RANMA, I HATE YOU!!

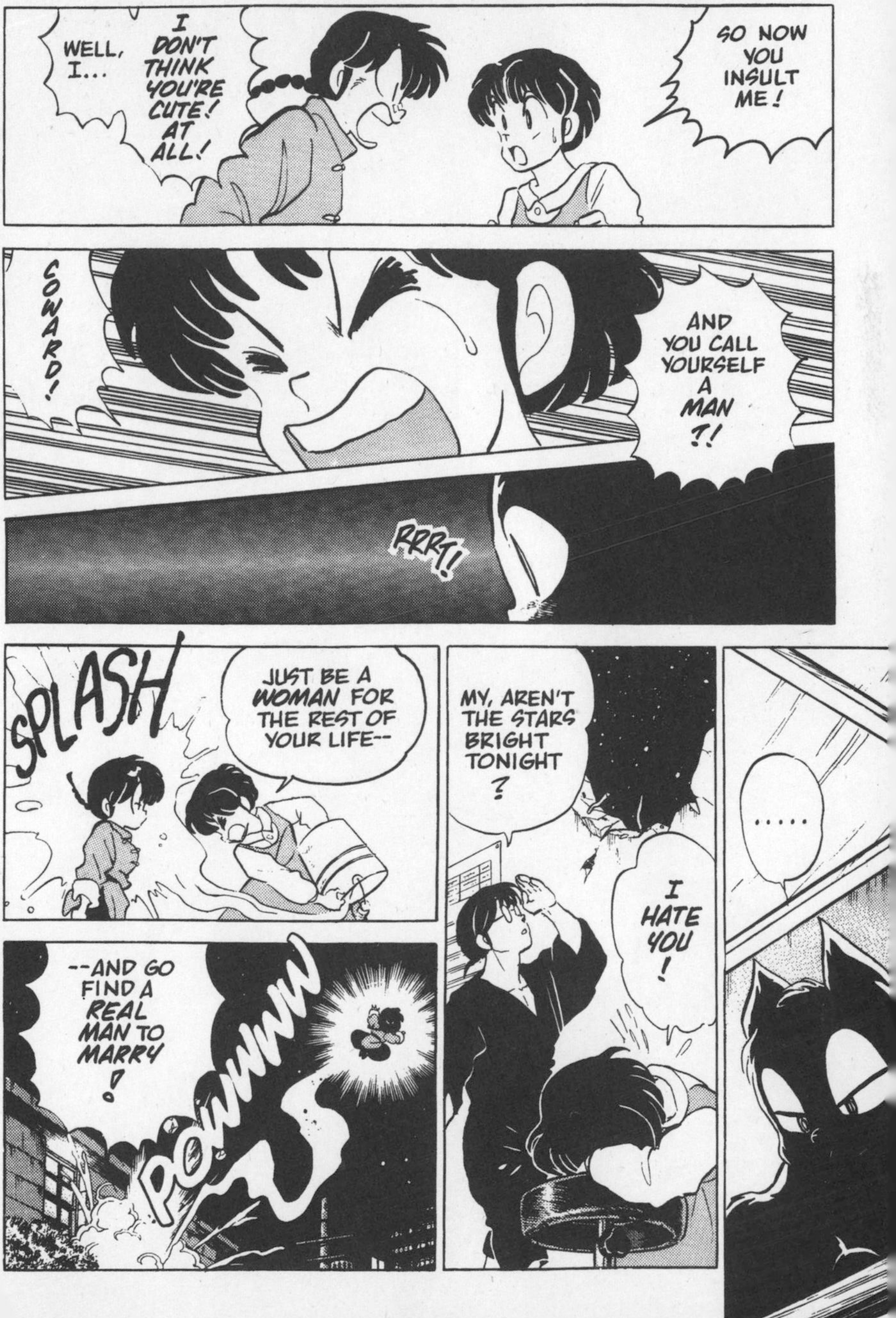
WELL, I...
I DON'T THINK YOU'RE CUTE! AT ALL!
SO NOW YOU INSULT ME!
COWARD!
AND YOU CALL YOURSELF A MAN ?!
RRRT!
SPLASH
JUST BE A WOMAN FOR THE REST OF YOUR LIFE--
--AND GO FIND A REAL MAN TO MARRY!
POWWW
MY, AREN'T THE STARS BRIGHT TONIGHT?
I HATE YOU!
.....

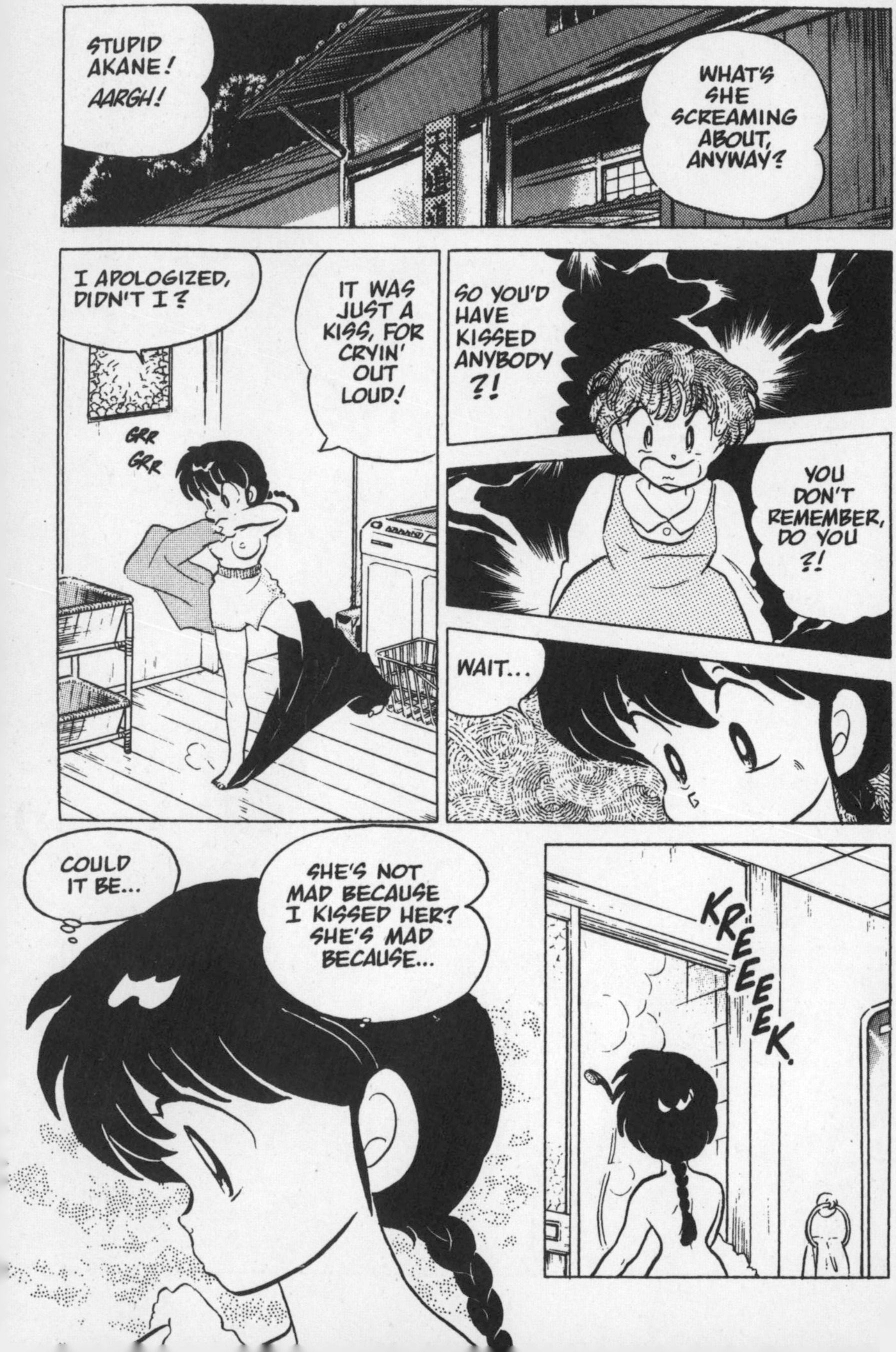
STUPID AKANE! AARGH!
WHAT'S SHE SCREAMING ABOUT, ANYWAY?
I APOLOGIZED, DIDN'T I?
IT WAS JUST A KISS, FOR CRYIN' OUT LOUD!
GRR GRR
SO YOU'D HAVE KISSED ANYBODY ?!
YOU DON'T REMEMBER, DO YOU ?!
WAIT...
COULD IT BE...
SHE'S NOT MAD BECAUSE I KISSED HER? SHE'S MAD BECAUSE...
KREEEEEK.

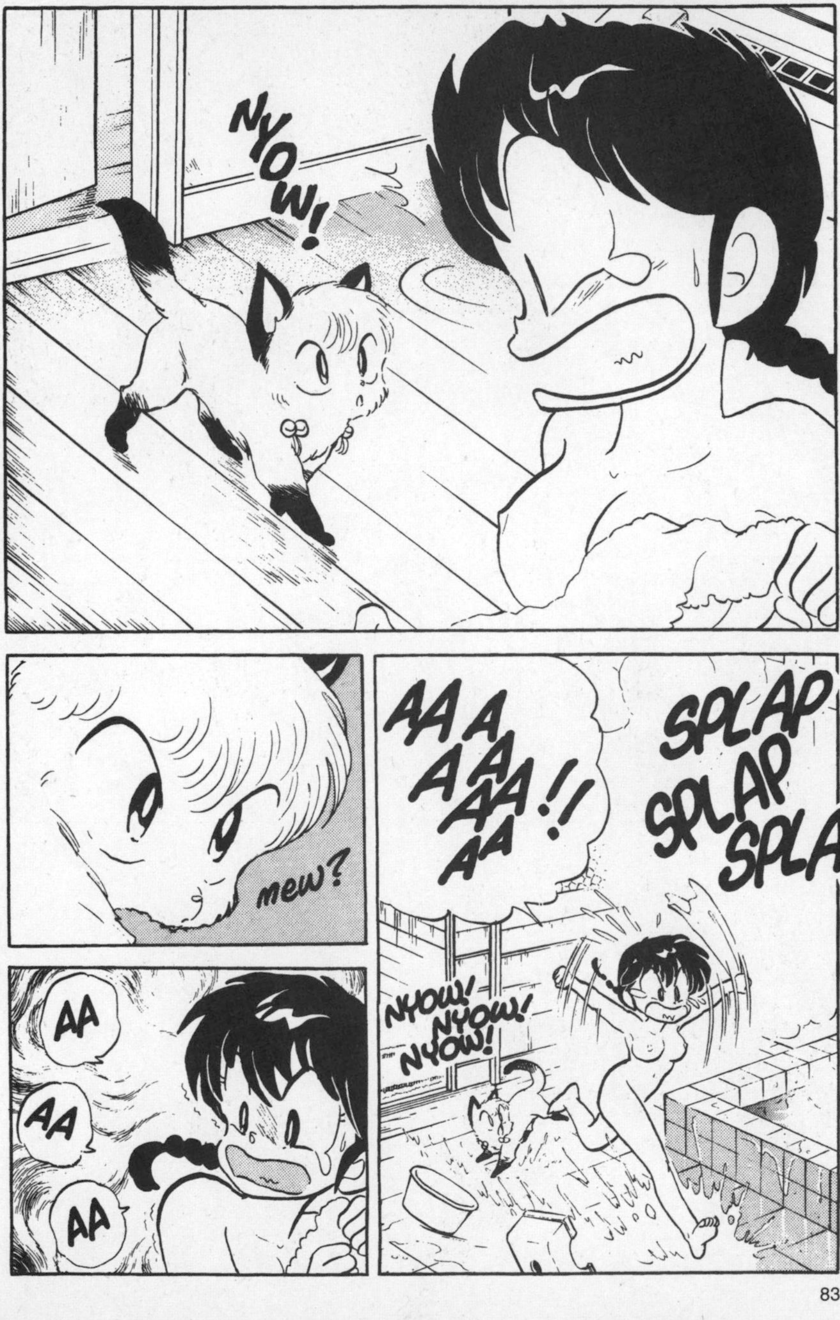
NYOW!
mew?
AA
AA
AA
AAAAAAAAAA!!
SPLAP
SPLAP
SPLAP
NYOW! NYOW! NYOW!

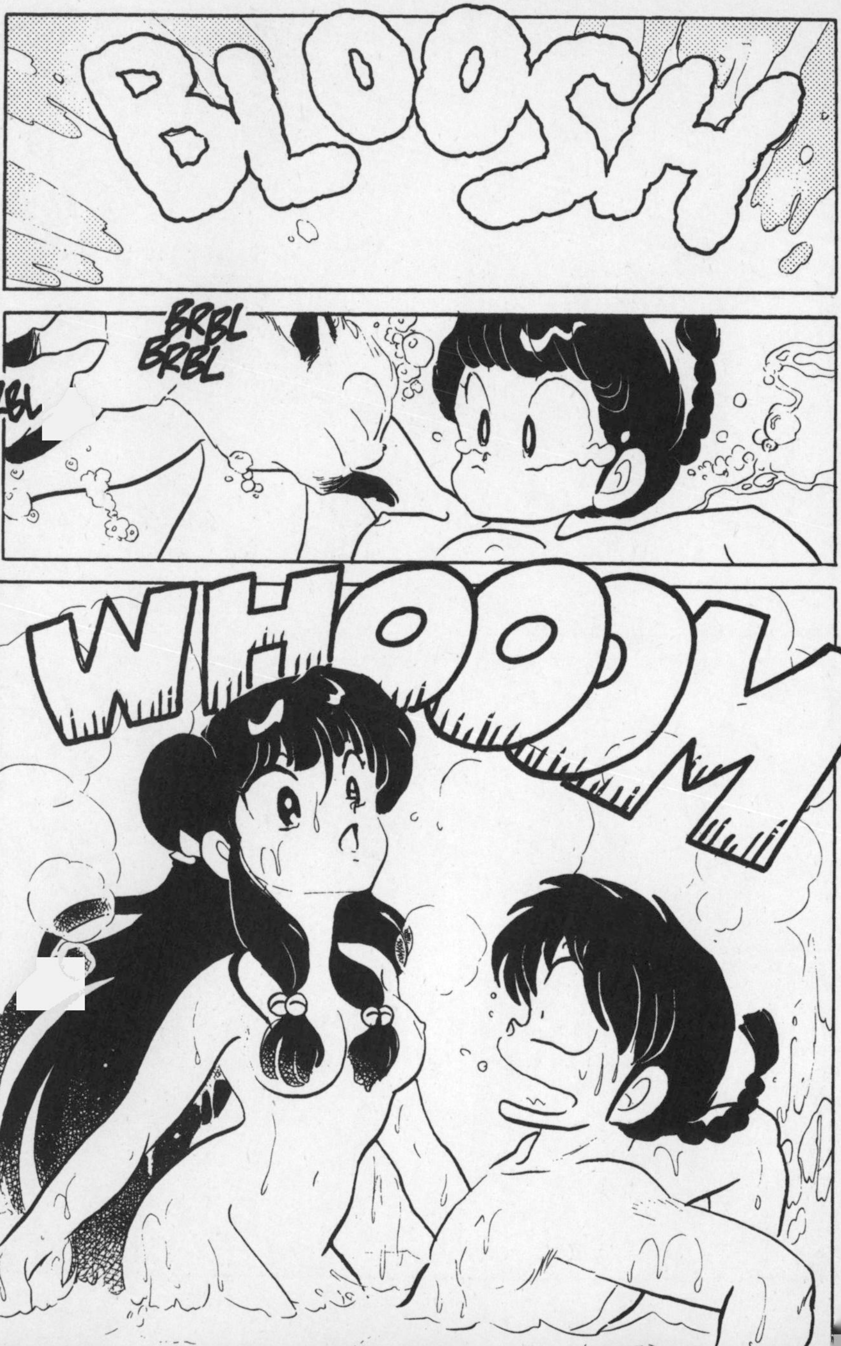
BLOOSH!
BRBL
BRBL
BRBL
WHOOM

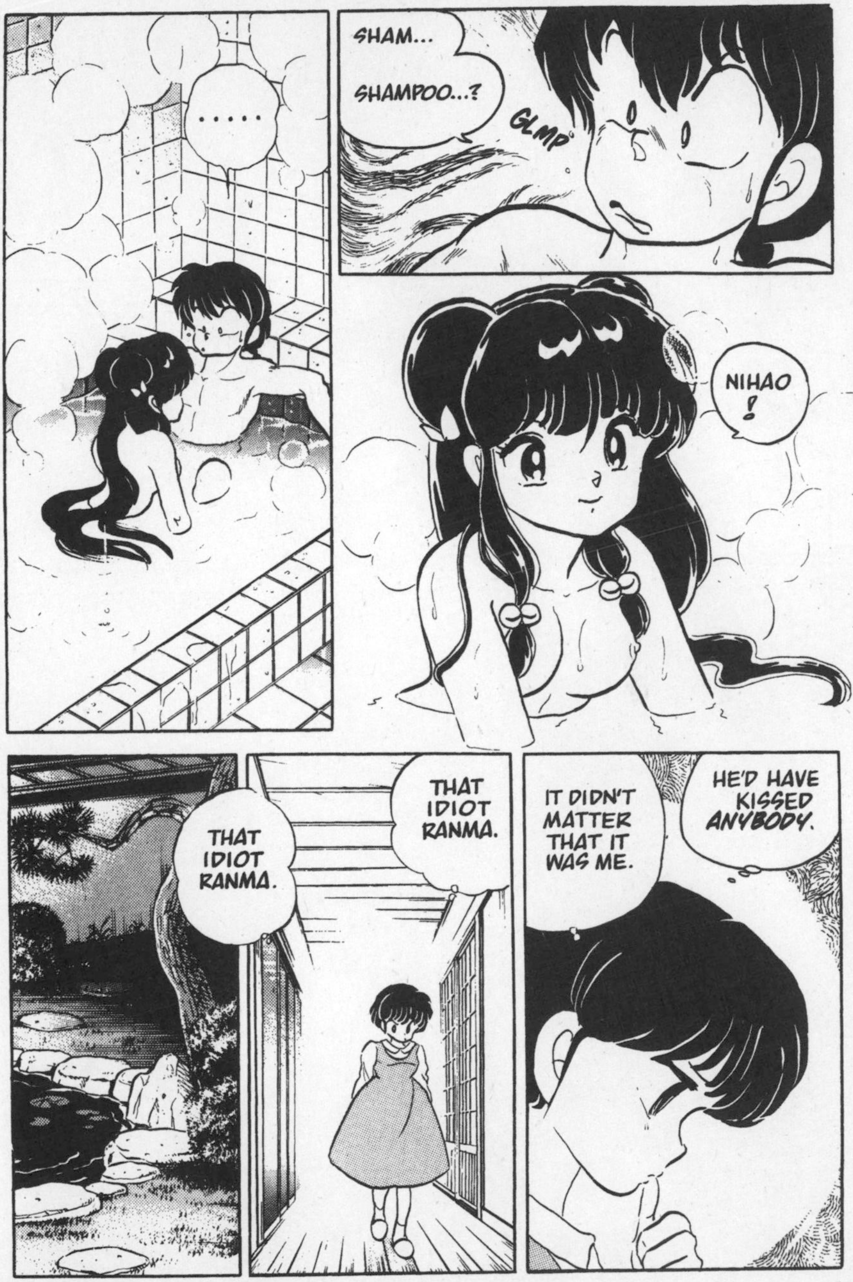
.....
SHAM...
SHAMPOO...?
GLMP
NIHAO!
THAT IDIOT RANMA.
THAT IDIOT RANMA.
IT DIDN'T MATTER THAT IT WAS ME.
HE'D HAVE KISSED ANYBODY.

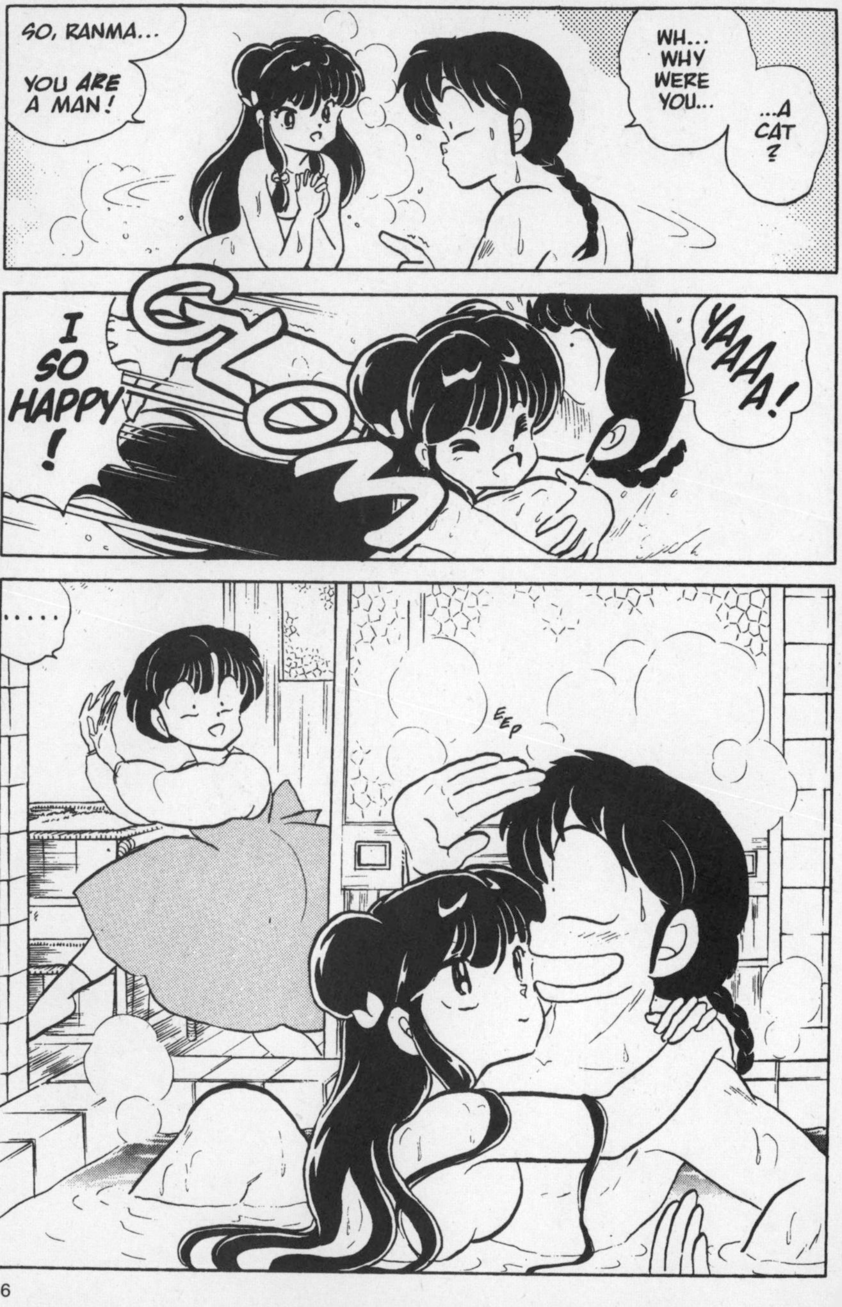
SO, RANMA...
YOU ARE A MAN!
WH... WHY WERE YOU...
...A CAT?
GLOMP
I SO HAPPY!
YAAAAA!
......
EEP

Part 6

SHAMPOO RIDES AGAIN

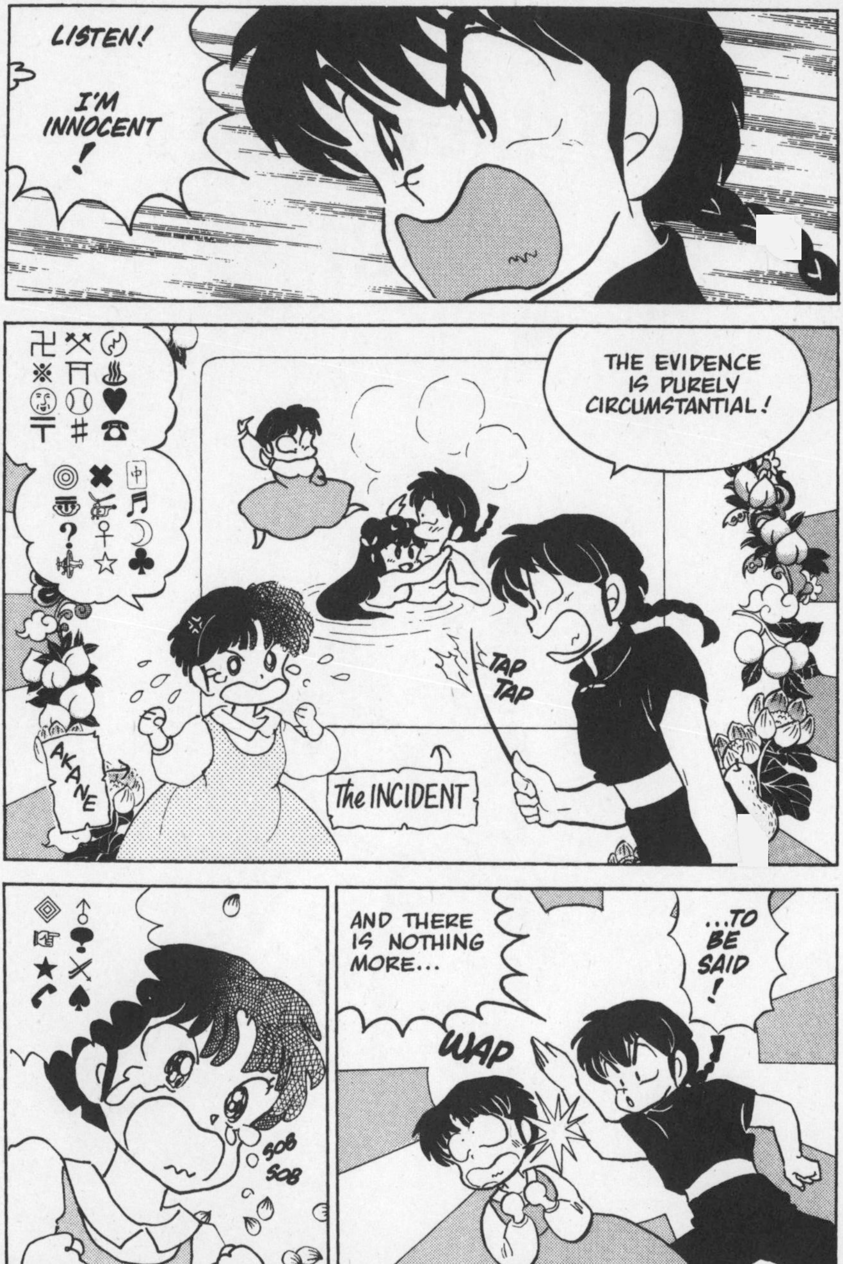
LISTEN!
I'M INNOCENT!
THE EVIDENCE IS PURELY CIRCUMSTANTIAL!
TAP TAP
AKANE
The INCIDENT
SOB SOB
AND THERE IS NOTHING MORE...
WAP
...TO BE SAID!

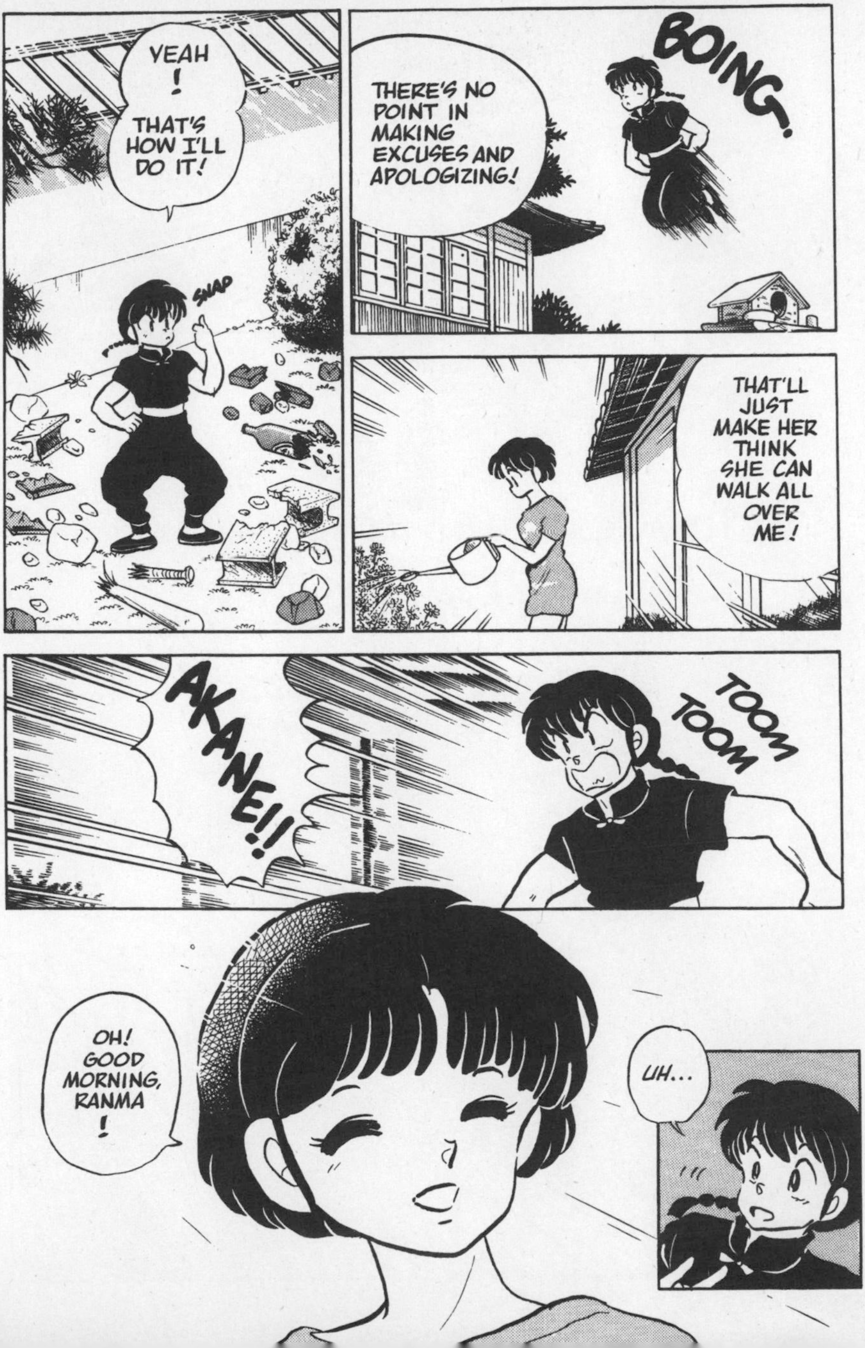
YEAH!
THAT'S HOW I'LL DO IT!
SNAP
THERE'S NO POINT IN MAKING EXCUSES AND APOLOGIZING!
BOING!
THAT'LL JUST MAKE HER THINK SHE CAN WALK ALL OVER ME!
AKANE!!
TOOM TOOM
OH! GOOD MORNING, RANMA!
UH...

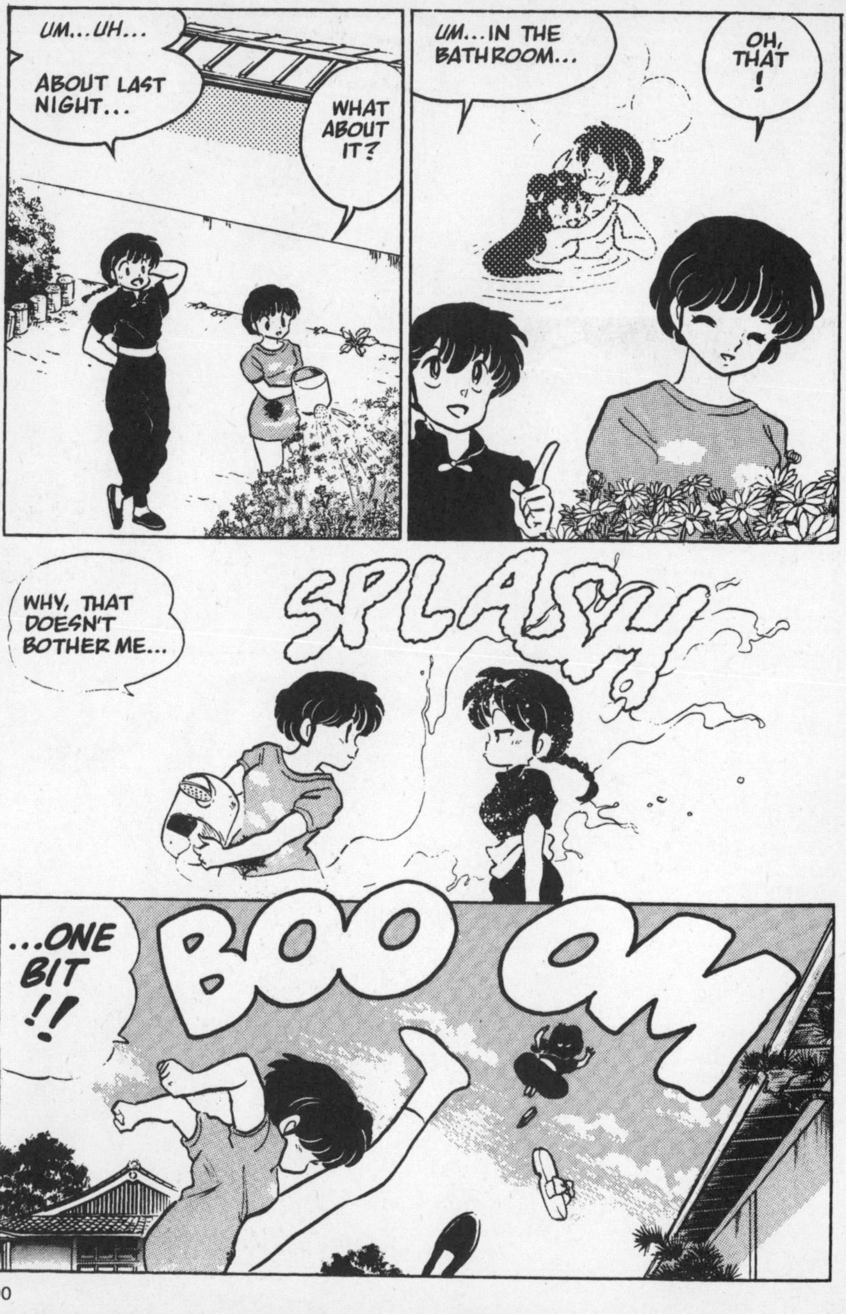
UM...UH...
ABOUT LAST NIGHT...
WHAT ABOUT IT?
UM...IN THE BATHROOM...
OH, THAT!
WHY, THAT DOESN'T BOTHER ME...
SPLASH
...ONE BIT!!
BOO OM

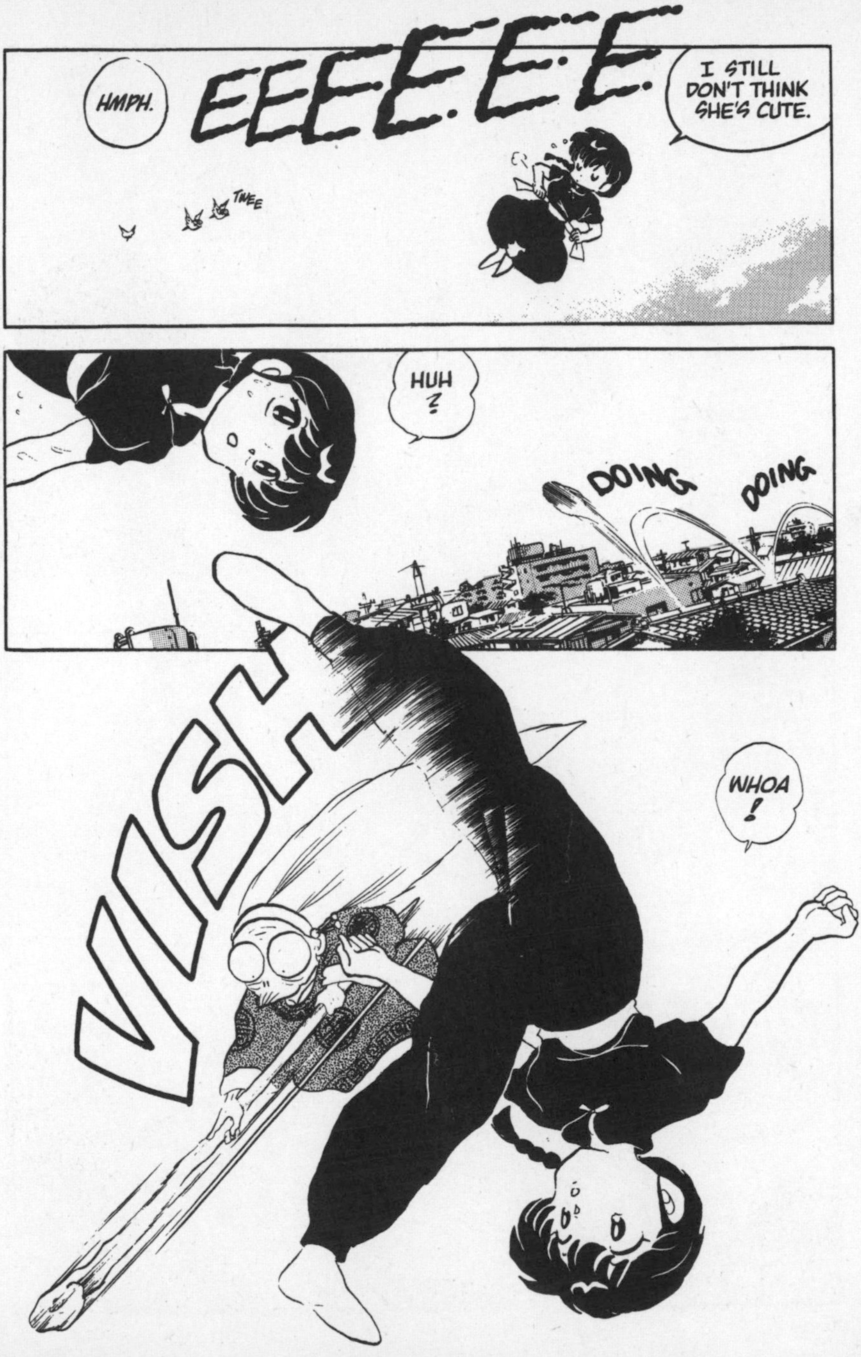
HMPH.
EEEEE-E-E
TWEE
I STILL DON'T THINK SHE'S CUTE.
HUH ?
DOING
DOING
VUSH
WHOA !

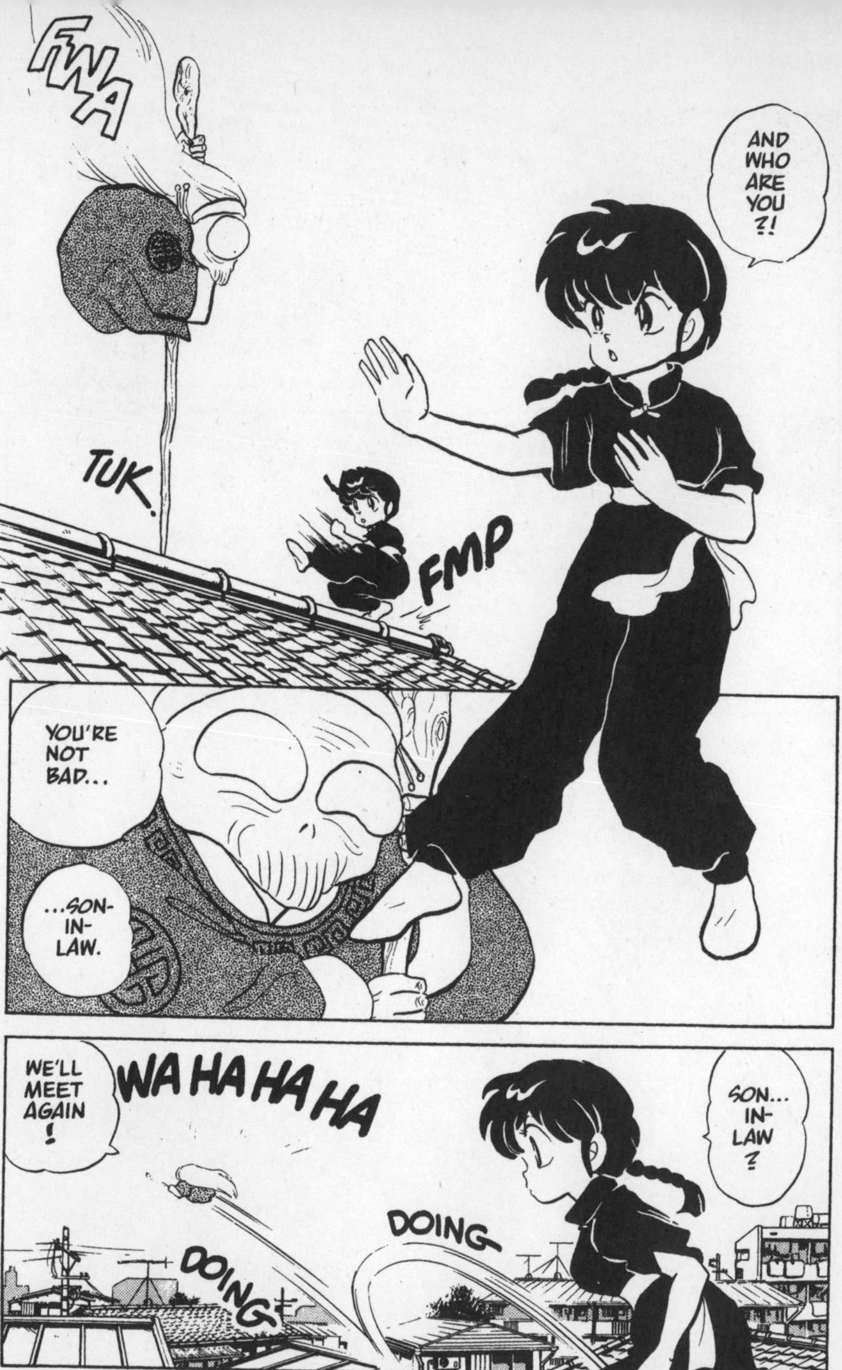
FWA
AND WHO ARE YOU ?!
TUK
FMP
YOU'RE NOT BAD...
...SON-IN-LAW.
WE'LL MEET AGAIN !
WA HA HA HA HA
SON... IN-LAW ?
DOING
DOING

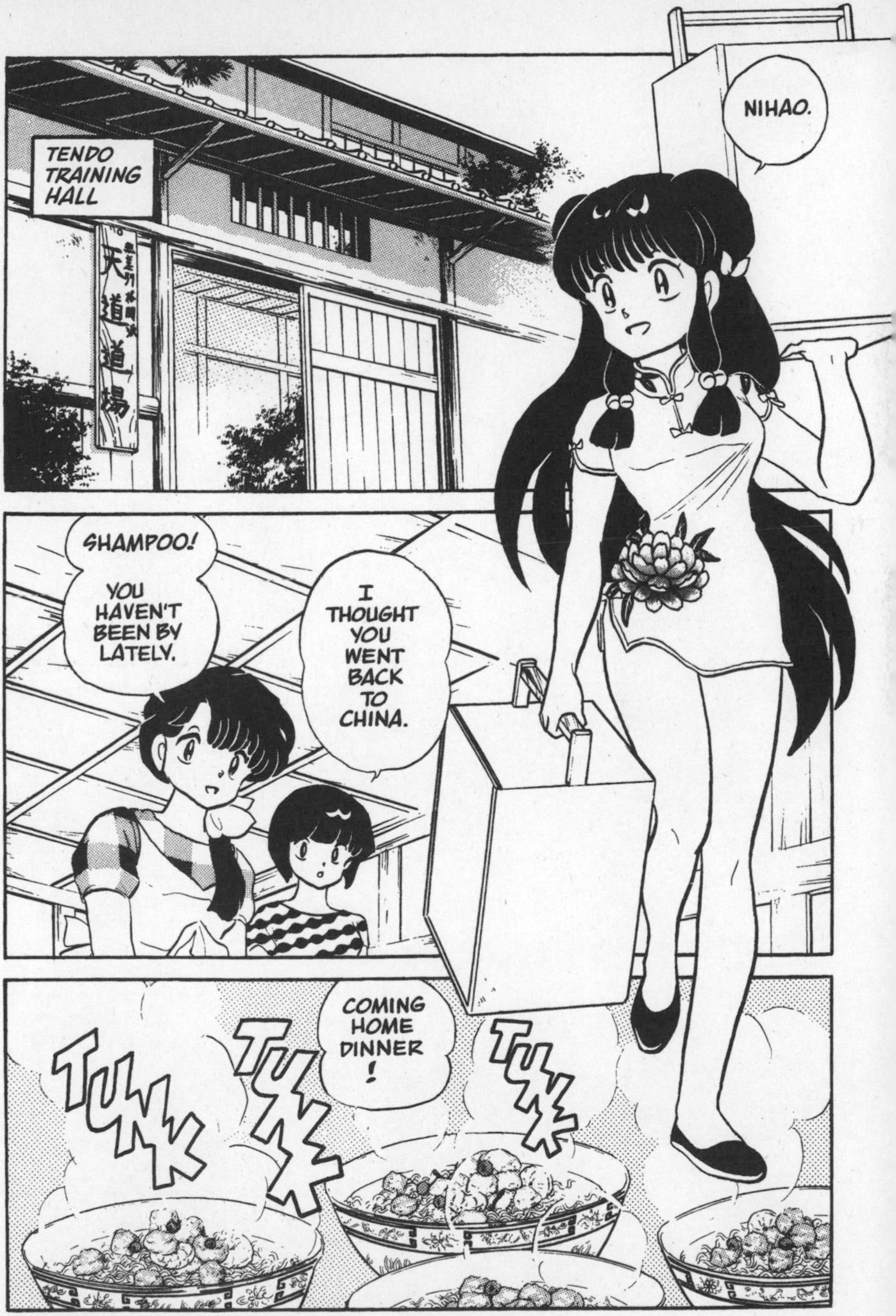
TENDO TRAINING HALL
天道道場
NIHAO.
SHAMPOO! YOU HAVEN'T BEEN BY LATELY.
I THOUGHT YOU WENT BACK TO CHINA.
TUNK
TUNK
COMING HOME DINNER!
TUNK

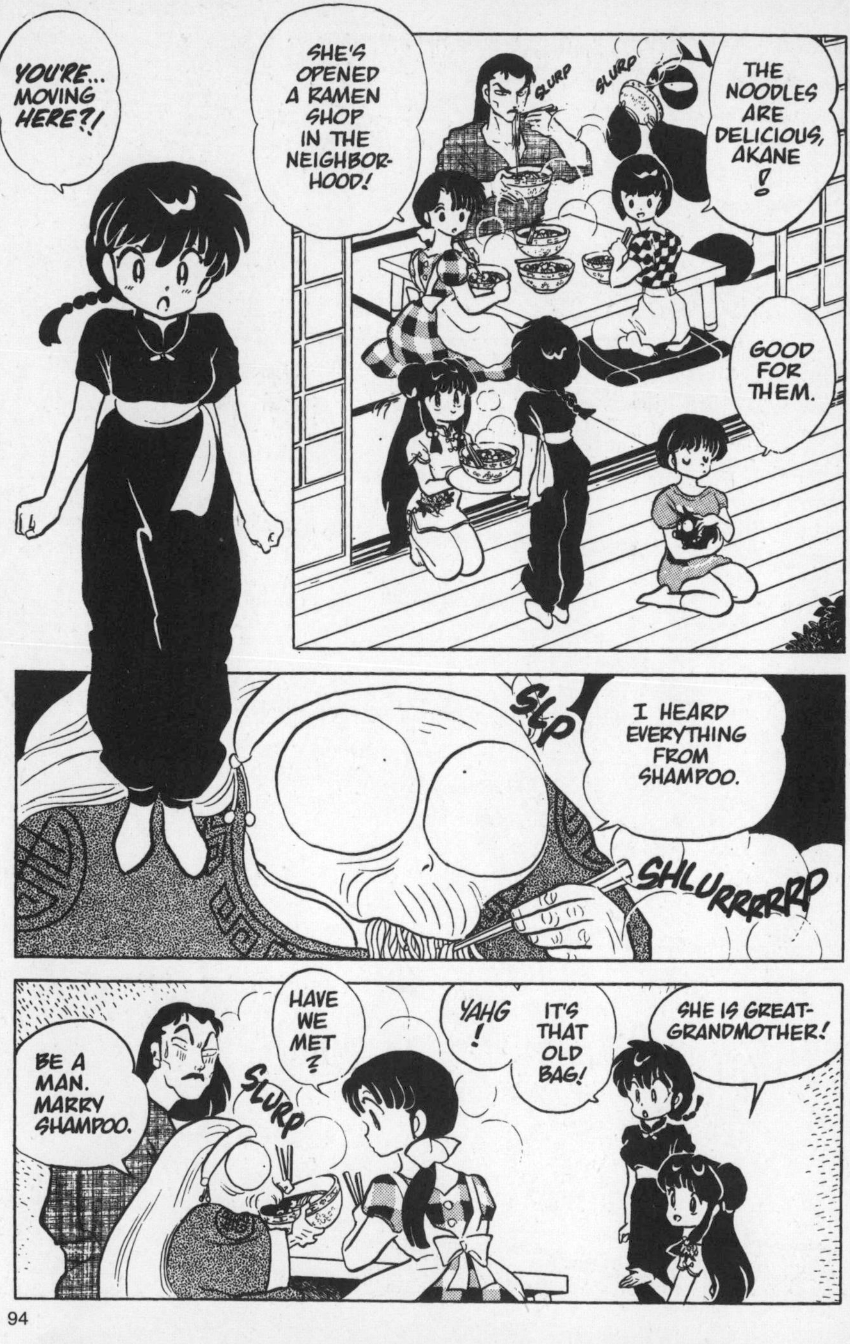
YOU'RE... MOVING HERE?!
SHE'S OPENED A RAMEN SHOP IN THE NEIGHBOR-HOOD!
SLURP
SLURP
THE NOODLES ARE DELICIOUS, AKANE!
GOOD FOR THEM.
SLP
I HEARD EVERYTHING FROM SHAMPOO.
SHLURRRRRP
BE A MAN. MARRY SHAMPOO.
HAVE WE MET?
SLURP
YAHG!
IT'S THAT OLD BAG!
SHE IS GREAT-GRANDMOTHER!

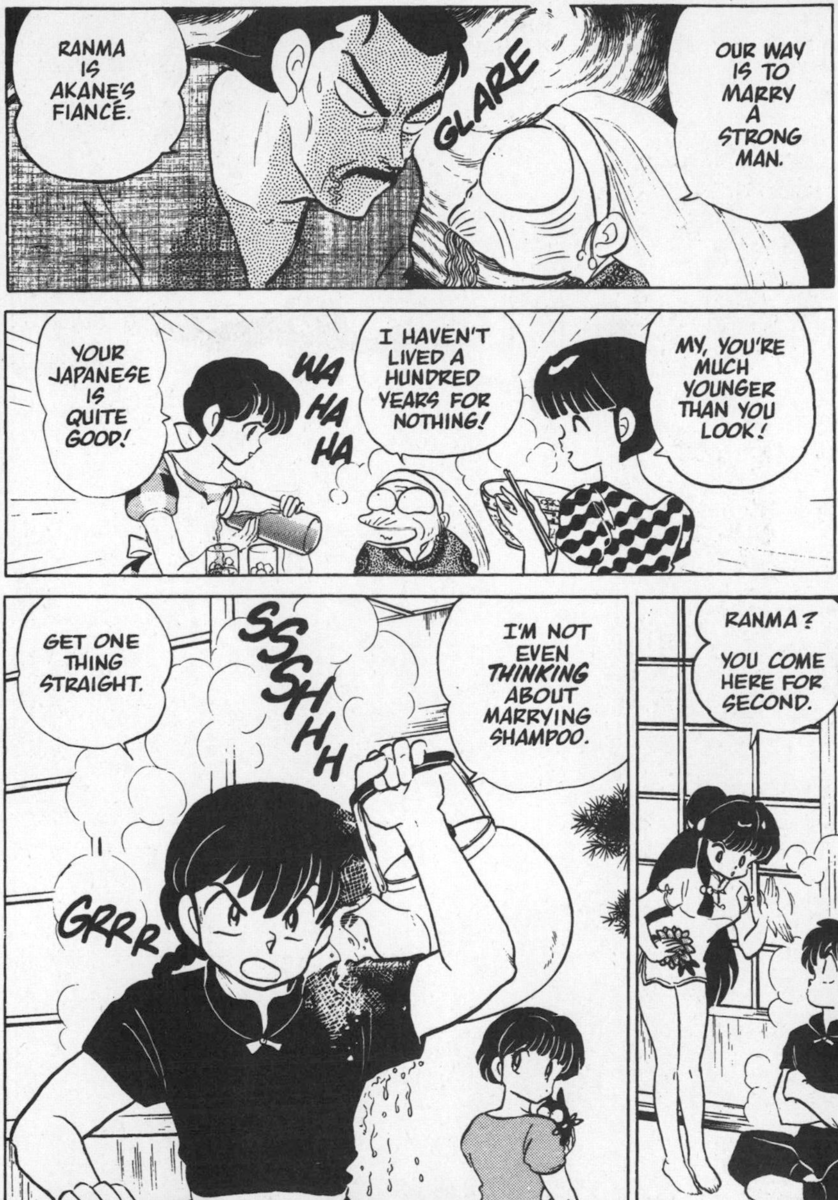
RANMA IS AKANE'S FIANCÉ.
GLARE
OUR WAY IS TO MARRY A STRONG MAN.
YOUR JAPANESE IS QUITE GOOD!
WA HA HA
I HAVEN'T LIVED A HUNDRED YEARS FOR NOTHING!
MY, YOU'RE MUCH YOUNGER THAN YOU LOOK!
GET ONE THING STRAIGHT.
SSSHHH
I'M NOT EVEN THINKING ABOUT MARRYING SHAMPOO.
GRRR
RANMA? YOU COME HERE FOR SECOND.

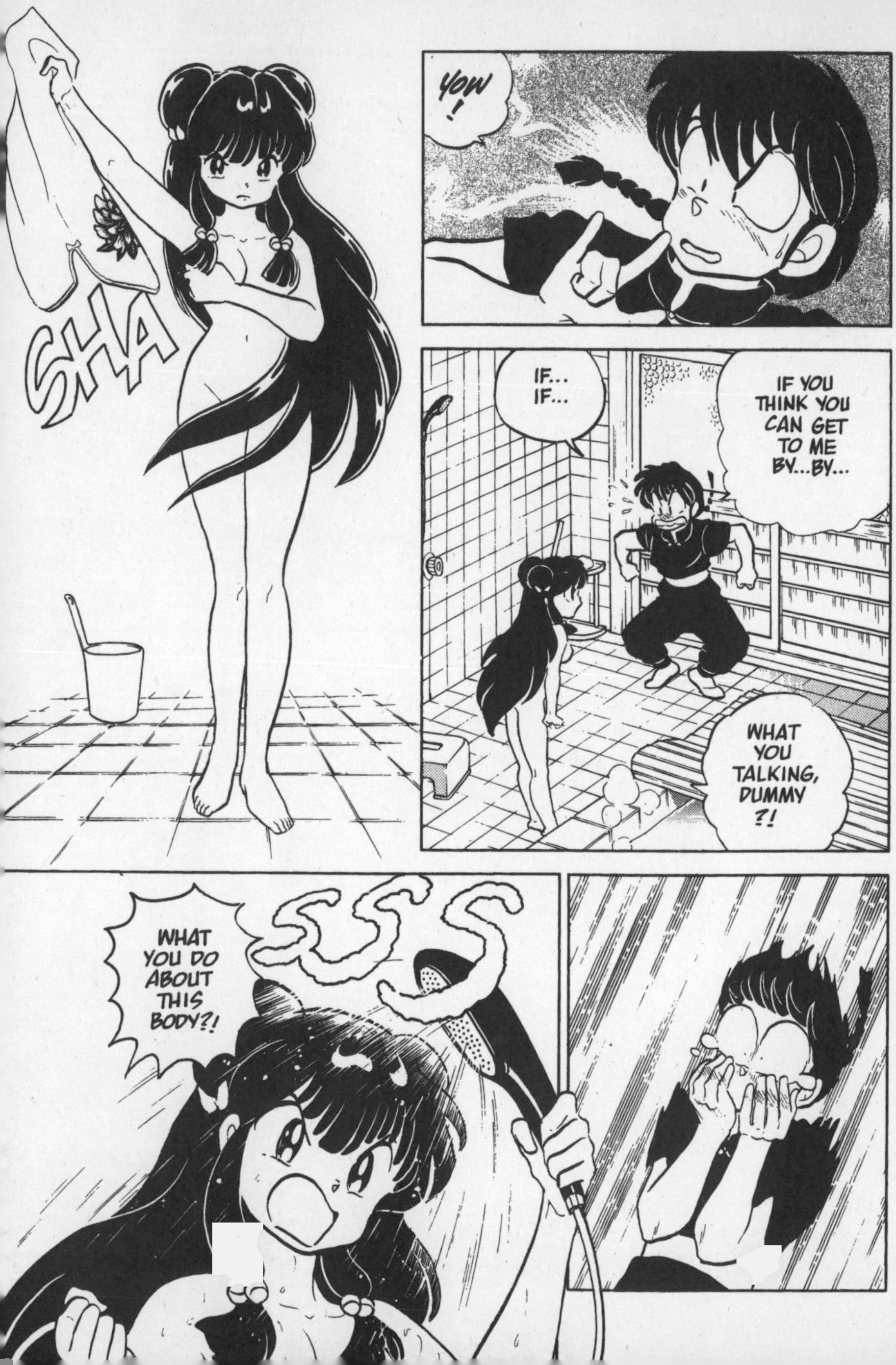
SHA
YOW!
IF... IF...
IF YOU THINK YOU CAN GET TO ME BY...BY...
WHAT YOU TALKING, DUMMY?!
WHAT YOU DO ABOUT THIS BODY?!
SSS

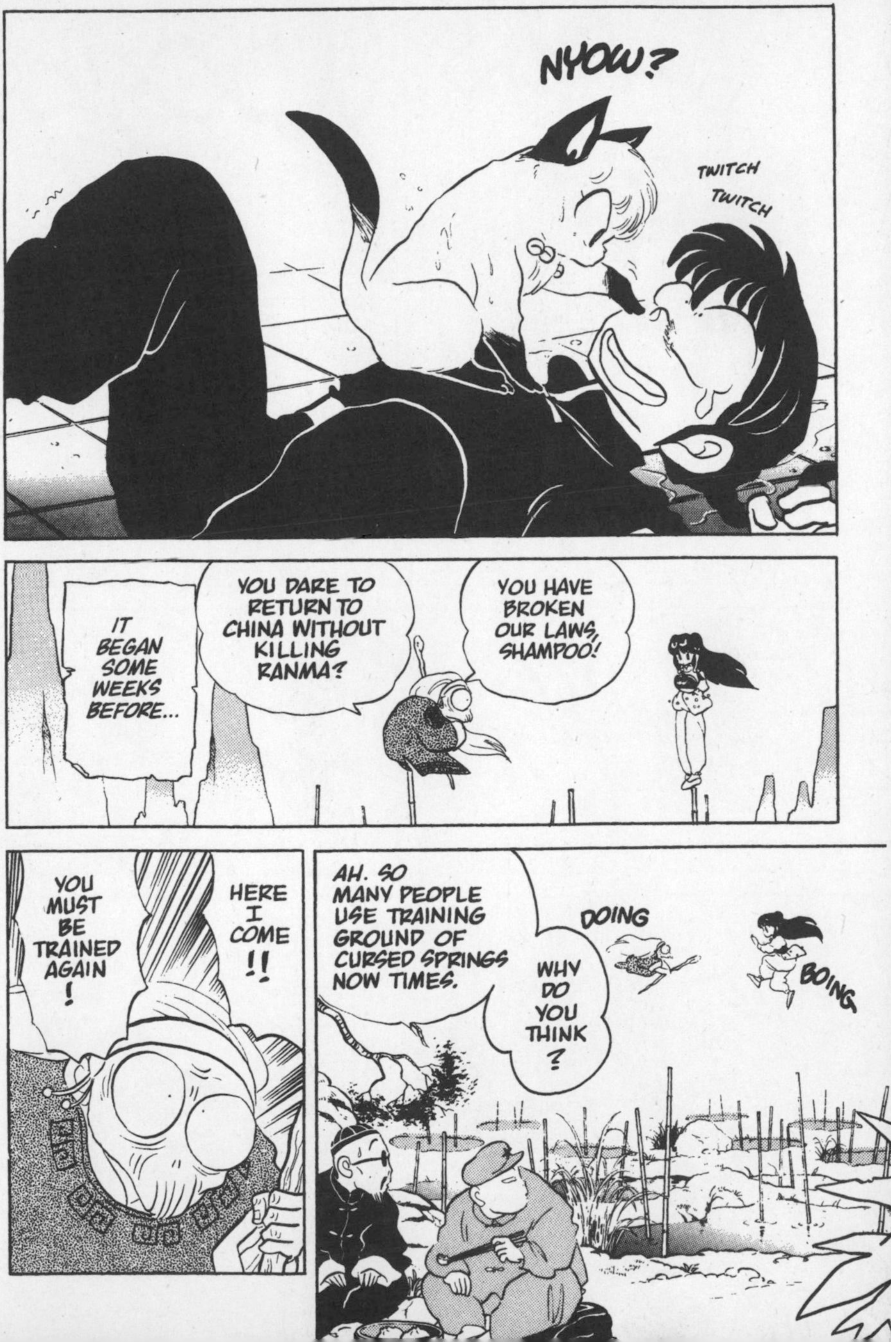
NYOW?
TWITCH
TWITCH
IT BEGAN SOME WEEKS BEFORE...
YOU DARE TO RETURN TO CHINA WITHOUT KILLING RANMA?
YOU HAVE BROKEN OUR LAWS, SHAMPOO!
YOU MUST BE TRAINED AGAIN!
HERE I COME!!
AH. SO MANY PEOPLE USE TRAINING GROUND OF CURSED SPRINGS NOW TIMES.
WHY DO YOU THINK?
DOING
BOING

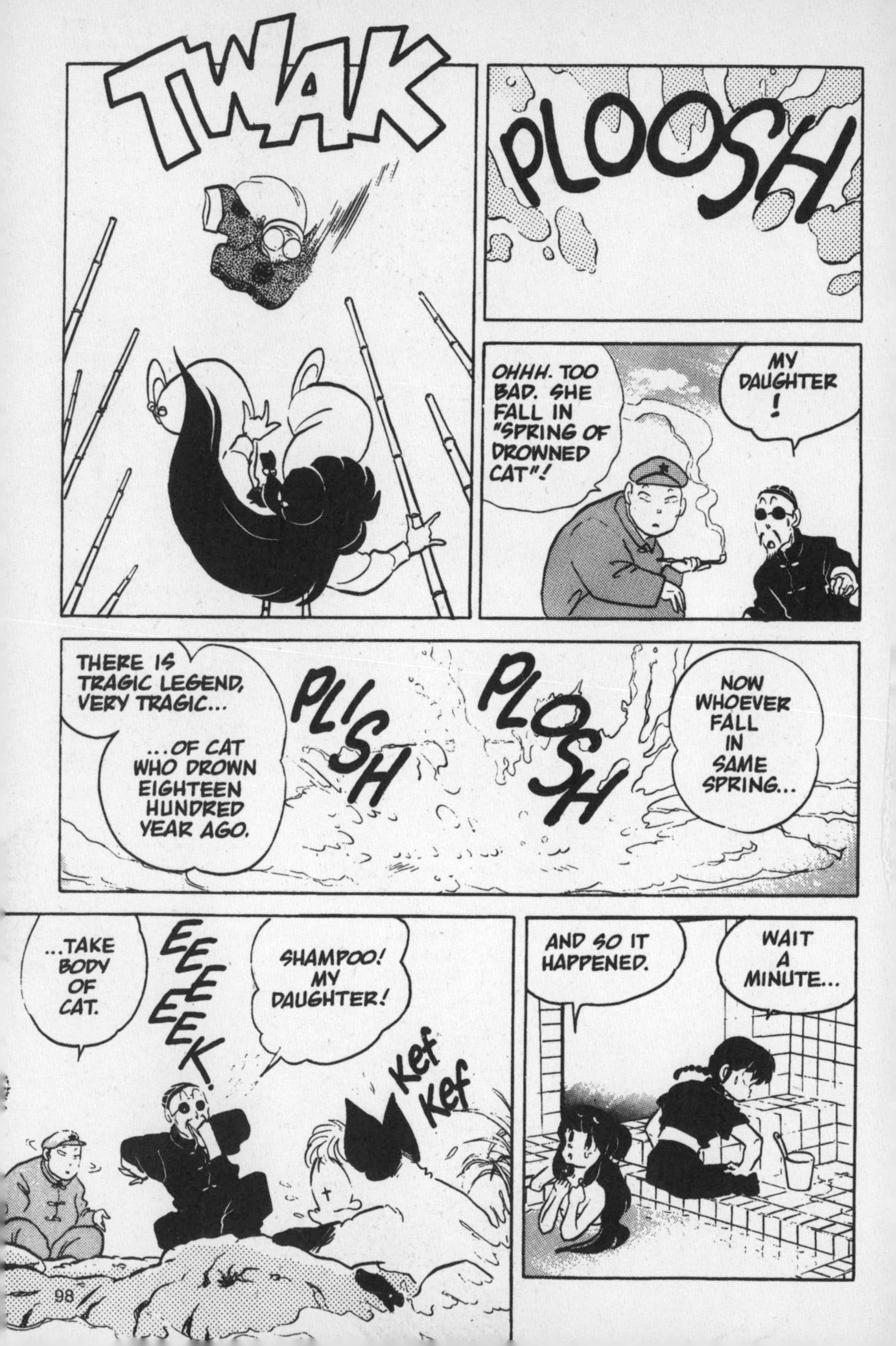

TWAK
PLOOSH
OHHH. TOO BAD. SHE FALL IN "SPRING OF DROWNED CAT"!
MY DAUGHTER!
THERE IS TRAGIC LEGEND, VERY TRAGIC...
...OF CAT WHO DROWN EIGHTEEN HUNDRED YEAR AGO.
PLISH
PLOSH
NOW WHOEVER FALL IN SAME SPRING...
...TAKE BODY OF CAT.
EEEEEEK!
SHAMPOO! MY DAUGHTER!
Kef Kef
AND SO IT HAPPENED.
WAIT A MINUTE...

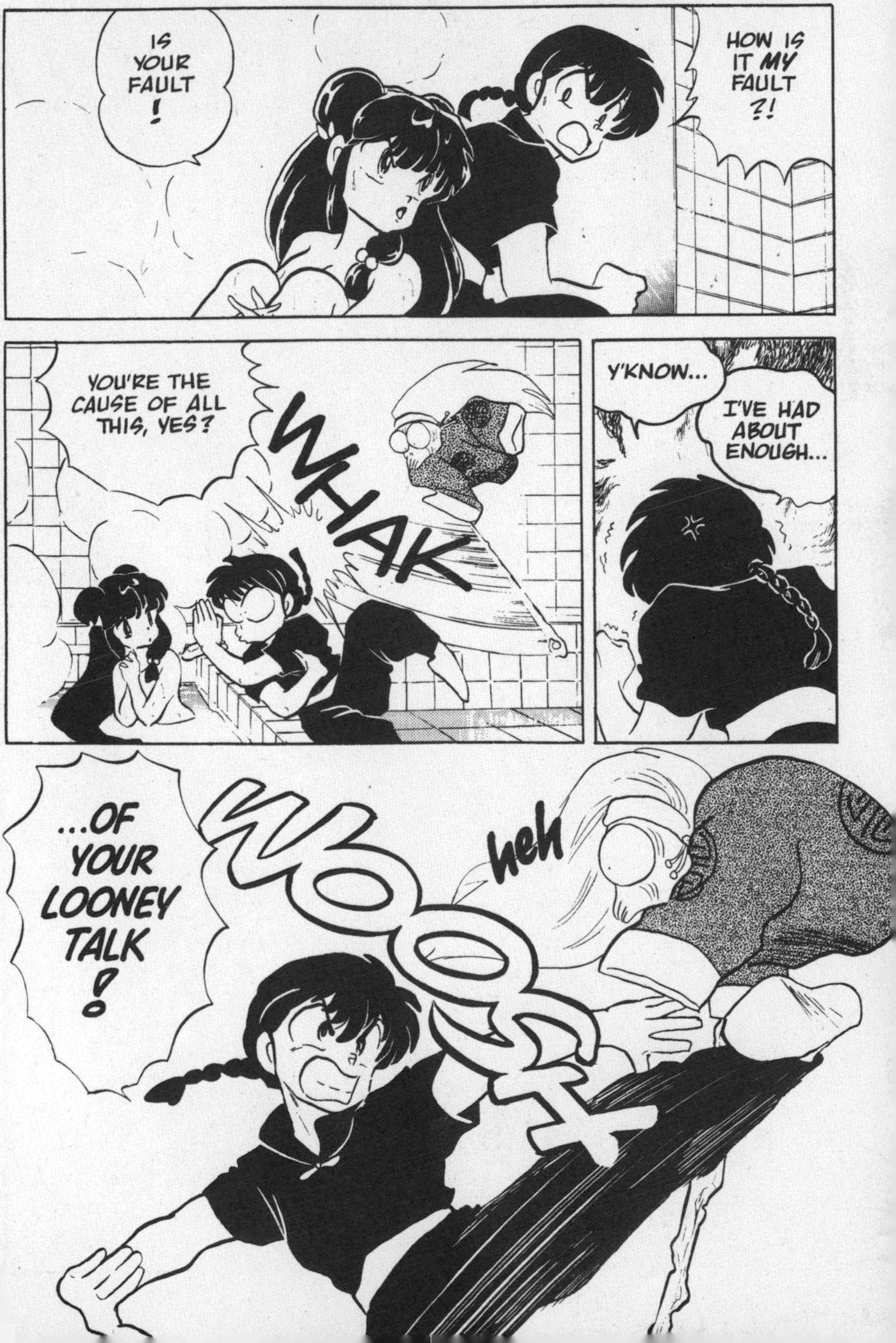
IS YOUR FAULT !
HOW IS IT MY FAULT ?!
YOU'RE THE CAUSE OF ALL THIS, YES?
WHAK
Y'KNOW...
I'VE HAD ABOUT ENOUGH...
...OF YOUR LOONEY TALK !
WOOOSH
heh

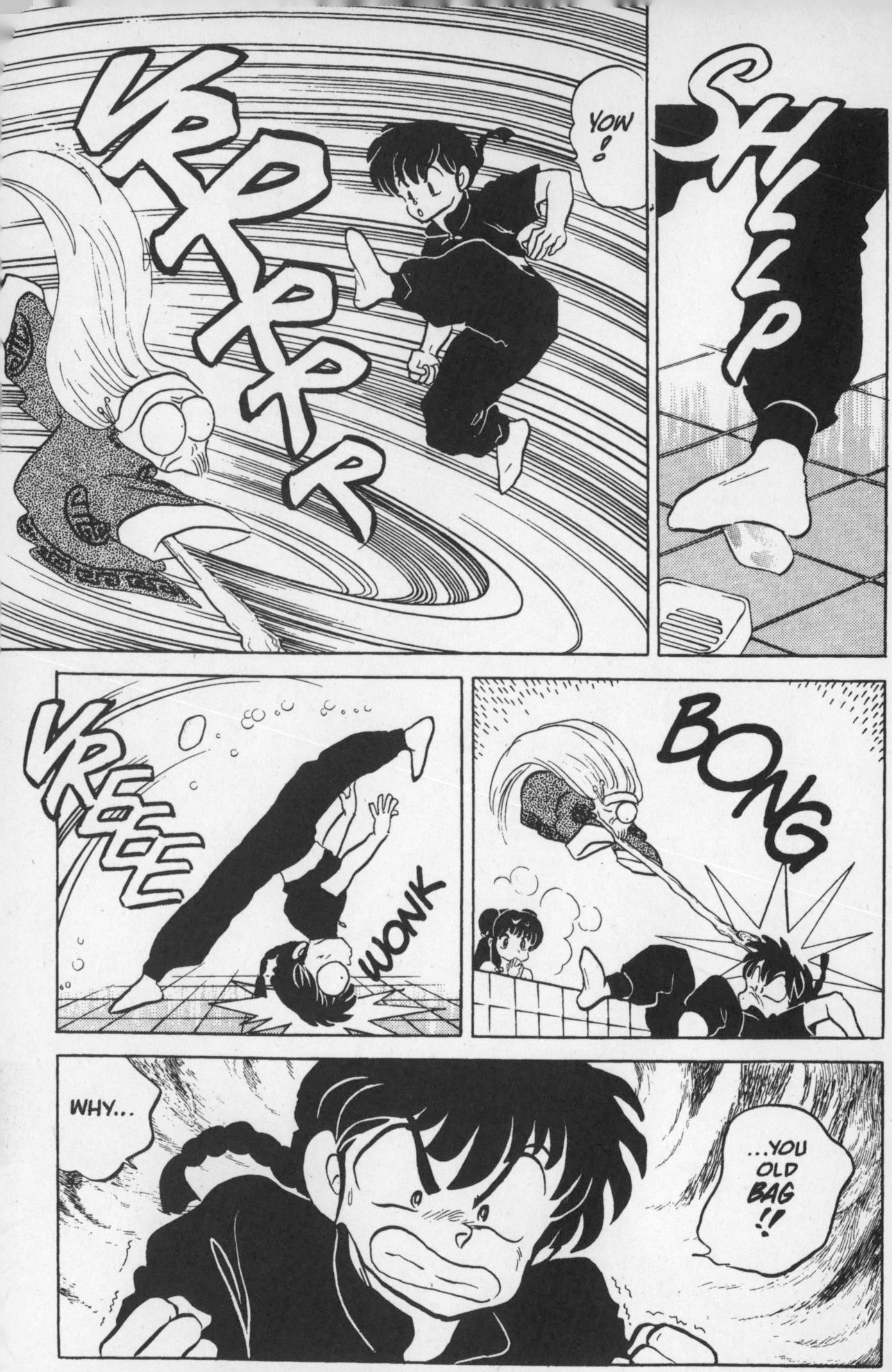
VRRRRR
YOW!
SHLLP
VREEEE
WONK
BONG
WHY...
...YOU OLD BAG!!

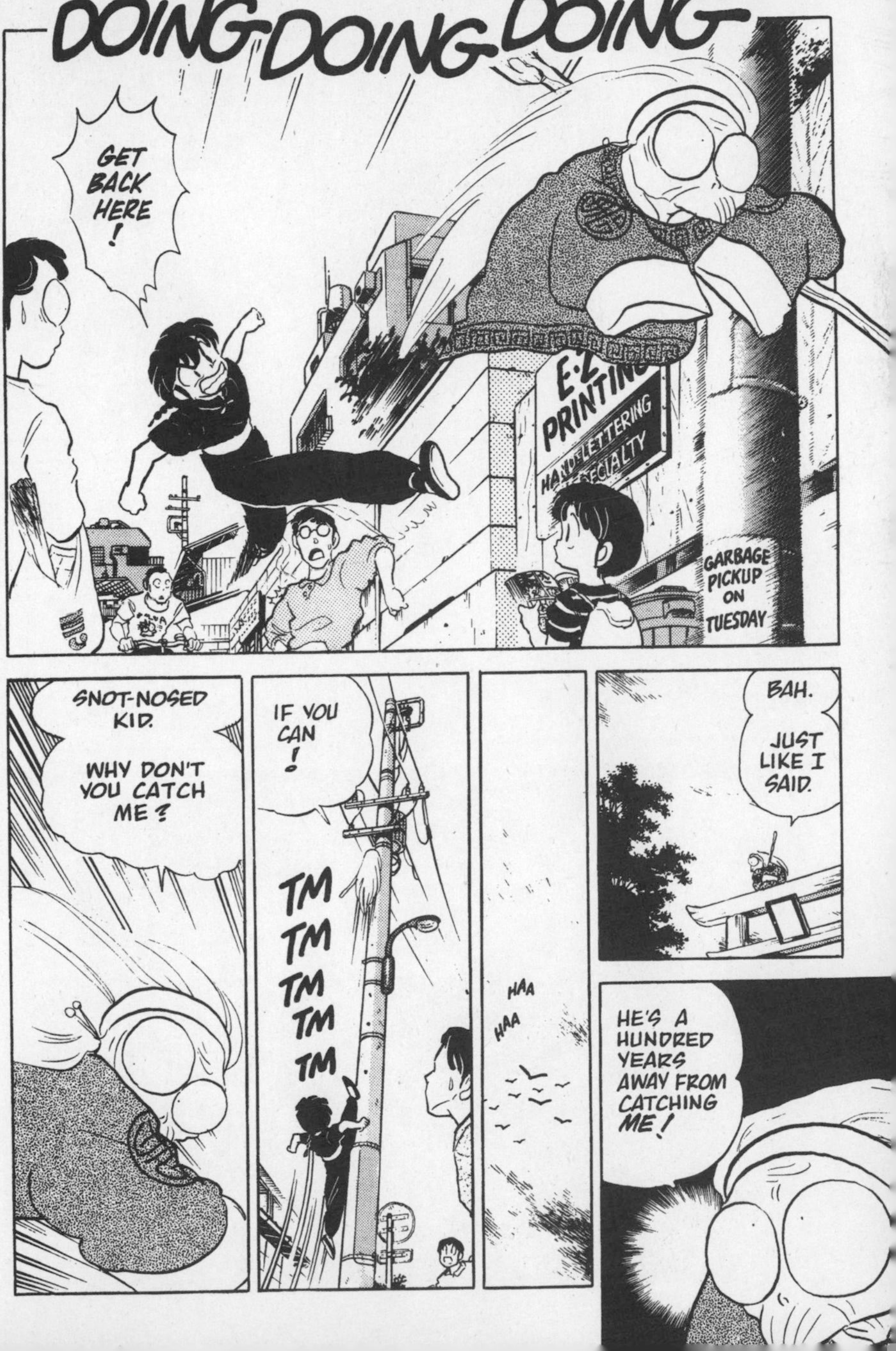
DOING DOING DOING
GET BACK HERE!
PRINTING
LETTERING
GARBAGE PICKUP ON TUESDAY
SNOT-NOSED KID.
WHY DON'T YOU CATCH ME?
IF YOU CAN!
TM TM TM TM TM
HAA HAA
BAH.
JUST LIKE I SAID.
HE'S A HUNDRED YEARS AWAY FROM CATCHING ME!

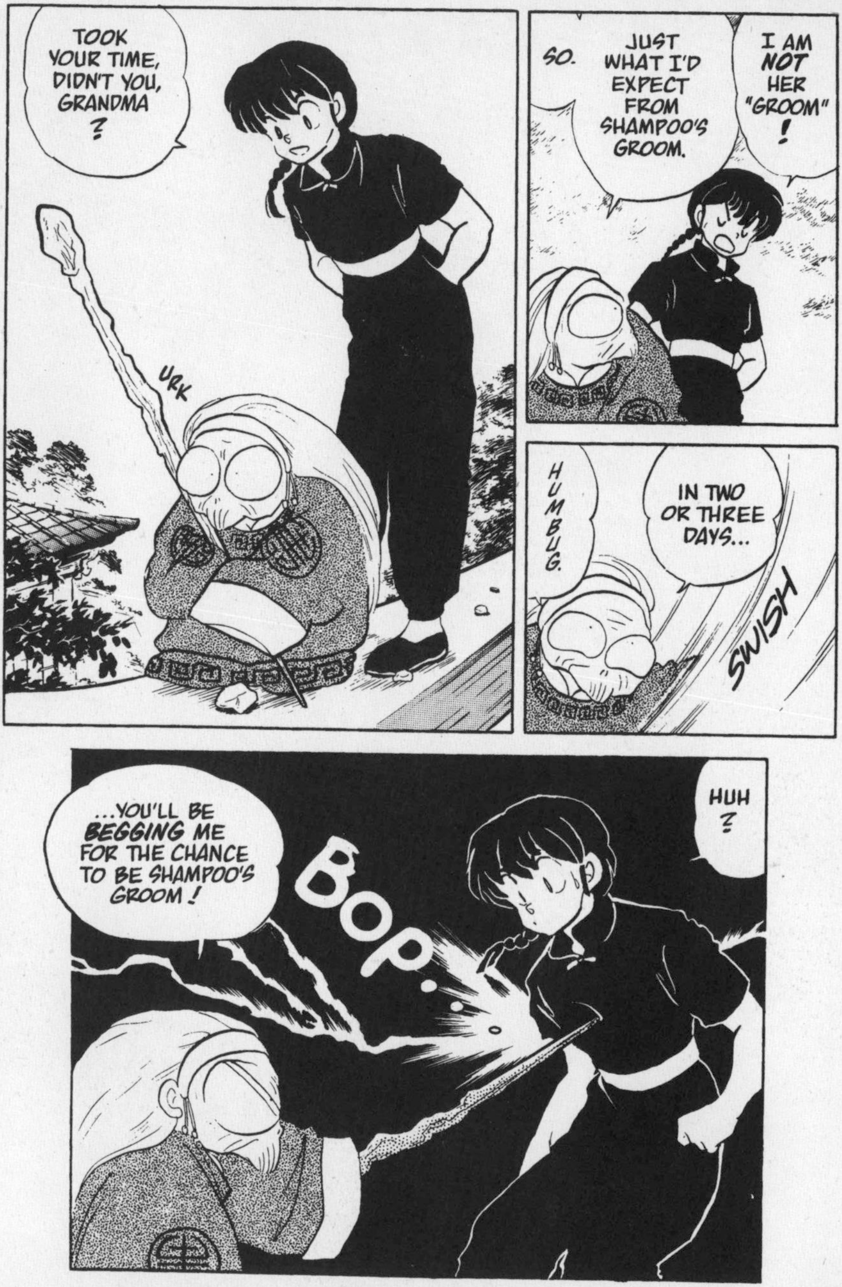
TOOK YOUR TIME, DIDN'T YOU, GRANDMA?
URK
SO.
JUST WHAT I'D EXPECT FROM SHAMPOO'S GROOM.
I AM NOT HER "GROOM"!
HUMBUG.
IN TWO OR THREE DAYS...
SWISH
...YOU'LL BE BEGGING ME FOR THE CHANCE TO BE SHAMPOO'S GROOM!
BOP...
HUH?

Part 7

ATTACK OF THE WILD MOUSSE

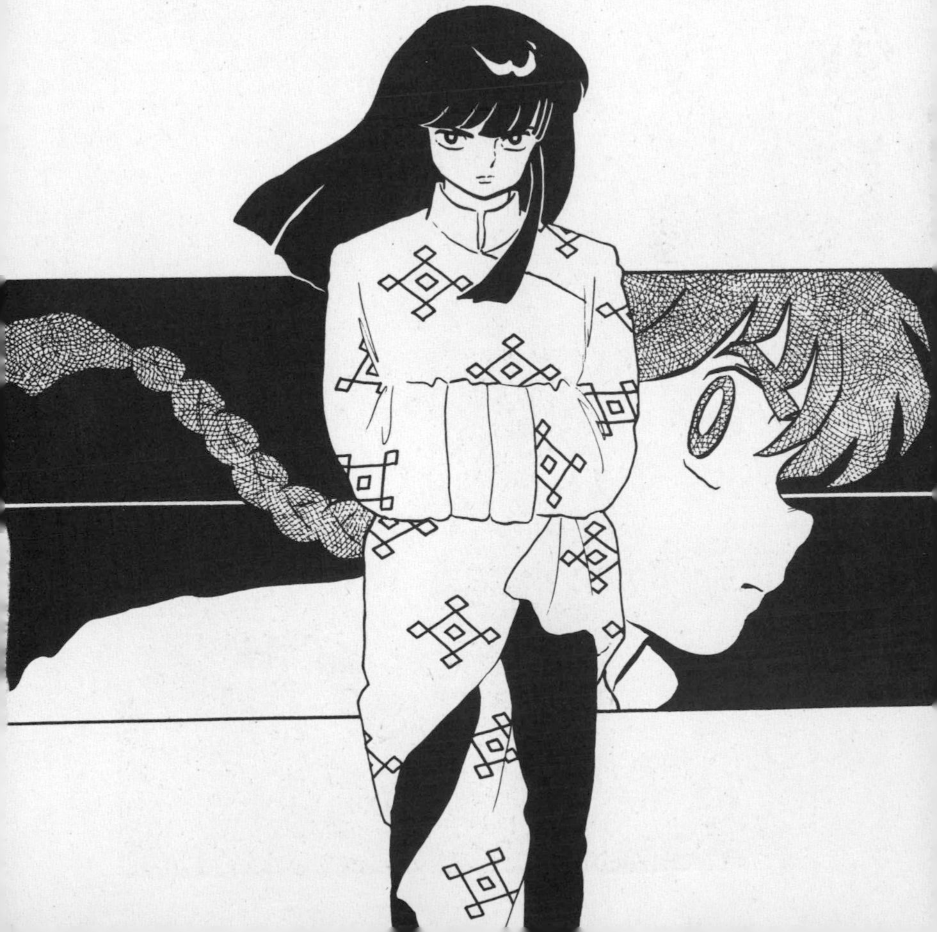

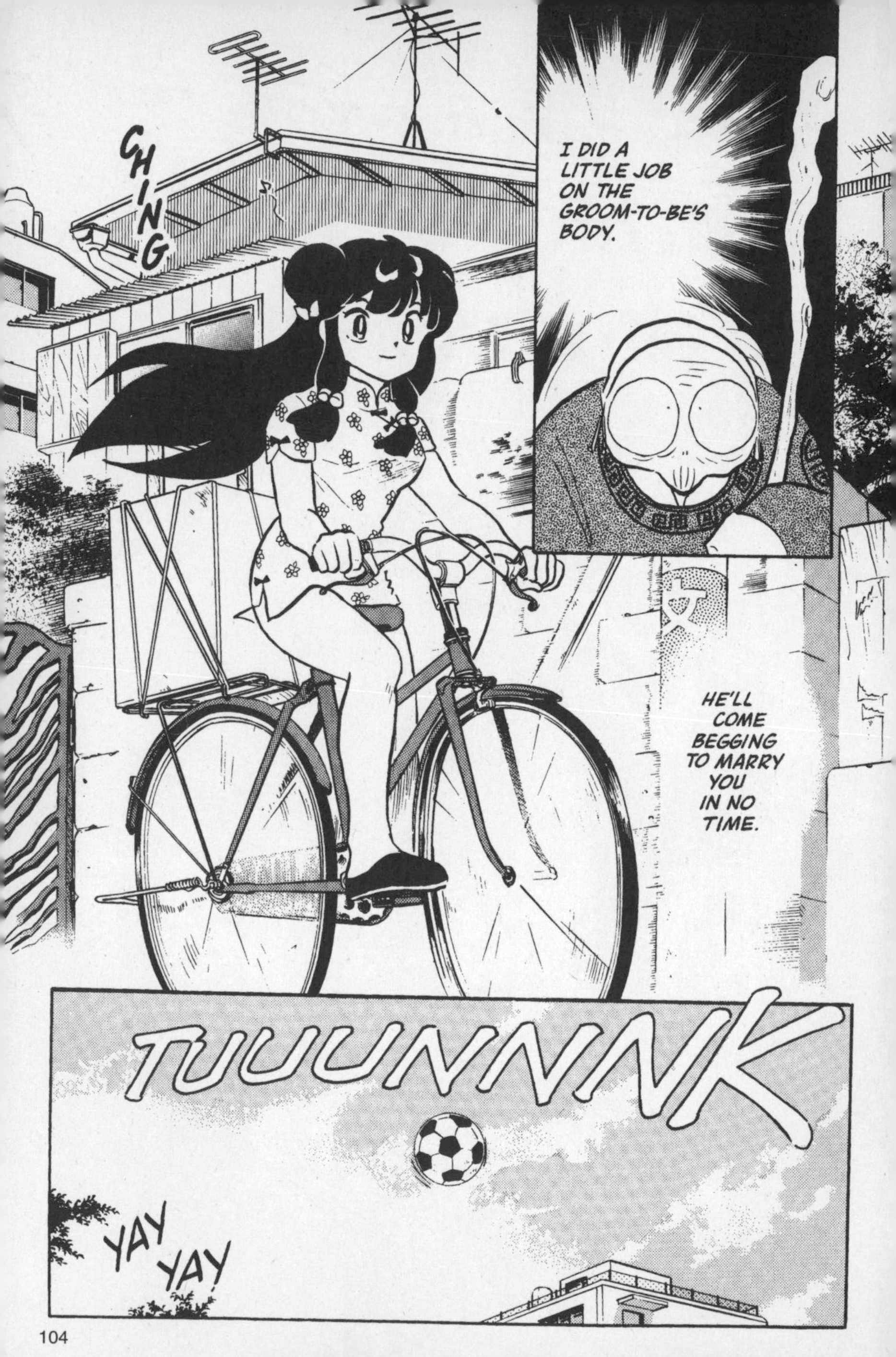
CHING
I DID A LITTLE JOB ON THE GROOM-TO-BE'S BODY.
HE'LL COME BEGGING TO MARRY YOU IN NO TIME.
TUUUNNNK
YAY YAY

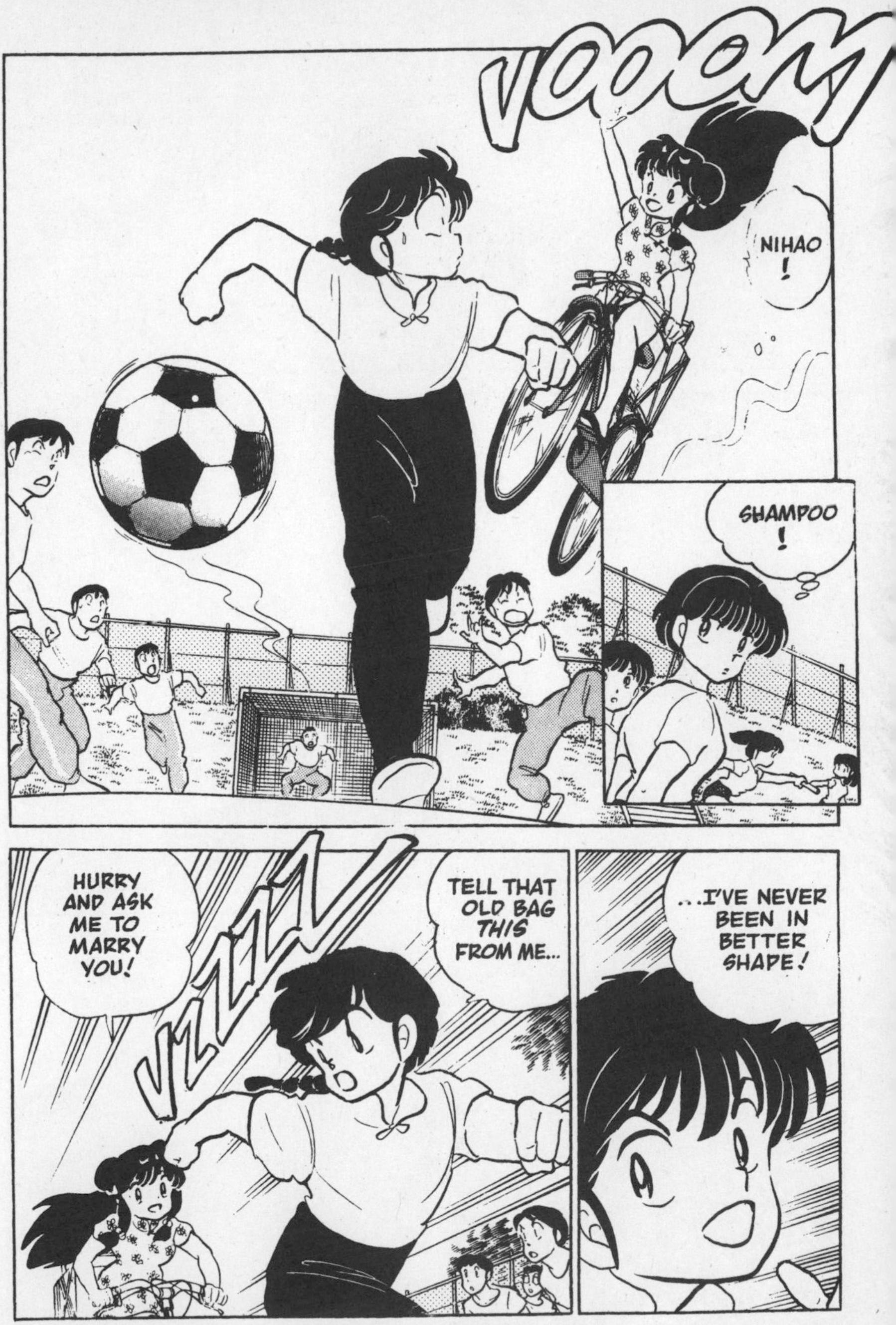
VOOOM
NIHAO!
SHAMPOO!
HURRY AND ASK ME TO MARRY YOU!
VZZZZN
TELL THAT OLD BAG THIS FROM ME...
...I'VE NEVER BEEN IN BETTER SHAPE!

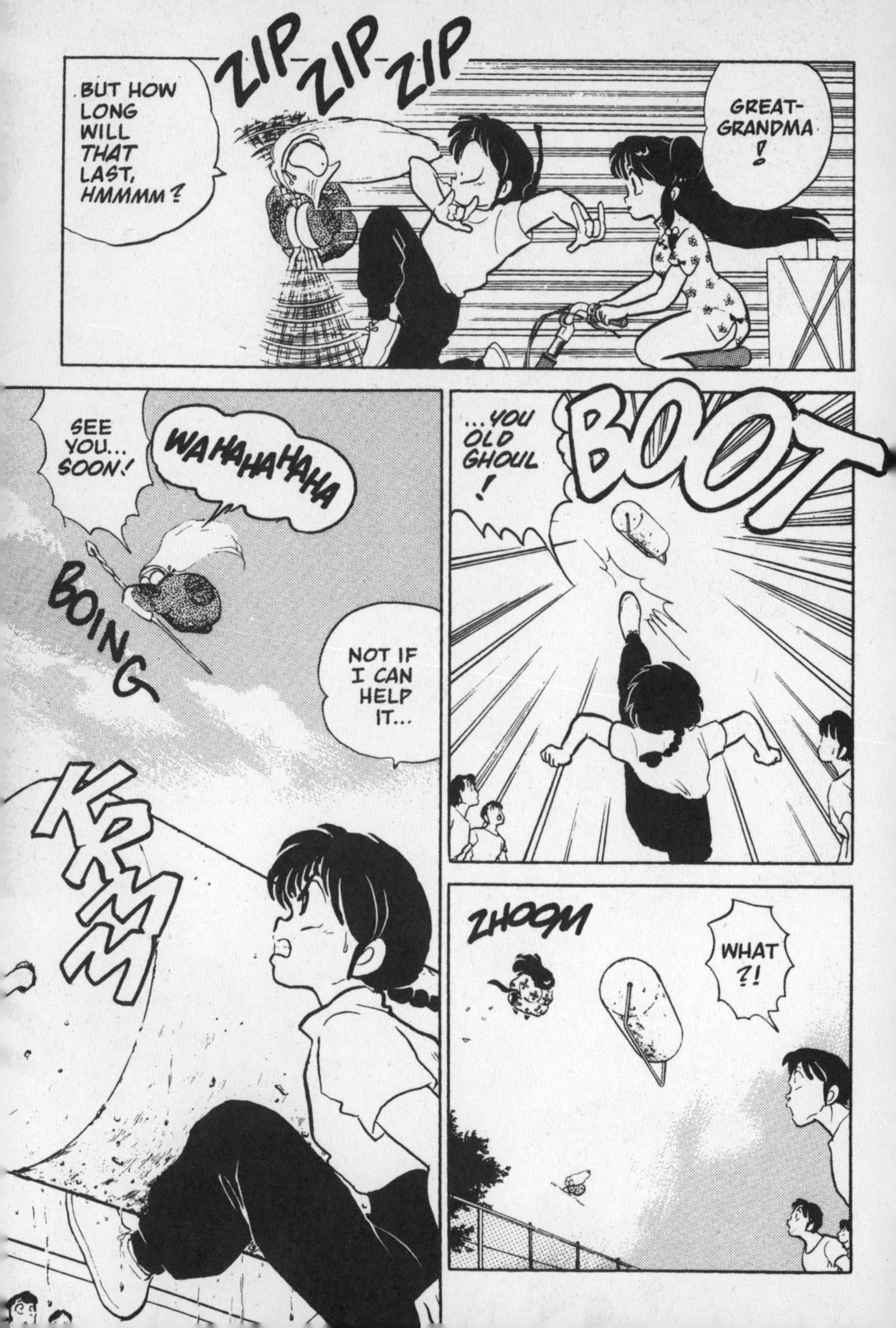

ZIP-ZIP-ZIP
BUT HOW LONG WILL THAT LAST, HMMMM?
GREAT-GRANDMA!
SEE YOU... SOON!
WAHAHAHAHAHA
BOING
NOT IF I CAN HELP IT...
KRMM
...YOU OLD GHOUL!
BOOT
ZHOOM
WHAT?!

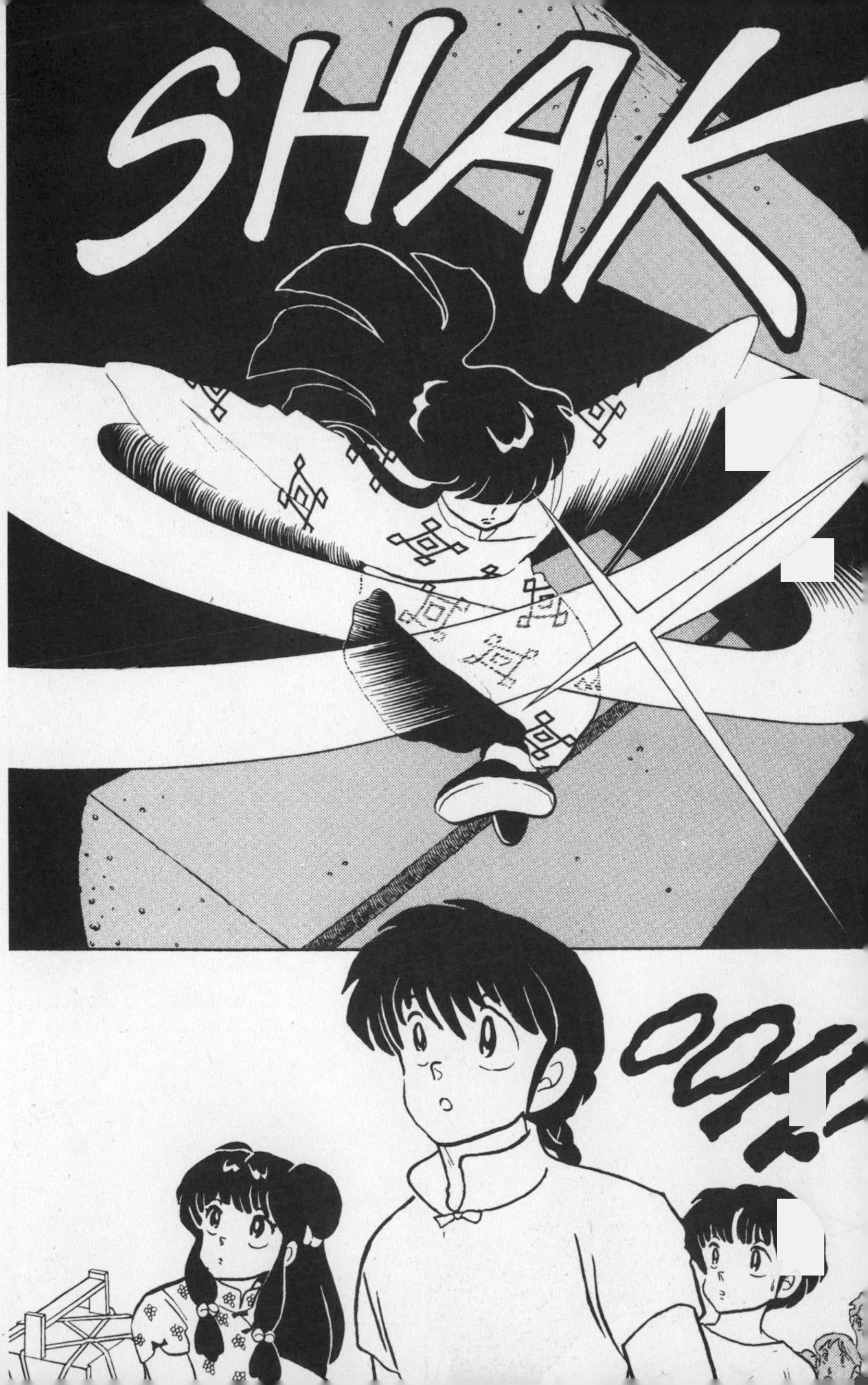
SHAK
OOH!!

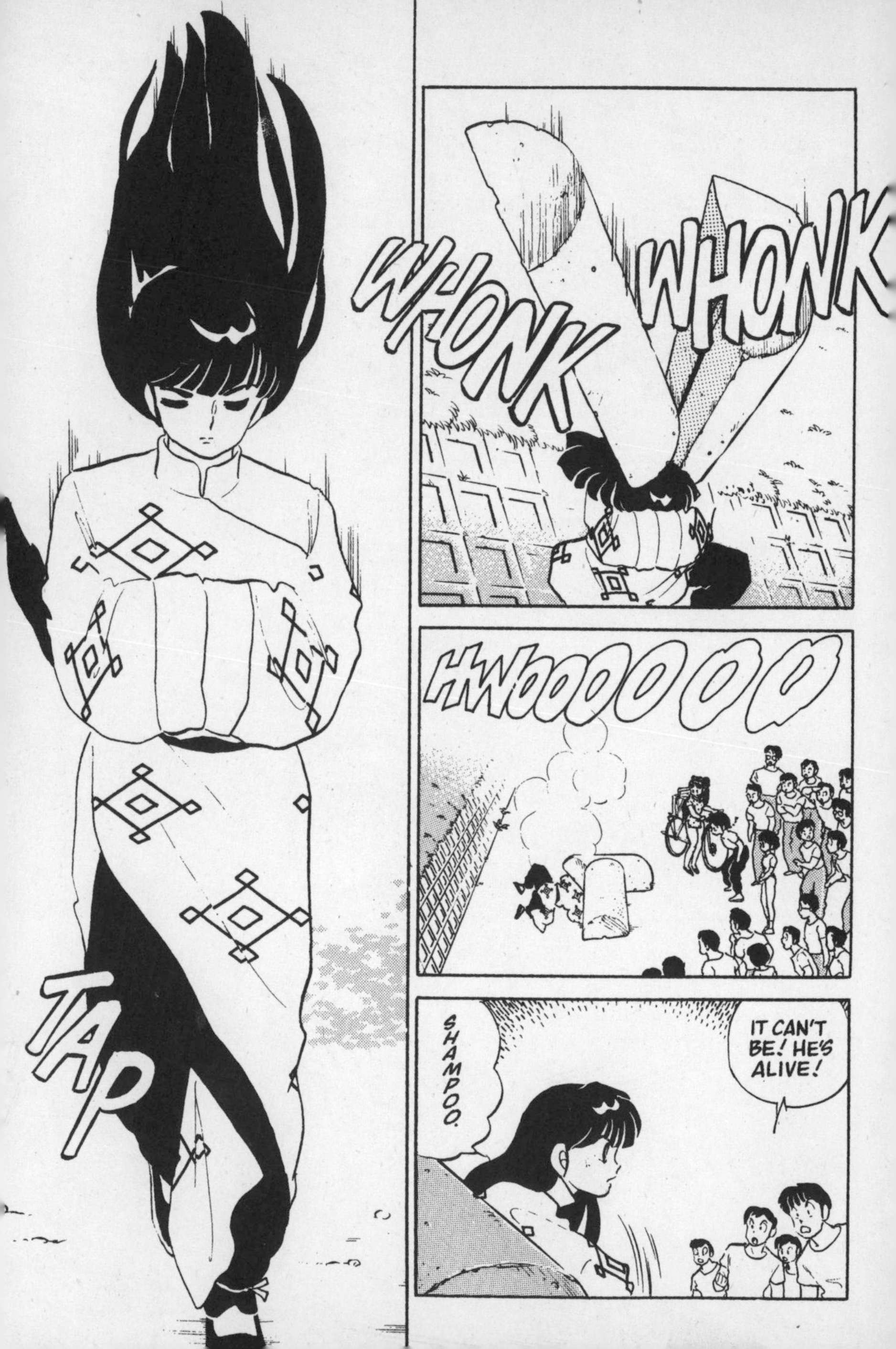
TAP
WHONK
WHONK
HWOOOOOOO
SHAMPOO.
IT CAN'T BE! HE'S ALIVE!

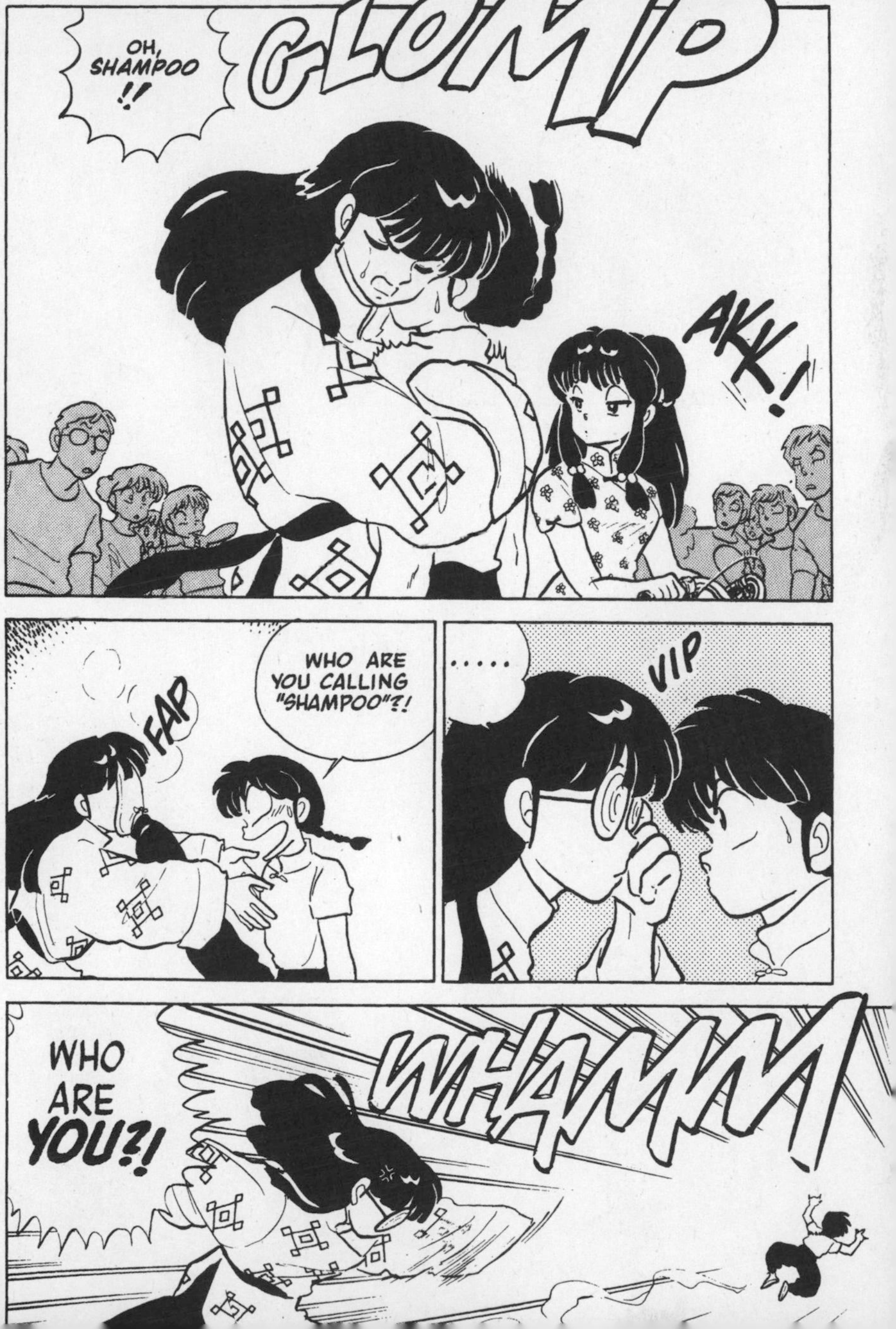
OH, SHAMPOO !!
CLOMP
AKK!
FAP
WHO ARE YOU CALLING "SHAMPOO"?!
.....
VIP
WHO ARE YOU?!
WHAMM!

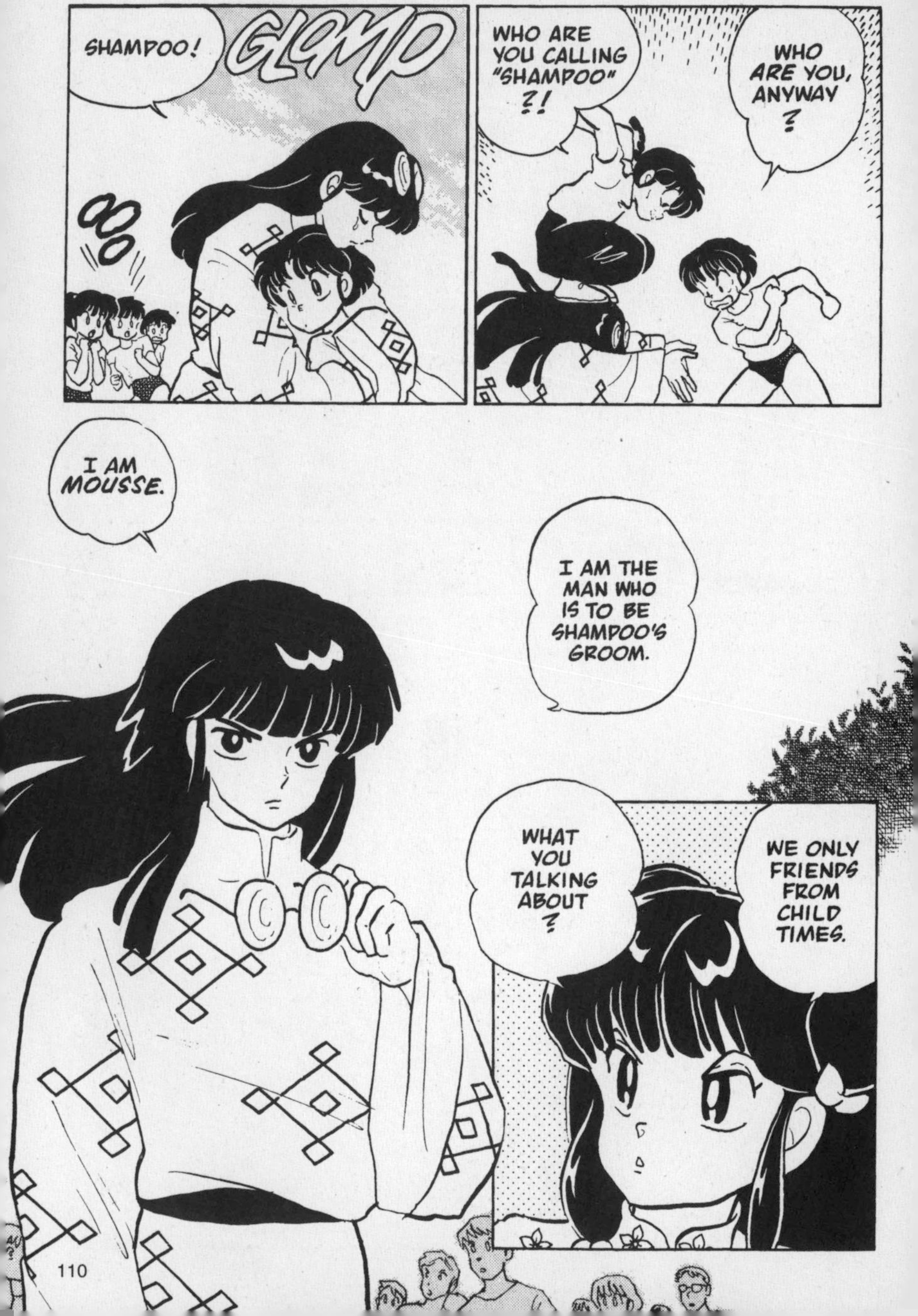
SHAMPOO!
GLOMP
WHO ARE YOU CALLING "SHAMPOO" ?!
WHO ARE YOU, ANYWAY ?
I AM MOUSSE.
I AM THE MAN WHO IS TO BE SHAMPOO'S GROOM.
WHAT YOU TALKING ABOUT ?
WE ONLY FRIENDS FROM CHILD TIMES.

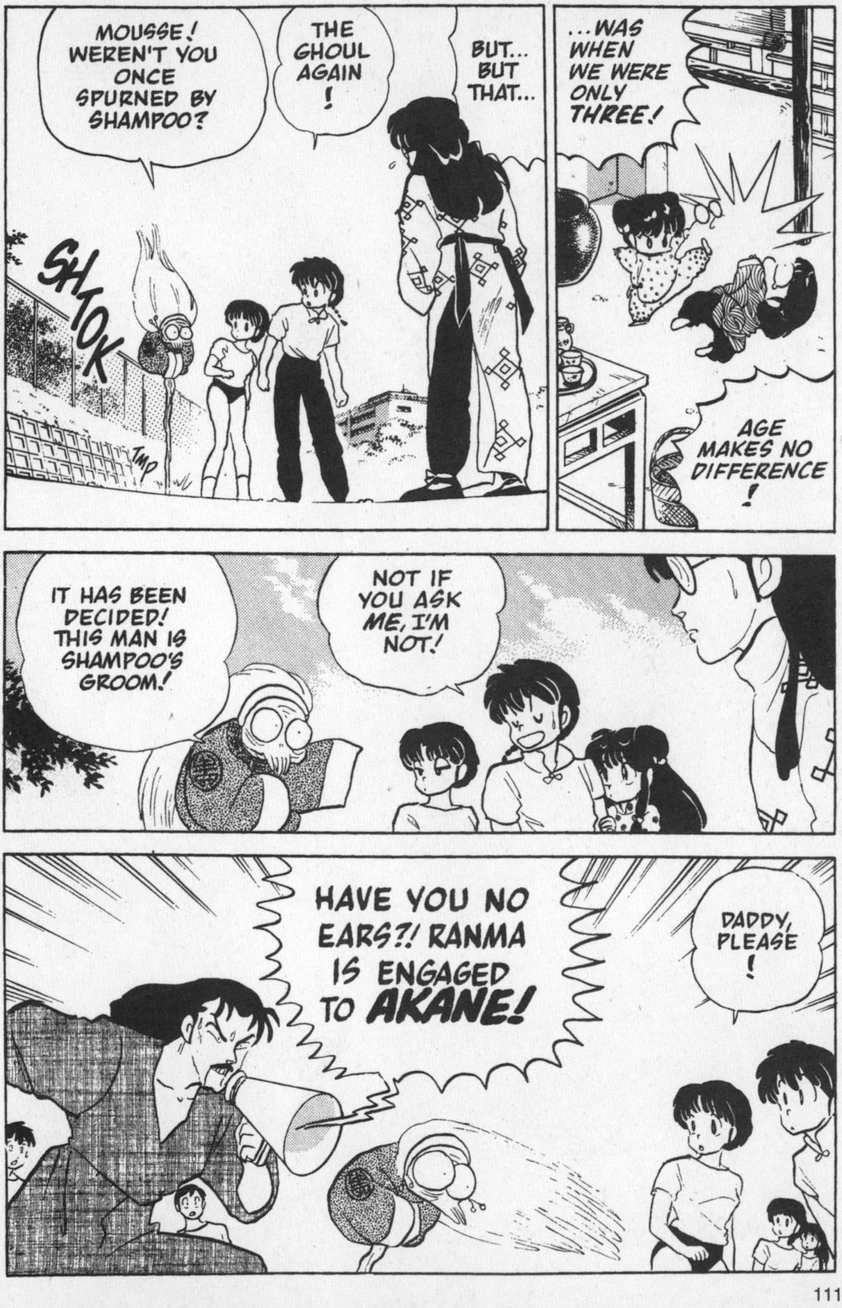
MOUSSE! WEREN'T YOU ONCE SPURNED BY SHAMPOO?
THE GHOUL AGAIN!
BUT... BUT THAT...
SHTOK
TMP
...WAS WHEN WE WERE ONLY THREE!
AGE MAKES NO DIFFERENCE!
IT HAS BEEN DECIDED! THIS MAN IS SHAMPOO'S GROOM!
NOT IF YOU ASK ME, I'M NOT!
HAVE YOU NO EARS?! RANMA IS ENGAGED TO AKANE!
DADDY, PLEASE!

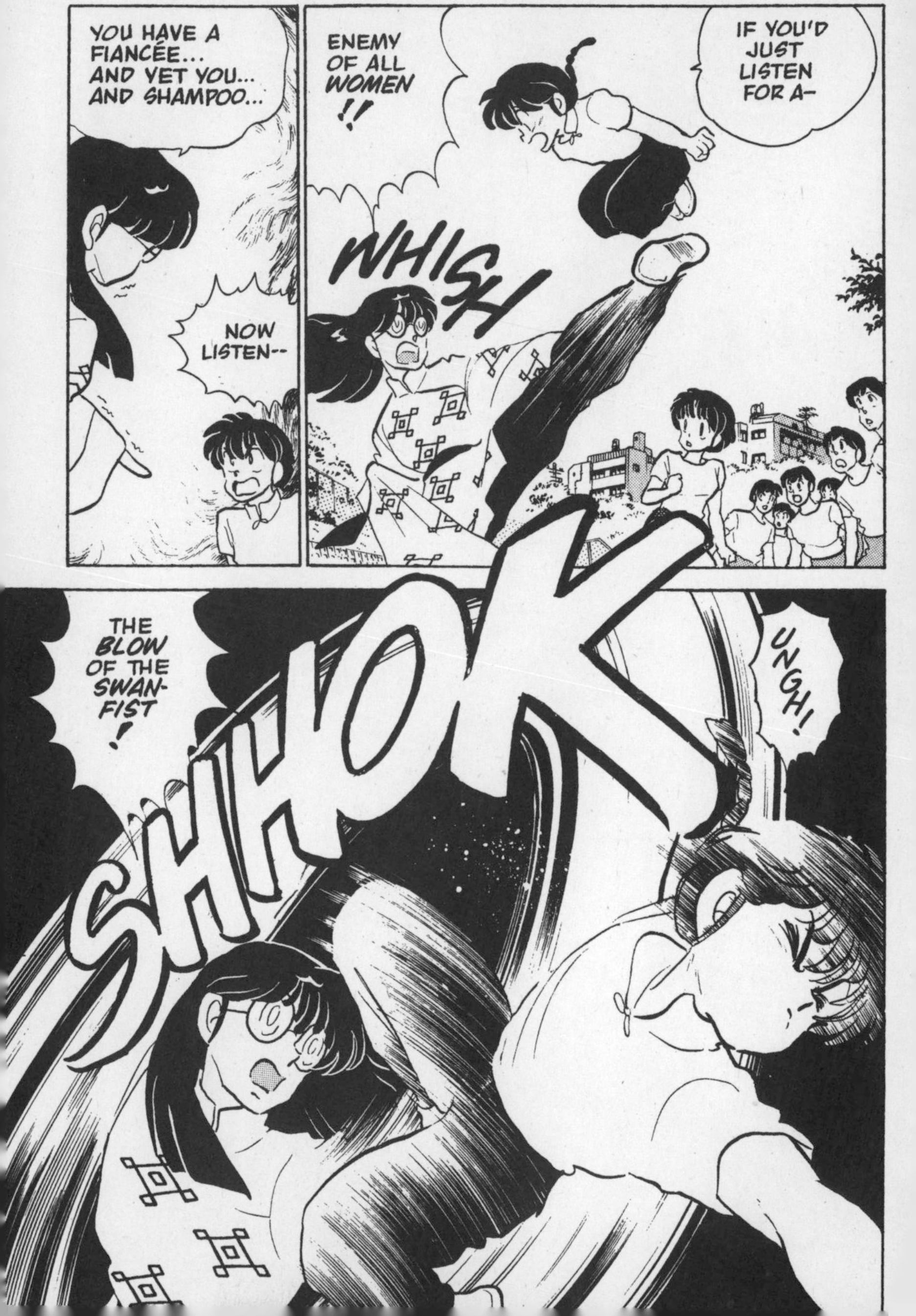
YOU HAVE A FIANCÉE... AND YET YOU... AND SHAMPOO...
NOW LISTEN--
ENEMY OF ALL WOMEN !!
IF YOU'D JUST LISTEN FOR A-
WHISH
THE BLOW OF THE SWAN-FIST!
SHHOK
UNGH!

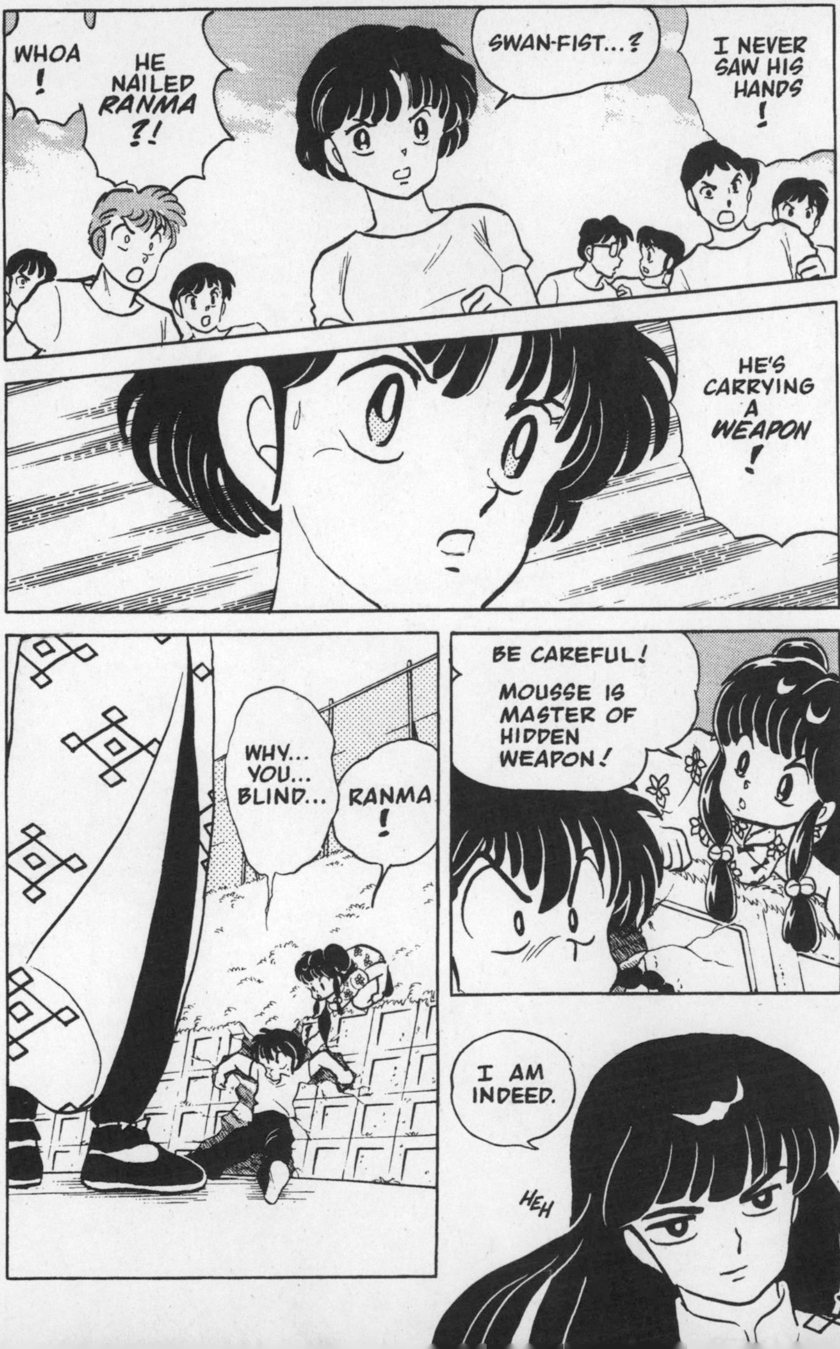
WHOA!
HE NAILED RANMA?!
SWAN-FIST...?
I NEVER SAW HIS HANDS!
HE'S CARRYING A WEAPON!
WHY... YOU... BLIND...
RANMA!
BE CAREFUL!
MOUSSE IS MASTER OF HIDDEN WEAPON!
I AM INDEED.
HEH

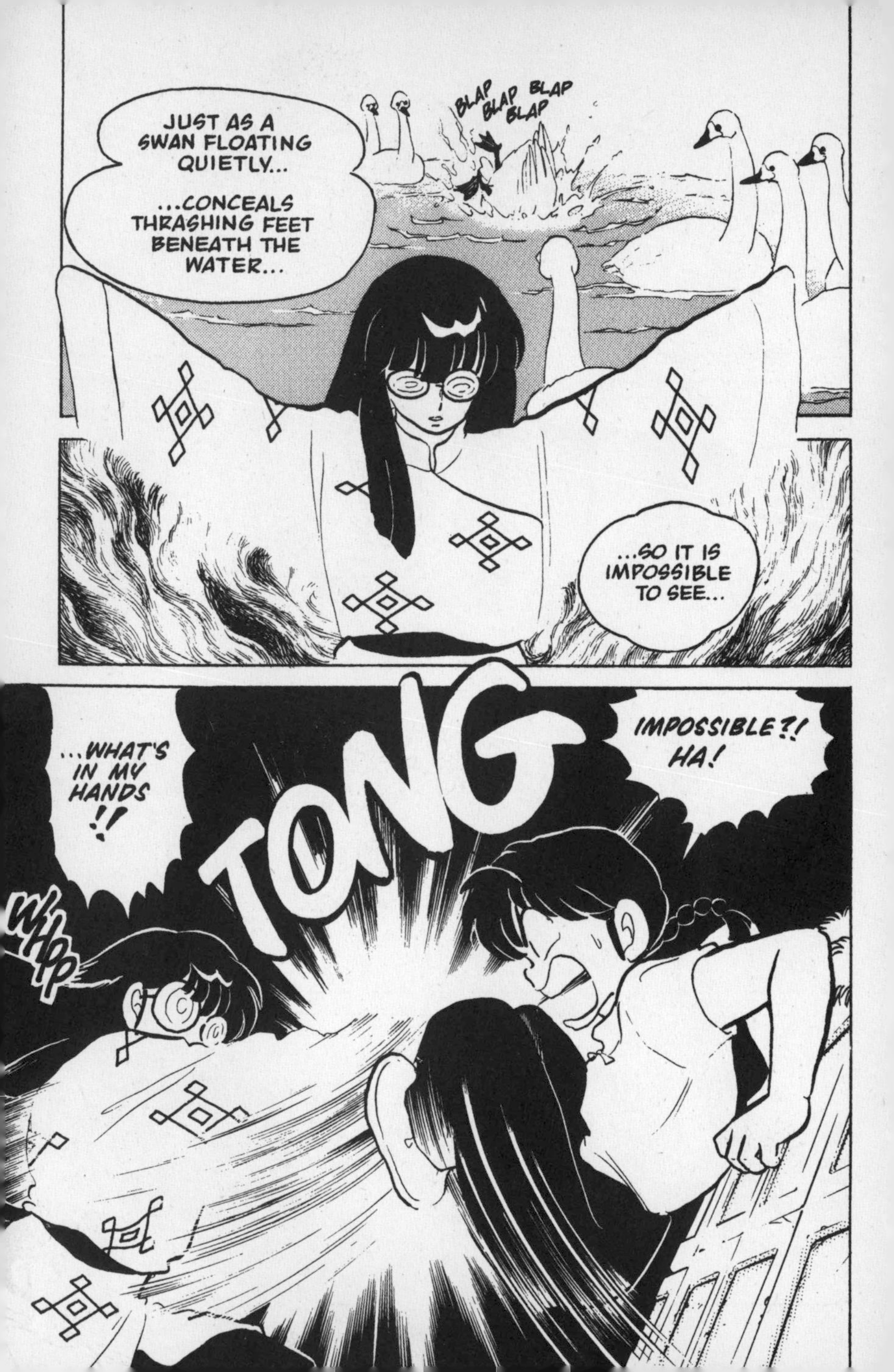
JUST AS A SWAN FLOATING QUIETLY...
...CONCEALS THRASHING FEET BENEATH THE WATER...
BLAP BLAP BLAP BLAP
...SO IT IS IMPOSSIBLE TO SEE...
...WHAT'S IN MY HANDS !!
TONG
IMPOSSIBLE?! HA!
WHPP

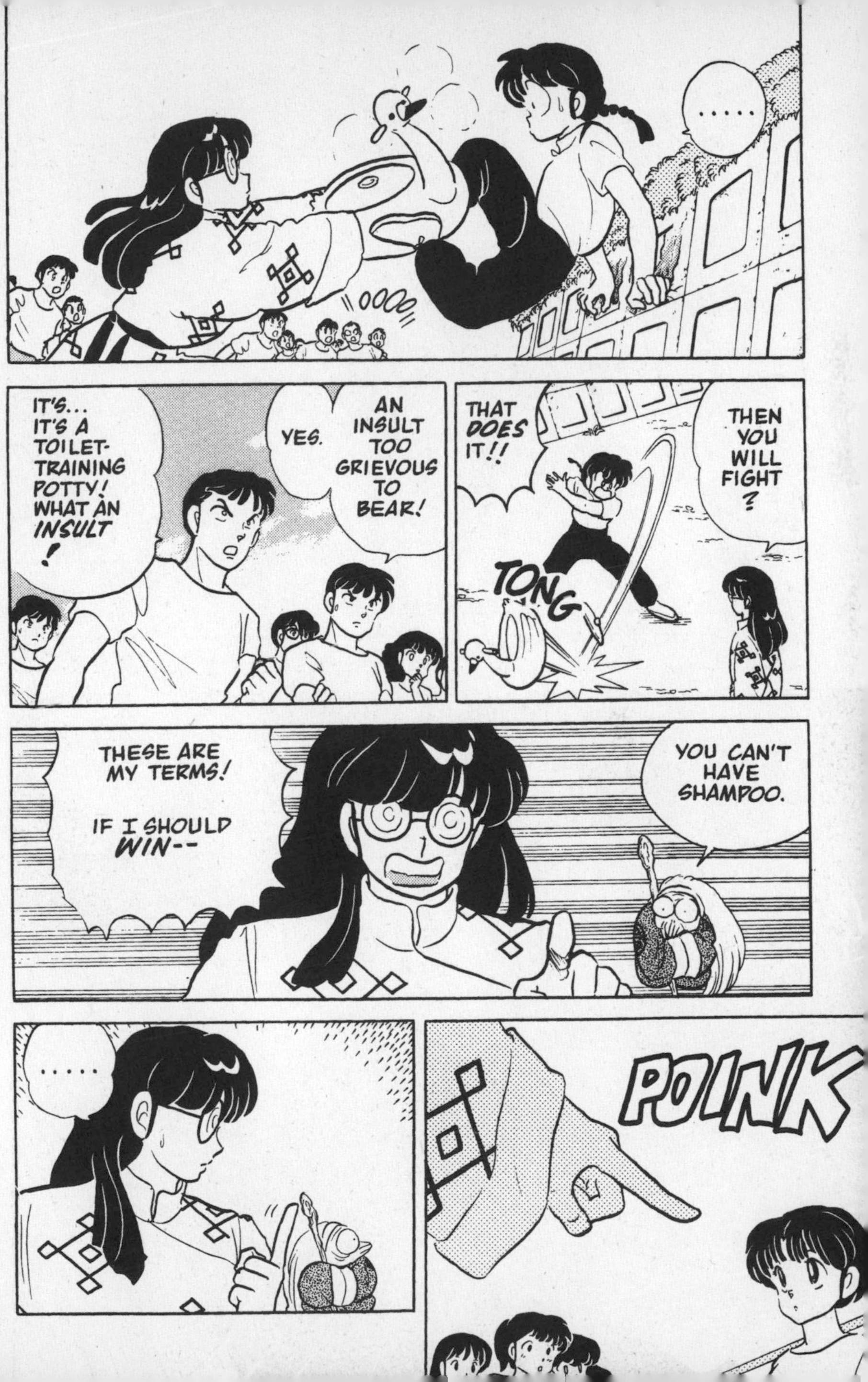
.....
OOOO
IT'S... IT'S A TOILET-TRAINING POTTY! WHAT AN INSULT!
YES.
AN INSULT TOO GRIEVOUS TO BEAR!
THAT DOES IT!!
THEN YOU WILL FIGHT?
TONG
THESE ARE MY TERMS!
IF I SHOULD WIN--
YOU CAN'T HAVE SHAMPOO.
.....
POINK

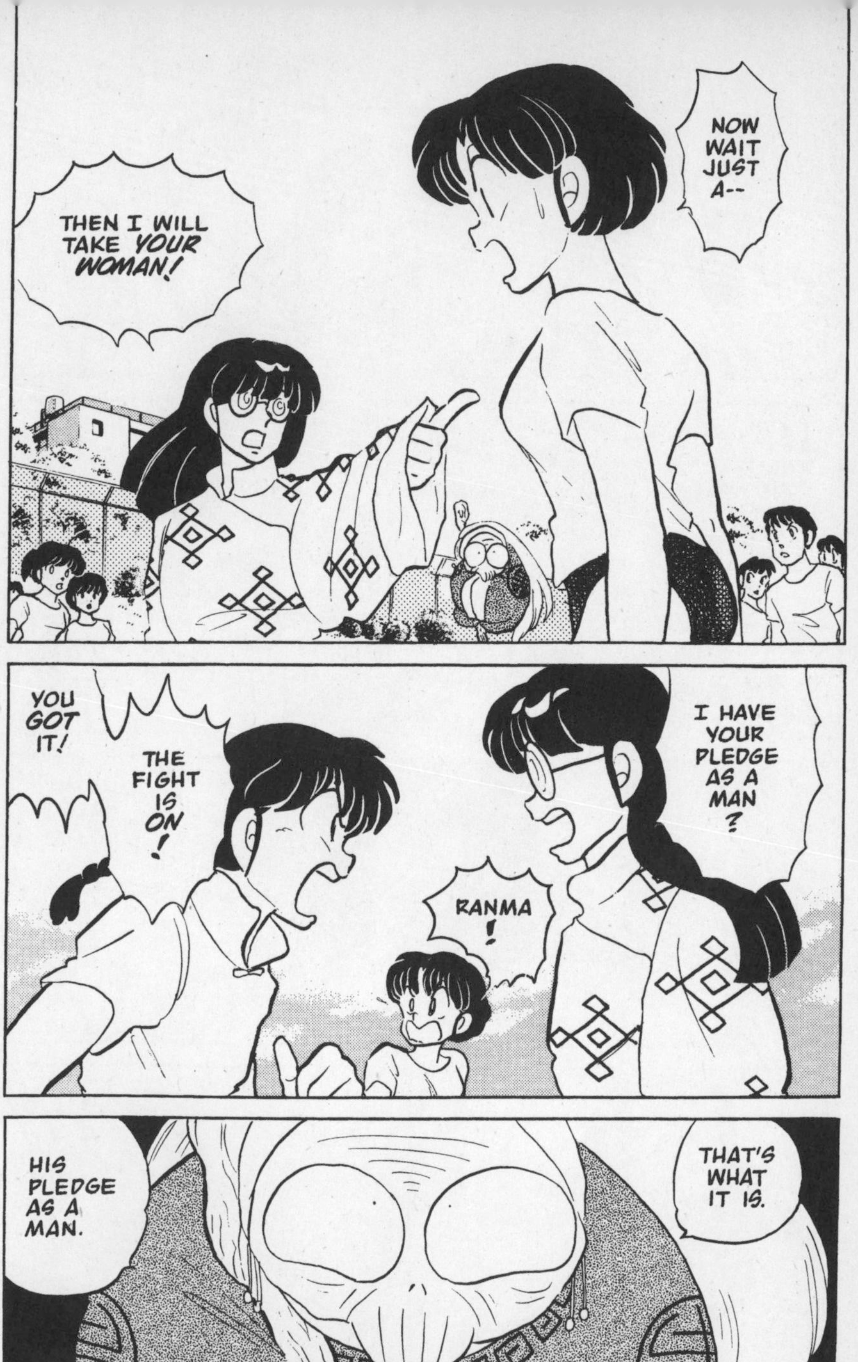
THEN I WILL TAKE *YOUR WOMAN!*
NOW WAIT JUST A--
YOU GOT IT!
THE FIGHT IS *ON!*
RANMA!
I HAVE YOUR PLEDGE AS A MAN?
HIS PLEDGE AS A MAN.
THAT'S WHAT IT IS.

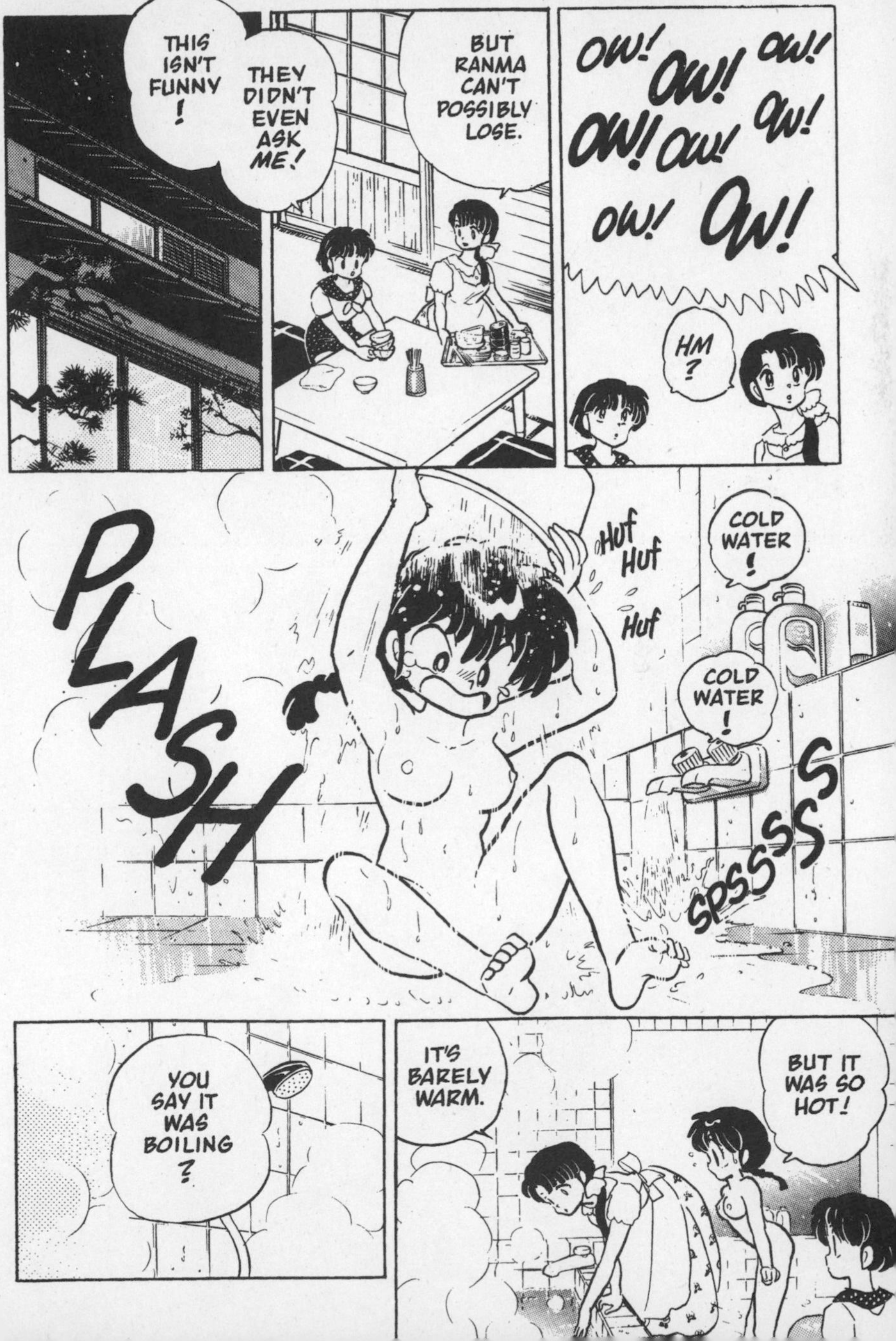
THIS ISN'T FUNNY!
THEY DIDN'T EVEN ASK ME!
BUT RANMA CAN'T POSSIBLY LOSE.
OW! OW! OW! OW! OW! OW! OW! OW! OW!
HM?
PLASH
HUF HUF HUF
COLD WATER!
COLD WATER!
SPSSSSSS
YOU SAY IT WAS BOILING?
IT'S BARELY WARM.
BUT IT WAS SO HOT!

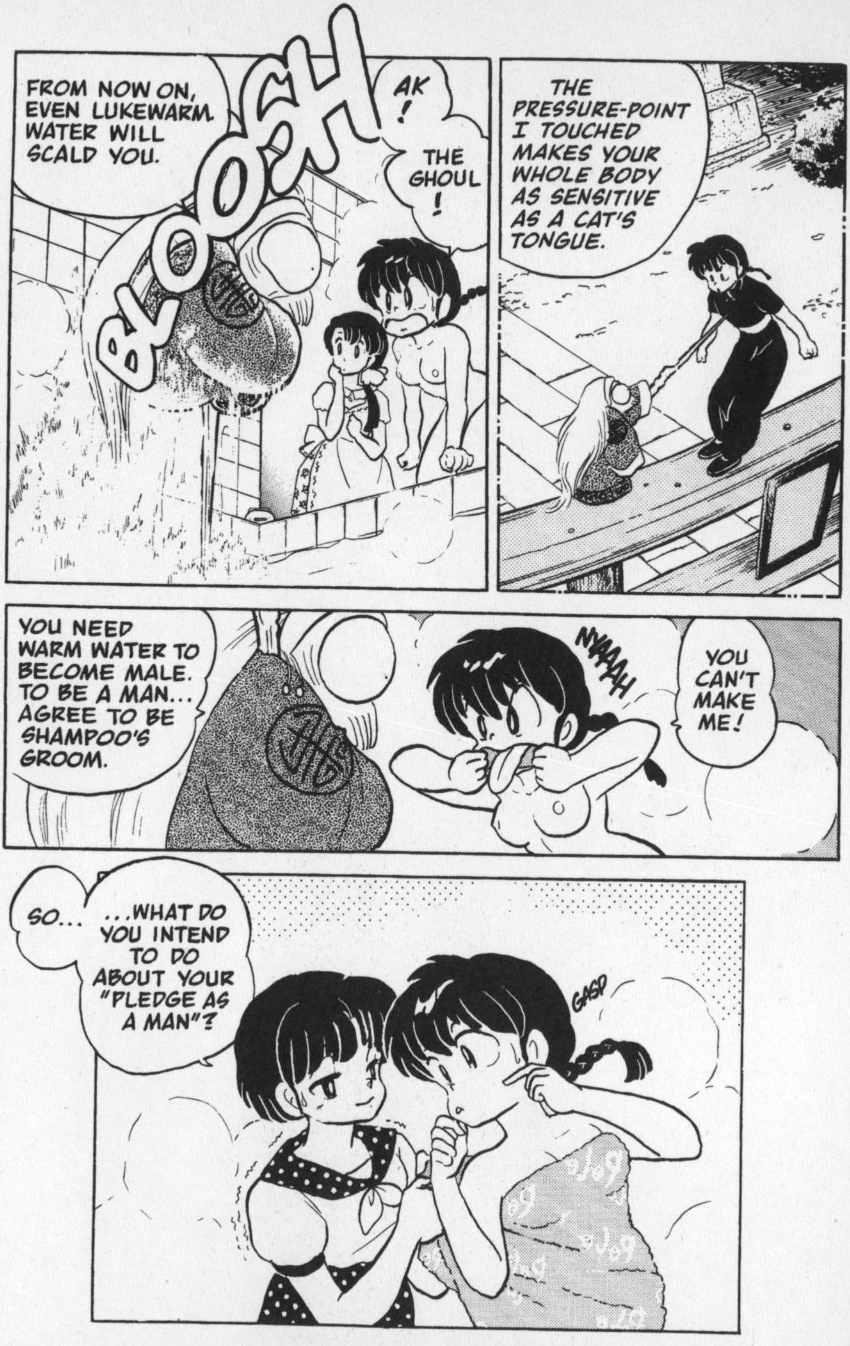
FROM NOW ON, EVEN LUKEWARM WATER WILL SCALD YOU.
BLOOOSH
AK!
THE GHOUL!
THE PRESSURE-POINT I TOUCHED MAKES YOUR WHOLE BODY AS SENSITIVE AS A CAT'S TONGUE.
YOU NEED WARM WATER TO BECOME MALE. TO BE A MAN... AGREE TO BE SHAMPOO'S GROOM.
NYAAAH
YOU CAN'T MAKE ME!
SO... ...WHAT DO YOU INTEND TO DO ABOUT YOUR "PLEDGE AS A MAN"?
GASP

Part 8
THE MARTIAL ARTS MAGIC SHOW

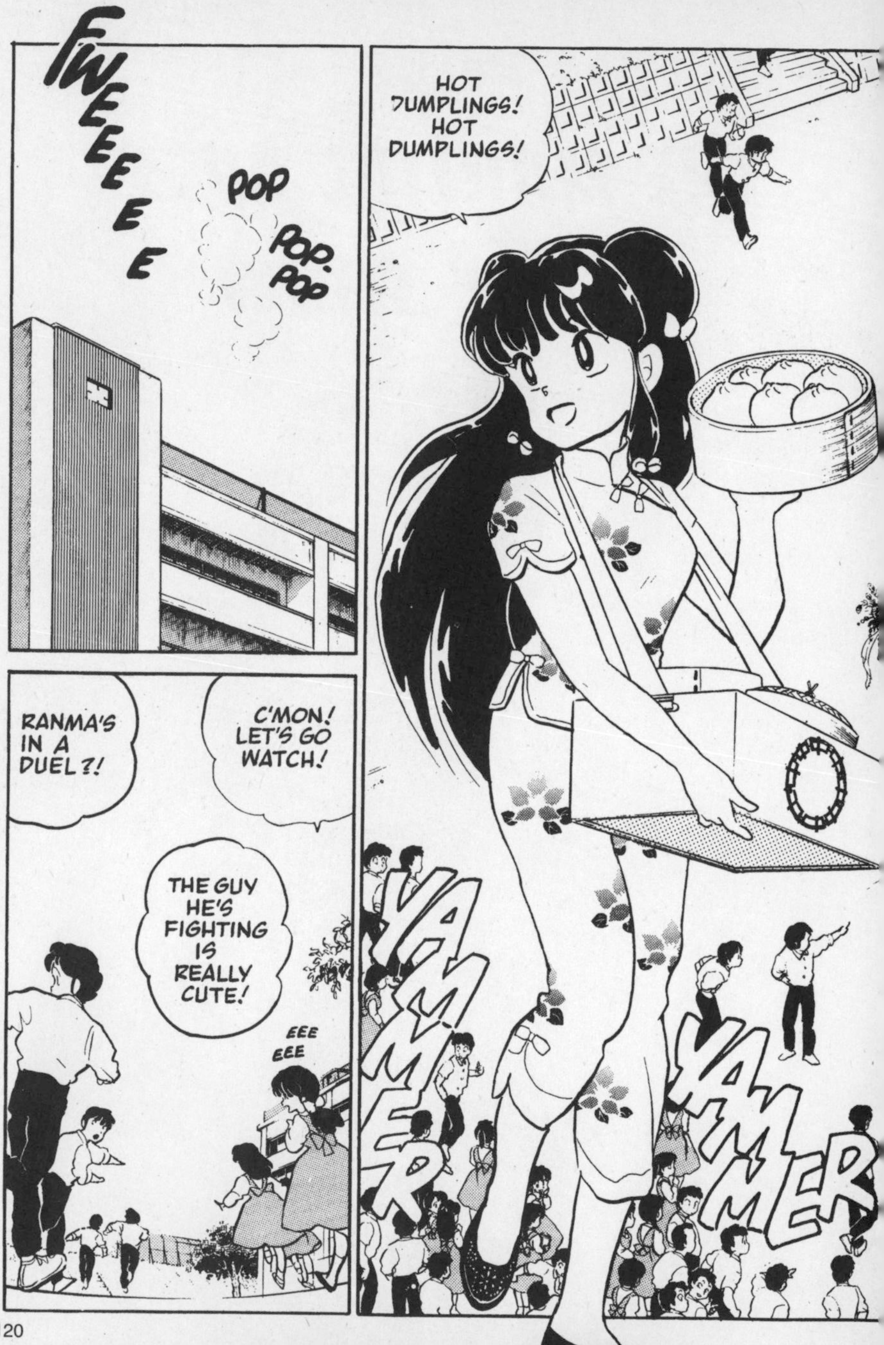
FWEEEEEE
POP
POP. POP
RANMA'S IN A DUEL?!
C'MON! LET'S GO WATCH!
THE GUY HE'S FIGHTING IS REALLY CUTE!
EEE EEE
HOT DUMPLINGS! HOT DUMPLINGS!
YAMMER
YAMMER

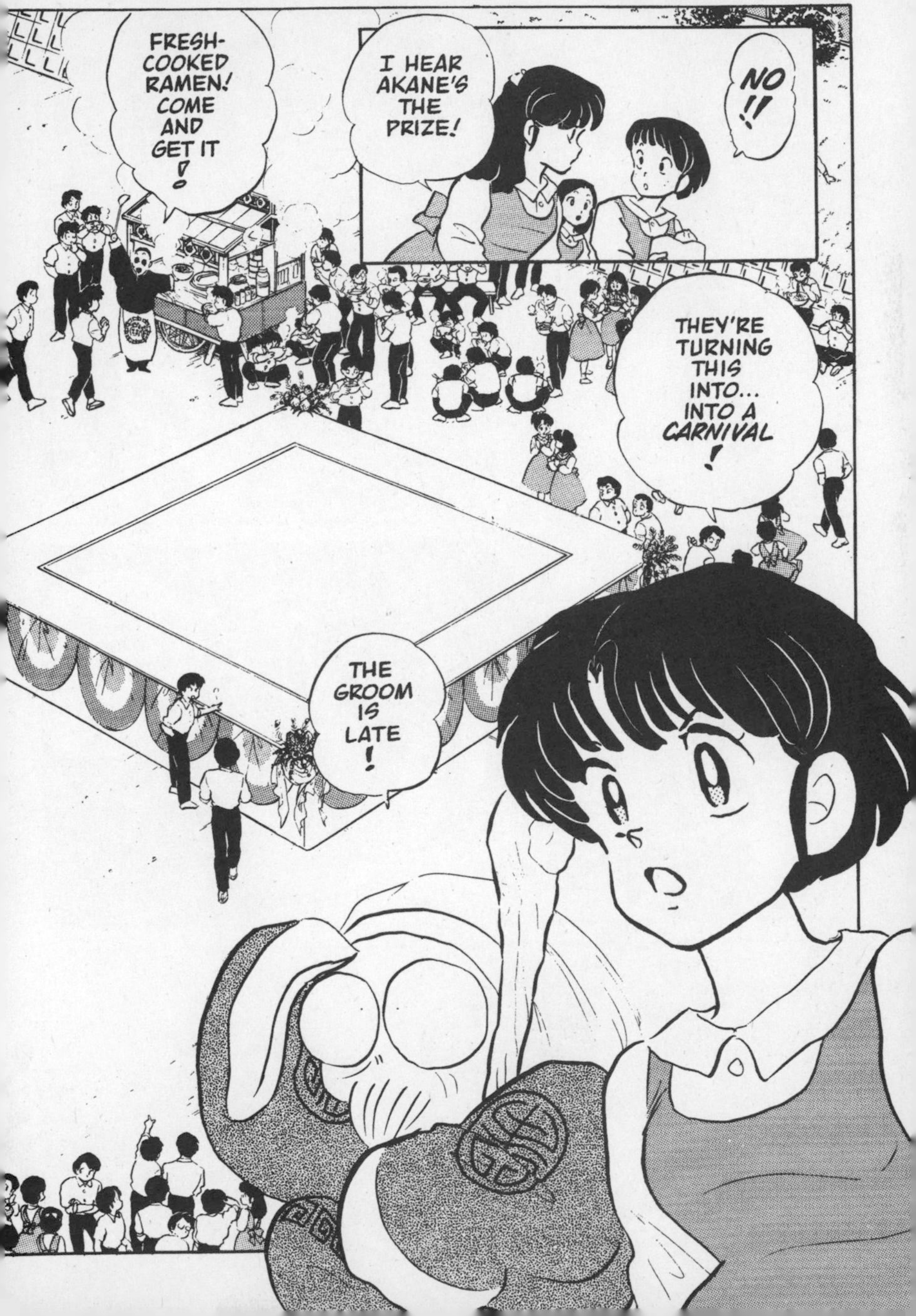
FRESH-COOKED RAMEN! COME AND GET IT !
I HEAR AKANE'S THE PRIZE!
NO !!
THEY'RE TURNING THIS INTO... INTO A CARNIVAL !
THE GROOM IS LATE !

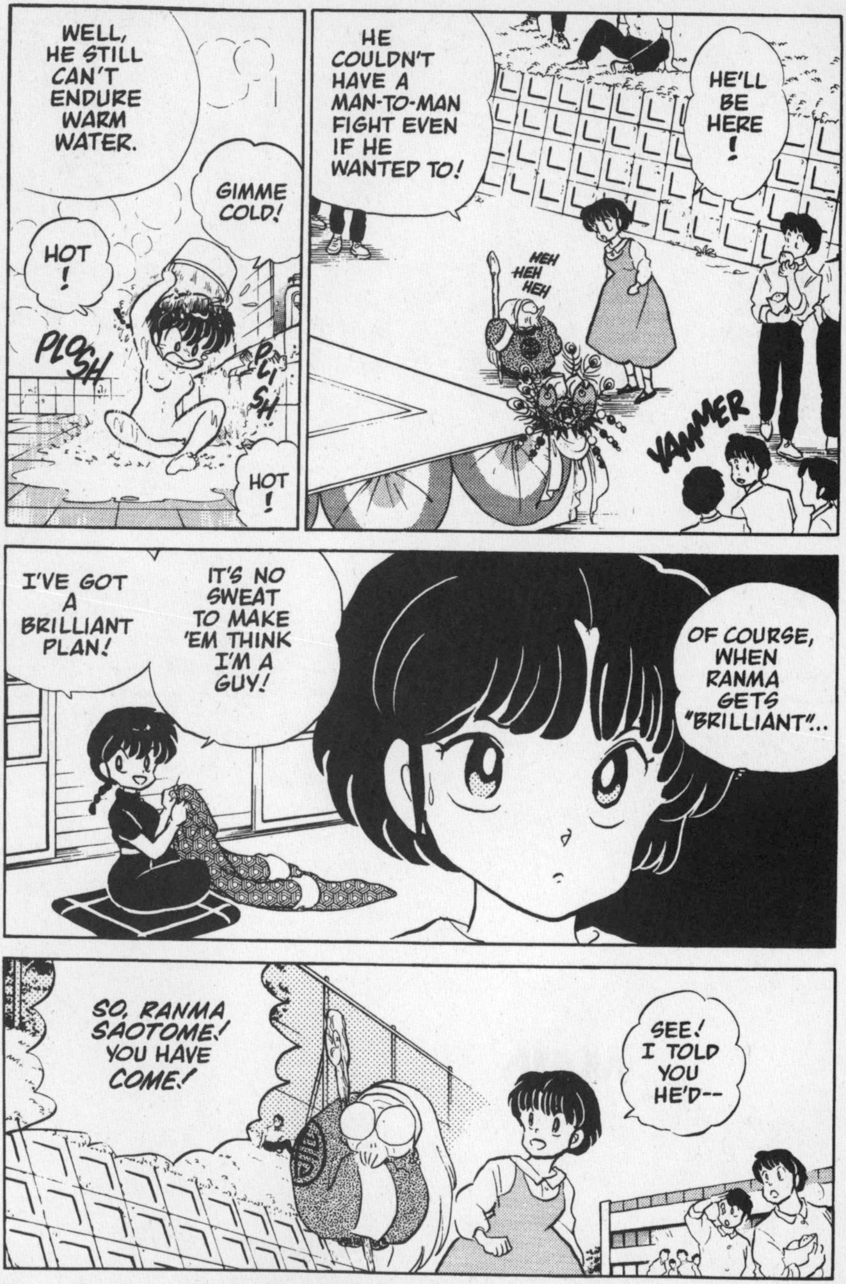
WELL, HE STILL CAN'T ENDURE WARM WATER.
HOT!
GIMME COLD!
PLOSH
PLISH
HOT!
HE COULDN'T HAVE A MAN-TO-MAN FIGHT EVEN IF HE WANTED TO!
HE'LL BE HERE!
HEH HEH HEH
YAMMER
I'VE GOT A BRILLIANT PLAN!
IT'S NO SWEAT TO MAKE 'EM THINK I'M A GUY!
OF COURSE, WHEN RANMA GETS "BRILLIANT"...
SO, RANMA SAOTOME! YOU HAVE COME!
SEE! I TOLD YOU HE'D--

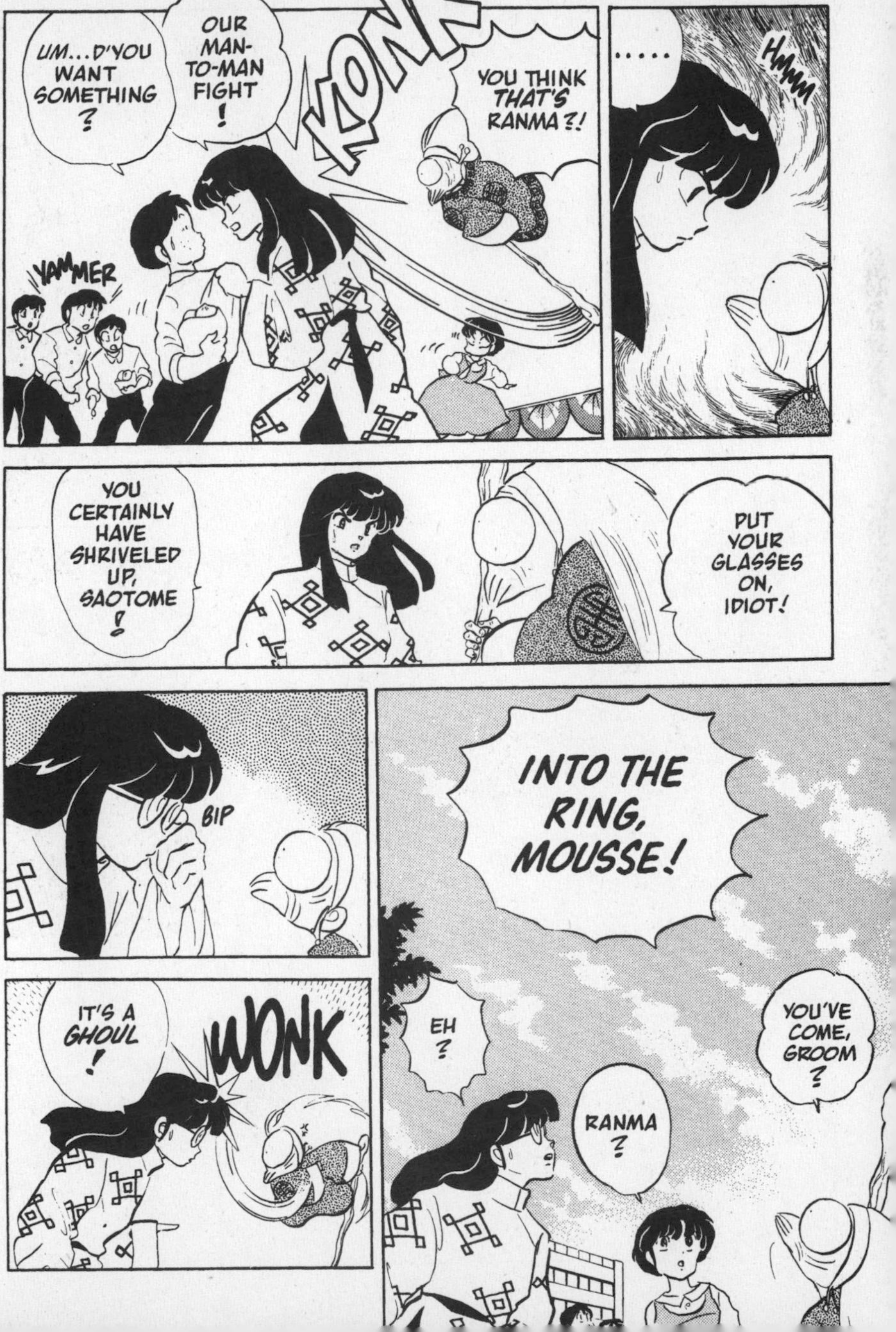
UM...D'YOU WANT SOMETHING?
OUR MAN-TO-MAN FIGHT!
KONK
YAMMER
YOU THINK THAT'S RANMA?!
.....
HMMM
YOU CERTAINLY HAVE SHRIVELED UP, SAOTOME!
PUT YOUR GLASSES ON, IDIOT!
BIP
IT'S A GHOUL!
WONK
INTO THE RING, MOUSSE!
EH?
YOU'VE COME, GROOM?
RANMA?

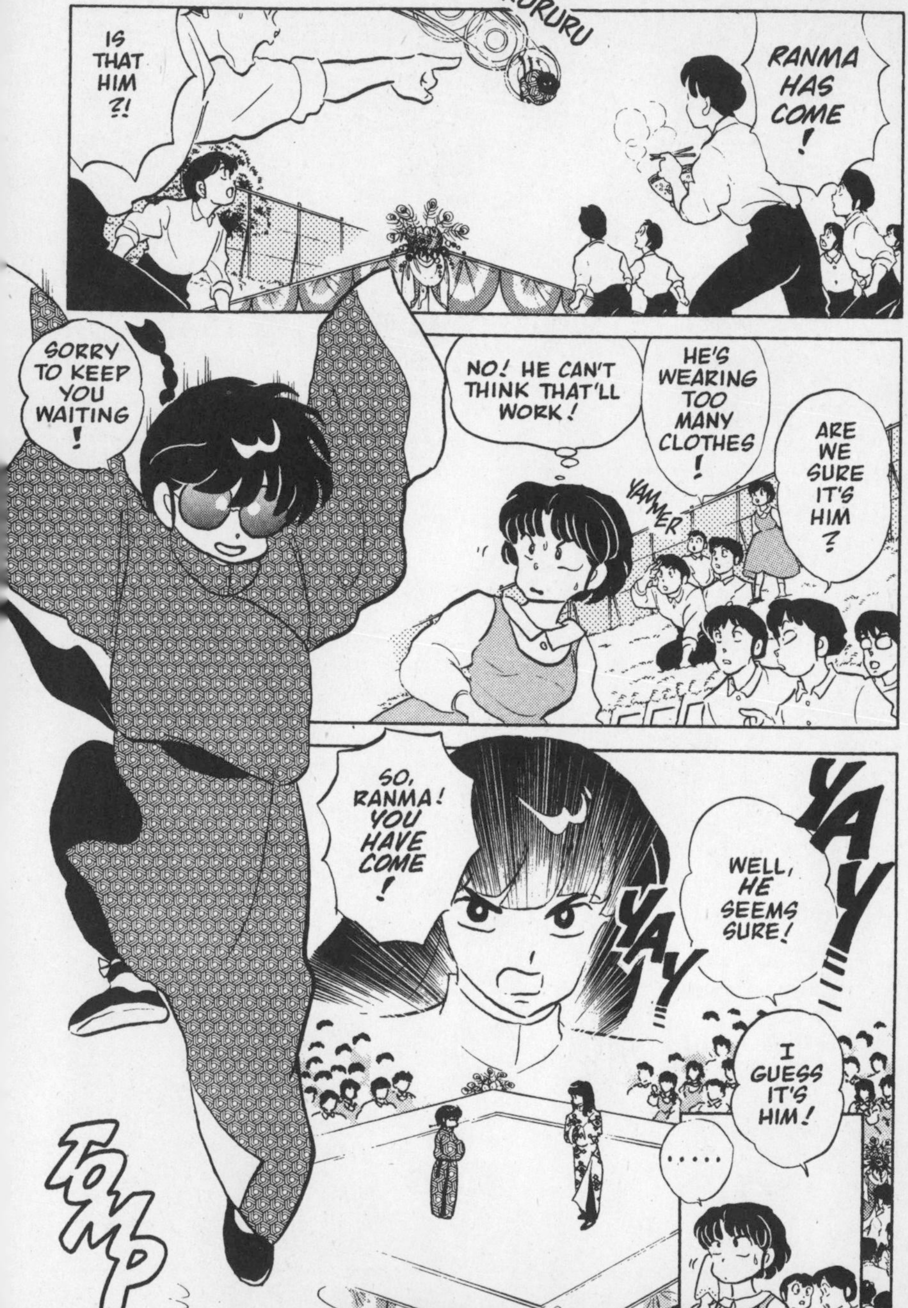
URURURU
IS THAT HIM ?!
RANMA HAS COME!
SORRY TO KEEP YOU WAITING!
NO! HE CAN'T THINK THAT'LL WORK!
HE'S WEARING TOO MANY CLOTHES!
YAMMER
ARE WE SURE IT'S HIM?
SO, RANMA! YOU HAVE COME!
WELL, HE SEEMS SURE!
YAY
YAY
I GUESS IT'S HIM!
.....
TOMP

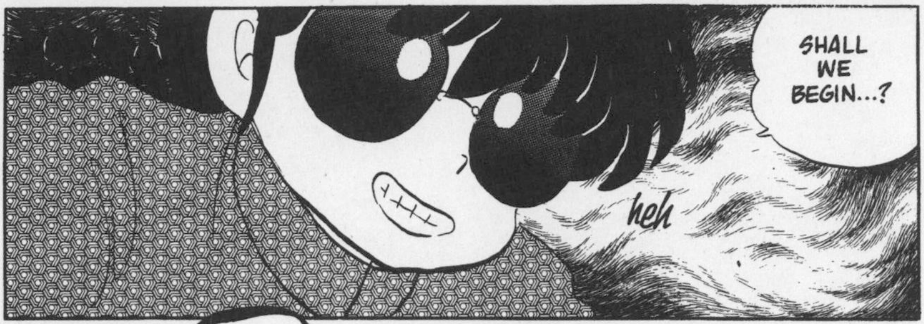
SHALL WE BEGIN...?
heh

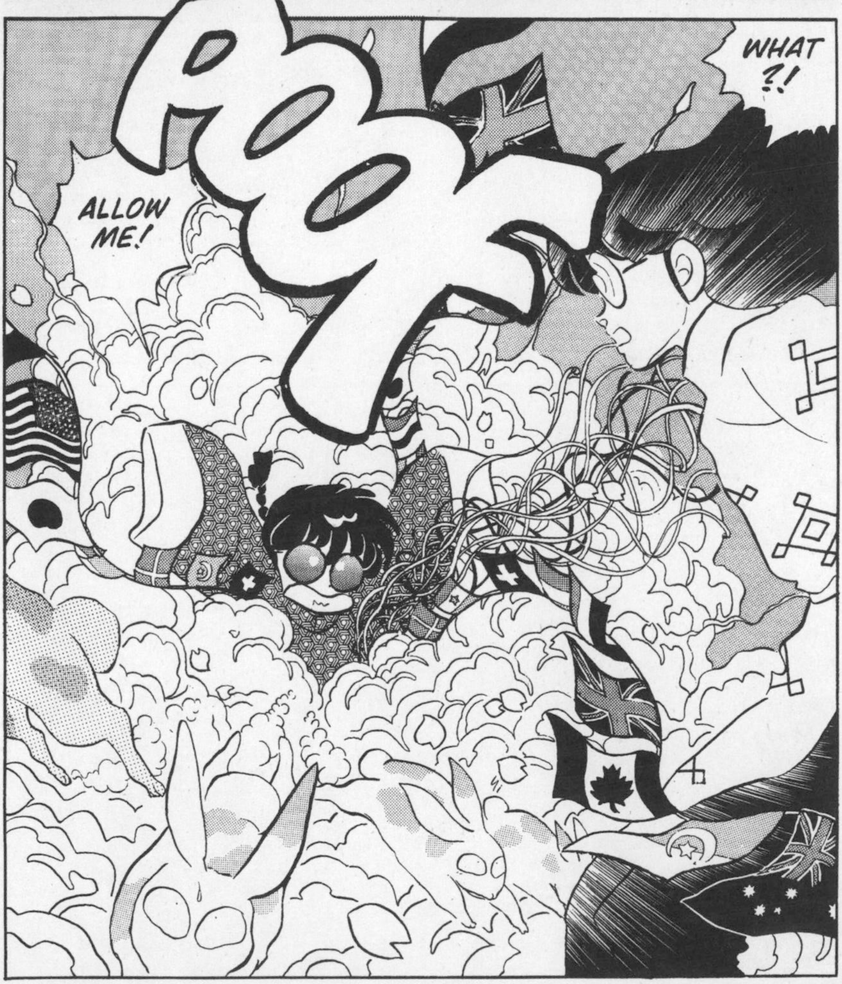
WHAT ?!
ALLOW ME!

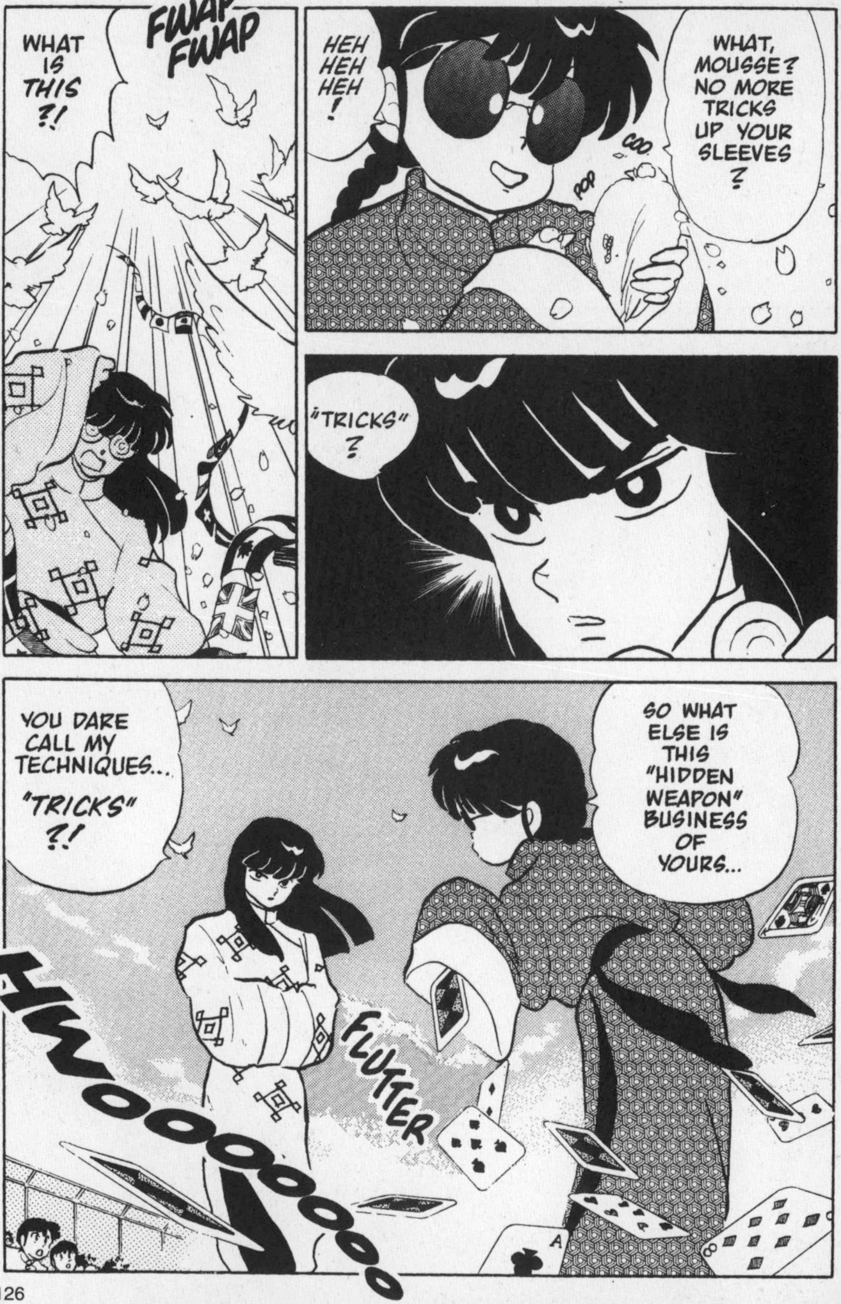
WHAT, MOUSSE? NO MORE TRICKS UP YOUR SLEEVES?
HEH HEH HEH!
COO
POP
"TRICKS"?
FWAP FWAP
WHAT IS THIS?!
SO WHAT ELSE IS THIS "HIDDEN WEAPON" BUSINESS OF YOURS...
YOU DARE CALL MY TECHNIQUES... "TRICKS"?!
FLUTTER
HWOOOOOOOOO

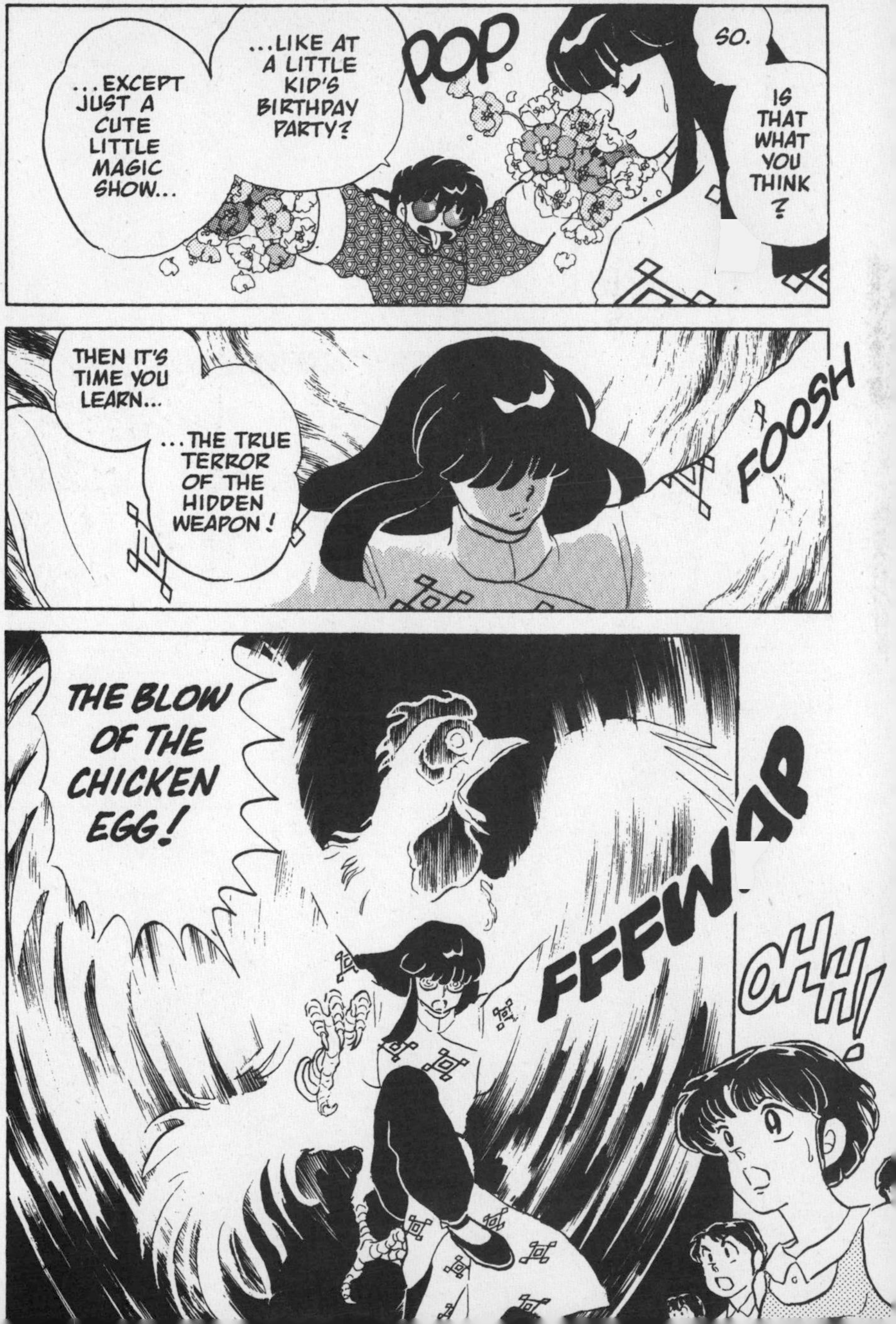
...EXCEPT JUST A CUTE LITTLE MAGIC SHOW...
...LIKE AT A LITTLE KID'S BIRTHDAY PARTY?
POP
SO.
IS THAT WHAT YOU THINK?
THEN IT'S TIME YOU LEARN...
...THE TRUE TERROR OF THE HIDDEN WEAPON!
FOOSH
THE BLOW OF THE CHICKEN EGG!
FFFWAP
OHH!

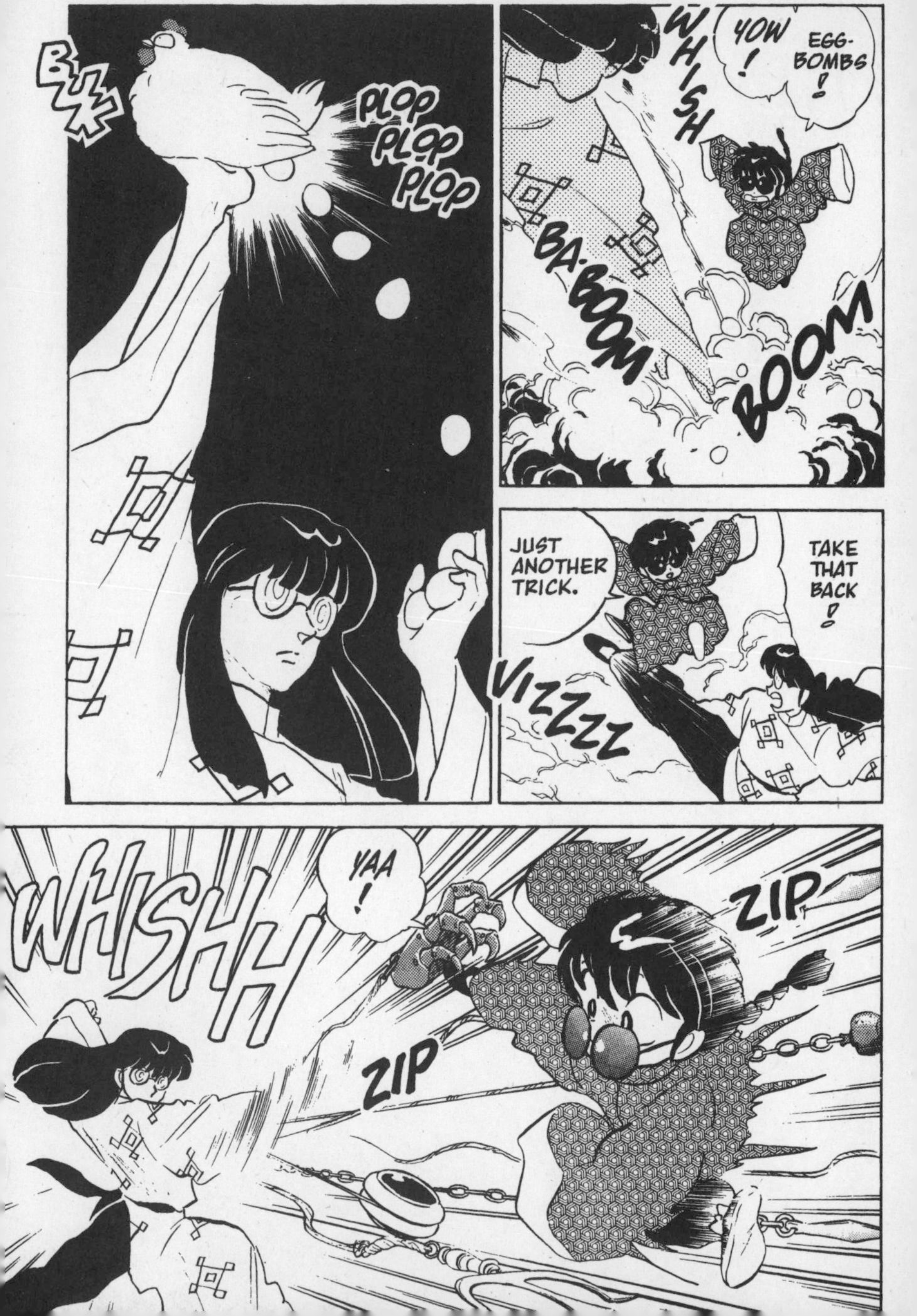
BUK
PLOP PLOP PLOP
WHISH
YOW!
EGG-BOMBS!
BA-BOOM
BOOM
JUST ANOTHER TRICK.
TAKE THAT BACK!
VIZZZZZ
WHISHH
YAA!
ZIP
ZIP

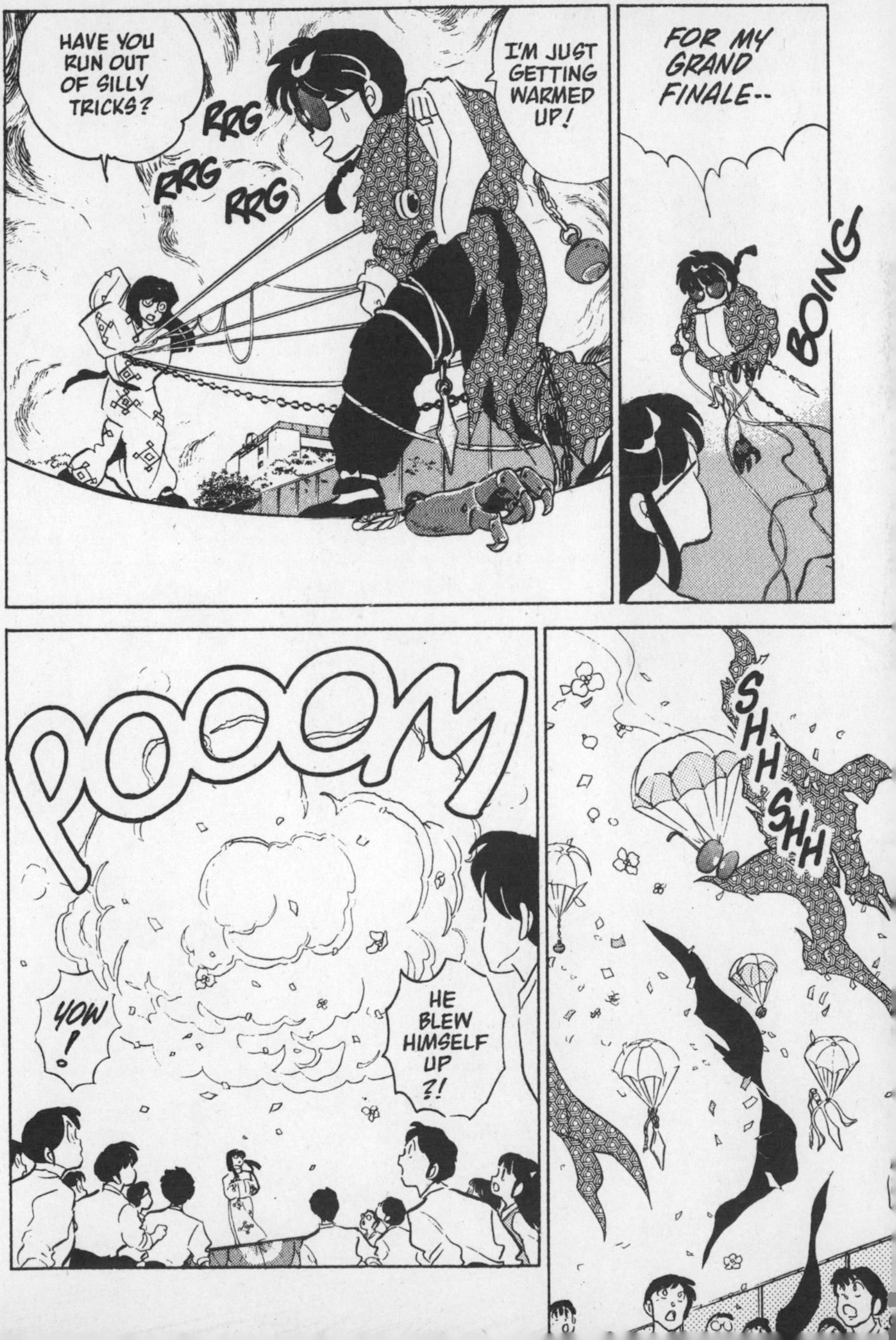
HAVE YOU RUN OUT OF SILLY TRICKS?
RRG
RRG
RRG
I'M JUST GETTING WARMED UP!
FOR MY GRAND FINALE--
BOING
POOOM
YOW!
HE BLEW HIMSELF UP?!
SHHSHH

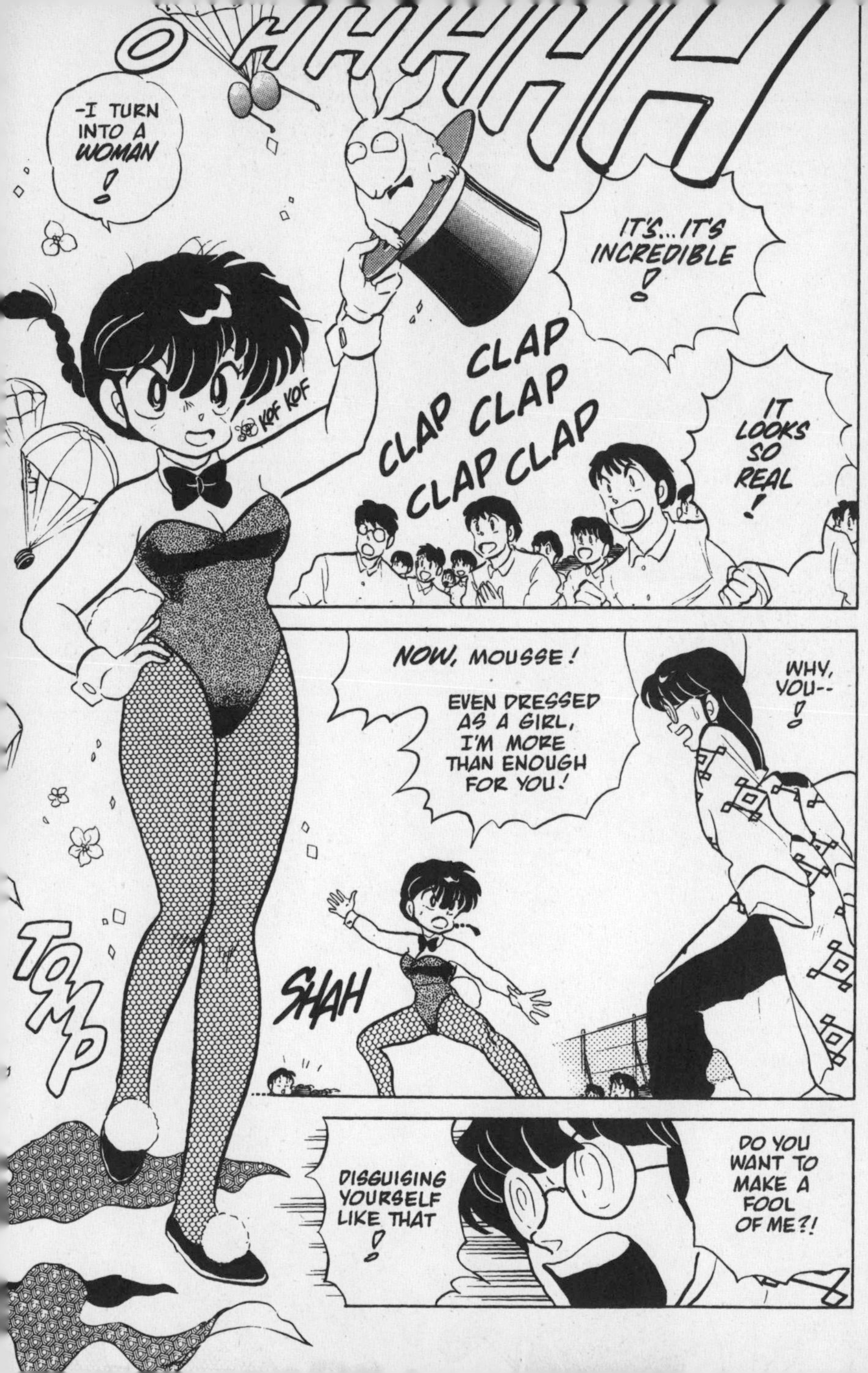

OHHHHHHH
-I TURN INTO A WOMAN!
KOF KOF
TOMP
IT'S...IT'S INCREDIBLE!
CLAP CLAP
CLAP CLAP
CLAP CLAP
IT LOOKS SO REAL!
NOW, MOUSSE!
EVEN DRESSED AS A GIRL, I'M MORE THAN ENOUGH FOR YOU!
SHAH
WHY, YOU--!
DISGUISING YOURSELF LIKE THAT!
DO YOU WANT TO MAKE A FOOL OF ME?!

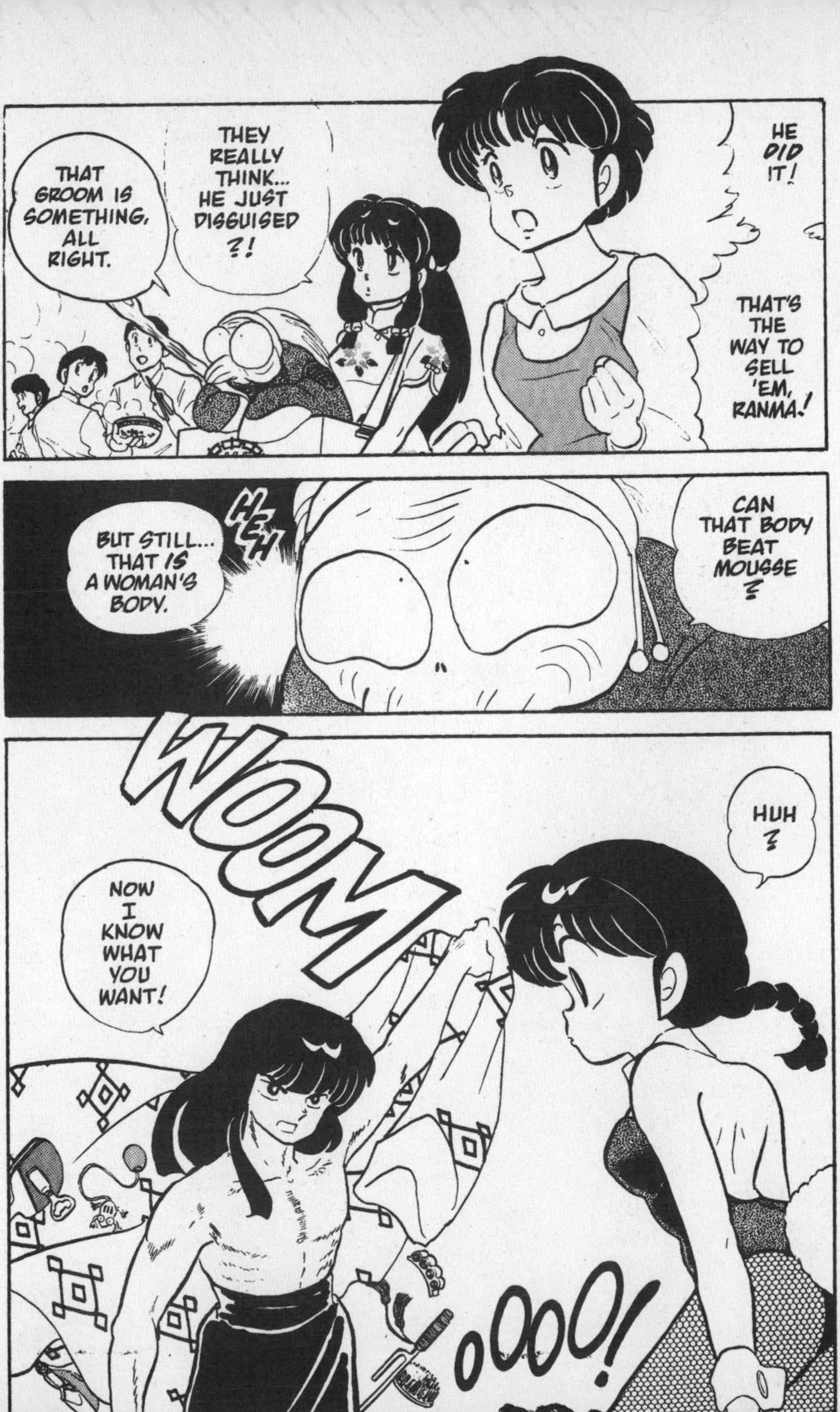
THAT GROOM IS SOMETHING, ALL RIGHT.
THEY REALLY THINK... HE JUST DISGUISED ?!
HE DID IT!
THAT'S THE WAY TO SELL 'EM, RANMA!
BUT STILL... THAT IS A WOMAN'S BODY.
HEH
CAN THAT BODY BEAT MOUSSE ?
WOOM
NOW I KNOW WHAT YOU WANT!
HUH ?
OOOO!

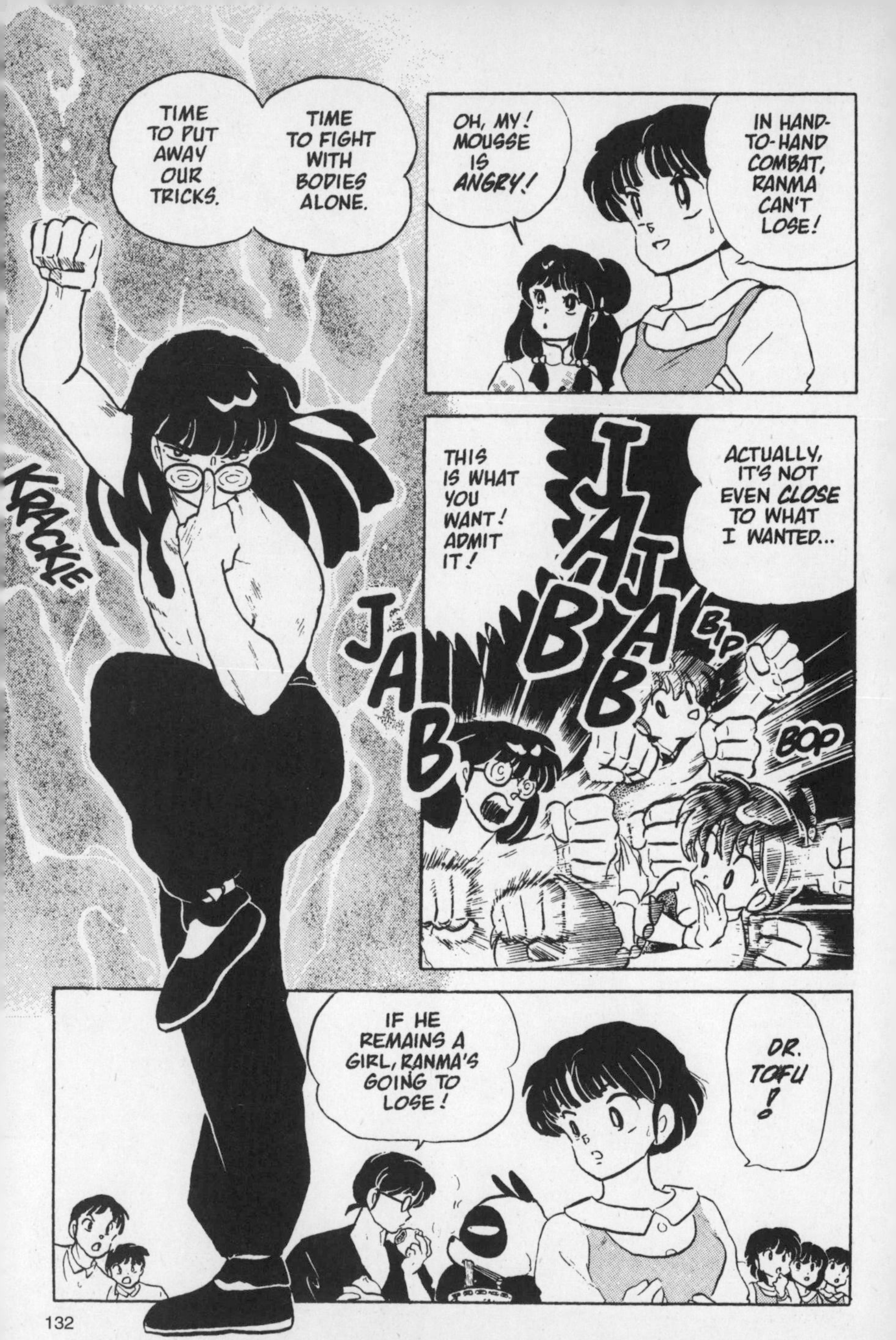
TIME TO PUT AWAY OUR TRICKS.
TIME TO FIGHT WITH BODIES ALONE.
KRACKLE
OH, MY! MOUSSE IS ANGRY!
IN HAND-TO-HAND COMBAT, RANMA CAN'T LOSE!
THIS IS WHAT YOU WANT! ADMIT IT!
ACTUALLY, IT'S NOT EVEN CLOSE TO WHAT I WANTED...
JAB
JAB
JAB
BIP
BOP
IF HE REMAINS A GIRL, RANMA'S GOING TO LOSE!
DR. TOFU!

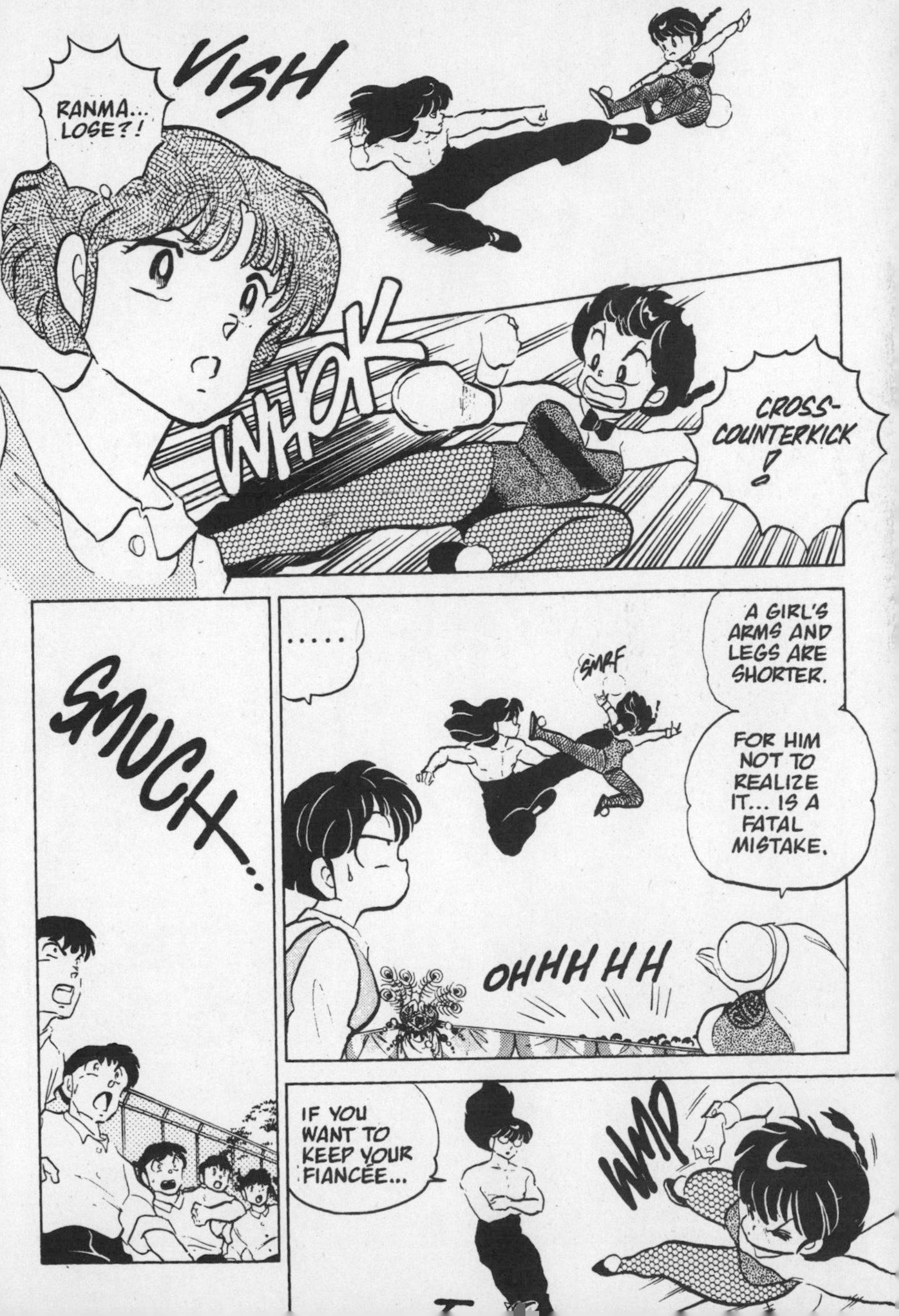
RANMA... LOSE?!
VISH
WHOK
CROSS-COUNTERKICK!
SMUCH...
......
SMRF
A GIRL'S ARMS AND LEGS ARE SHORTER.
FOR HIM NOT TO REALIZE IT... IS A FATAL MISTAKE.
OHHHHHH
IF YOU WANT TO KEEP YOUR FIANCÉE...
WMP

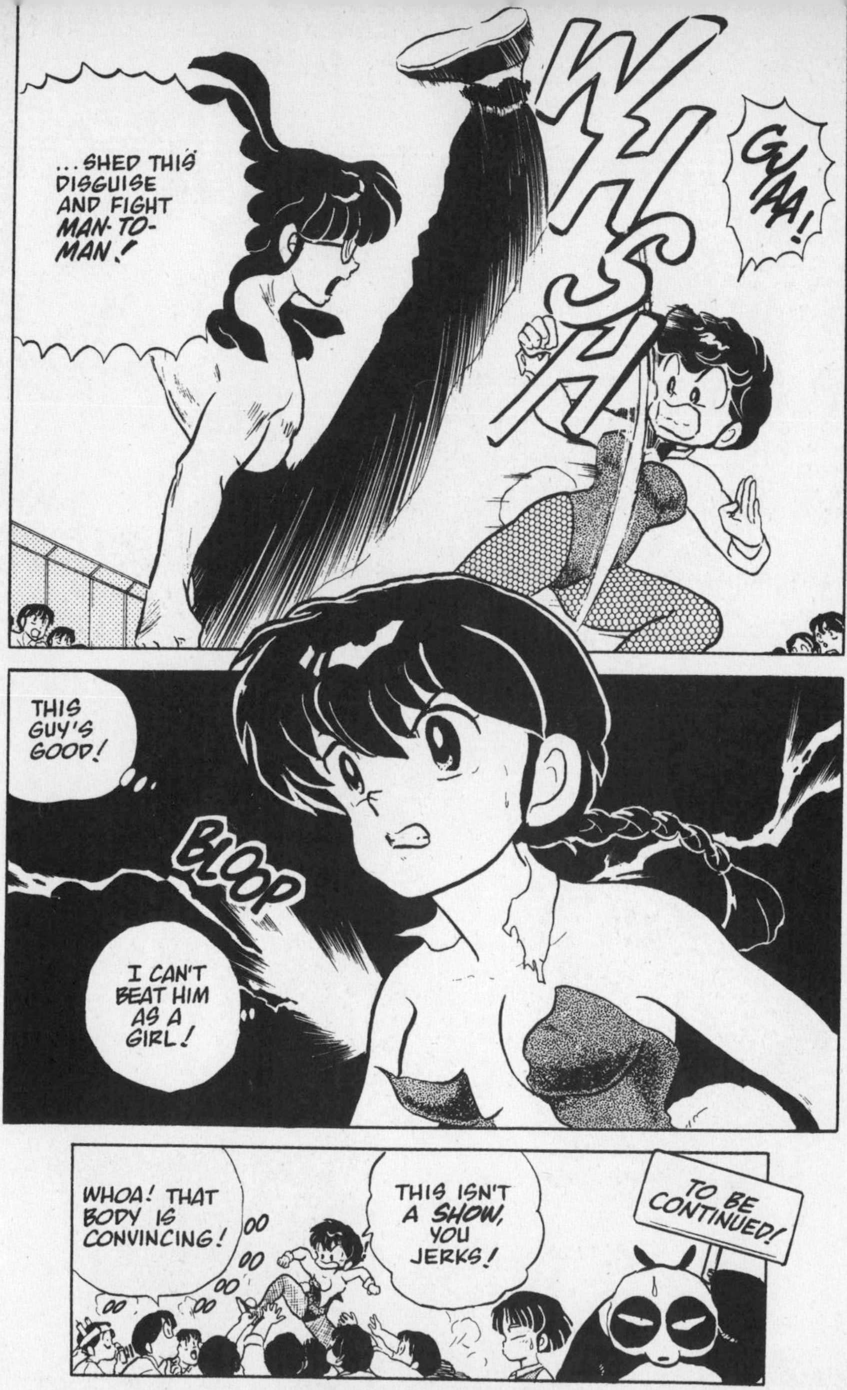
...SHED THIS DISGUISE AND FIGHT MAN-TO-MAN!
WHSSH
GUAA!
THIS GUY'S GOOD!
BLOOP
I CAN'T BEAT HIM AS A GIRL!
WHOA! THAT BODY IS CONVINCING!
OO
THIS ISN'T A SHOW, YOU JERKS!
TO BE CONTINUED!

Part 9

CAT'S TONGUE GOT YOU?

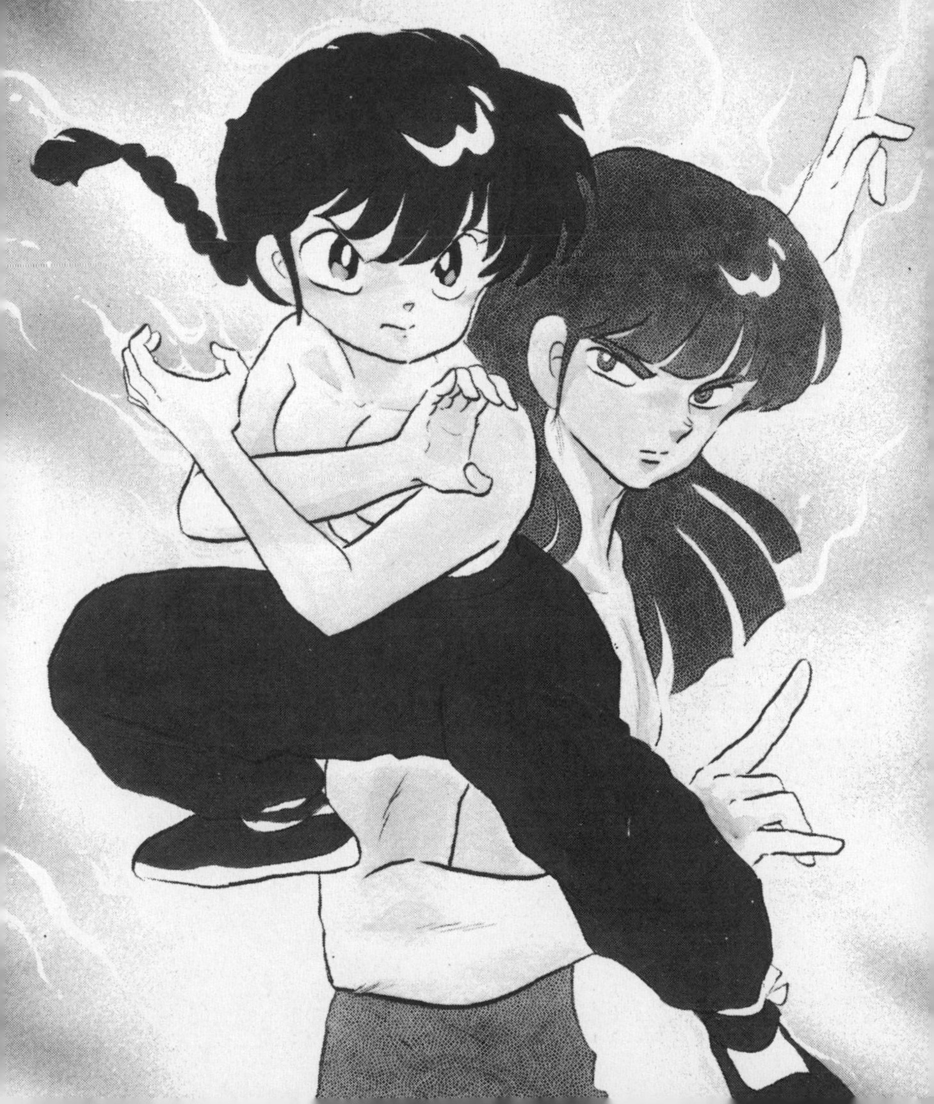

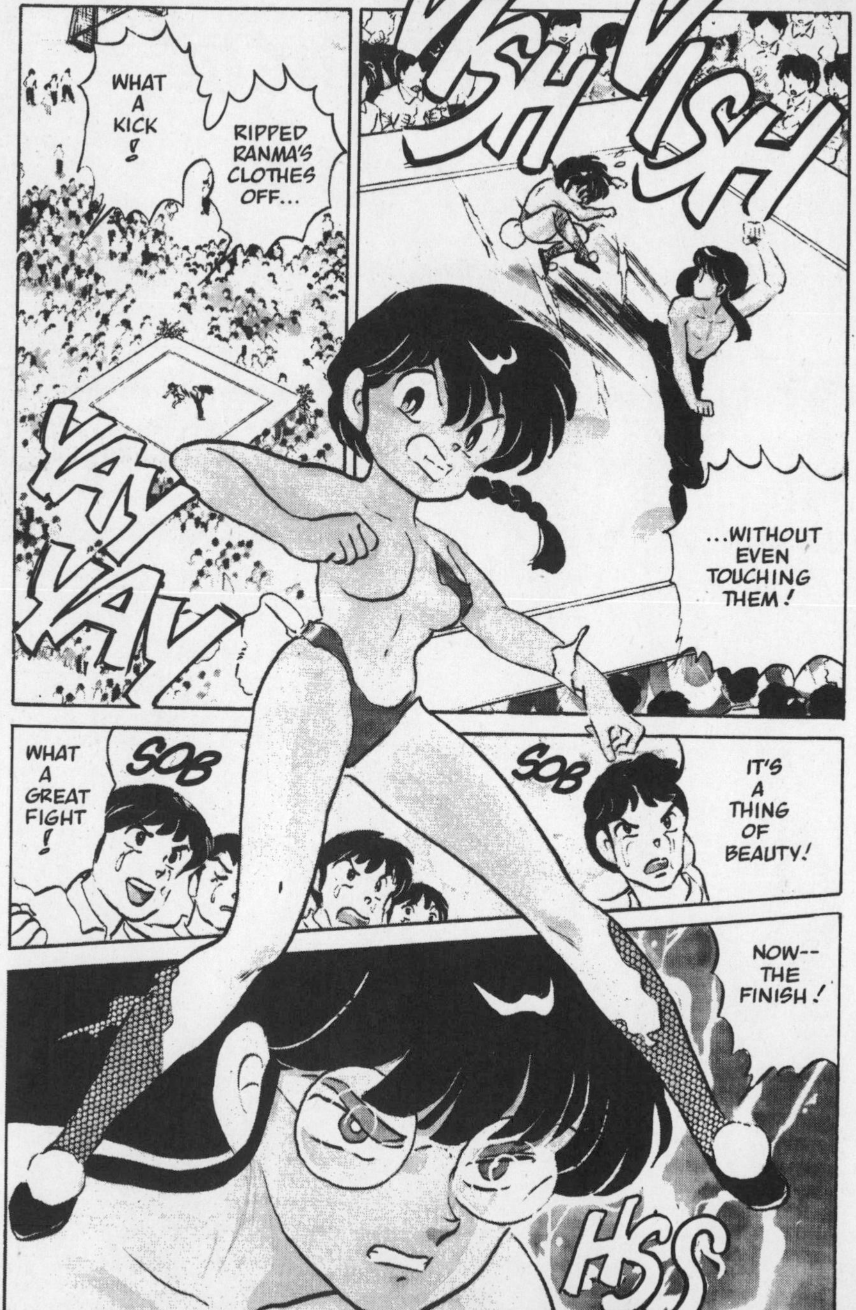
WHAT A KICK!
RIPPED RANMA'S CLOTHES OFF...
YAY YAY
YISH YISH
...WITHOUT EVEN TOUCHING THEM!
WHAT A GREAT FIGHT!
SOB
SOB
IT'S A THING OF BEAUTY!
NOW-- THE FINISH!
HSS

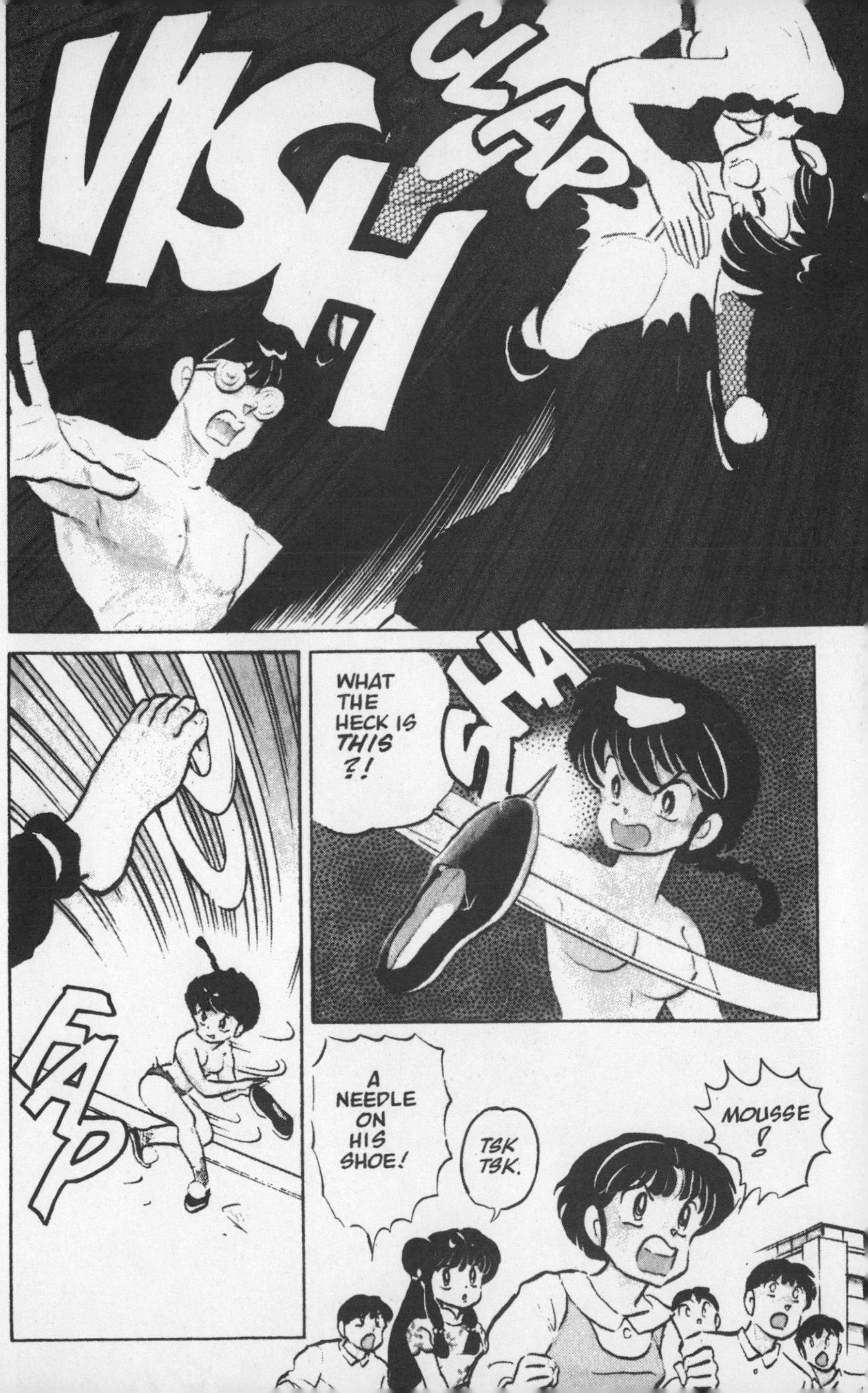
VISH
CLAP
FLAP
SHA
WHAT THE HECK IS *THIS* ?!
A NEEDLE ON HIS SHOE!
TSK TSK.
MOUSSE!

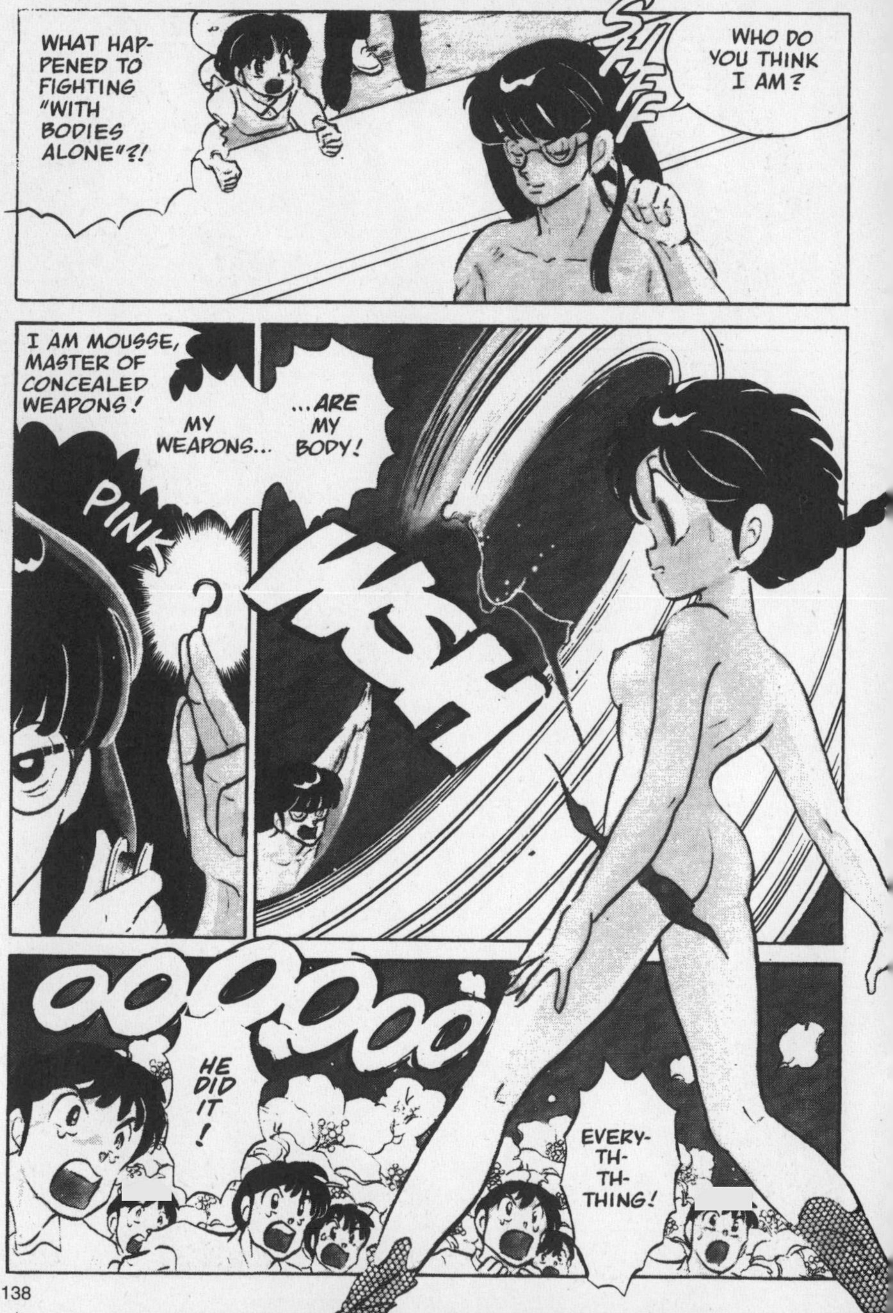
WHAT HAP-
PENED TO
FIGHTING
"WITH
BODIES
ALONE"?!
WHO DO
YOU THINK
I AM?
I AM MOUSSE,
MASTER OF
CONCEALED
WEAPONS!
MY
WEAPONS...
PINK
...ARE
MY
BODY!
HE
DID
IT
!
EVERY-
TH-
TH-
THING!

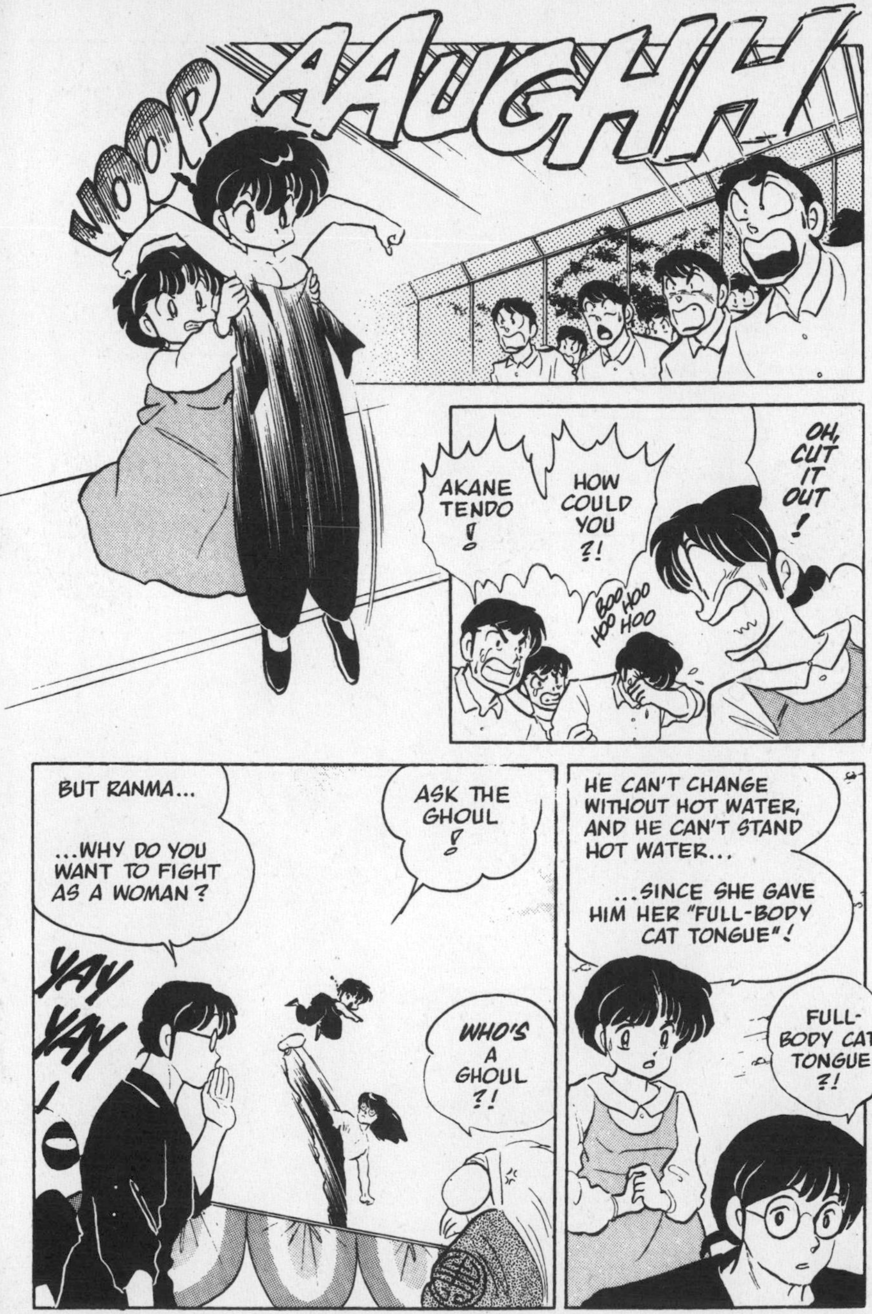
WOOOP
AAUGHH!
AKANE TENDO!
HOW COULD YOU?!
BOO HOO HOO
OH, CUT IT OUT!
BUT RANMA...
...WHY DO YOU WANT TO FIGHT AS A WOMAN?
ASK THE GHOUL!
YAY YAY!
WHO'S A GHOUL?!
HE CAN'T CHANGE WITHOUT HOT WATER, AND HE CAN'T STAND HOT WATER...
...SINCE SHE GAVE HIM HER "FULL-BODY CAT TONGUE"!
FULL-BODY CAT TONGUE?!

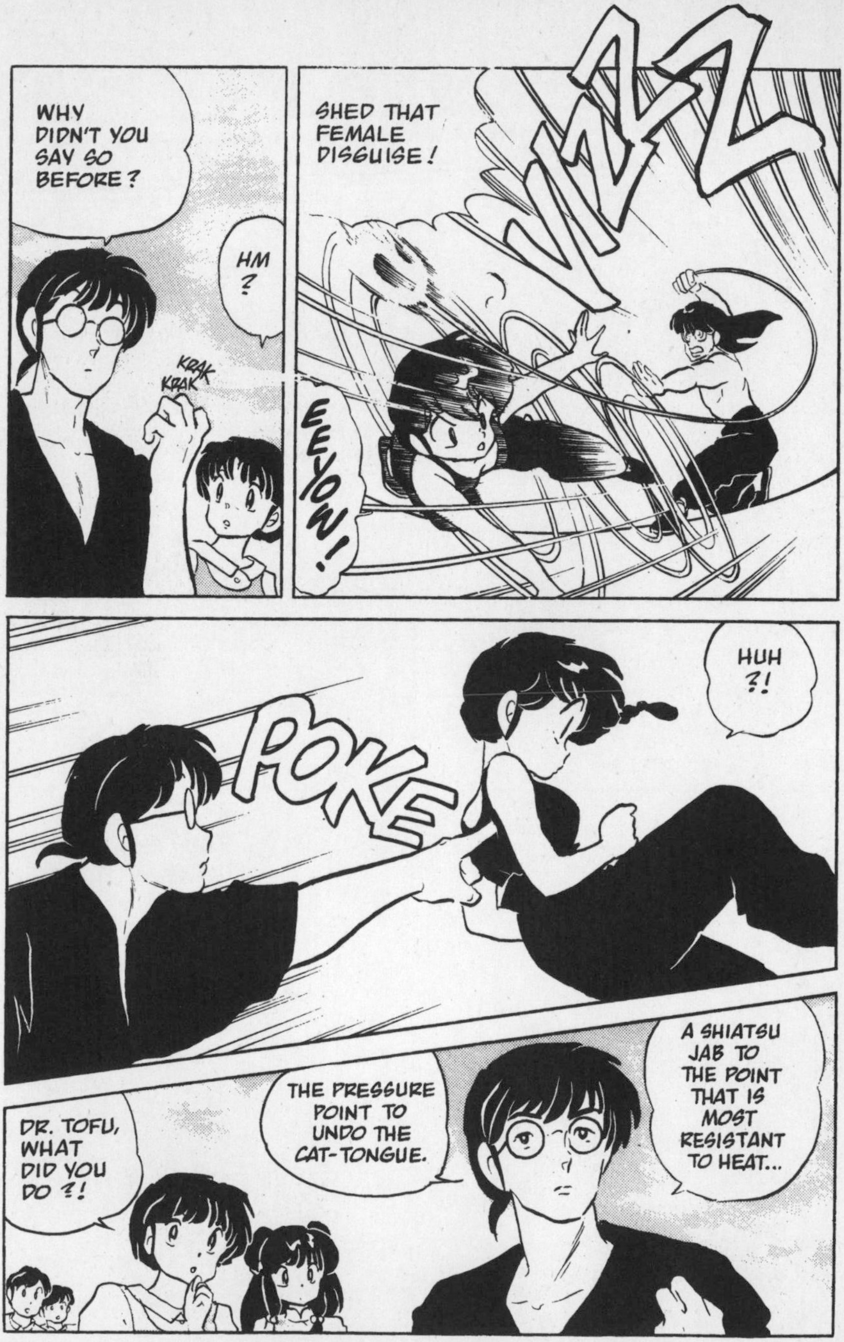
WHY DIDN'T YOU SAY SO BEFORE?
HM ?
KRAK KRAK
SHED THAT FEMALE DISGUISE!
WIZZ
EEYOW!
POKE
HUH ?!
DR. TOFU, WHAT DID YOU DO ?!
THE PRESSURE POINT TO UNDO THE CAT-TONGUE.
A SHIATSU JAB TO THE POINT THAT IS MOST RESISTANT TO HEAT...

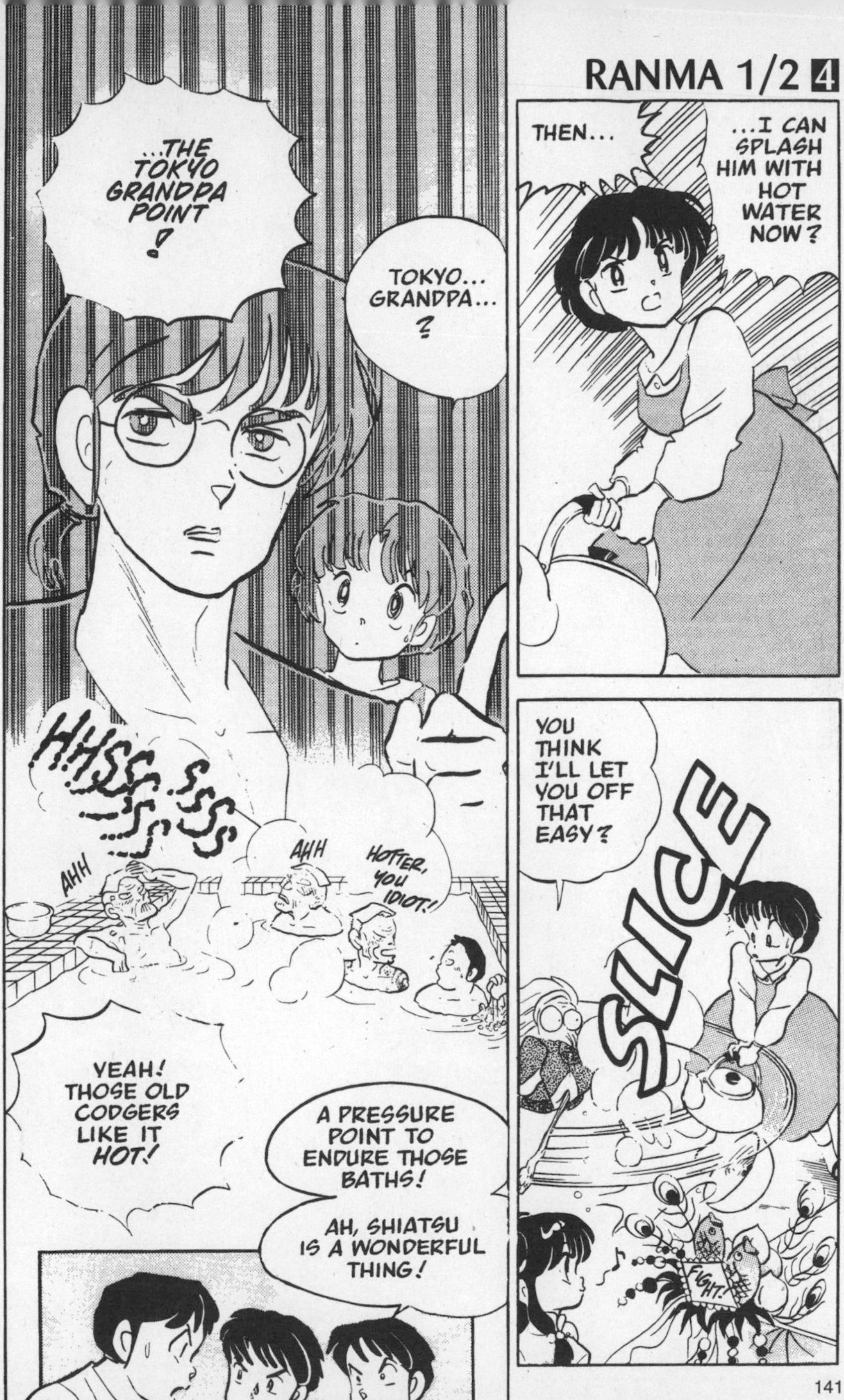
...THE TOKYO GRANDPA POINT !
TOKYO... GRANDPA... ?
HHSSSSSSSSS
AHH
AHH
HOTTER, YOU IDIOT!
YEAH! THOSE OLD CODGERS LIKE IT HOT!
A PRESSURE POINT TO ENDURE THOSE BATHS!
AH, SHIATSU IS A WONDERFUL THING!
THEN...
...I CAN SPLASH HIM WITH HOT WATER NOW?
YOU THINK I'LL LET YOU OFF THAT EASY?
SLICE
FIGHT!

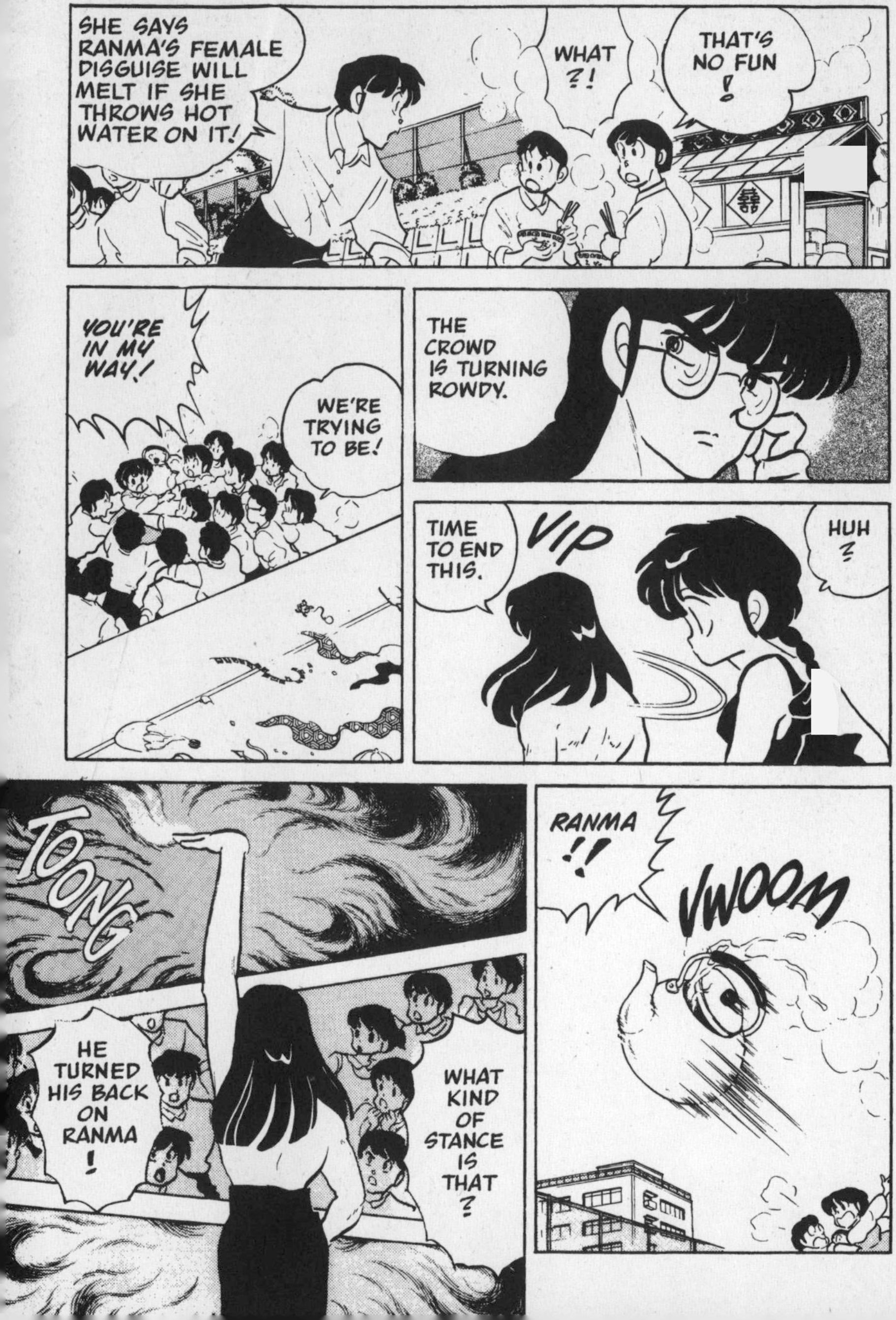
SHE SAYS RANMA'S FEMALE DISGUISE WILL MELT IF SHE THROWS HOT WATER ON IT!
WHAT ?!
THAT'S NO FUN !
YOU'RE IN MY WAY!
WE'RE TRYING TO BE!
THE CROWD IS TURNING ROWDY.
TIME TO END THIS.
VIP
HUH ?
TOONG
HE TURNED HIS BACK ON RANMA !
WHAT KIND OF STANCE IS THAT ?
RANMA !!
VWOOM

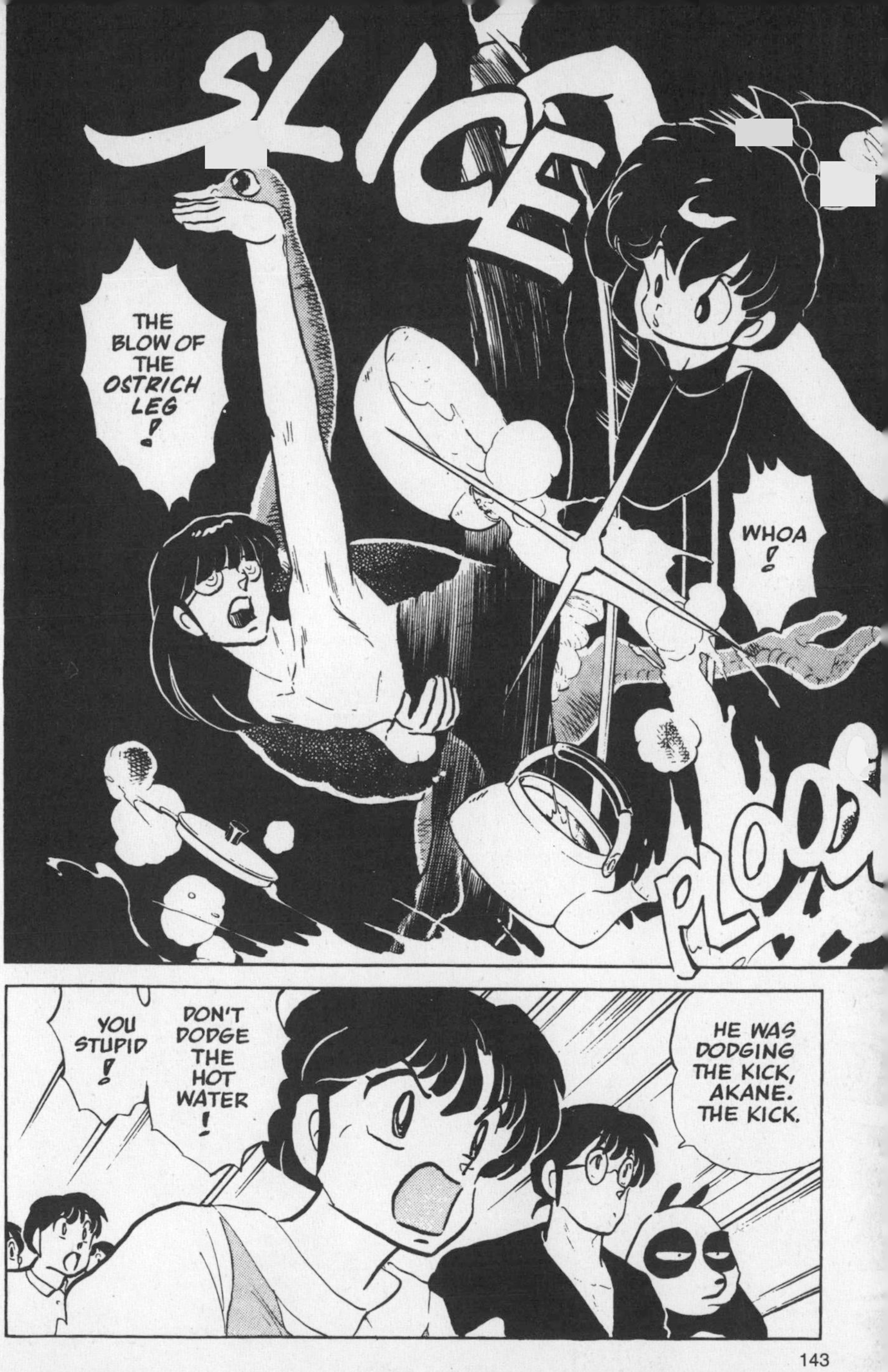

SLICE
THE BLOW OF THE OSTRICH LEG!
WHOA!
PLOOO
YOU STUPID!
DON'T DODGE THE HOT WATER!
HE WAS DODGING THE KICK, AKANE. THE KICK.

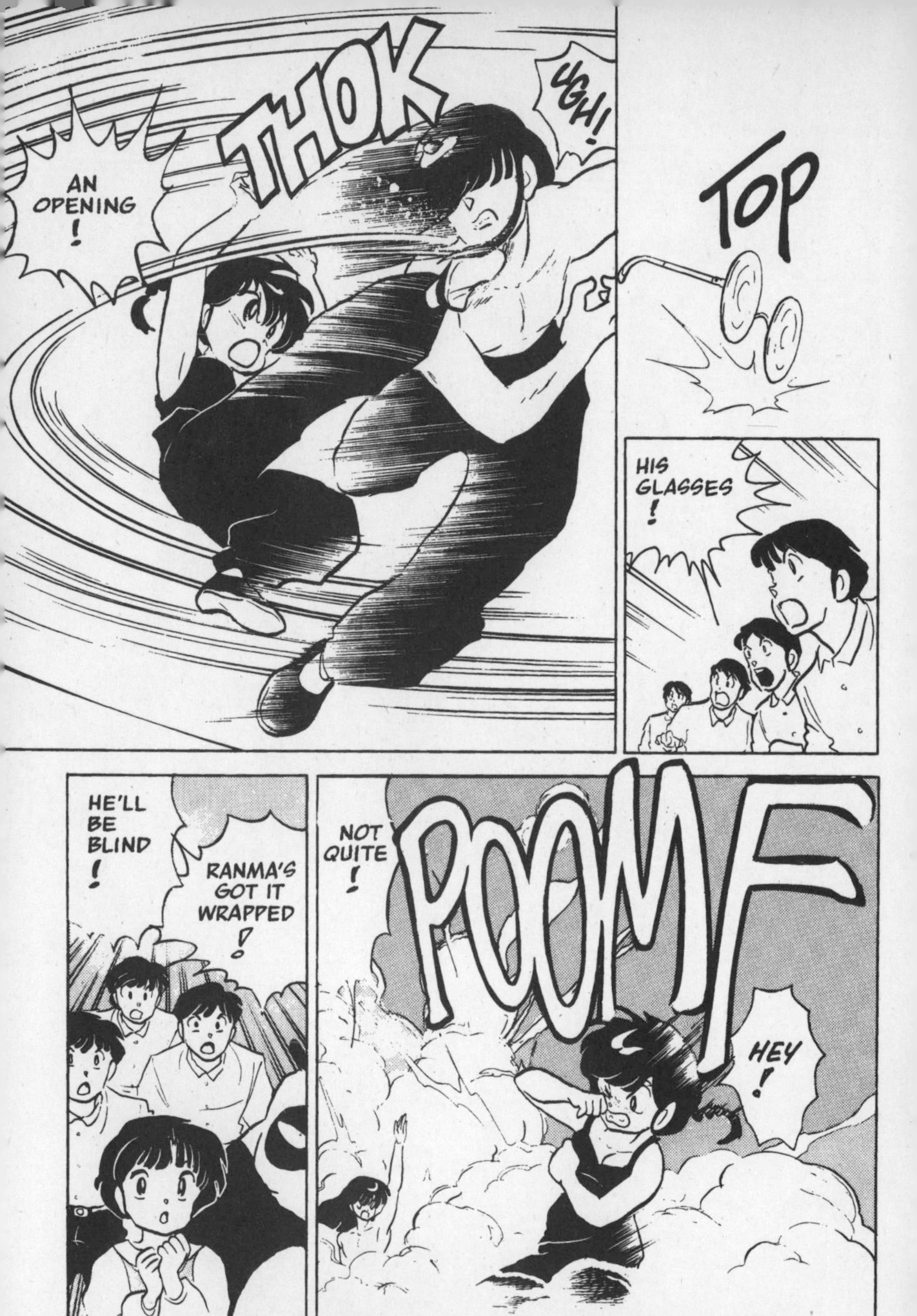

AN OPENING!
THOK
UGH!
TOP
HIS GLASSES!
HE'LL BE BLIND!
RANMA'S GOT IT WRAPPED!
NOT QUITE!
POOMF
HEY!

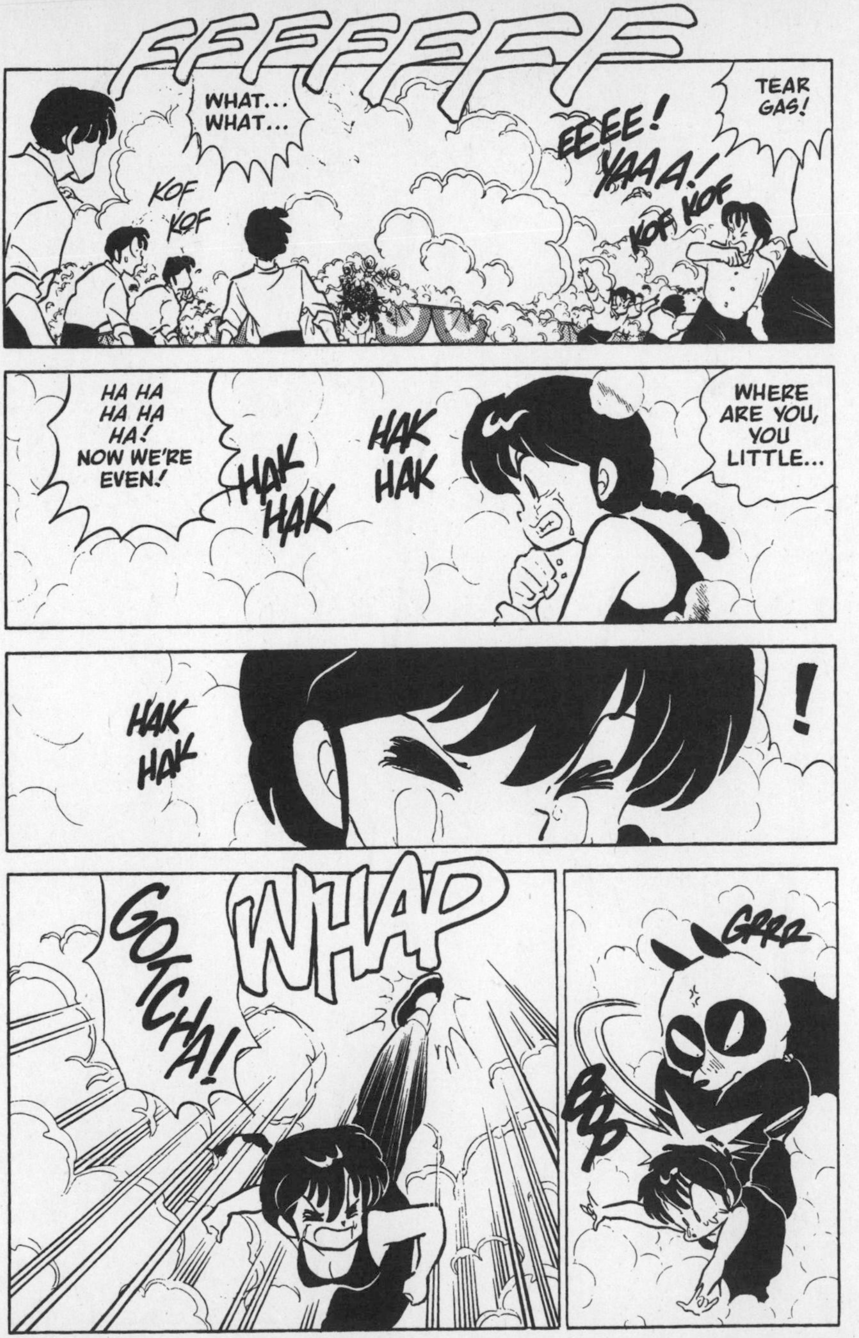
FFFFFFFF
WHAT... WHAT...
KOF KOF
EEEE!
YAAA!
KOF KOF
TEAR GAS!
HA HA HA HA HA! NOW WE'RE EVEN!
HAK HAK
HAK HAK
WHERE ARE YOU, YOU LITTLE...
HAK HAK
!
GOTCHA!
WHAP
GRRR
BOOP

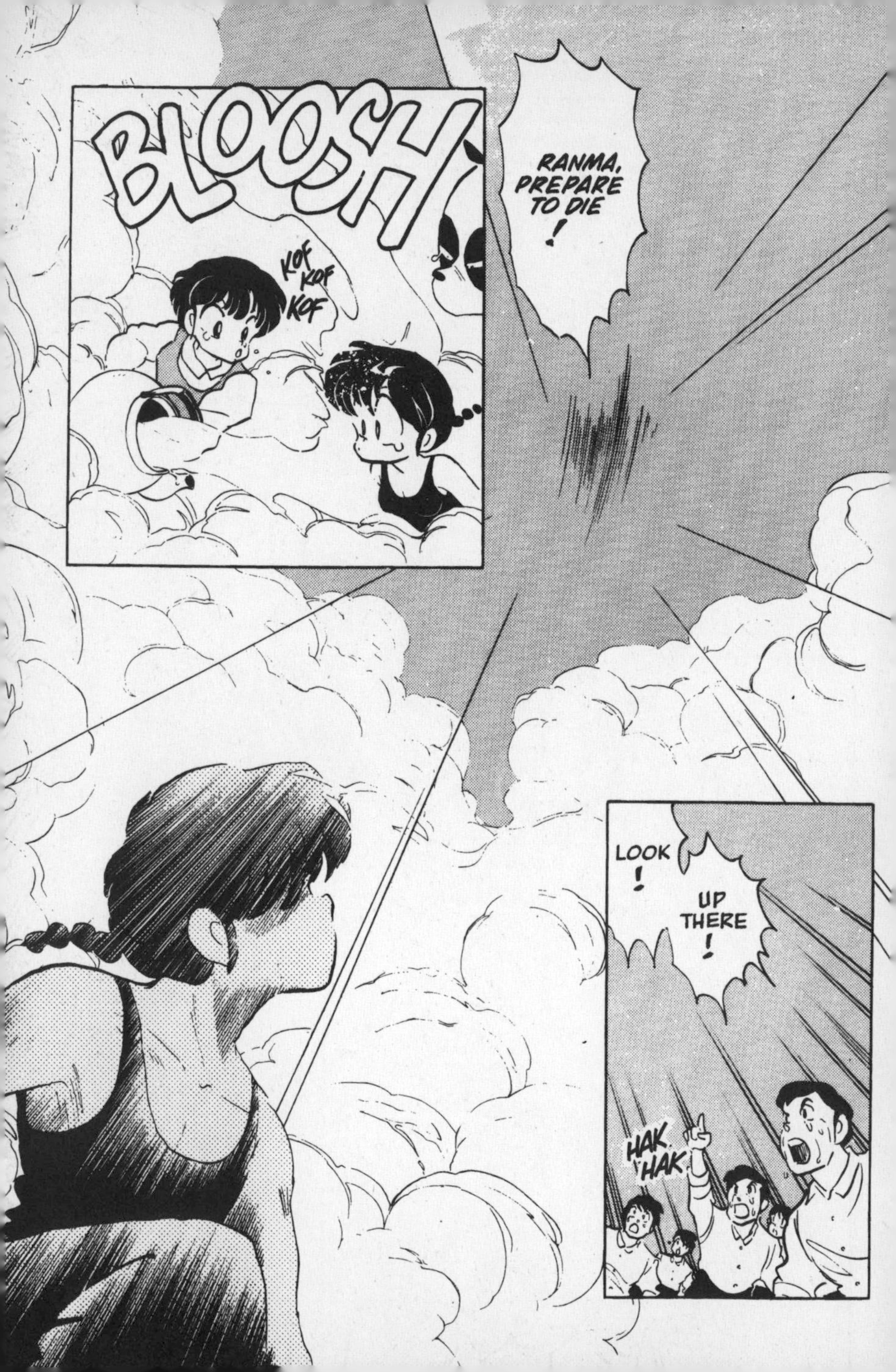
BLOOSH
KOF KOF KOF
RANMA, PREPARE TO DIE!
LOOK!
UP THERE!
HAK HAK

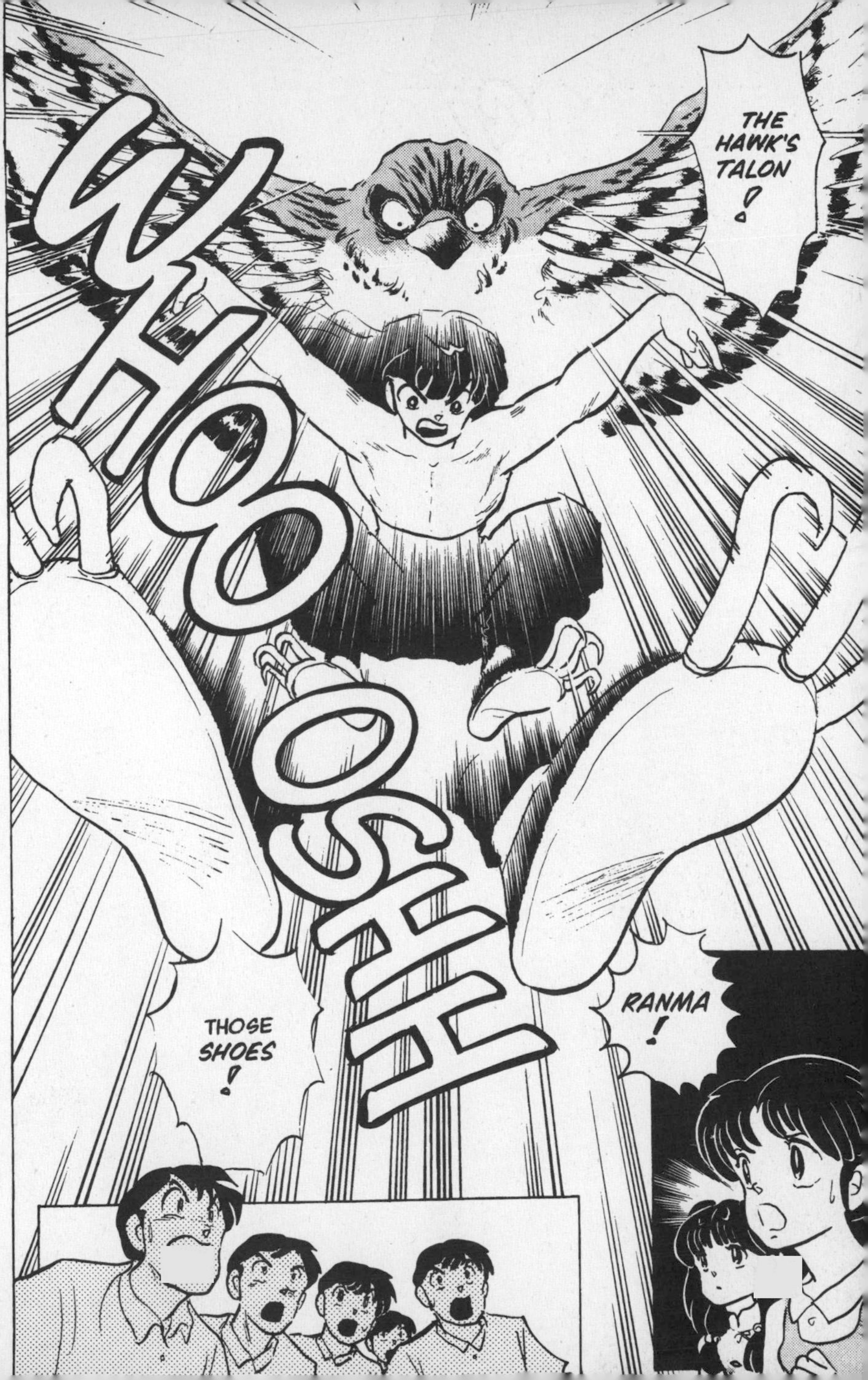
THE HAWK'S TALON!
WHOOOSH
THOSE SHOES!
RANMA!

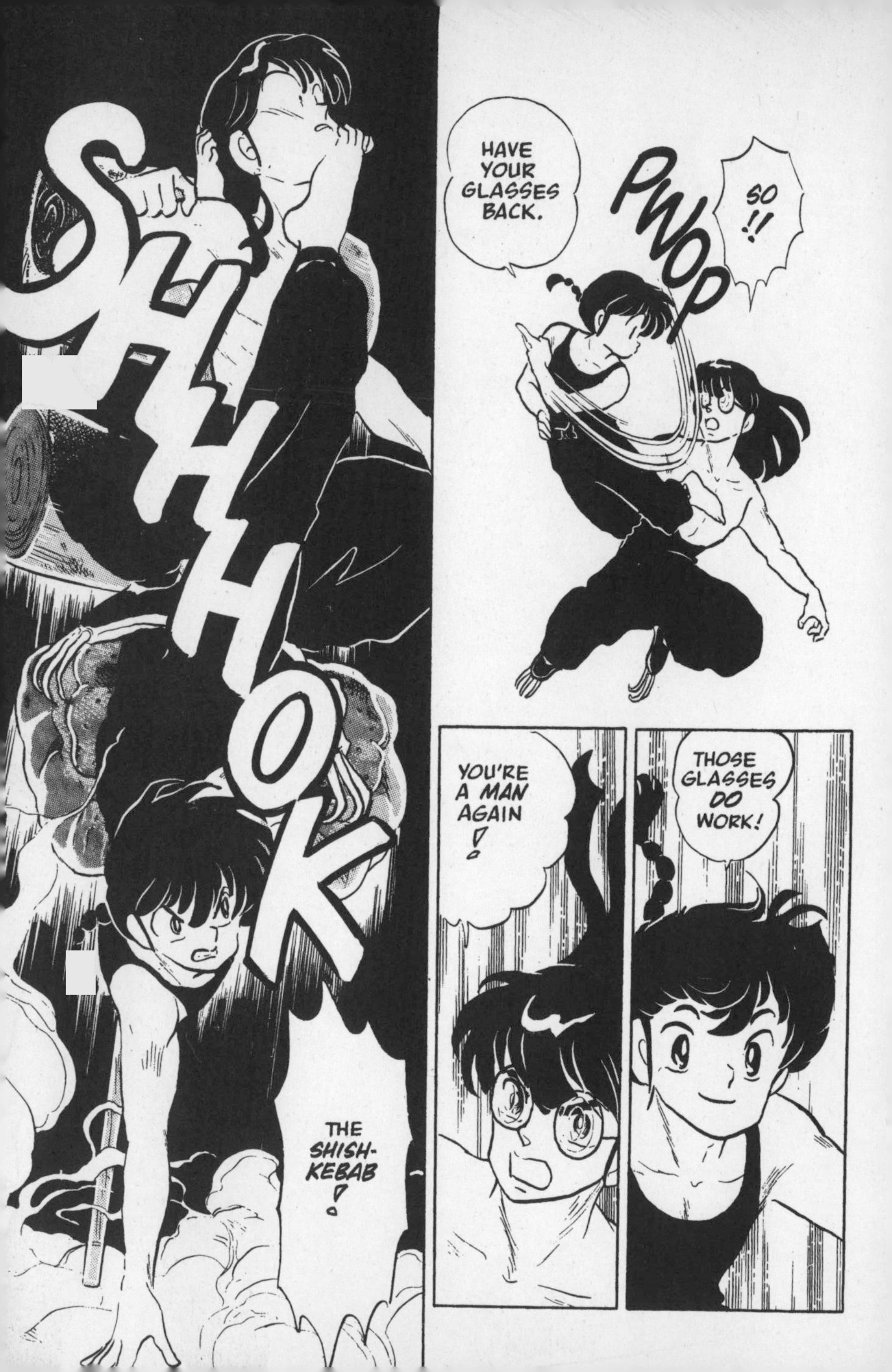
SHHOK
THE SHISH-KEBAB!
HAVE YOUR GLASSES BACK.
PWOP
SO!!
YOU'RE A MAN AGAIN!
THOSE GLASSES DO WORK!

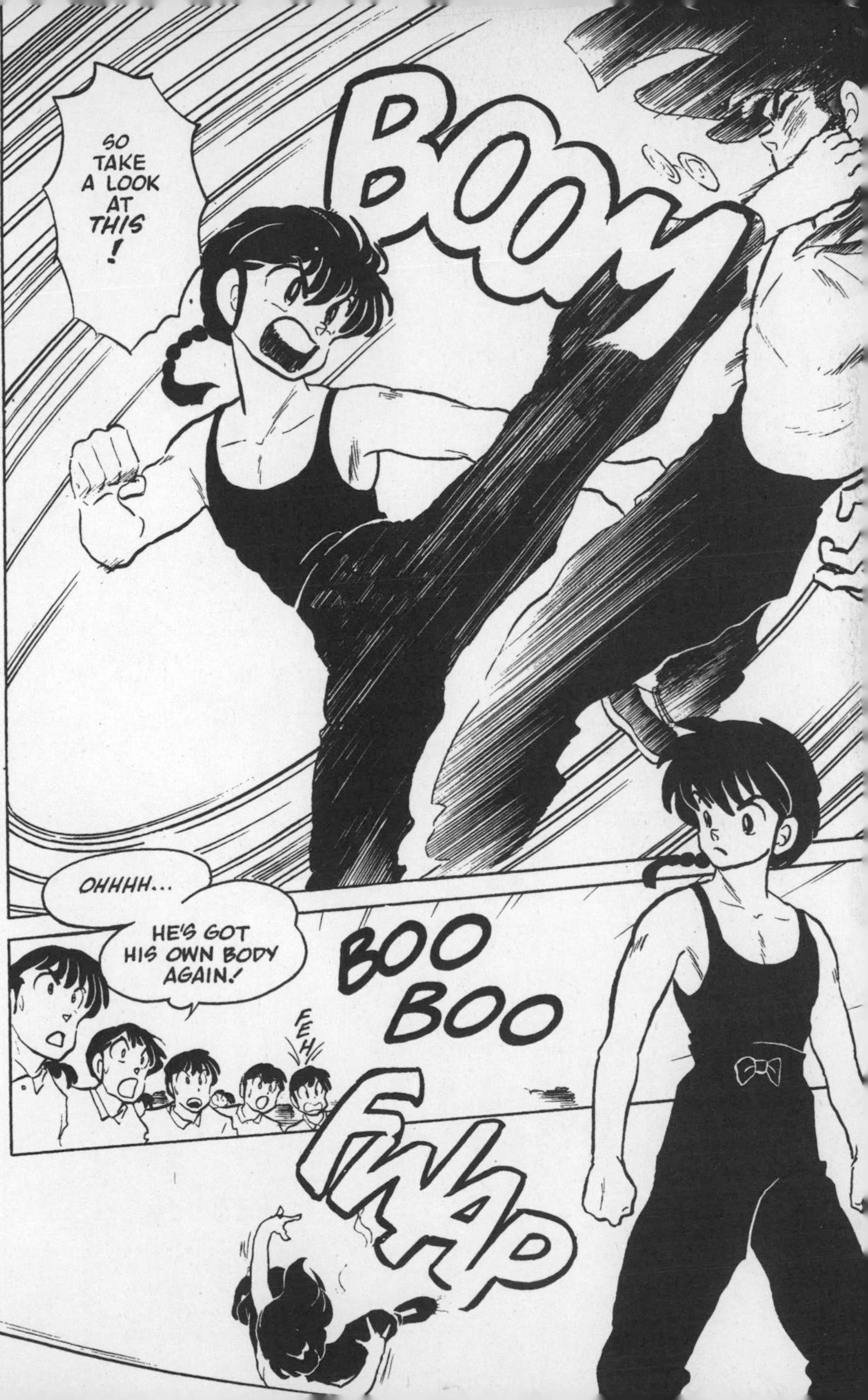
SO TAKE A LOOK AT THIS!
BOOM
OHHHH...
HE'S GOT HIS OWN BODY AGAIN!
BOO BOO
FEH
FWAP

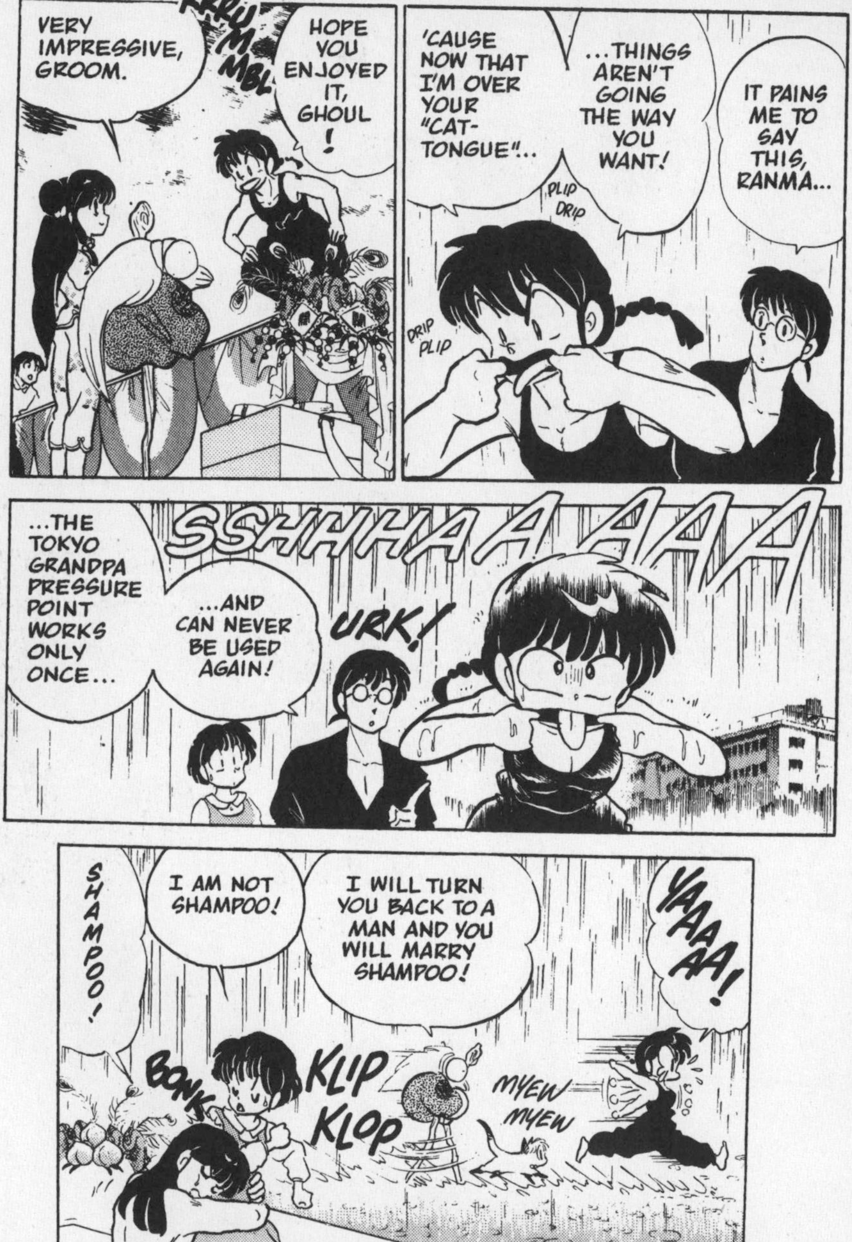
VERY IMPRESSIVE, GROOM.
RRRUMMBL
HOPE YOU ENJOYED IT, GHOUL!
'CAUSE NOW THAT I'M OVER YOUR "CAT-TONGUE"...
...THINGS AREN'T GOING THE WAY YOU WANT!
IT PAINS ME TO SAY THIS, RANMA...
PLIP DRIP
DRIP PLIP
...THE TOKYO GRANDPA PRESSURE POINT WORKS ONLY ONCE...
...AND CAN NEVER BE USED AGAIN!
SSHHHAAAAA
URK!
SHAMPOO!
I AM NOT SHAMPOO!
I WILL TURN YOU BACK TO A MAN AND YOU WILL MARRY SHAMPOO!
YAAAAA!
BONK
KLIP KLOP
MYEW MYEW

Part 10

THE PHOENIX PILL

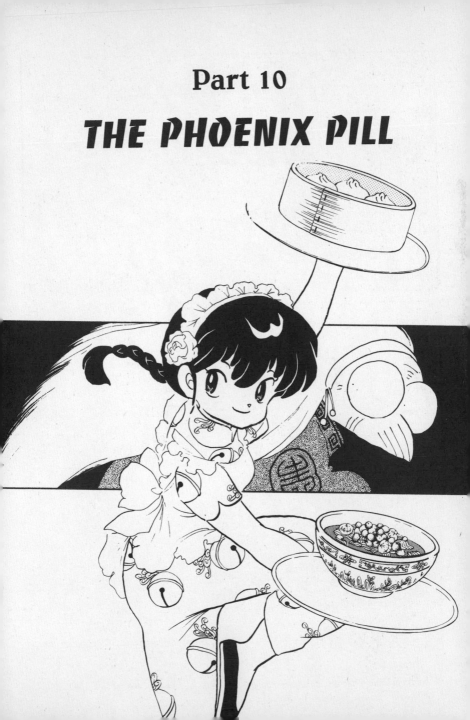

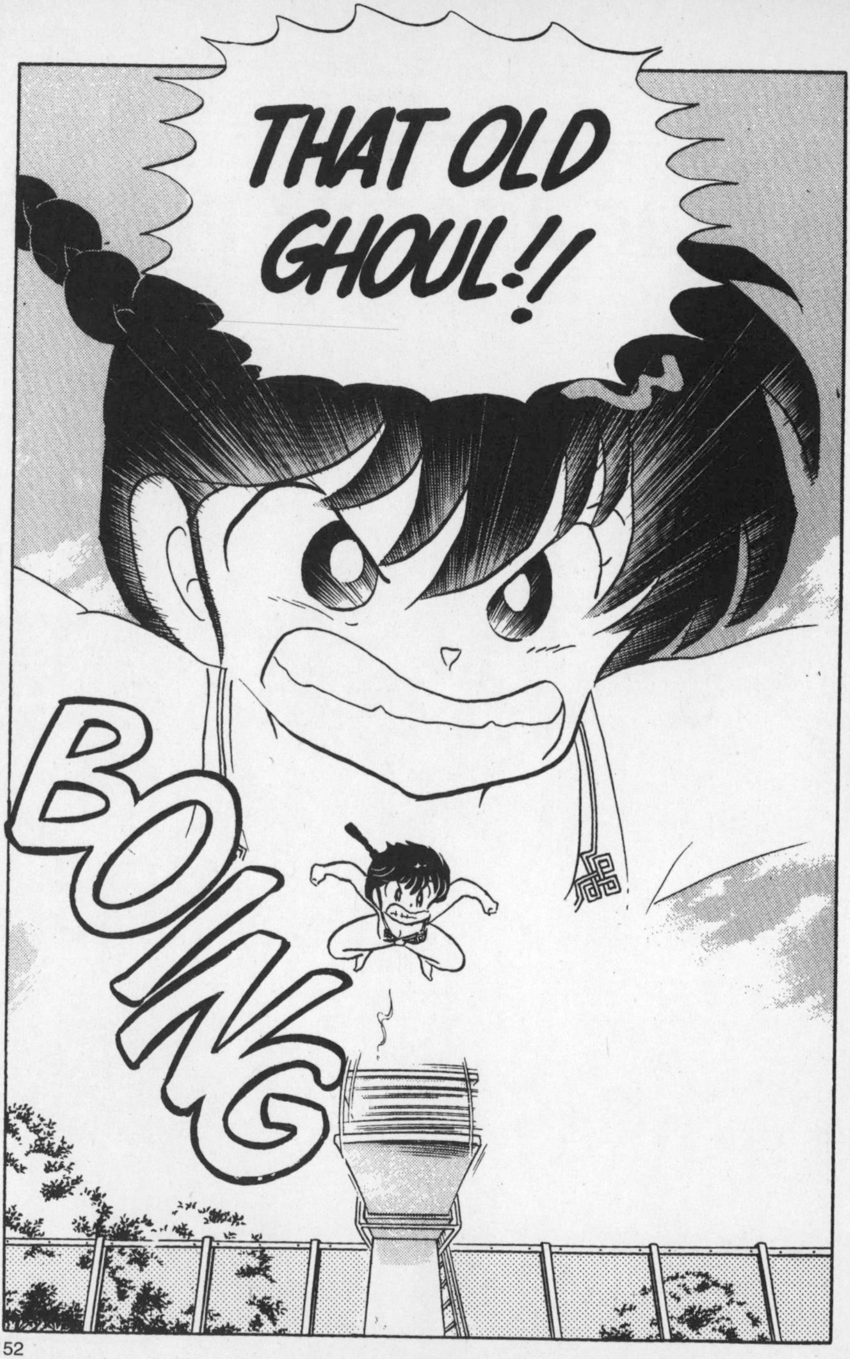
THAT OLD GHOUL!!
BOING

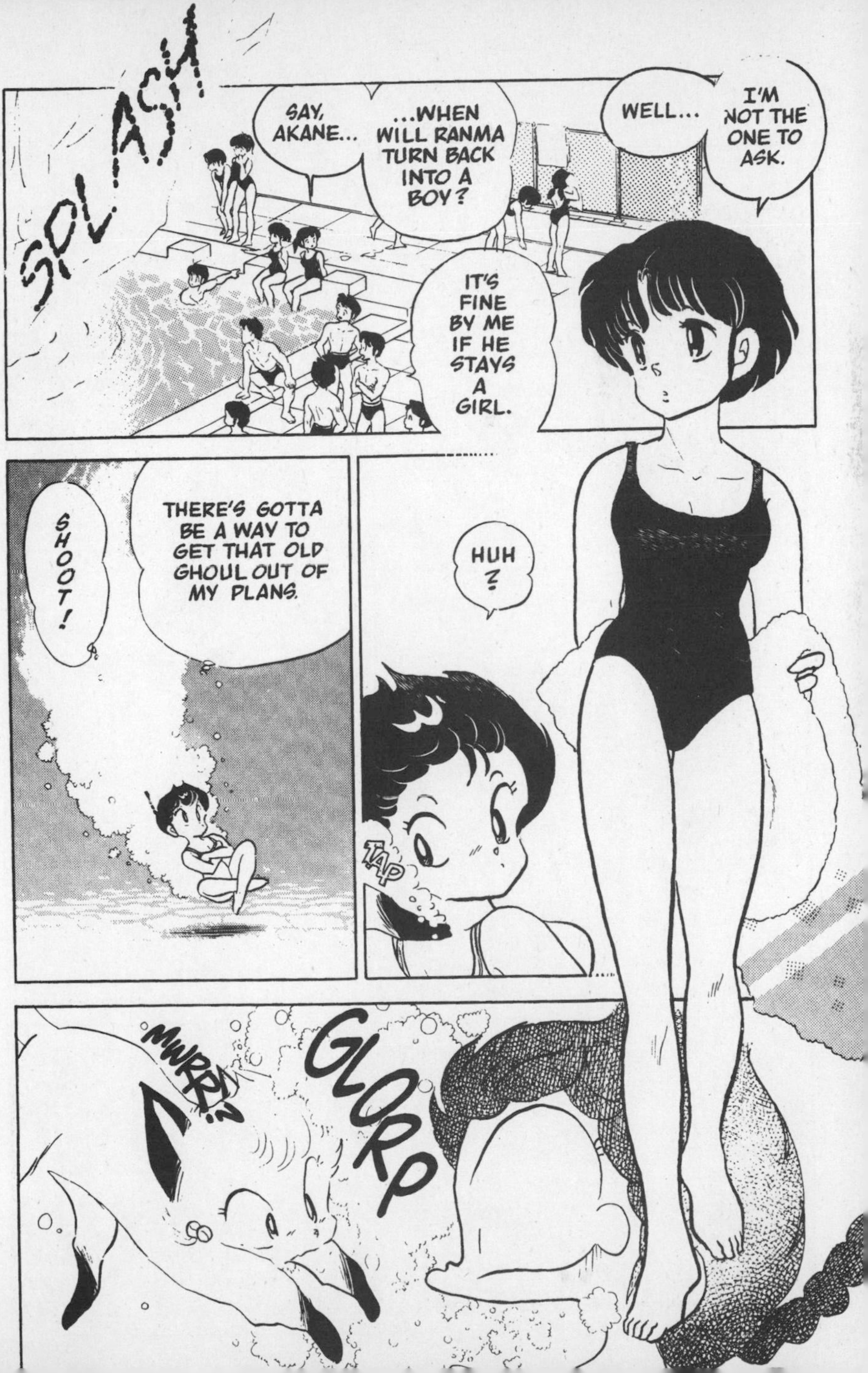
SPLASH
SAY, AKANE...
...WHEN WILL RANMA TURN BACK INTO A BOY?
WELL...
I'M NOT THE ONE TO ASK.
IT'S FINE BY ME IF HE STAYS A GIRL.
SHOOT!
THERE'S GOTTA BE A WAY TO GET THAT OLD GHOUL OUT OF MY PLANS.
HUH?
TAP
MWRR!?
GLORP

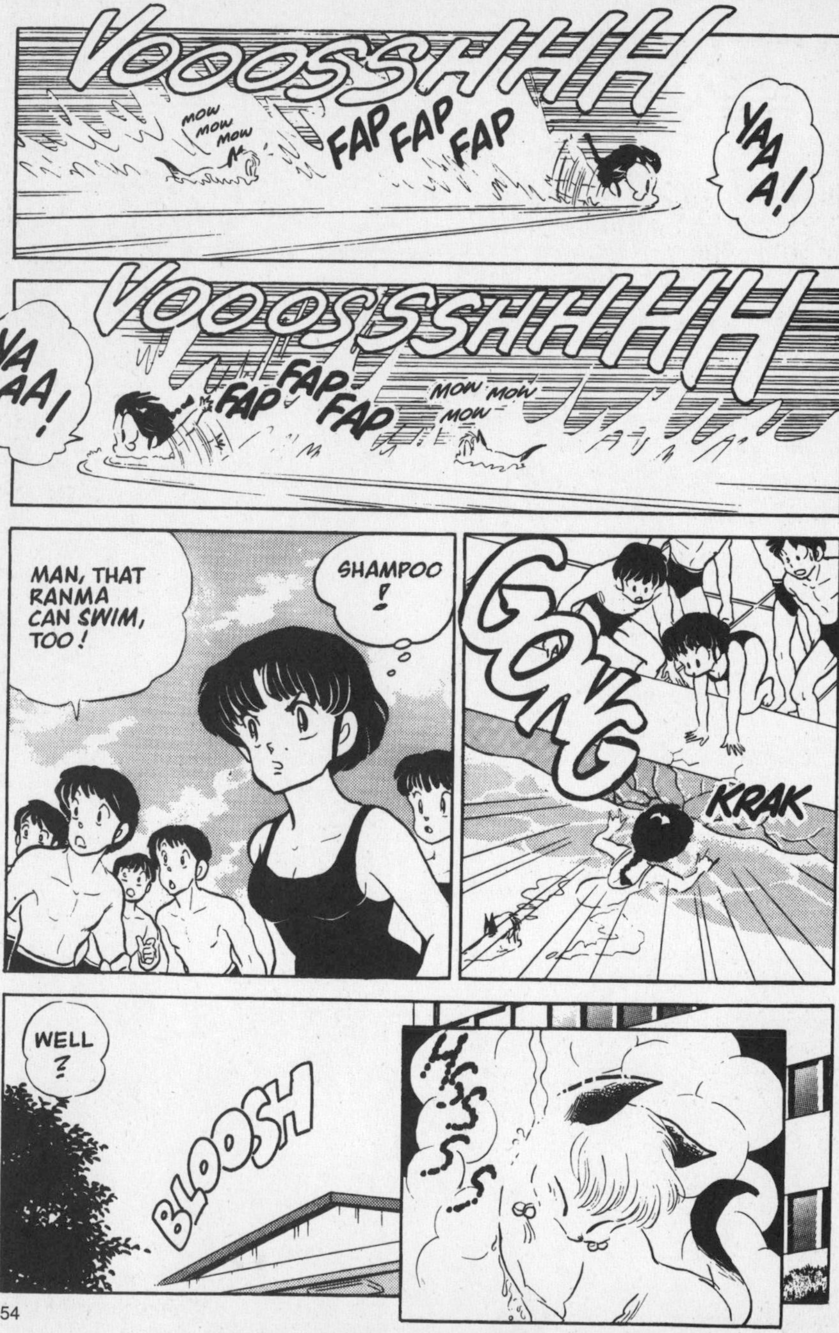
VOOOSSHHH
MOW MOW MOW
FAP FAP FAP
YAAAA!
VOOOSSHHHH
YAAAA!
FAP FAP FAP
MOW MOW MOW
MAN, THAT RANMA CAN SWIM, TOO!
SHAMPOO!
GONG
KRAK
WELL?
BLOOSH
HSSSSS...

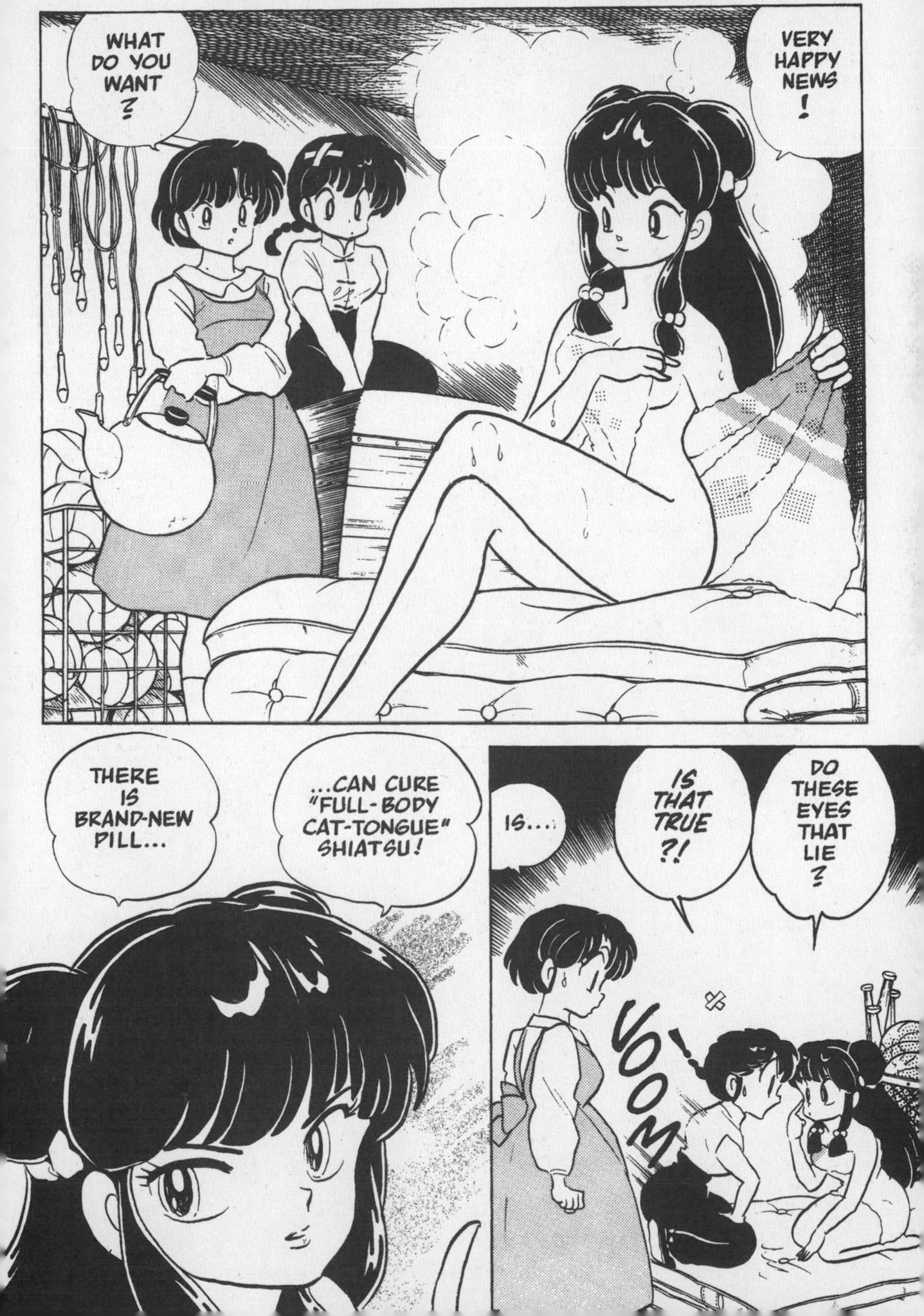
WHAT DO YOU WANT ?
VERY HAPPY NEWS !
THERE IS BRAND-NEW PILL...
...CAN CURE "FULL-BODY CAT-TONGUE" SHIATSU!
IS...
IS THAT TRUE ?!
DO THESE EYES THAT LIE ?
VOOM

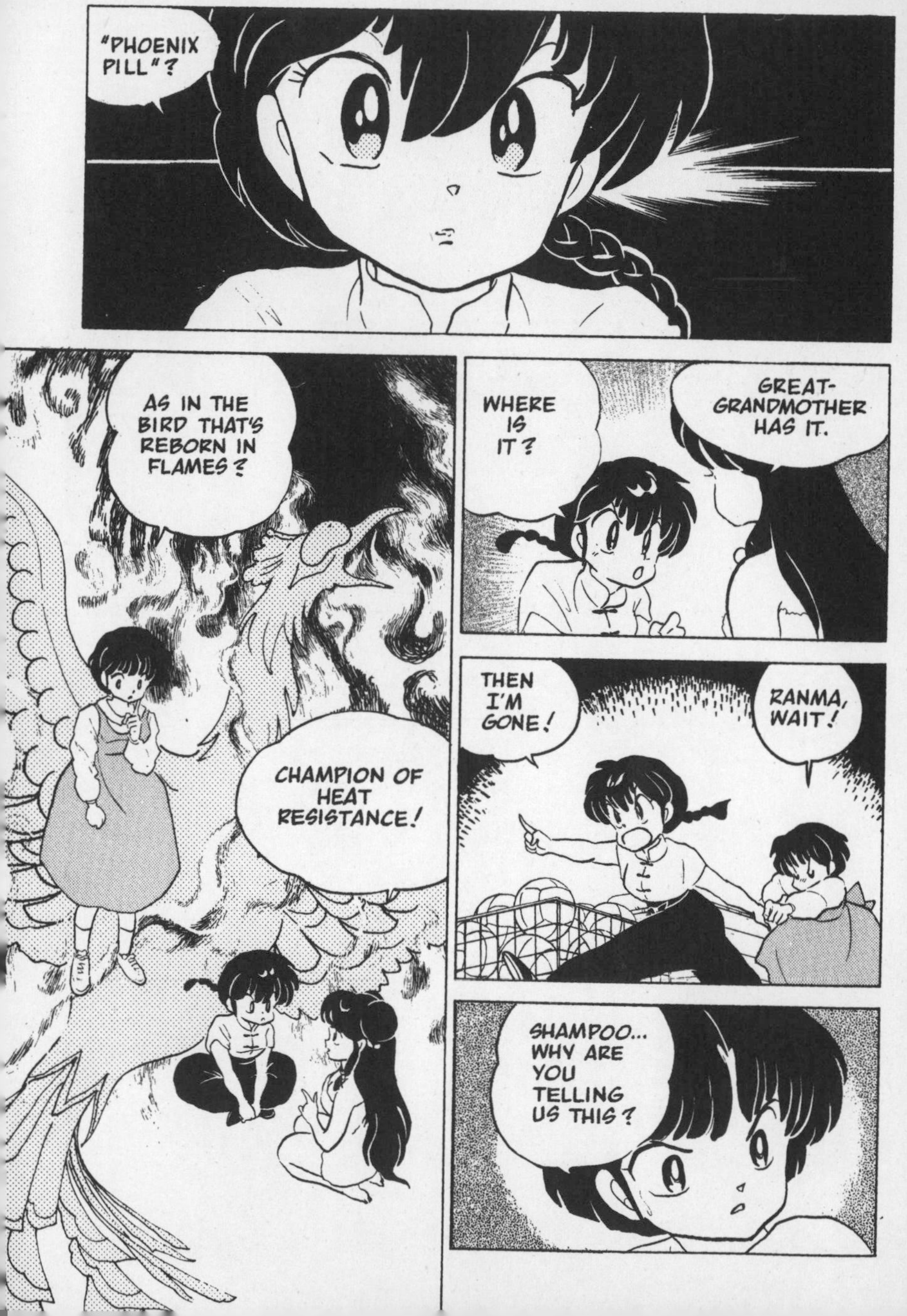
"PHOENIX PILL"?
AS IN THE BIRD THAT'S REBORN IN FLAMES?
CHAMPION OF HEAT RESISTANCE!
WHERE IS IT?
GREAT-GRANDMOTHER HAS IT.
THEN I'M GONE!
RANMA, WAIT!
SHAMPOO... WHY ARE YOU TELLING US THIS?

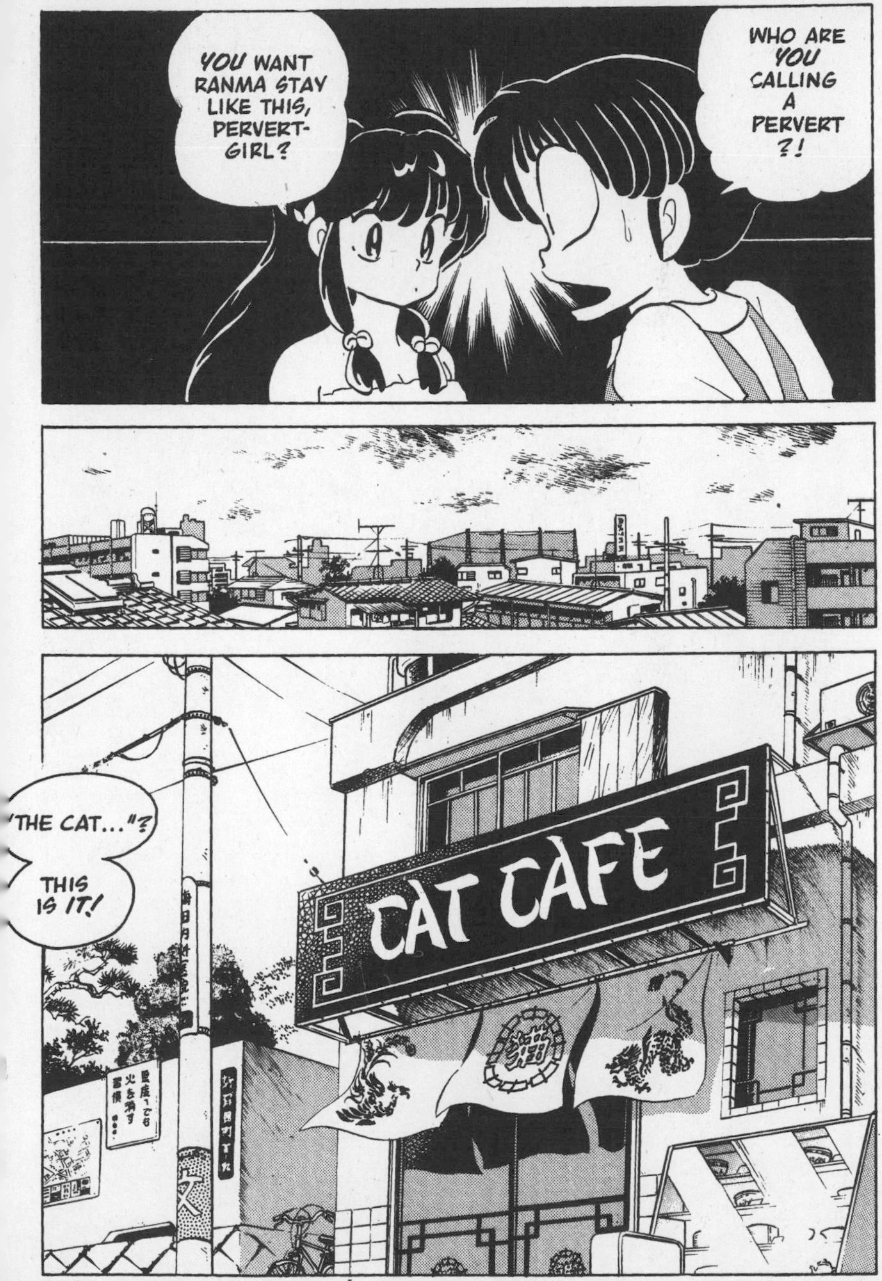
YOU WANT RANMA STAY LIKE THIS, PERVERT-GIRL?
WHO ARE YOU CALLING A PERVERT ?!
"THE CAT..."?
THIS IS IT!
CAT CAFE

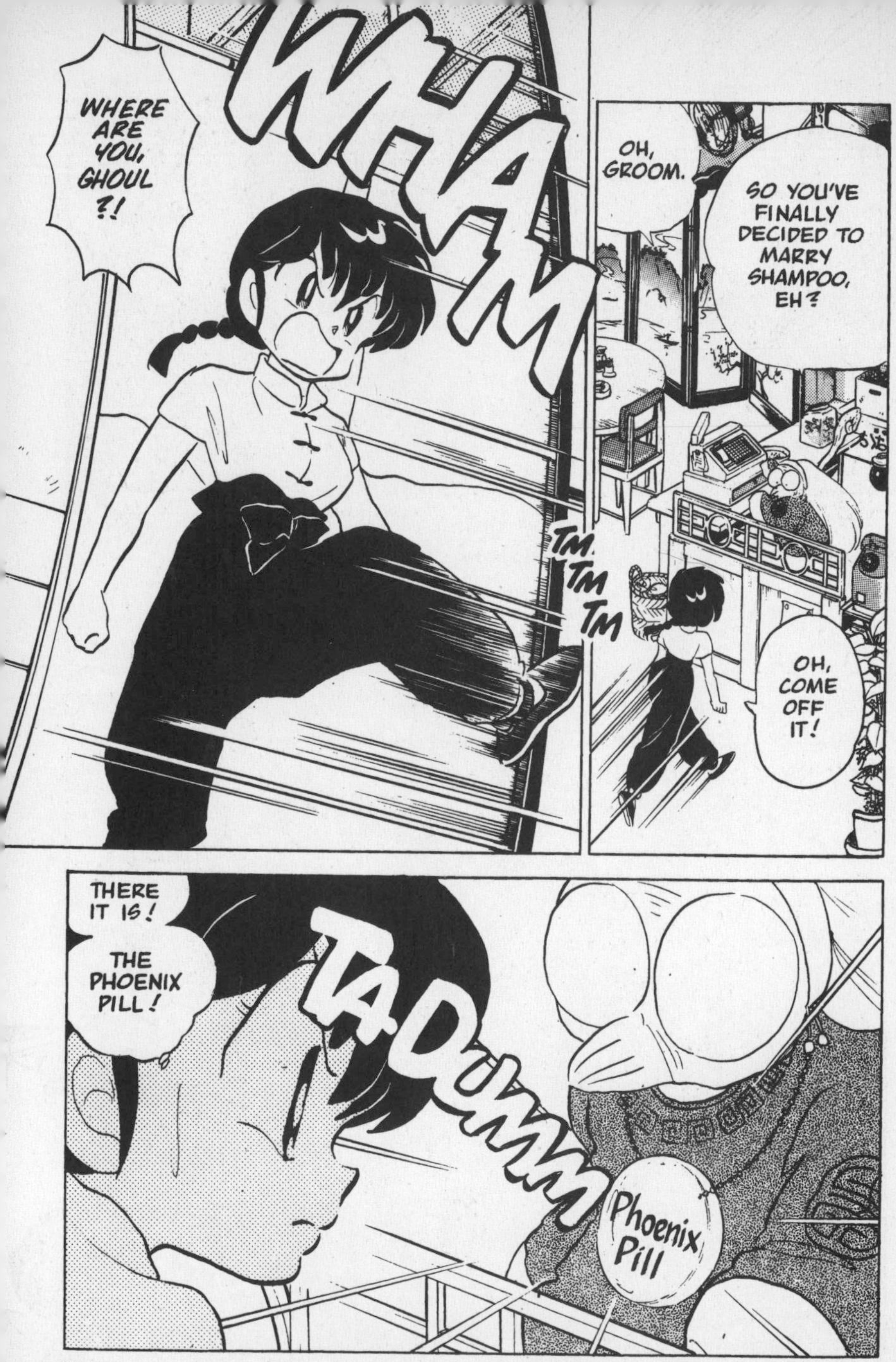
WHERE ARE YOU, GHOUL ?!
WHAM
OH, GROOM.
SO YOU'VE FINALLY DECIDED TO MARRY SHAMPOO, EH?
TM TM TM TM
OH, COME OFF IT!
THERE IT IS!
THE PHOENIX PILL!
TADUMM
Phoenix Pill

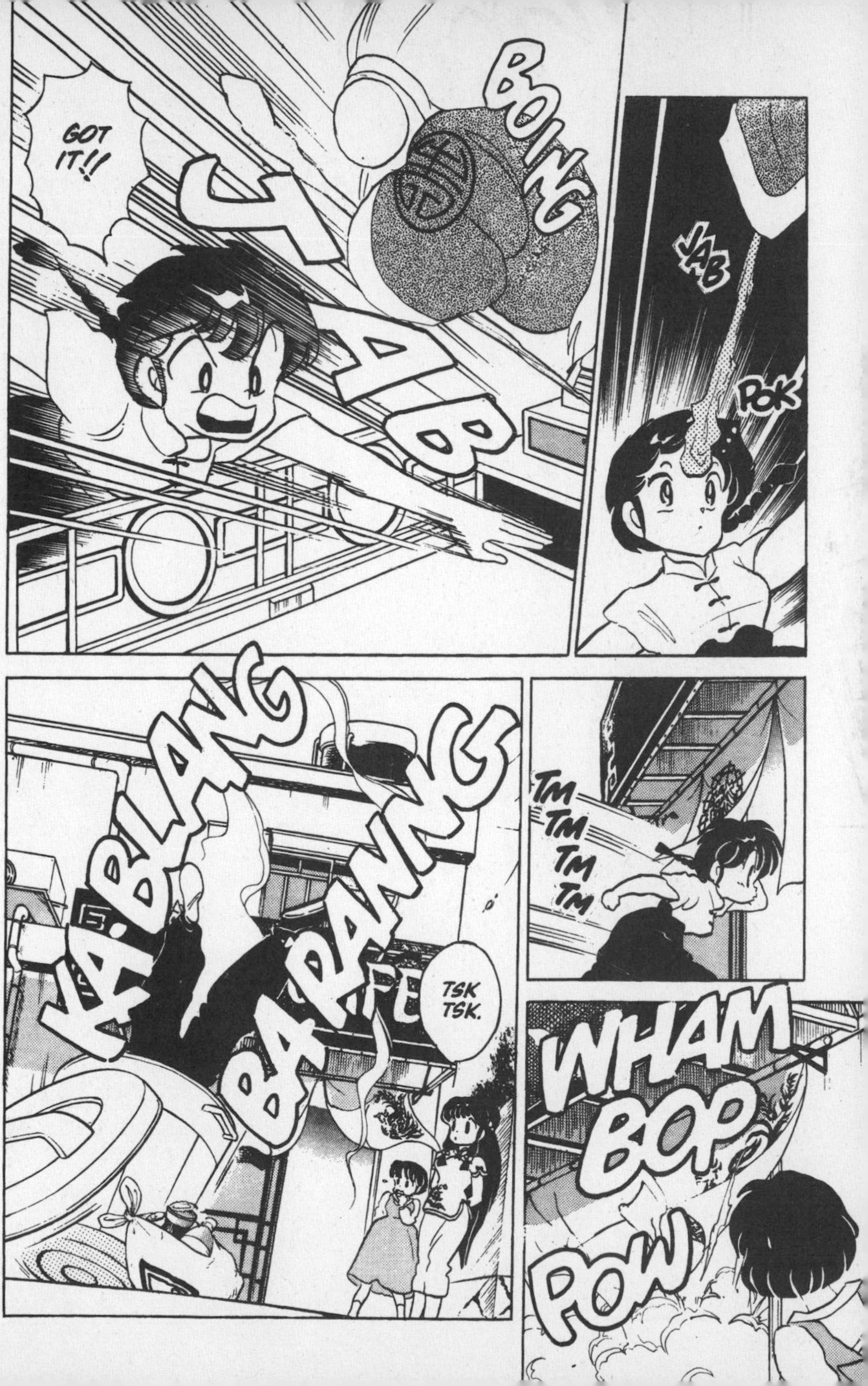
GOT IT!!
BOING
JAB
JAB
POK
KABLANG
BARANNG
TSK TSK.
TM TM TM TM TM
WHAM
BOP
POW

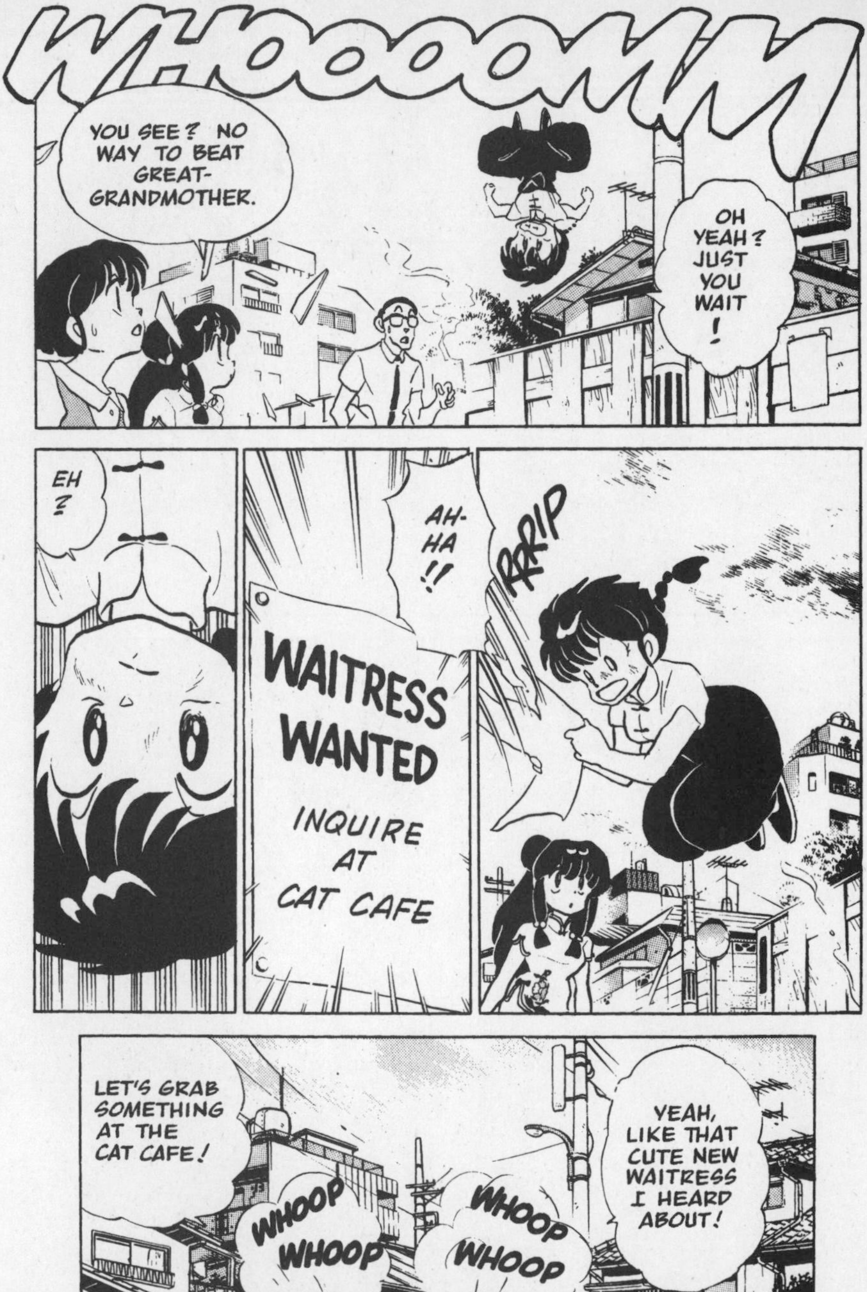
WHOOOOMM
YOU SEE? NO WAY TO BEAT GREAT-GRANDMOTHER.
OH YEAH? JUST YOU WAIT!
EH?
AH-HA!!
WAITRESS WANTED
INQUIRE AT CAT CAFE
RRRIP
LET'S GRAB SOMETHING AT THE CAT CAFE!
WHOOP WHOOP
WHOOP WHOOP
YEAH, LIKE THAT CUTE NEW WAITRESS I HEARD ABOUT!

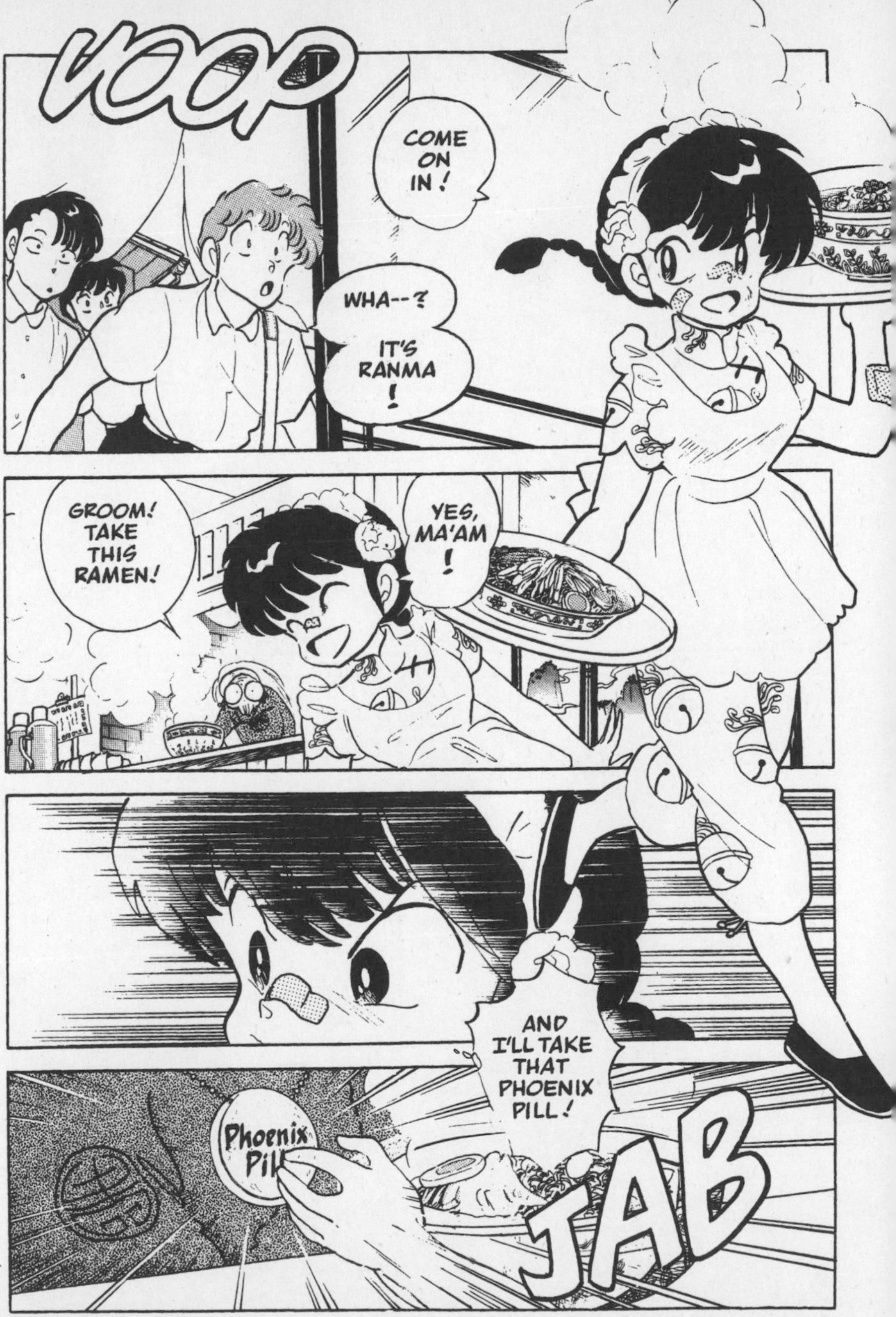
VOOP
COME ON IN!
WHA--?
IT'S RANMA!
GROOM! TAKE THIS RAMEN!
YES, MA'AM!
AND I'LL TAKE THAT PHOENIX PILL!
Phoenix Pill
JAB

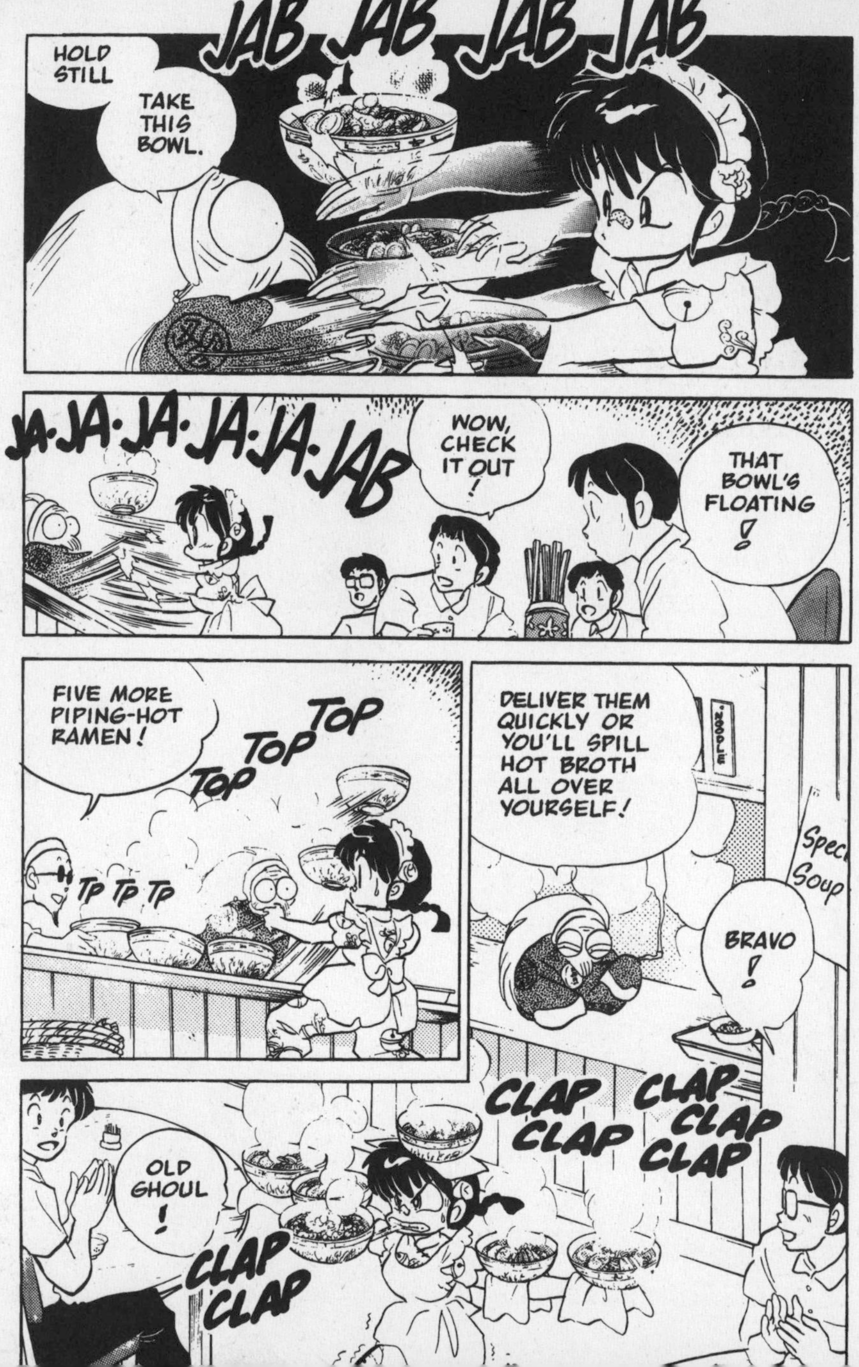
JAB JAB JAB JAB
HOLD STILL
TAKE THIS BOWL.
JA·JA·JA·JA·JA·JAB
WOW, CHECK IT OUT!
THAT BOWL'S FLOATING!
FIVE MORE PIPING-HOT RAMEN!
TOP TOP TOP
TP TP TP
DELIVER THEM QUICKLY OR YOU'LL SPILL HOT BROTH ALL OVER YOURSELF!
NOODLE
Speci Soup
BRAVO!
CLAP CLAP
CLAP CLAP CLAP
OLD GHOUL!
CLAP CLAP

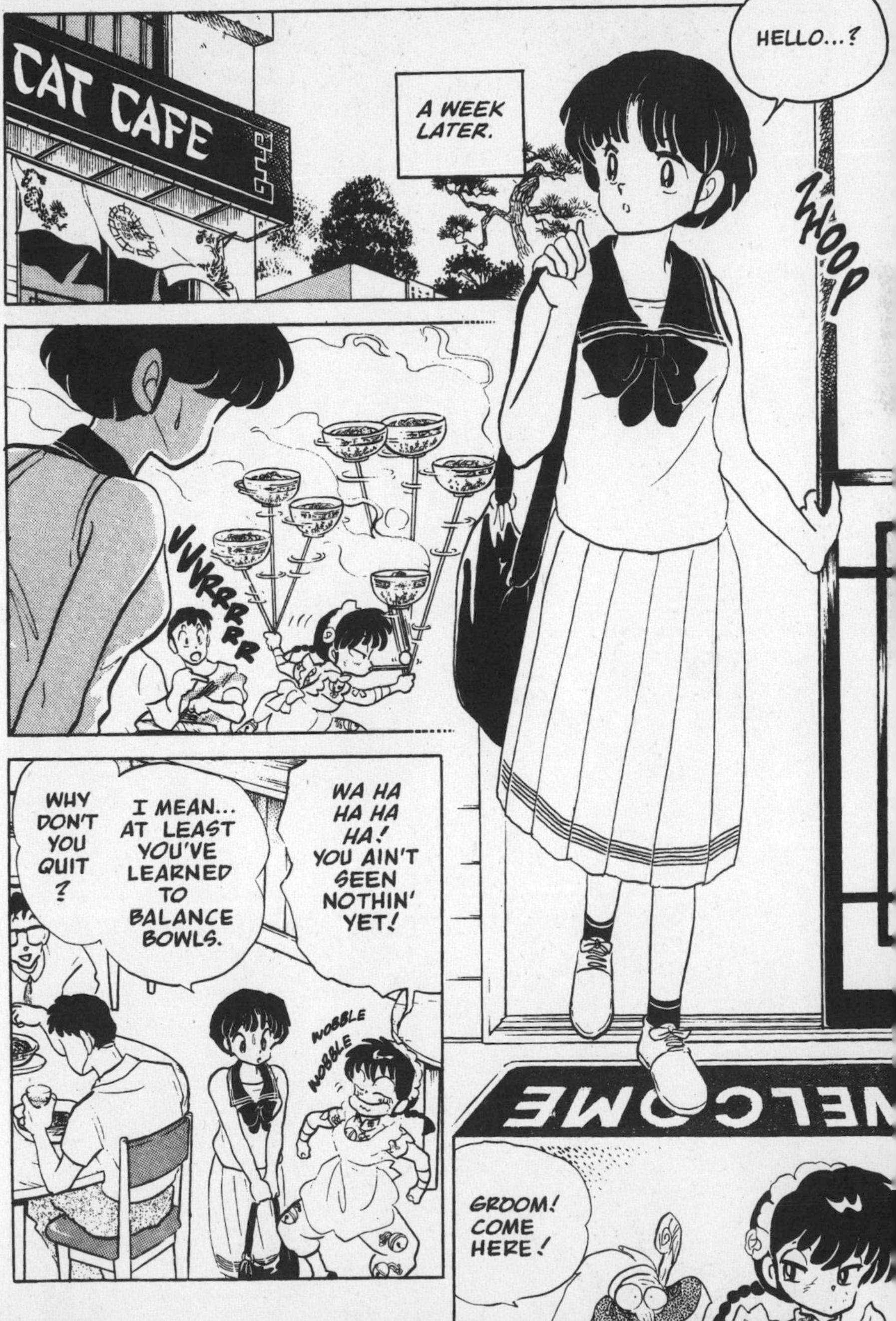
CAT CAFE
A WEEK LATER.
VVVRRRRR
WHY DON'T YOU QUIT ?
I MEAN... AT LEAST YOU'VE LEARNED TO BALANCE BOWLS.
WA HA HA HA HA! YOU AIN'T SEEN NOTHIN' YET!
WOBBLE WOBBLE
HELLO...?
ZHOOP
WELCOME
GROOM! COME HERE!

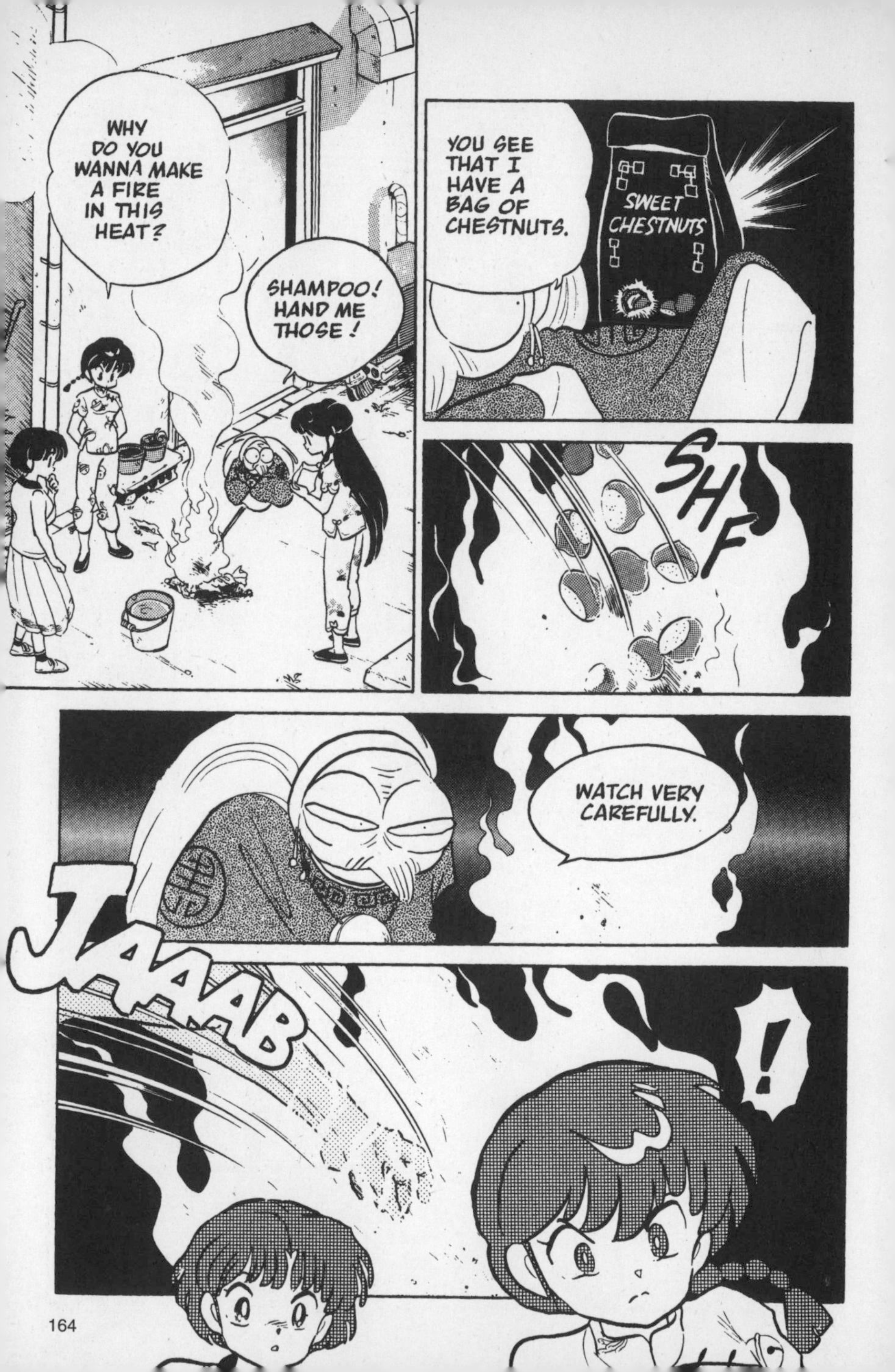
WHY DO YOU WANNA MAKE A FIRE IN THIS HEAT?
SHAMPOO! HAND ME THOSE!
YOU SEE THAT I HAVE A BAG OF CHESTNUTS.
SWEET CHESTNUTS
SHF
WATCH VERY CAREFULLY.
JAAAB
!

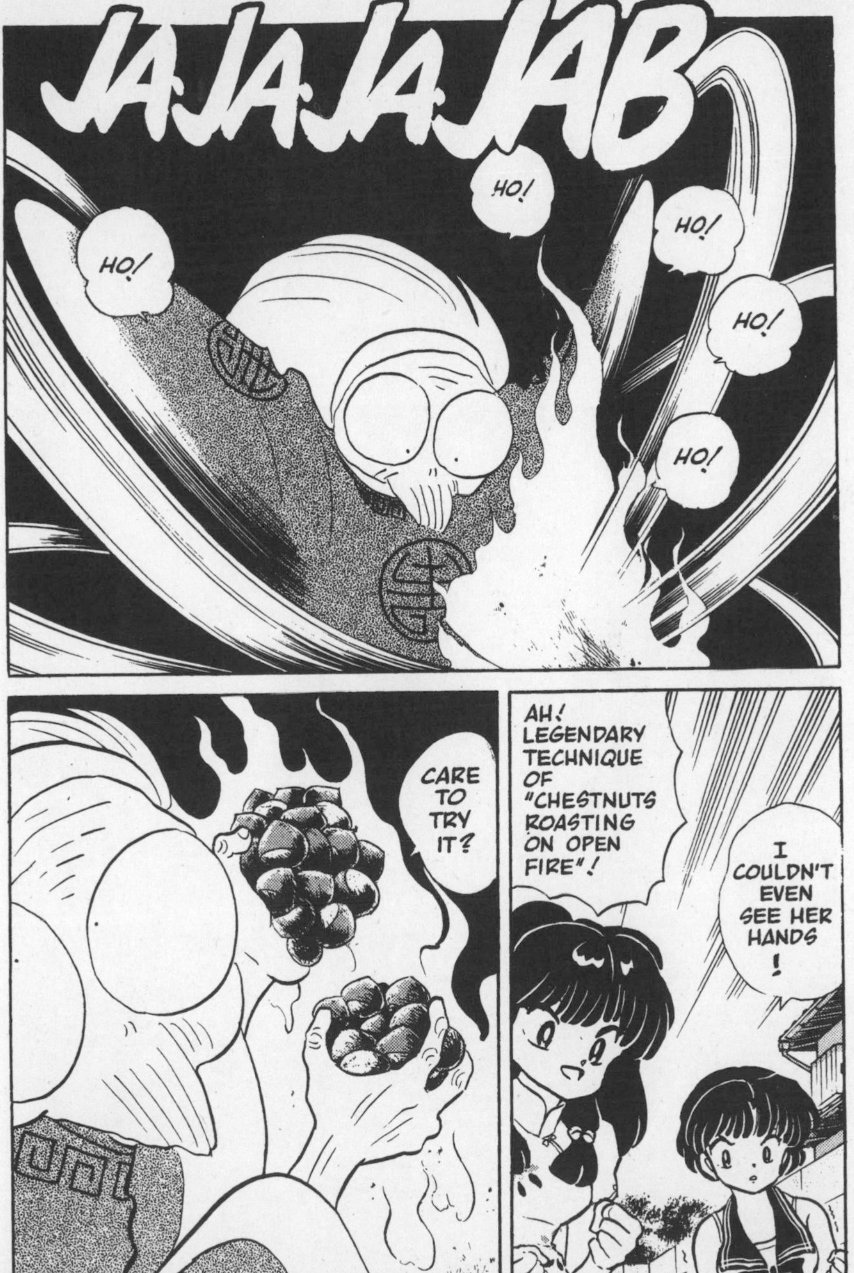
JAJAJAJAB
HO!
HO!
HO!
HO!
HO!
CARE TO TRY IT?
AH! LEGENDARY TECHNIQUE OF "CHESTNUTS ROASTING ON OPEN FIRE"!
I COULDN'T EVEN SEE HER HANDS!

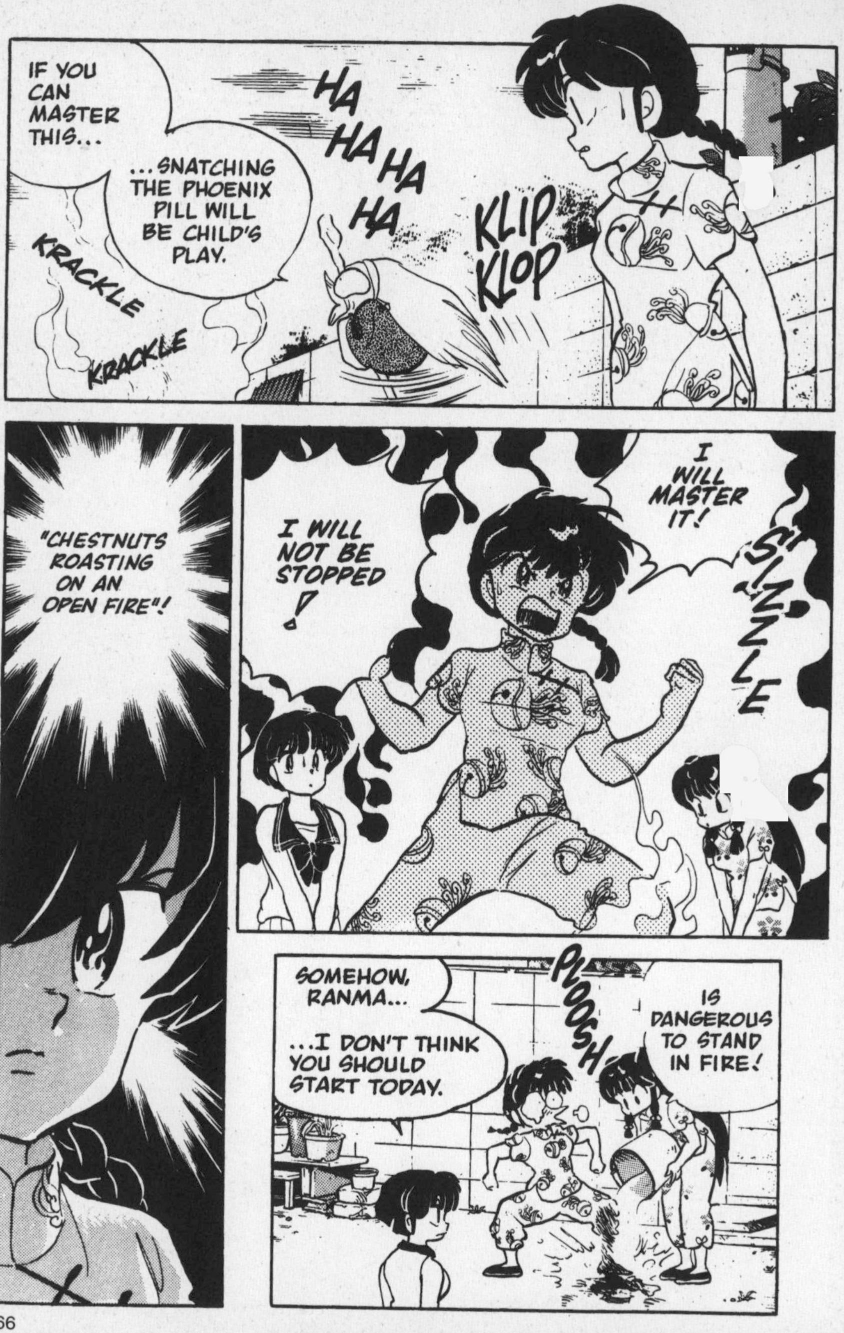
IF YOU CAN MASTER THIS...
...SNATCHING THE PHOENIX PILL WILL BE CHILD'S PLAY.
KRACKLE
KRACKLE
HA HA HA HA
KLIP KLOP
"CHESTNUTS ROASTING ON AN OPEN FIRE"!
I WILL NOT BE STOPPED!
I WILL MASTER IT!
SIZZLE
SOMEHOW, RANMA...
...I DON'T THINK YOU SHOULD START TODAY.
PLOOSH
IS DANGEROUS TO STAND IN FIRE!

Part 11

ALL'S FAIR AT THE FAIR

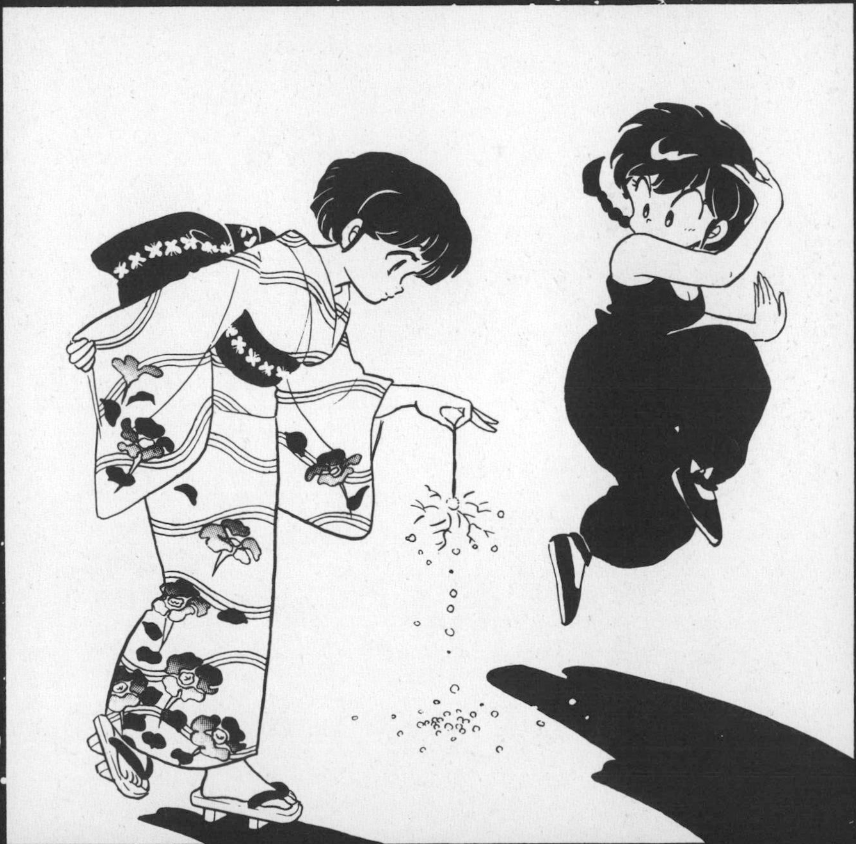

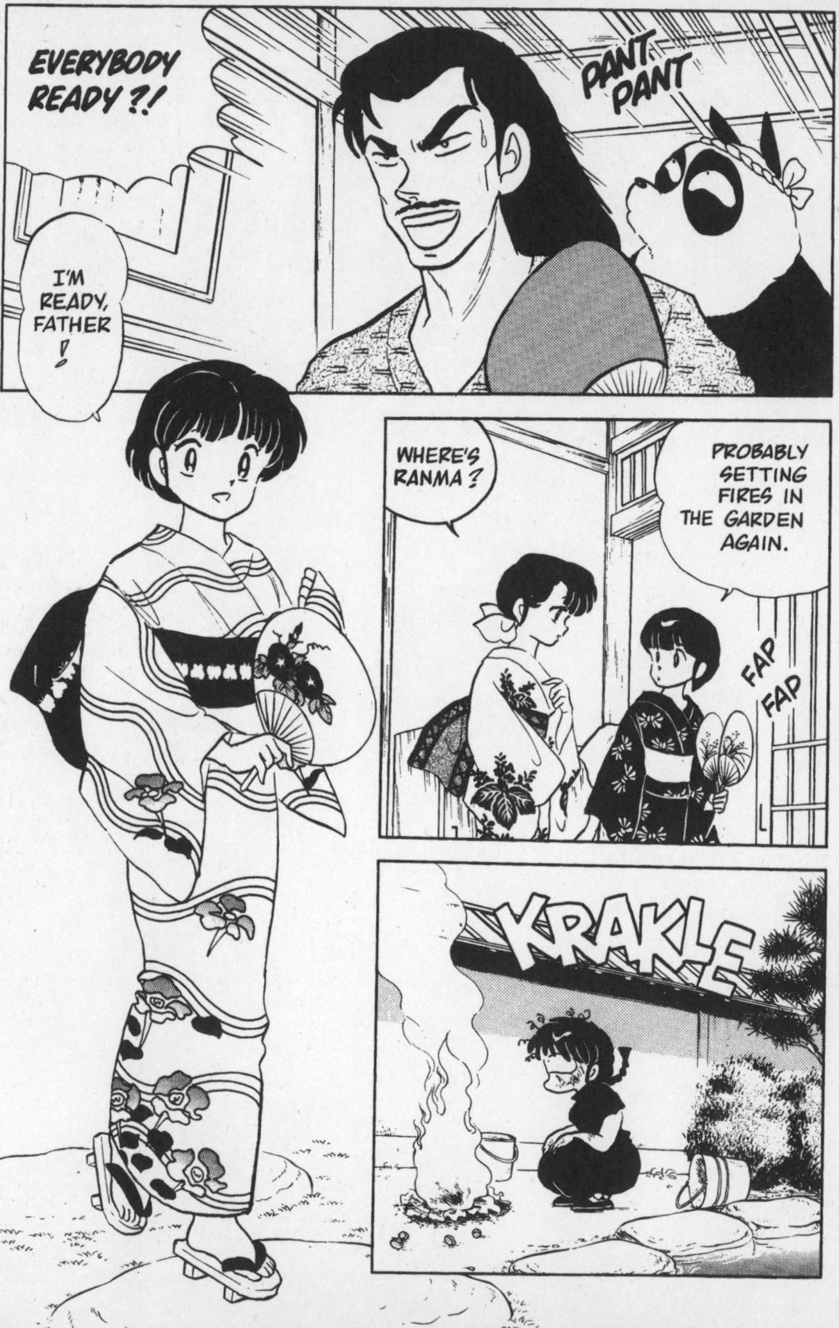
EVERYBODY READY?!
PANT PANT
I'M READY, FATHER!
WHERE'S RANMA?
PROBABLY SETTING FIRES IN THE GARDEN AGAIN.
FAP FAP
KRAKLE

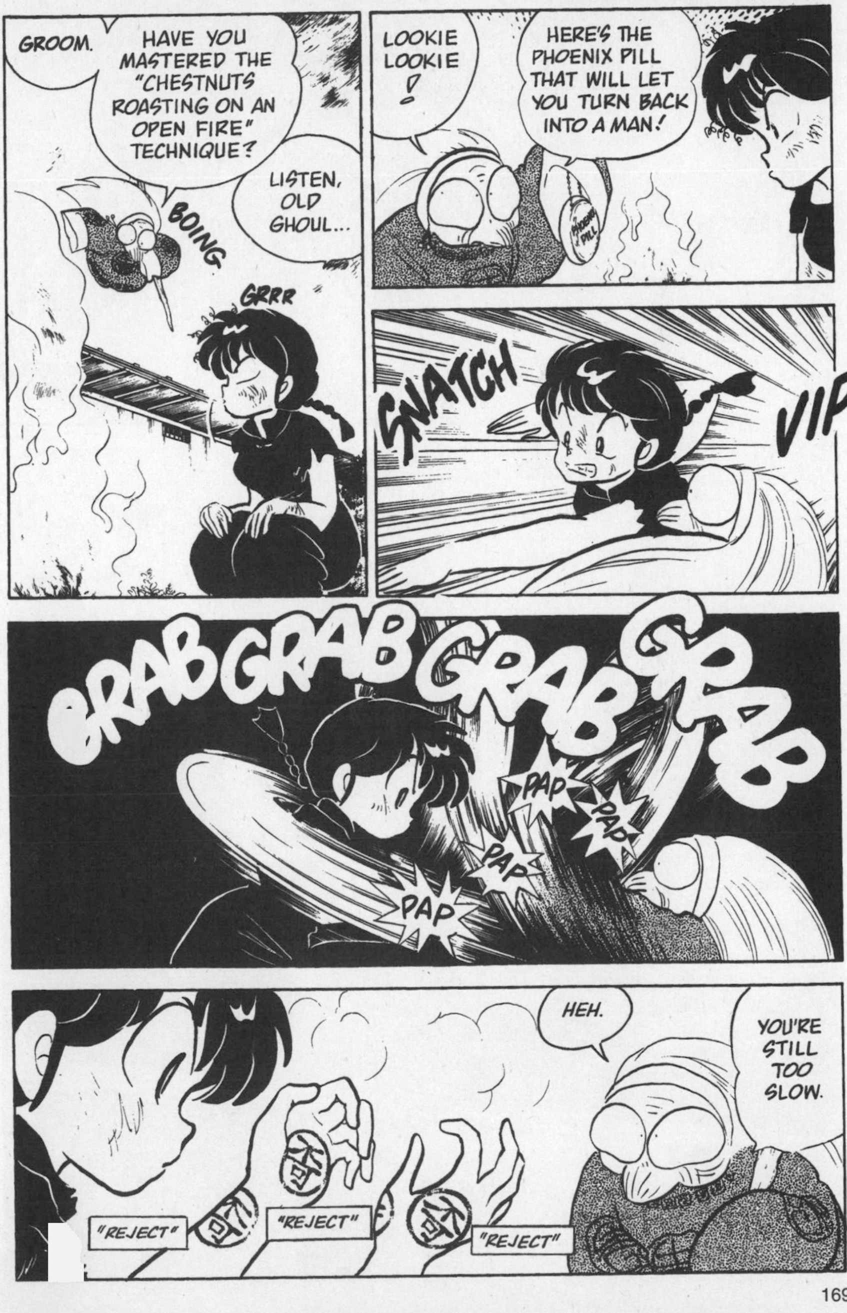
GROOM.
HAVE YOU MASTERED THE "CHESTNUTS ROASTING ON AN OPEN FIRE" TECHNIQUE?
BOING
LISTEN, OLD GHOUL...
GRRR
LOOKIE LOOKIE !
HERE'S THE PHOENIX PILL THAT WILL LET YOU TURN BACK INTO A MAN!
PHOENIX PILL
SNATCH
VIP
GRAB GRAB GRAB GRAB GRAB
PAP
PAP
PAP
PAP
"REJECT"
"REJECT"
"REJECT"
HEH.
YOU'RE STILL TOO SLOW.

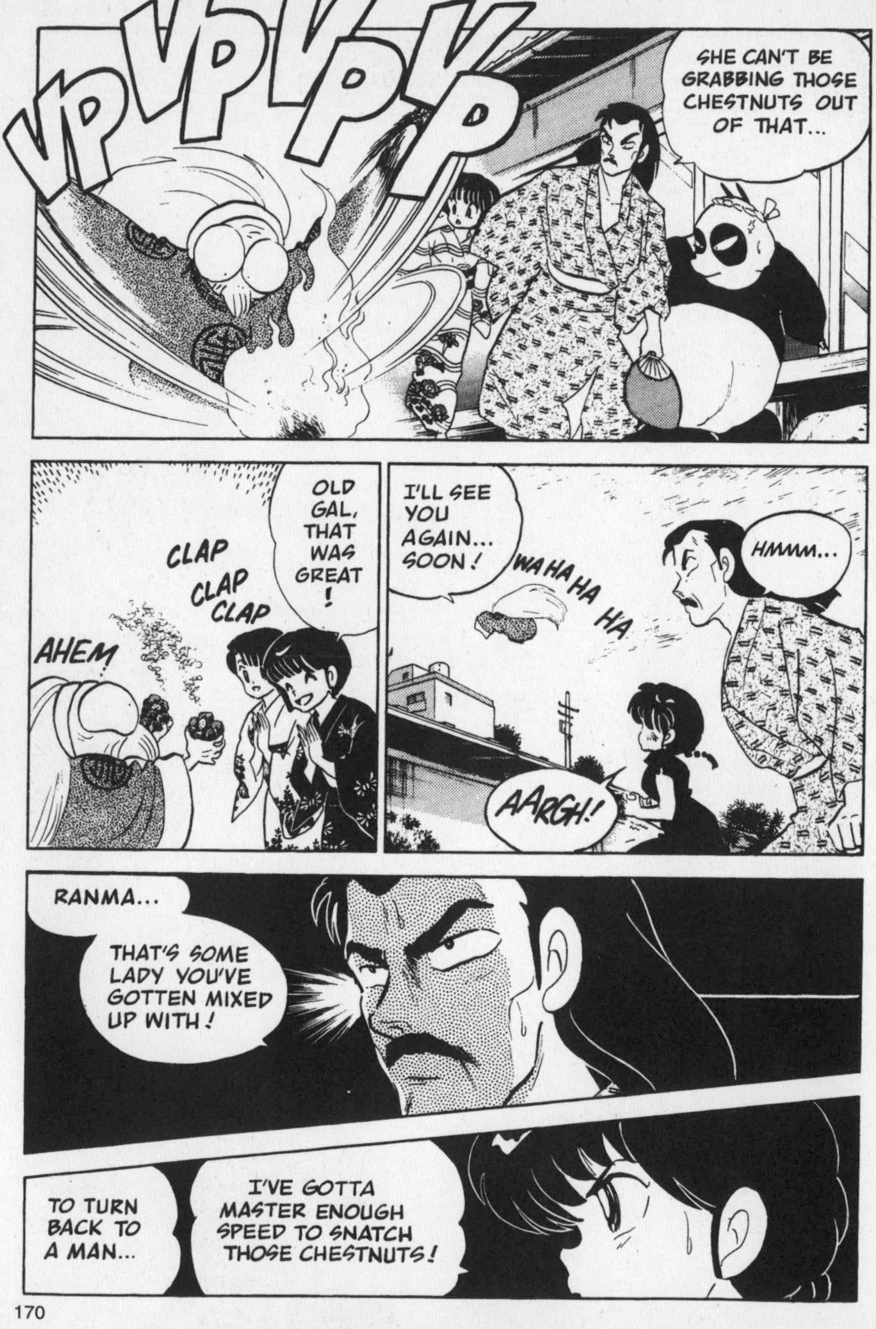
VPVPVPVPVP
SHE CAN'T BE GRABBING THOSE CHESTNUTS OUT OF THAT...
AHEM
CLAP
CLAP
CLAP
OLD GAL, THAT WAS GREAT!
I'LL SEE YOU AGAIN... SOON!
WA HA HA HA
HMMM...
AARGH!
RANMA...
THAT'S SOME LADY YOU'VE GOTTEN MIXED UP WITH!
TO TURN BACK TO A MAN...
I'VE GOTTA MASTER ENOUGH SPEED TO SNATCH THOSE CHESTNUTS!

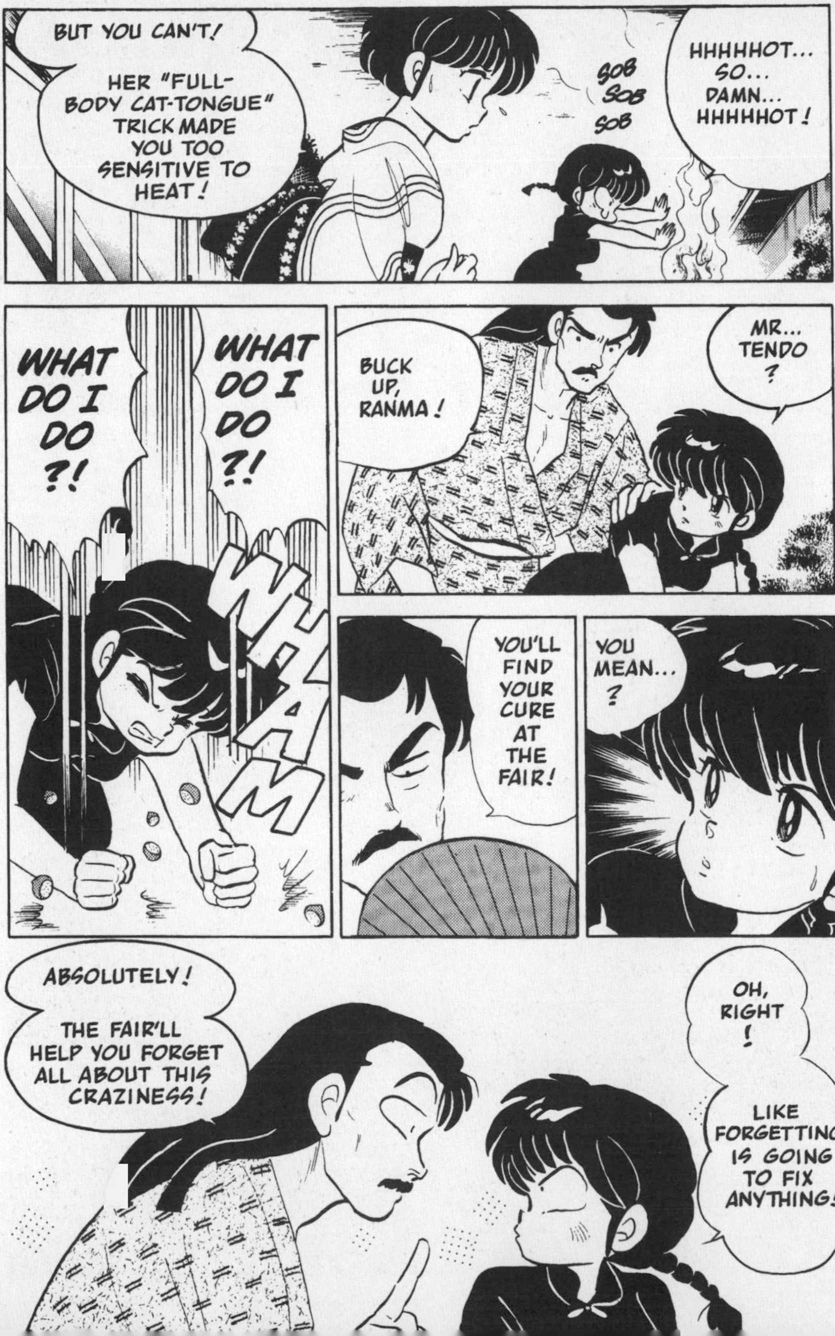
BUT YOU CAN'T!
HER "FULL-BODY CAT-TONGUE" TRICK MADE YOU TOO SENSITIVE TO HEAT!
SOB SOB SOB
HHHHHOT... SO... DAMN... HHHHHOT!
WHAT DO I DO ?!
WHAT DO I DO ?!
WHAM
BUCK UP, RANMA!
MR... TENDO ?
YOU'LL FIND YOUR CURE AT THE FAIR!
YOU MEAN... ?
ABSOLUTELY!
THE FAIR'LL HELP YOU FORGET ALL ABOUT THIS CRAZINESS!
OH, RIGHT!
LIKE FORGETTING IS GOING TO FIX ANYTHING!

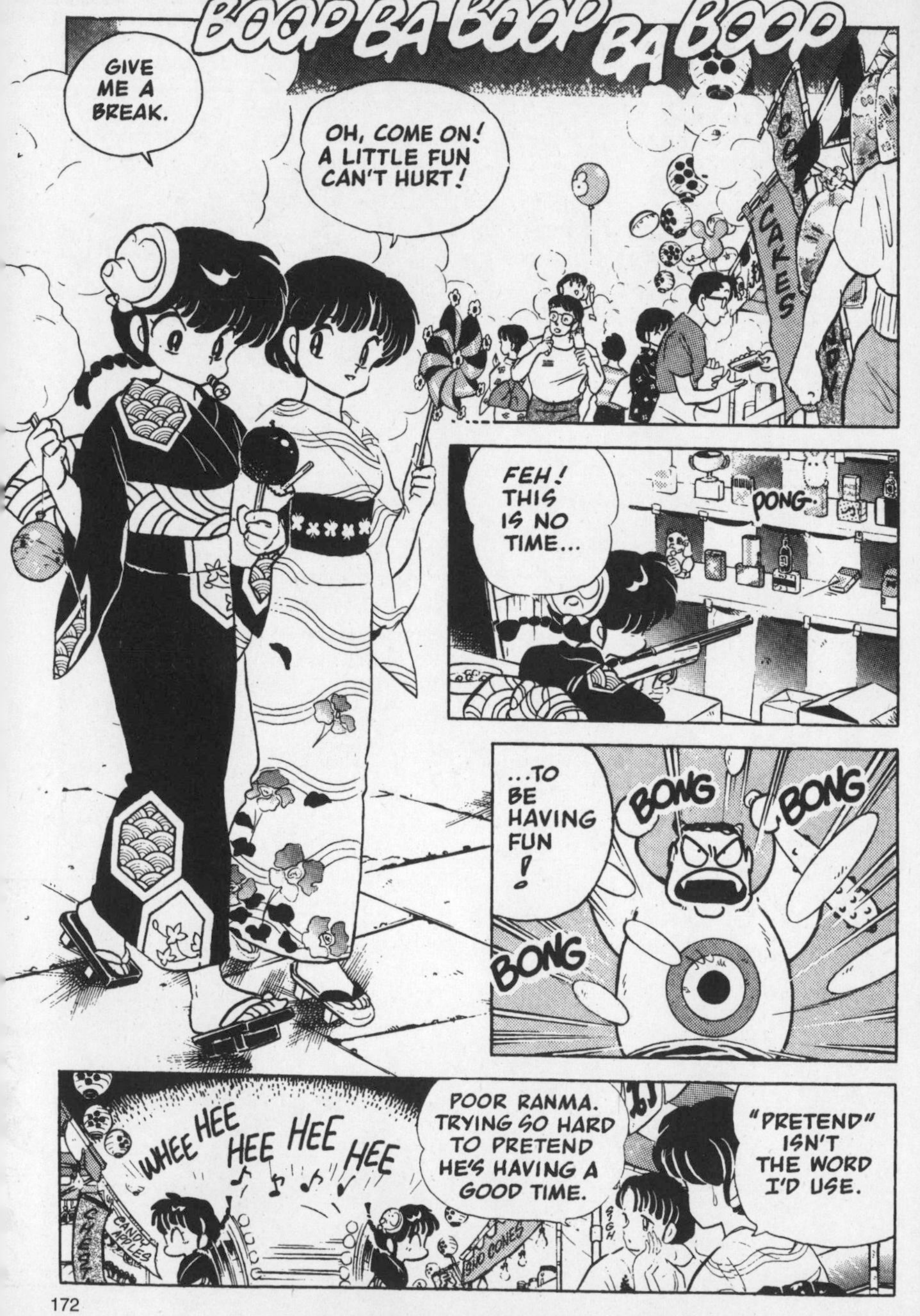
BOOP BA BOOP BA BOOP
GIVE ME A BREAK.
OH, COME ON! A LITTLE FUN CAN'T HURT!
CAKES
FEH! THIS IS NO TIME...
PONG
...TO BE HAVING FUN!
BONG
BONG
BONG
WHEE HEE HEE HEE HEE
CANDY APPLES
SNO CONES
POOR RANMA. TRYING SO HARD TO PRETEND HE'S HAVING A GOOD TIME.
SIGH
"PRETEND" ISN'T THE WORD I'D USE.

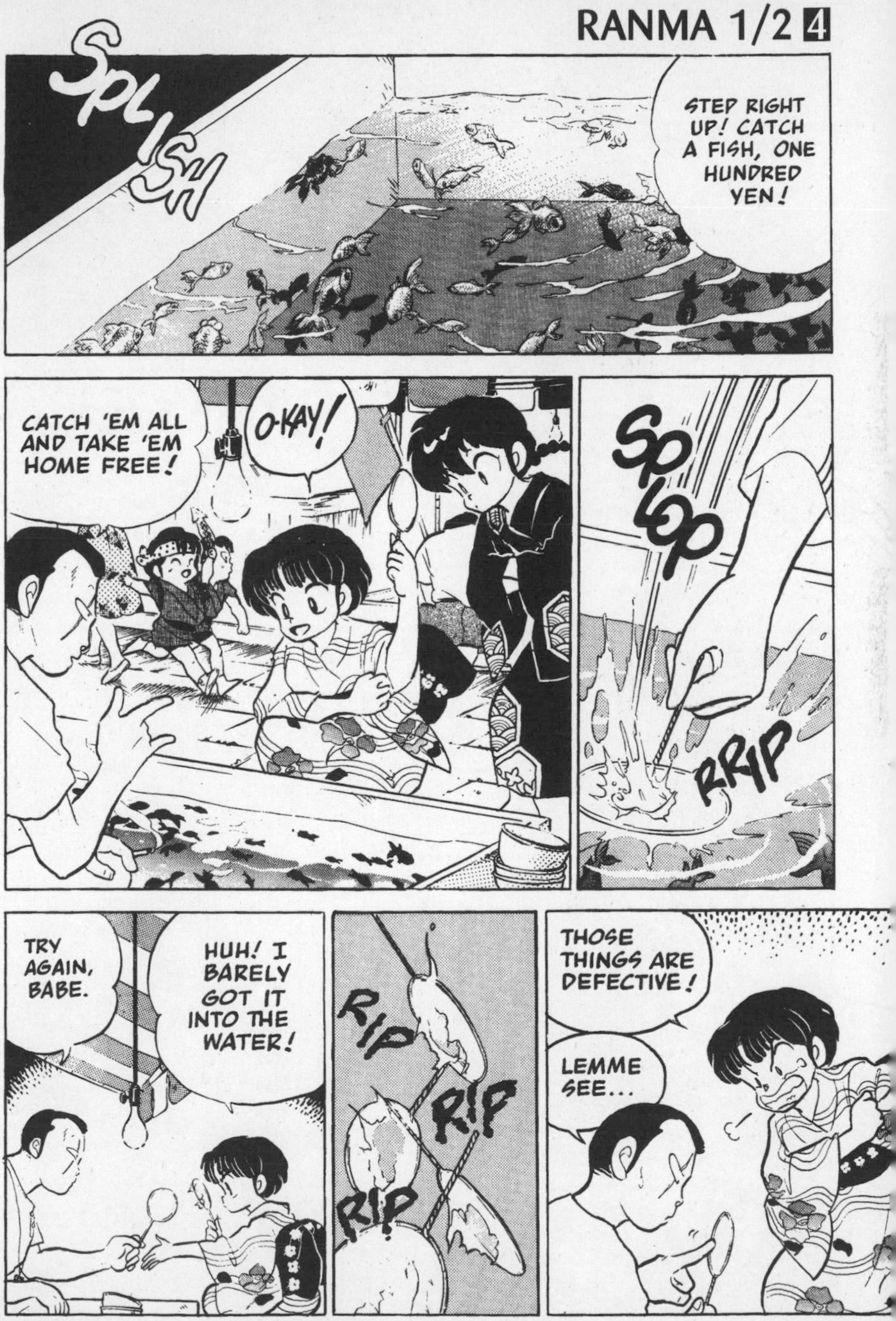
SPLISH
STEP RIGHT UP! CATCH A FISH, ONE HUNDRED YEN!
CATCH 'EM ALL AND TAKE 'EM HOME FREE!
O-KAY!
SPLOP
RRIP
TRY AGAIN, BABE.
HUH! I BARELY GOT IT INTO THE WATER!
RIP
RIP
RIP
THOSE THINGS ARE DEFECTIVE!
LEMME SEE...

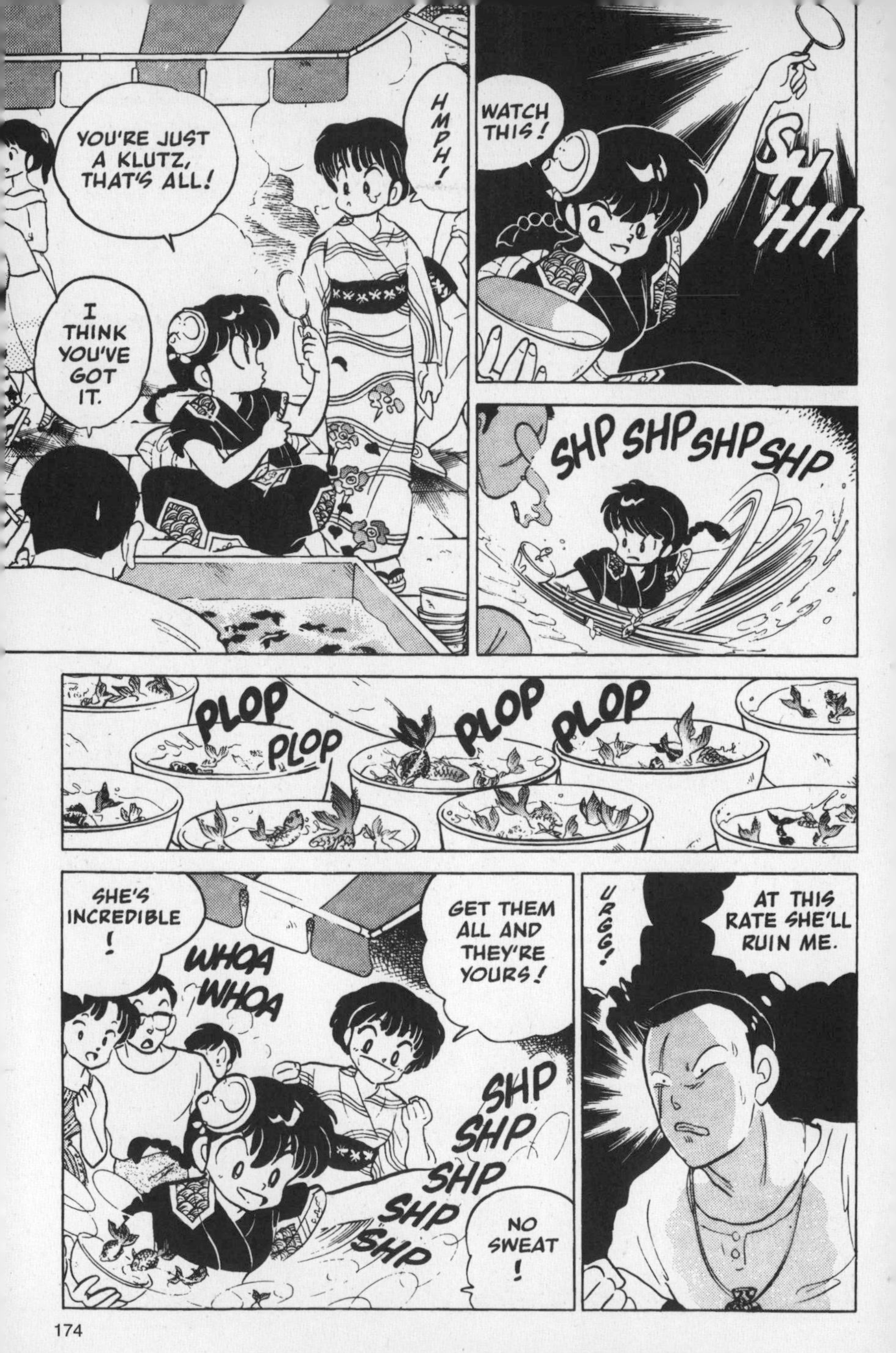
YOU'RE JUST A KLUTZ, THAT'S ALL!
HMPH!
I THINK YOU'VE GOT IT.
WATCH THIS!
SHHHH
SHP SHP SHP SHP
PLOP
PLOP
PLOP
PLOP
SHE'S INCREDIBLE!
WHOA WHOA
GET THEM ALL AND THEY'RE YOURS!
SHP SHP SHP SHP SHP
NO SWEAT!
URGG!
AT THIS RATE SHE'LL RUIN ME.

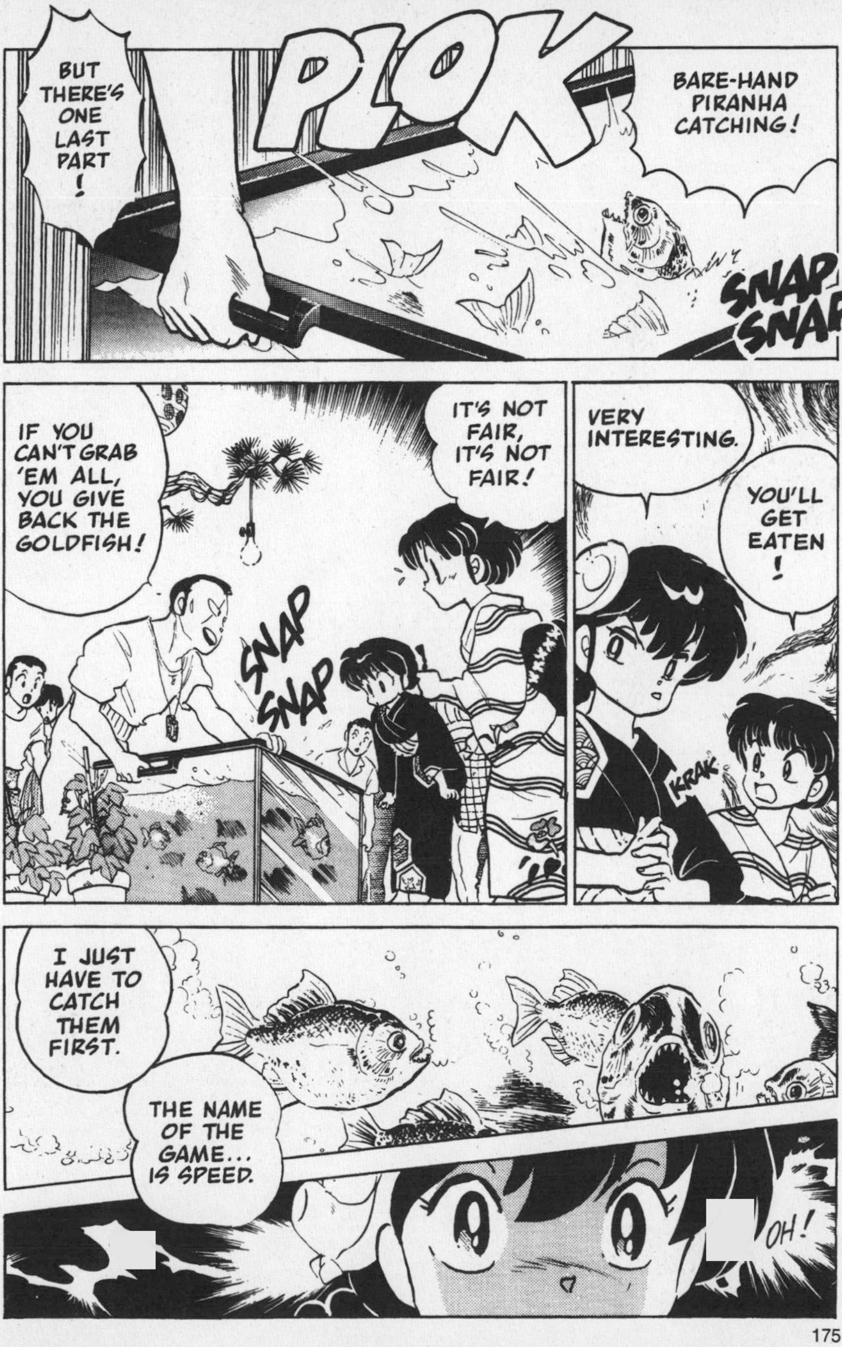
BUT THERE'S ONE LAST PART!
PLOK
BARE-HAND PIRANHA CATCHING!
SNAP SNAP
IF YOU CAN'T GRAB 'EM ALL, YOU GIVE BACK THE GOLDFISH!
IT'S NOT FAIR, IT'S NOT FAIR!
SNAP SNAP
VERY INTERESTING.
YOU'LL GET EATEN!
KRAK
I JUST HAVE TO CATCH THEM FIRST.
THE NAME OF THE GAME... IS SPEED.
OH!

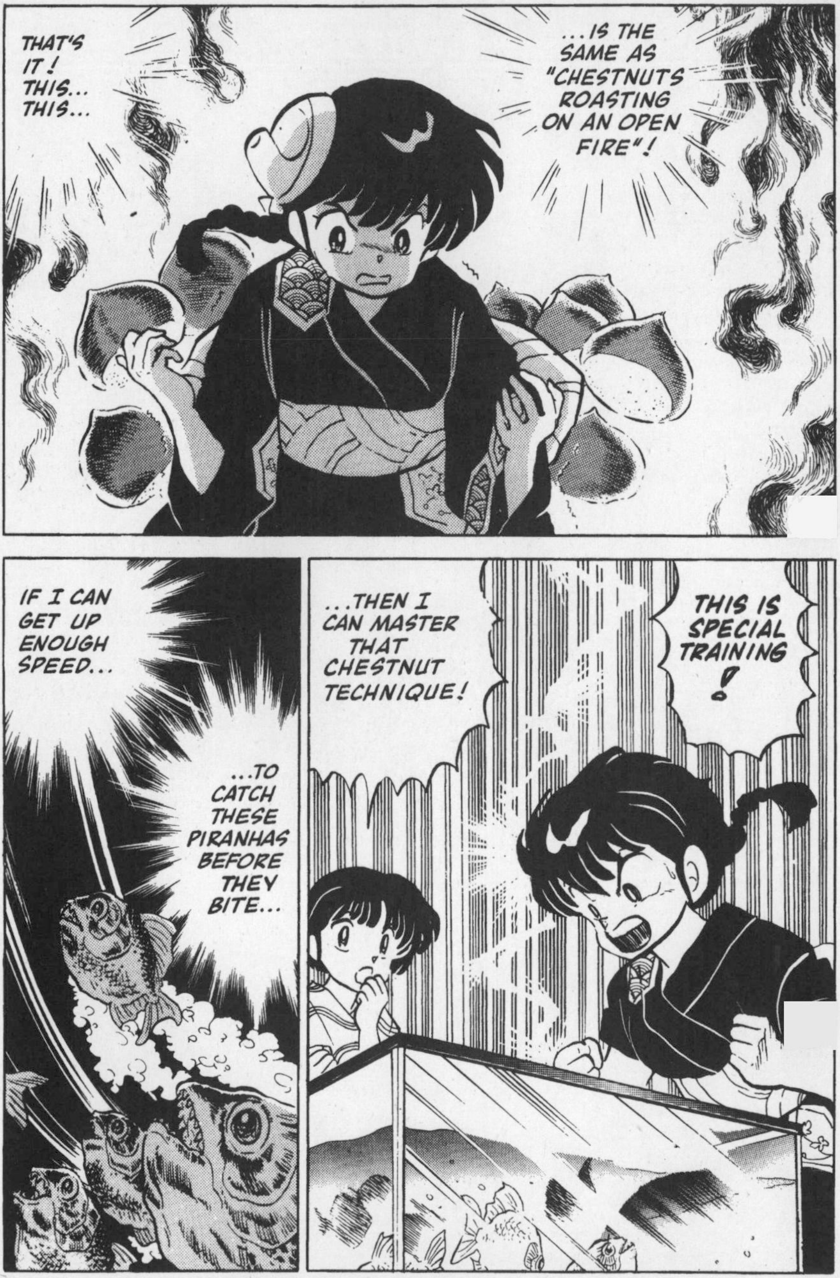
THAT'S IT! THIS... THIS...
...IS THE SAME AS "CHESTNUTS ROASTING ON AN OPEN FIRE"!
IF I CAN GET UP ENOUGH SPEED...
...TO CATCH THESE PIRANHAS BEFORE THEY BITE...
...THEN I CAN MASTER THAT CHESTNUT TECHNIQUE!
THIS IS SPECIAL TRAINING!

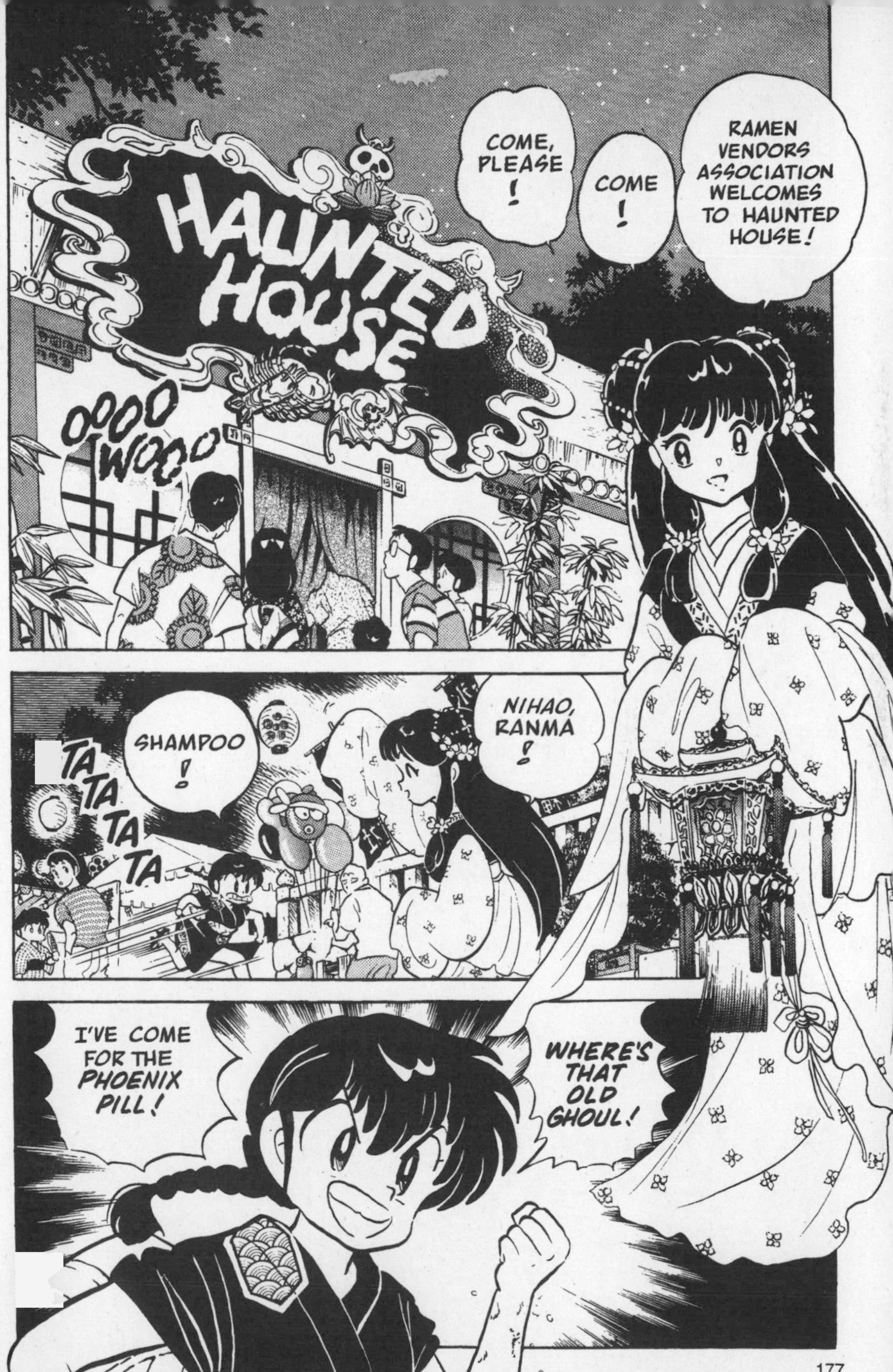
HAUNTED HOUSE
COME, PLEASE!
COME!
RAMEN VENDORS ASSOCIATION WELCOMES TO HAUNTED HOUSE!
OOOO WOOO
TA TA TA TA TA
SHAMPOO!
NIHAO, RANMA!
I'VE COME FOR THE PHOENIX PILL!
WHERE'S THAT OLD GHOUL!

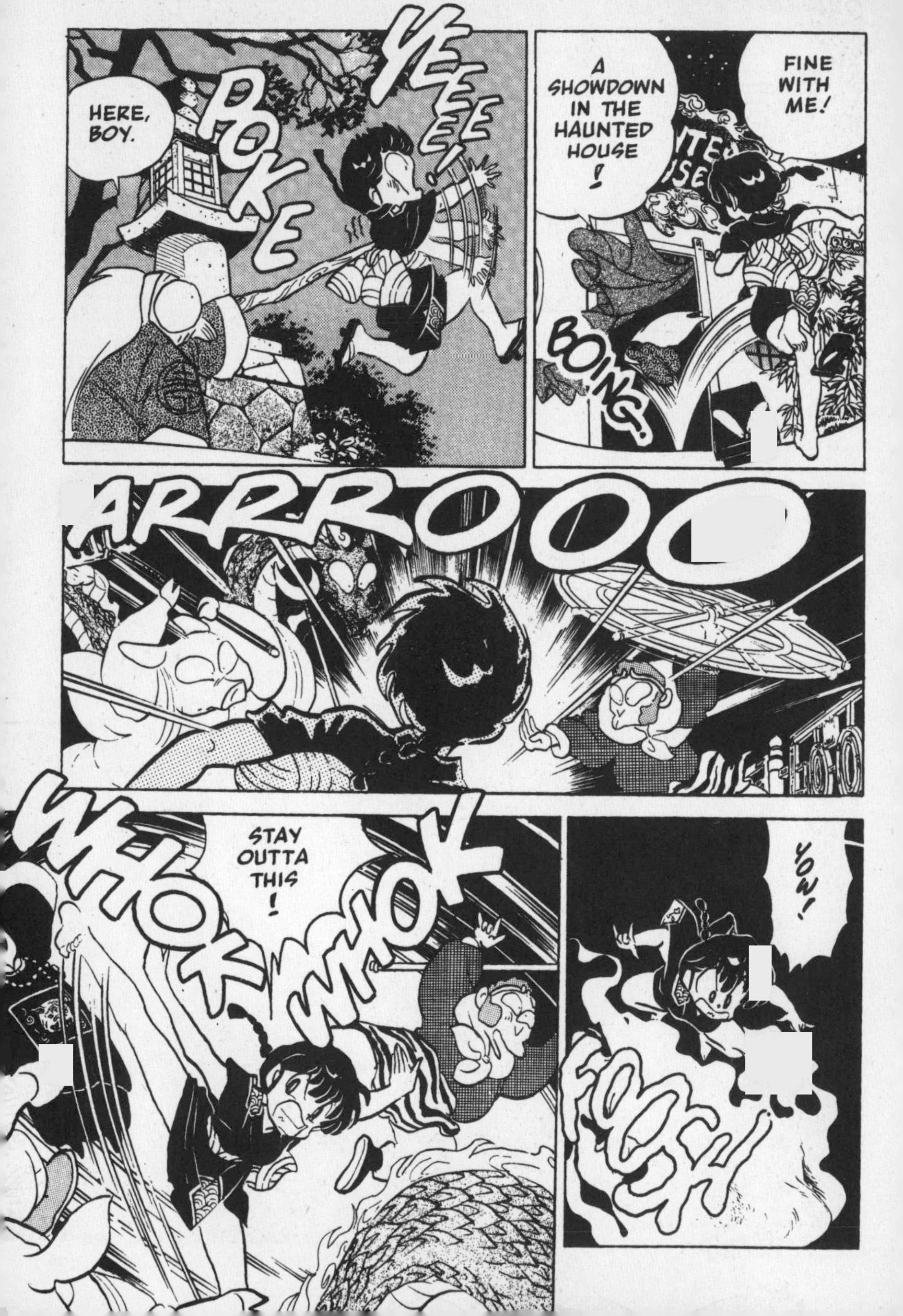
HERE, BOY.
POKE
YEEEEE!
A SHOWDOWN IN THE HAUNTED HOUSE!
FINE WITH ME!
BOING!
ARRROOO
WHOK
STAY OUTTA THIS!
WHOK
YOW!
FOOSH!

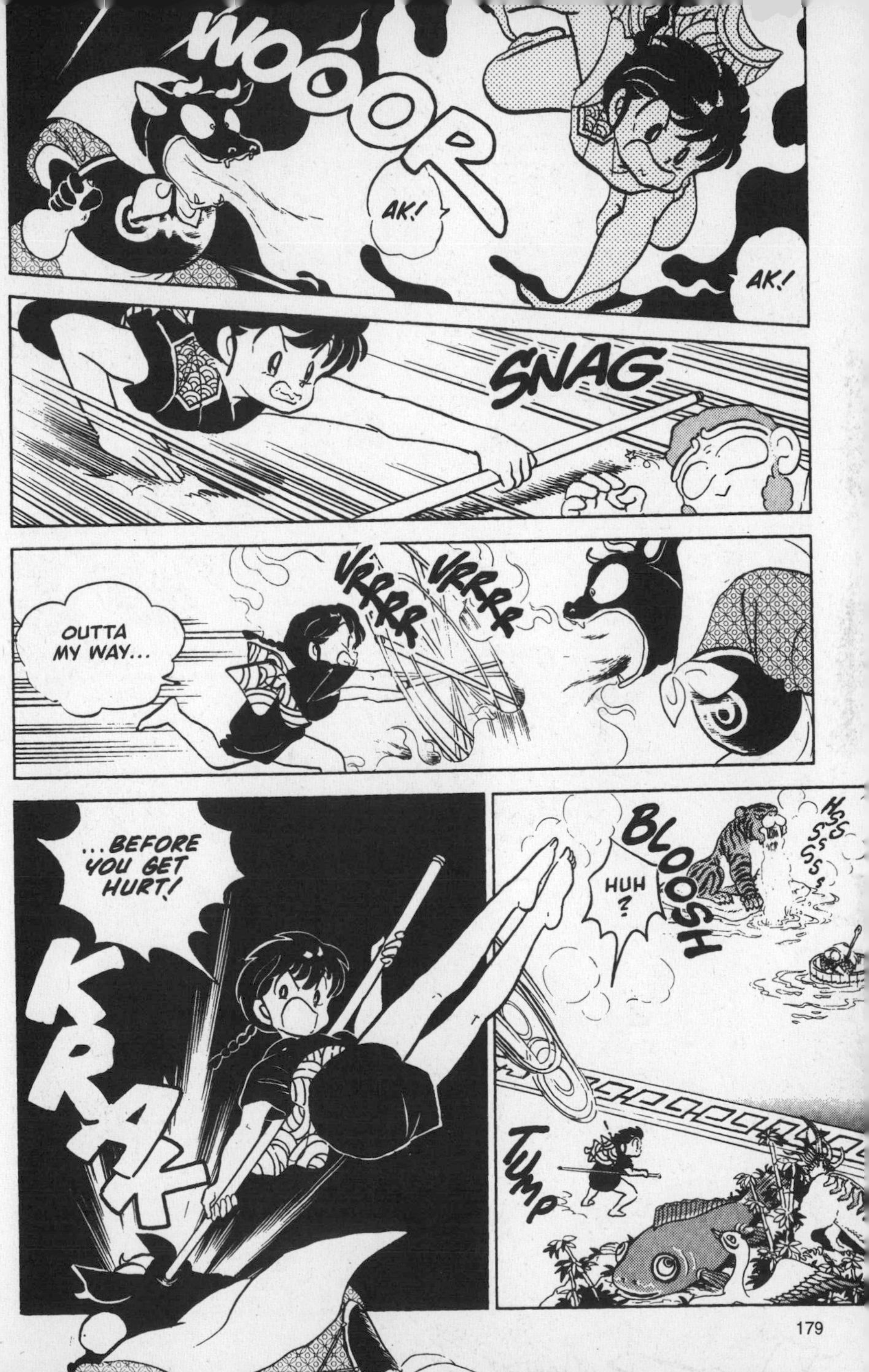
WOOOR
AK!
AK!
SNAG
OUTTA MY WAY...
VRRRRR
VRRRRR
...BEFORE YOU GET HURT!
KRAK
BLOOSH
HUH ?
HSSSSS
TUMP

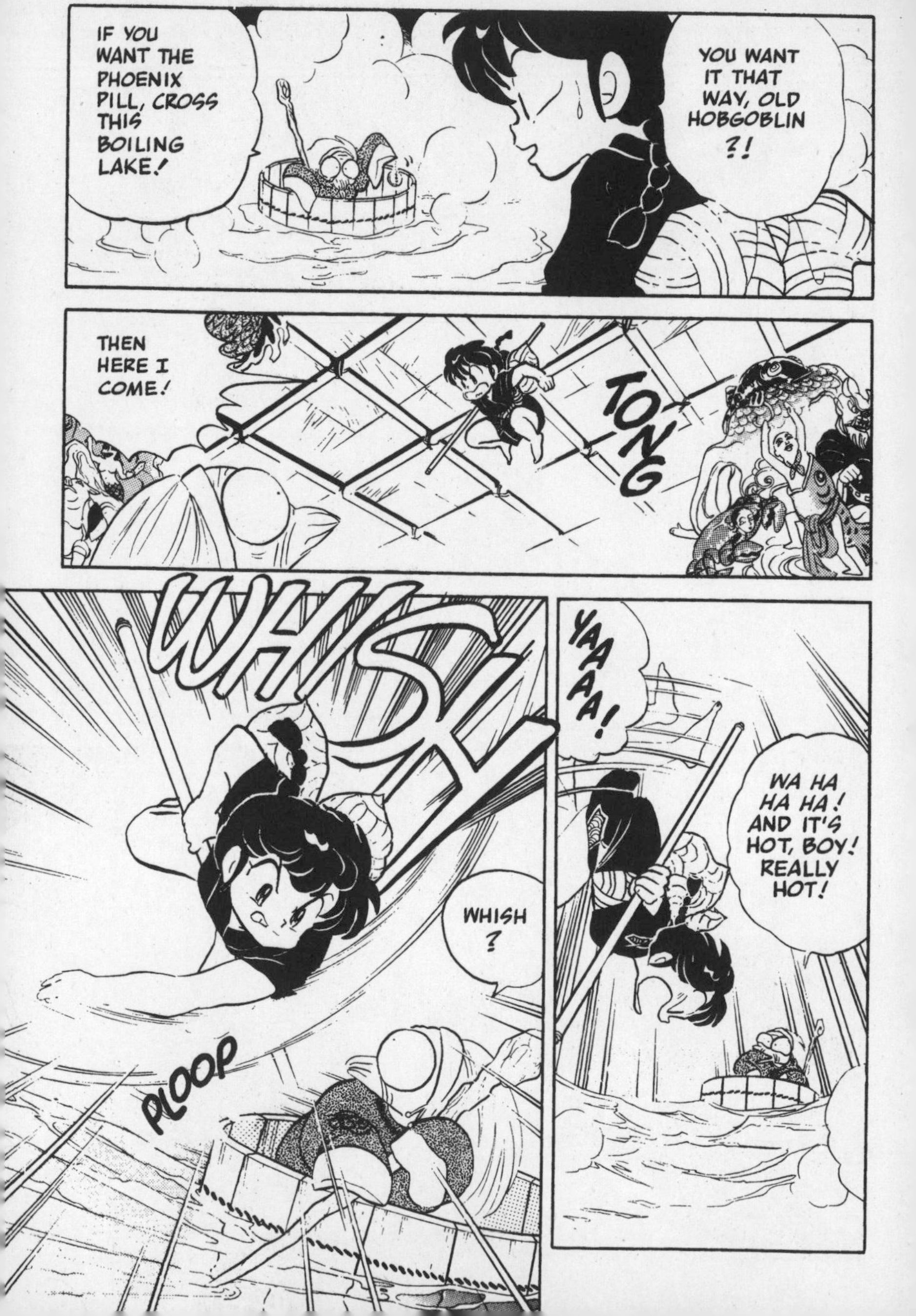
IF YOU WANT THE PHOENIX PILL, CROSS THIS BOILING LAKE!
YOU WANT IT THAT WAY, OLD HOBGOBLIN ?!
THEN HERE I COME!
TONG
WHISH
WHISH ?
PLOOP
YAAAAA!
WA HA HA HA! AND IT'S HOT, BOY! REALLY HOT!

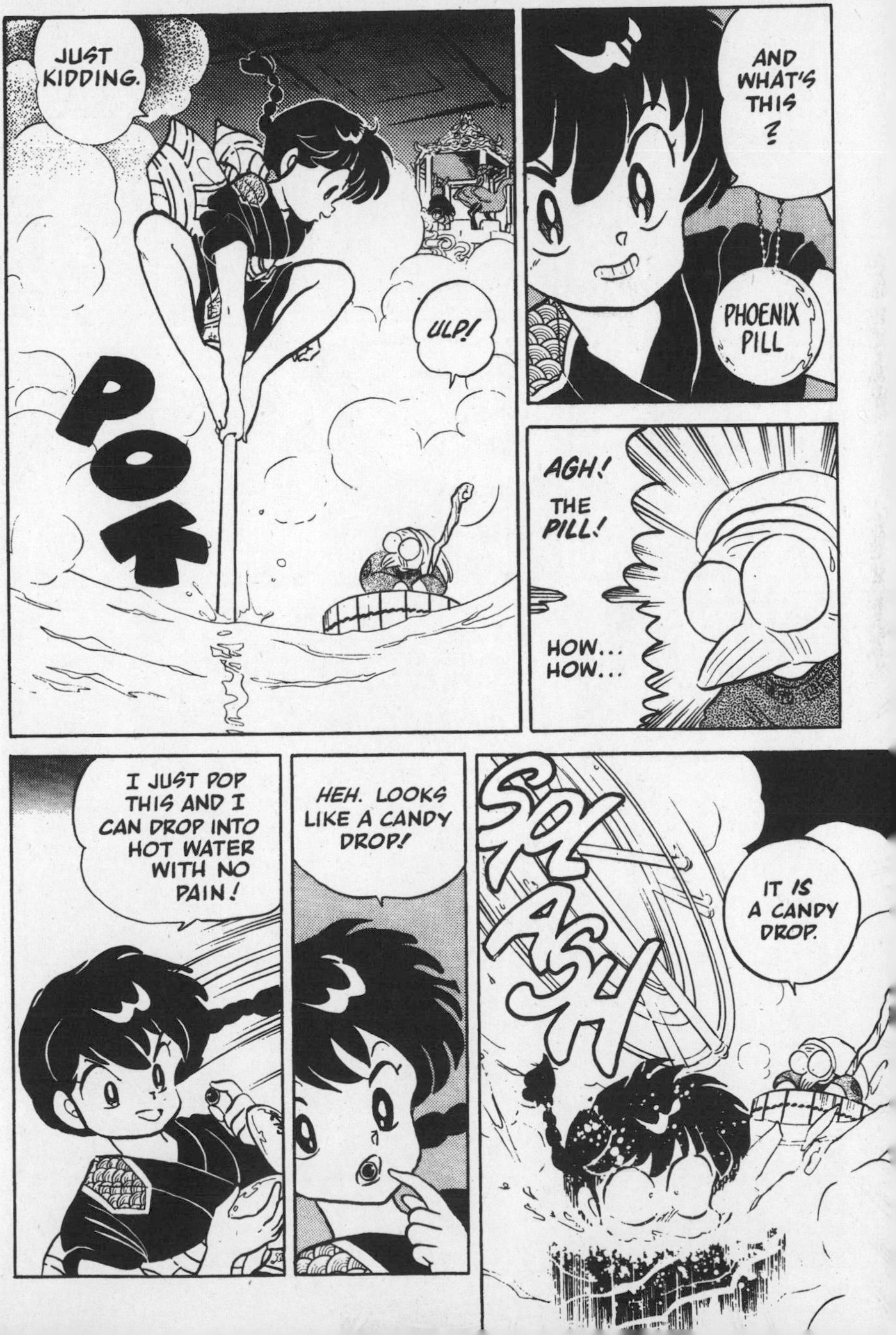
JUST KIDDING.
ULP!
POK
AND WHAT'S THIS ?
PHOENIX PILL
AGH! THE PILL!
HOW... HOW...
I JUST POP THIS AND I CAN DROP INTO HOT WATER WITH NO PAIN!
HEH. LOOKS LIKE A CANDY DROP!
SPLASH
IT IS A CANDY DROP.

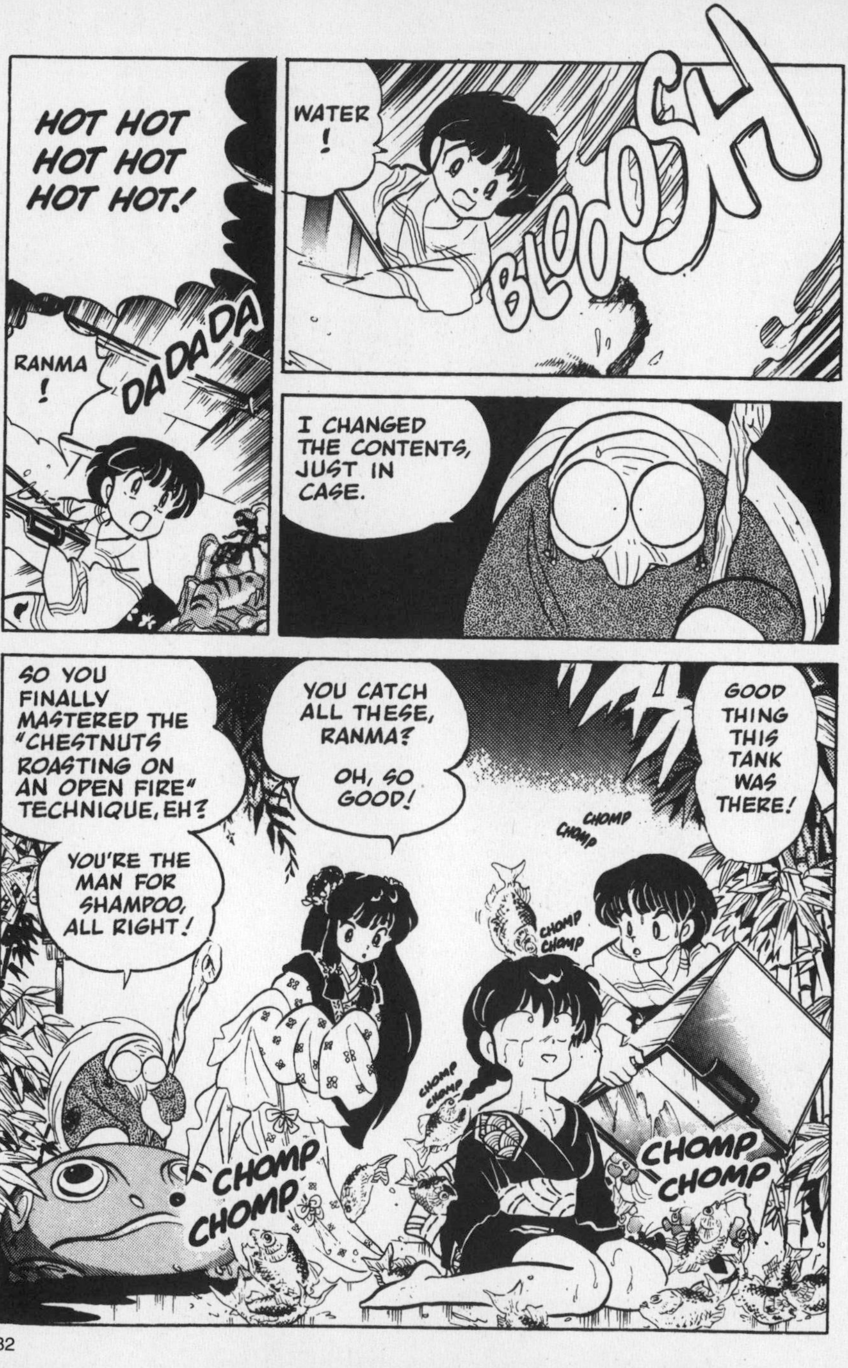
HOT HOT HOT HOT HOT HOT!
RANMA!
DADADA
WATER!
BLOOOSH
I CHANGED THE CONTENTS, JUST IN CASE.
SO YOU FINALLY MASTERED THE "CHESTNUTS ROASTING ON AN OPEN FIRE" TECHNIQUE, EH?
YOU'RE THE MAN FOR SHAMPOO, ALL RIGHT!
YOU CATCH ALL THESE, RANMA?
OH, SO GOOD!
GOOD THING THIS TANK WAS THERE!
CHOMP CHOMP
CHOMP CHOMP
CHOMP CHOMP
CHOMP CHOMP
CHOMP CHOMP

Part 12

WAR OF THE MELONS

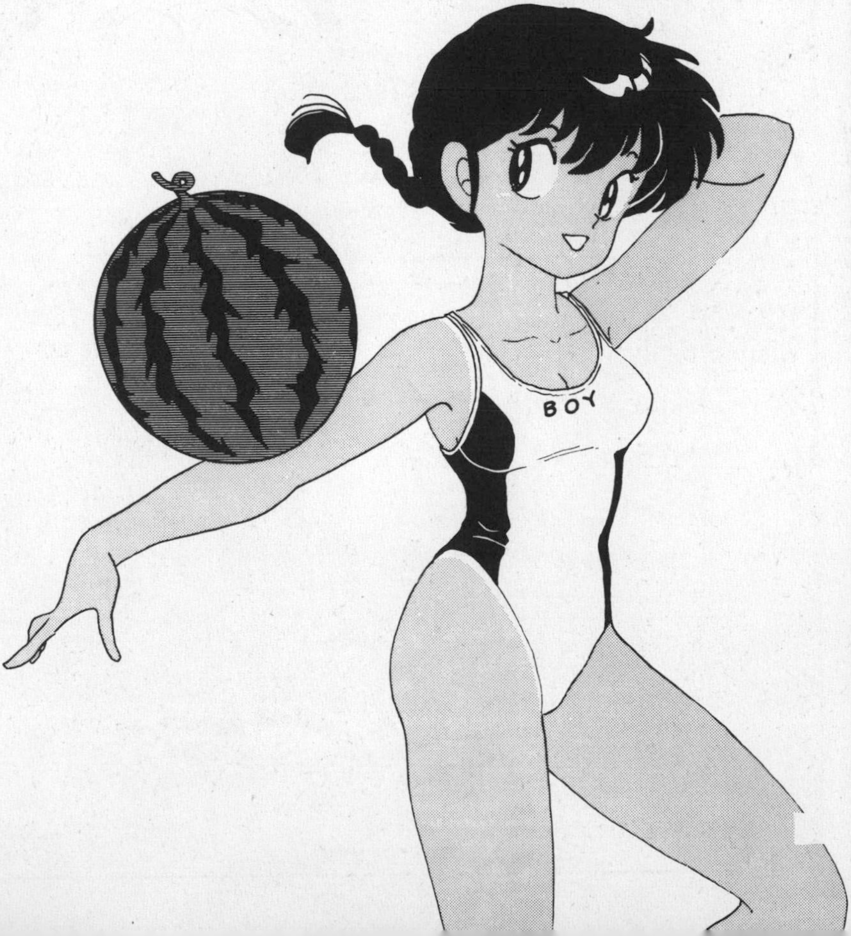
BOY

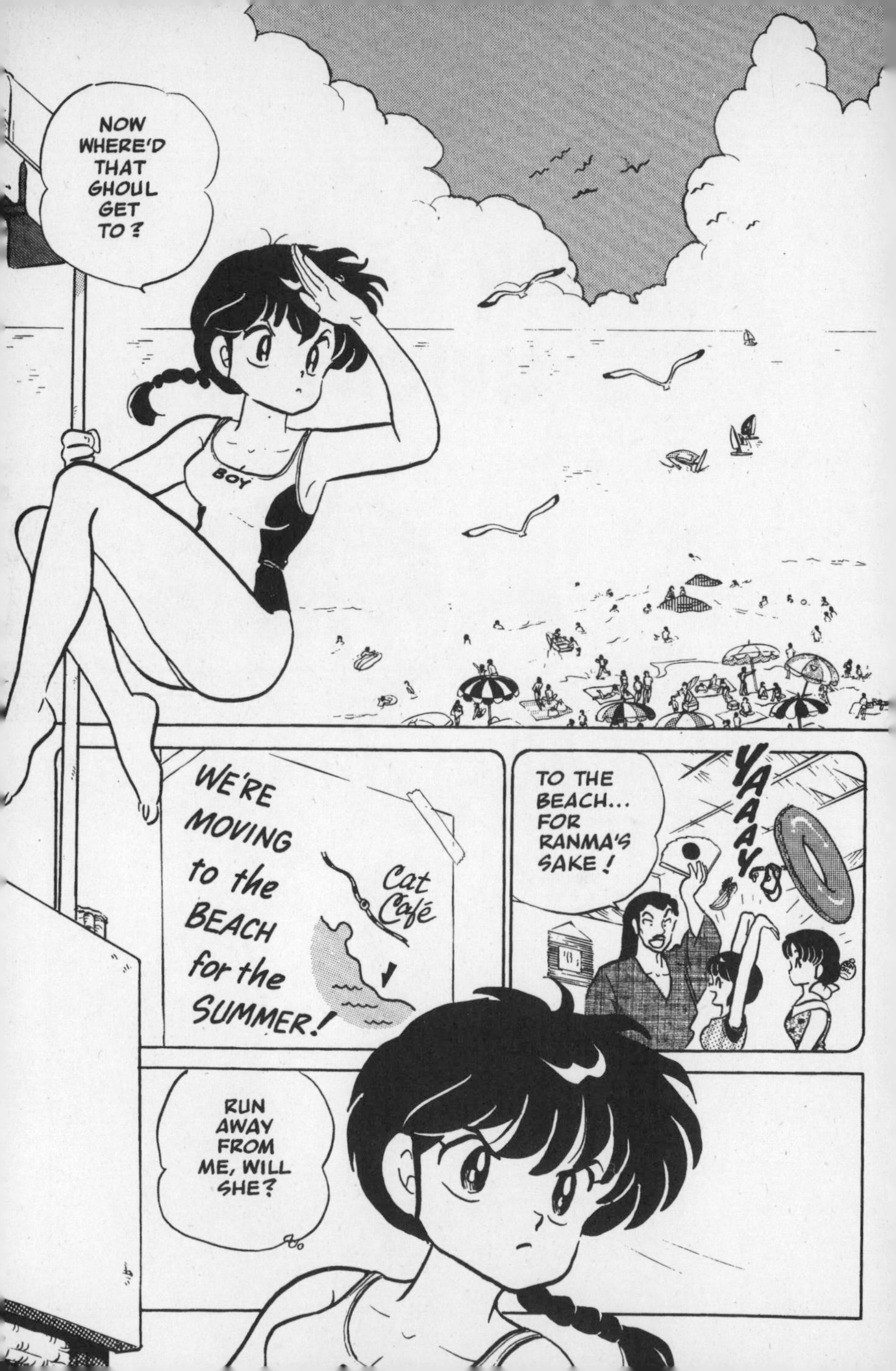
NOW WHERE'D THAT GHOUL GET TO?
BOY
WE'RE MOVING to the BEACH for the SUMMER!
Cat Café
TO THE BEACH... FOR RANMA'S SAKE!
YAAAAY
RUN AWAY FROM ME, WILL SHE?

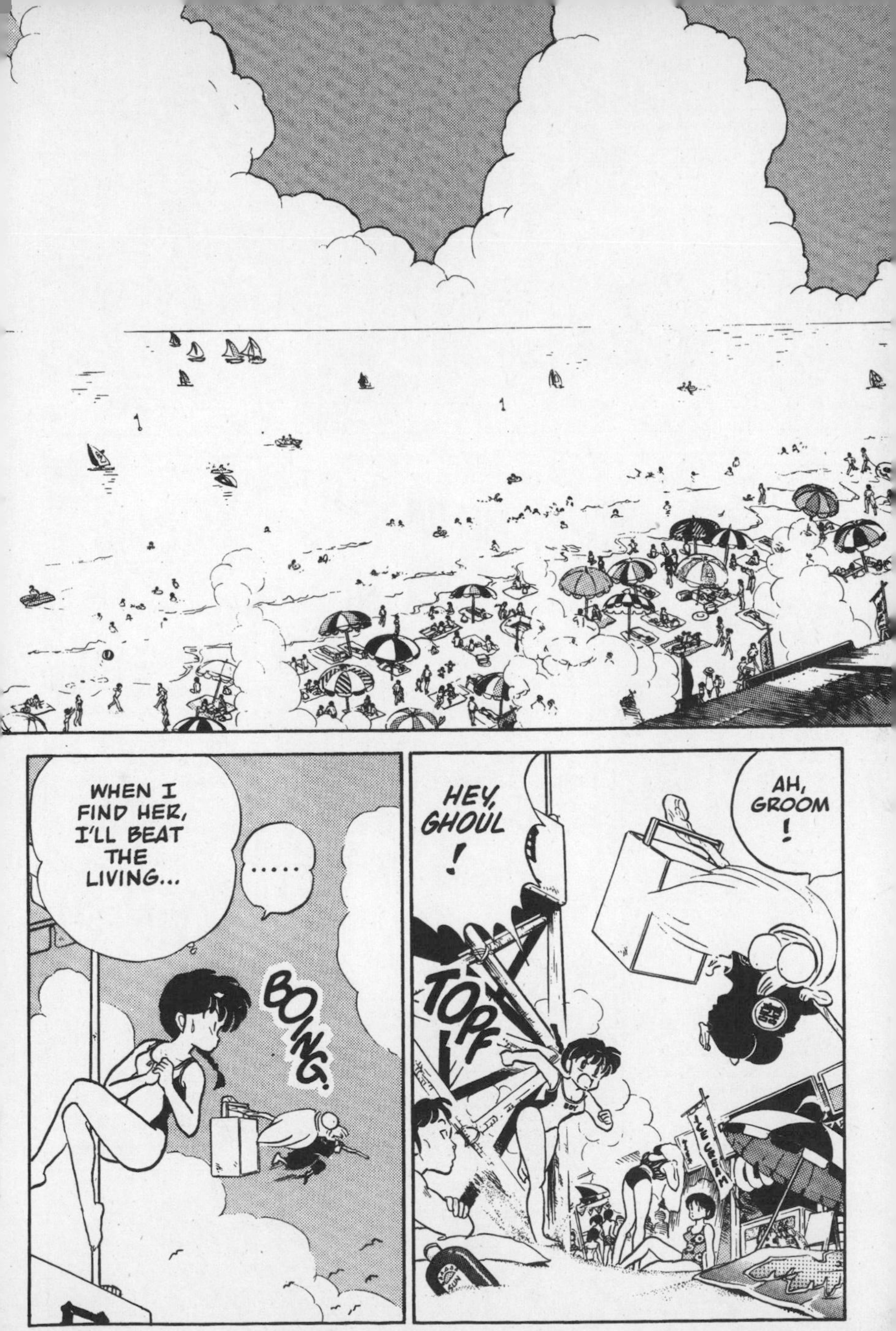
WHEN I FIND HER, I'LL BEAT THE LIVING...
......
BOING!
HEY, GHOUL!
TOPP
AH, GROOM!

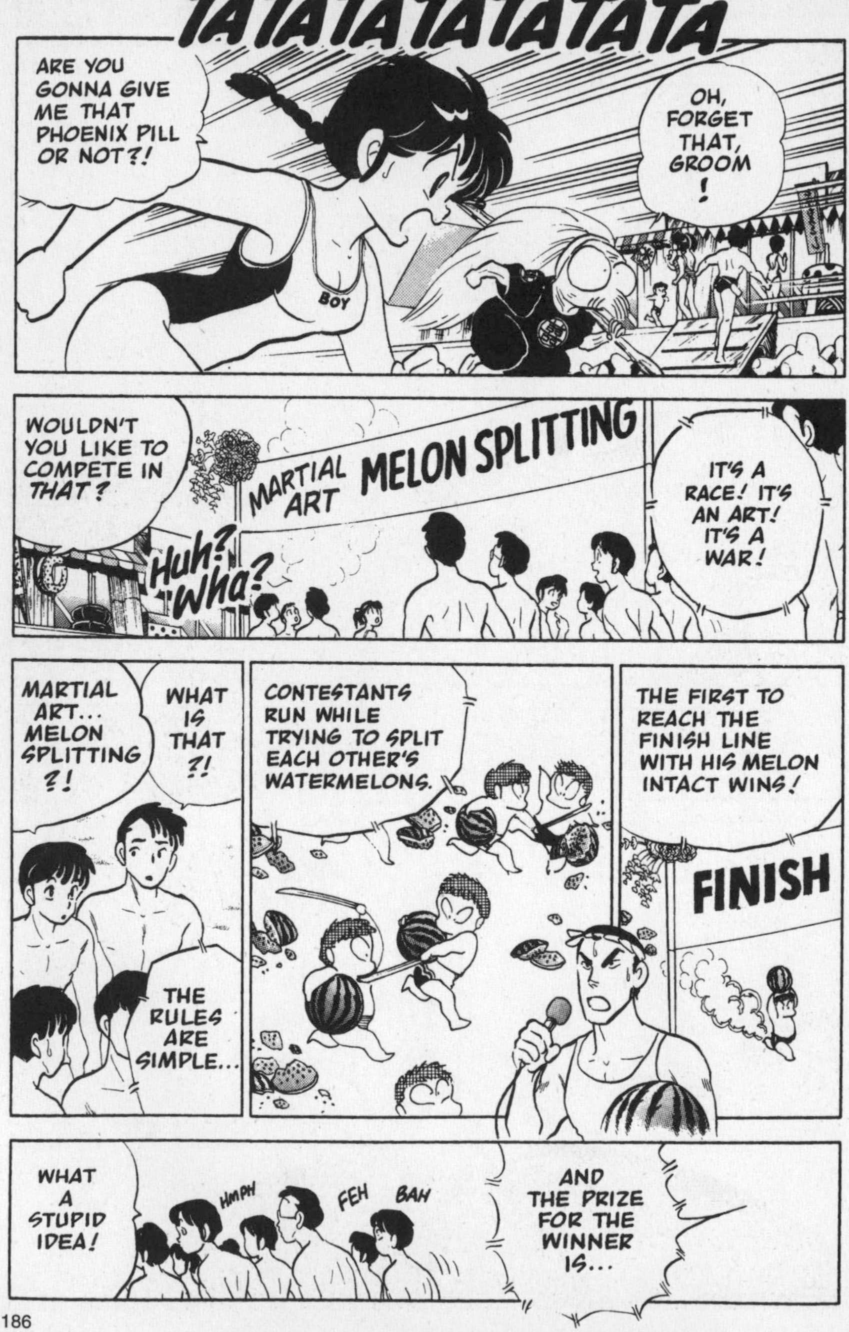

TATATATATATATA
ARE YOU GONNA GIVE ME THAT PHOENIX PILL OR NOT?!
OH, FORGET THAT, GROOM!
BOY
WOULDN'T YOU LIKE TO COMPETE IN THAT?
MARTIAL ART MELON SPLITTING
Huh? Wha?
IT'S A RACE! IT'S AN ART! IT'S A WAR!
MARTIAL ART... MELON SPLITTING?!
WHAT IS THAT?!
THE RULES ARE SIMPLE...
CONTESTANTS RUN WHILE TRYING TO SPLIT EACH OTHER'S WATERMELONS.
THE FIRST TO REACH THE FINISH LINE WITH HIS MELON INTACT WINS!
FINISH
WHAT A STUPID IDEA!
HMPH
FEH
BAH
AND THE PRIZE FOR THE WINNER IS...

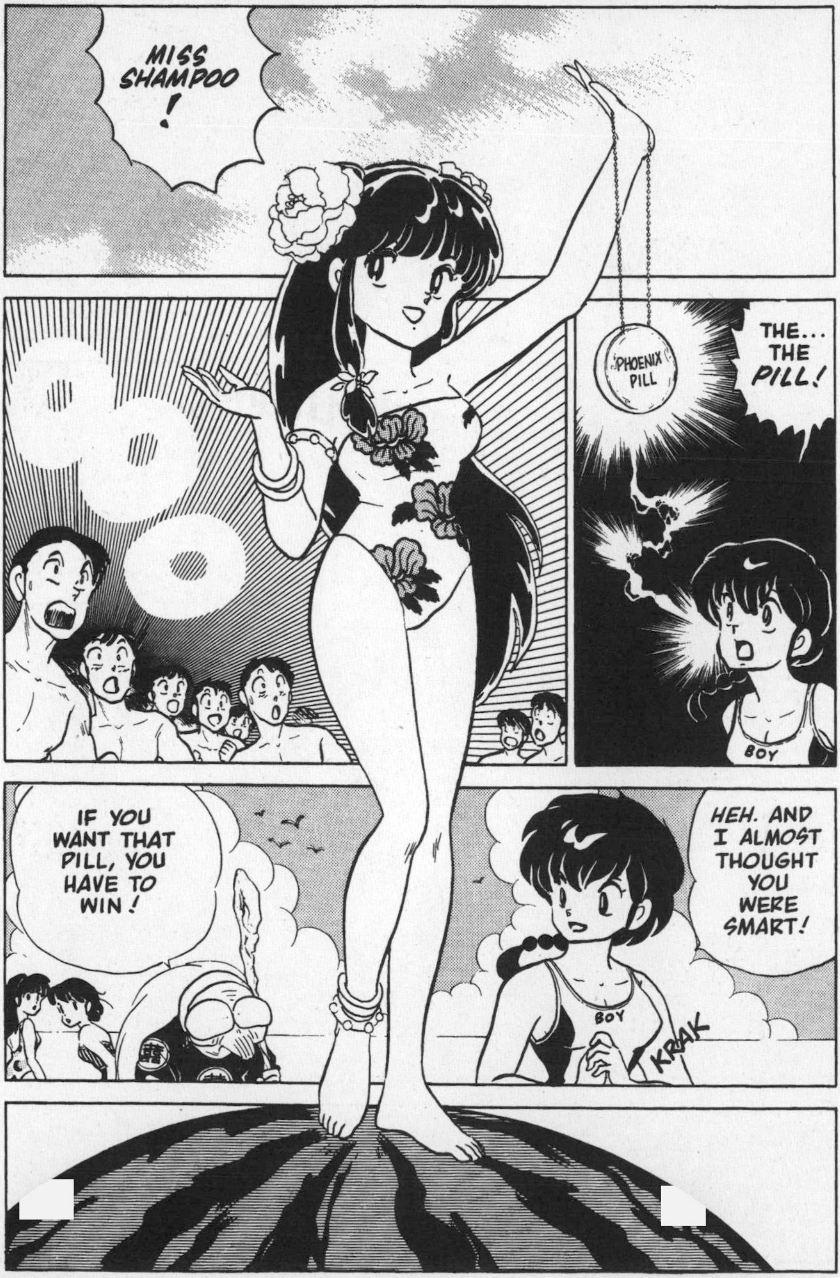
MISS SHAMPOO!
PHOENIX PILL
THE... THE PILL!
BOY
IF YOU WANT THAT PILL, YOU HAVE TO WIN!
HEH. AND I ALMOST THOUGHT YOU WERE SMART!
BOY
KRAK

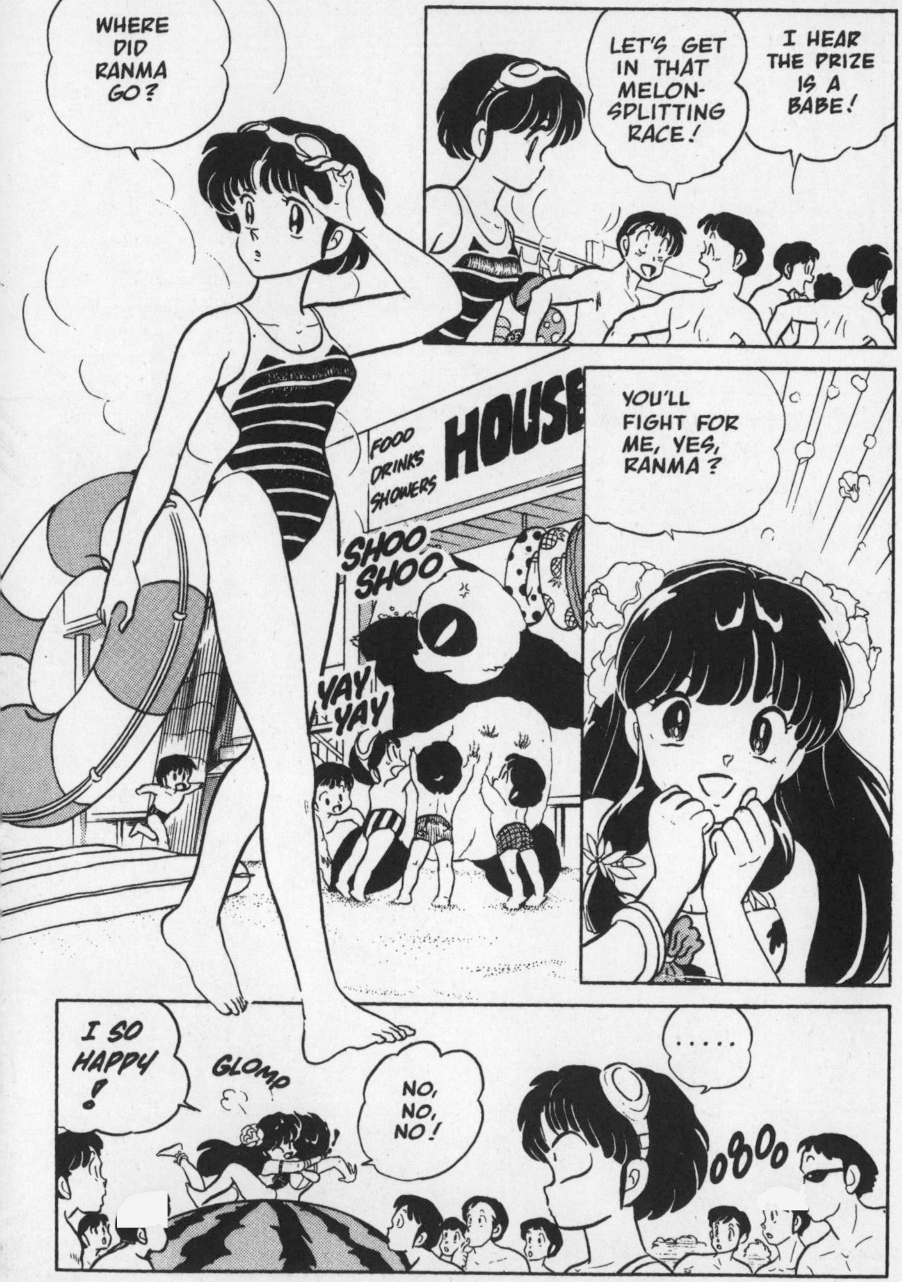
WHERE DID RANMA GO?
FOOD
DRINKS
SHOWERS
HOUSE
SHOO SHOO
YAY YAY
LET'S GET IN THAT MELON-SPLITTING RACE!
I HEAR THE PRIZE IS A BABE!
YOU'LL FIGHT FOR ME, YES, RANMA?
I SO HAPPY!
GLOMP
NO, NO, NO!
.....

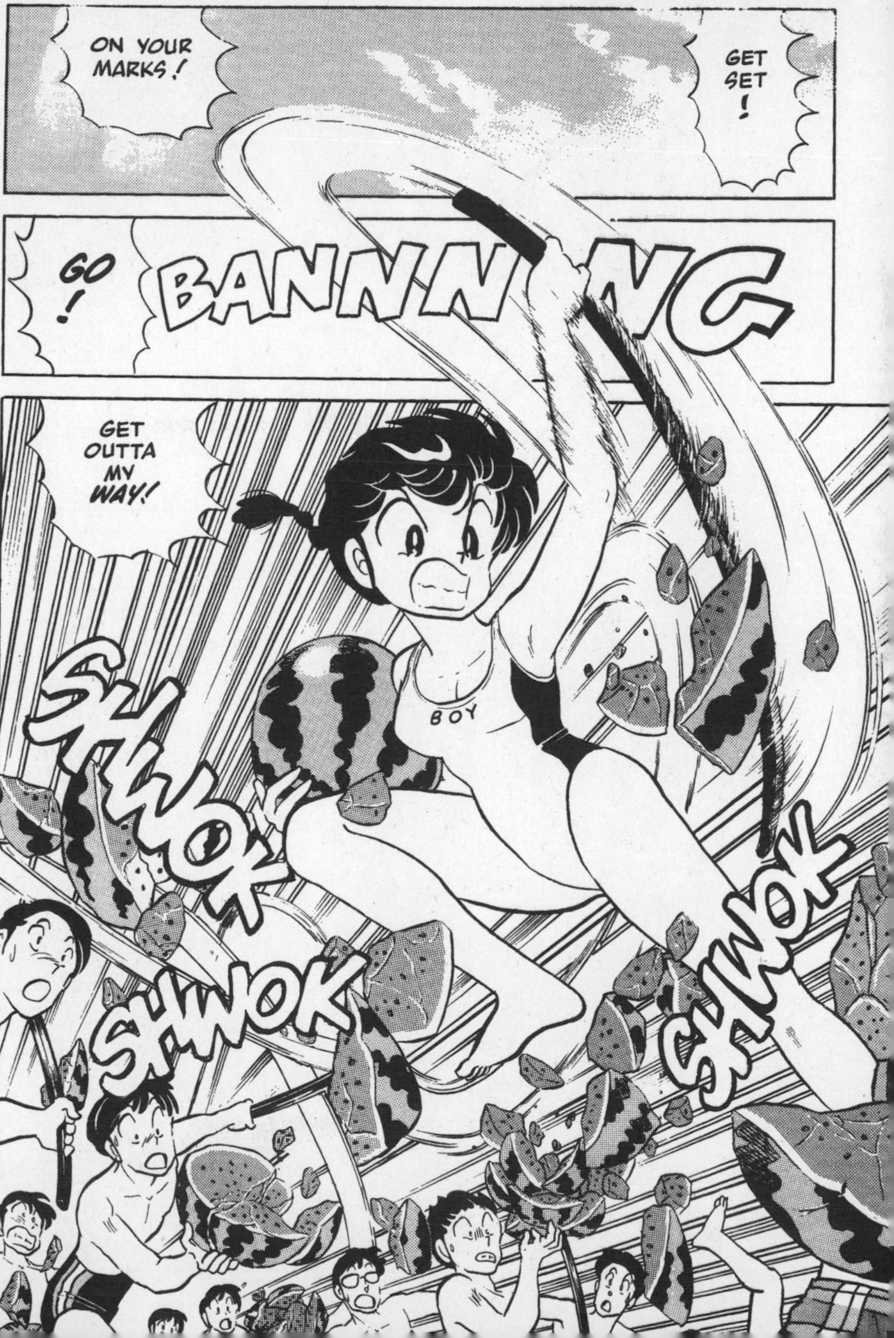
ON YOUR MARKS!
GET SET!
GO!
BANNNNNG
GET OUTTA MY WAY!
SHWOK
SHWOK
SHWOK
BOY

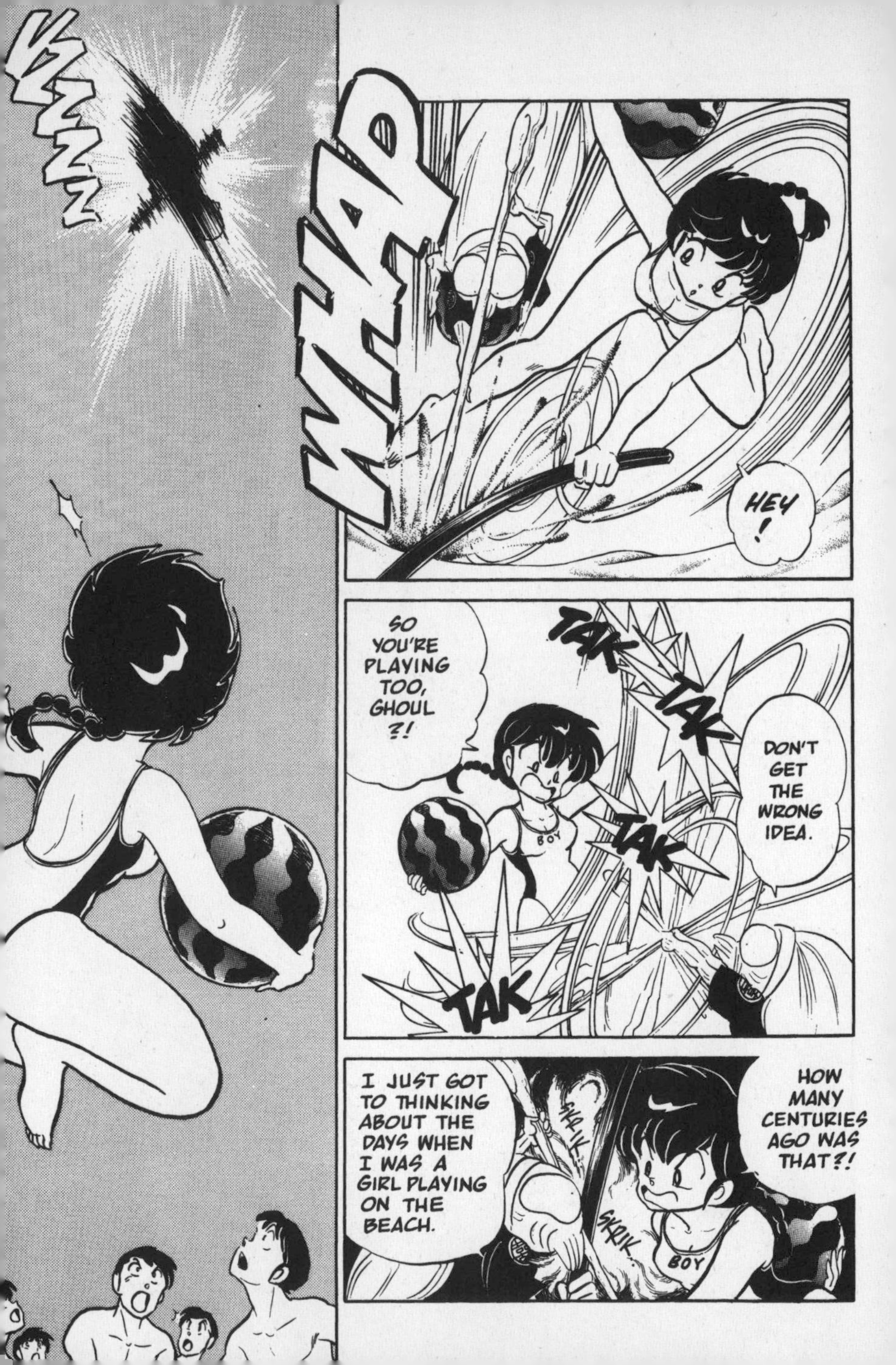
WHAP
HEY!
SO YOU'RE PLAYING TOO, GHOUL ?!
TAK
TAK
DON'T GET THE WRONG IDEA.
TAK
TAK
I JUST GOT TO THINKING ABOUT THE DAYS WHEN I WAS A GIRL PLAYING ON THE BEACH.
SKRIK
SKRIK
HOW MANY CENTURIES AGO WAS THAT?!

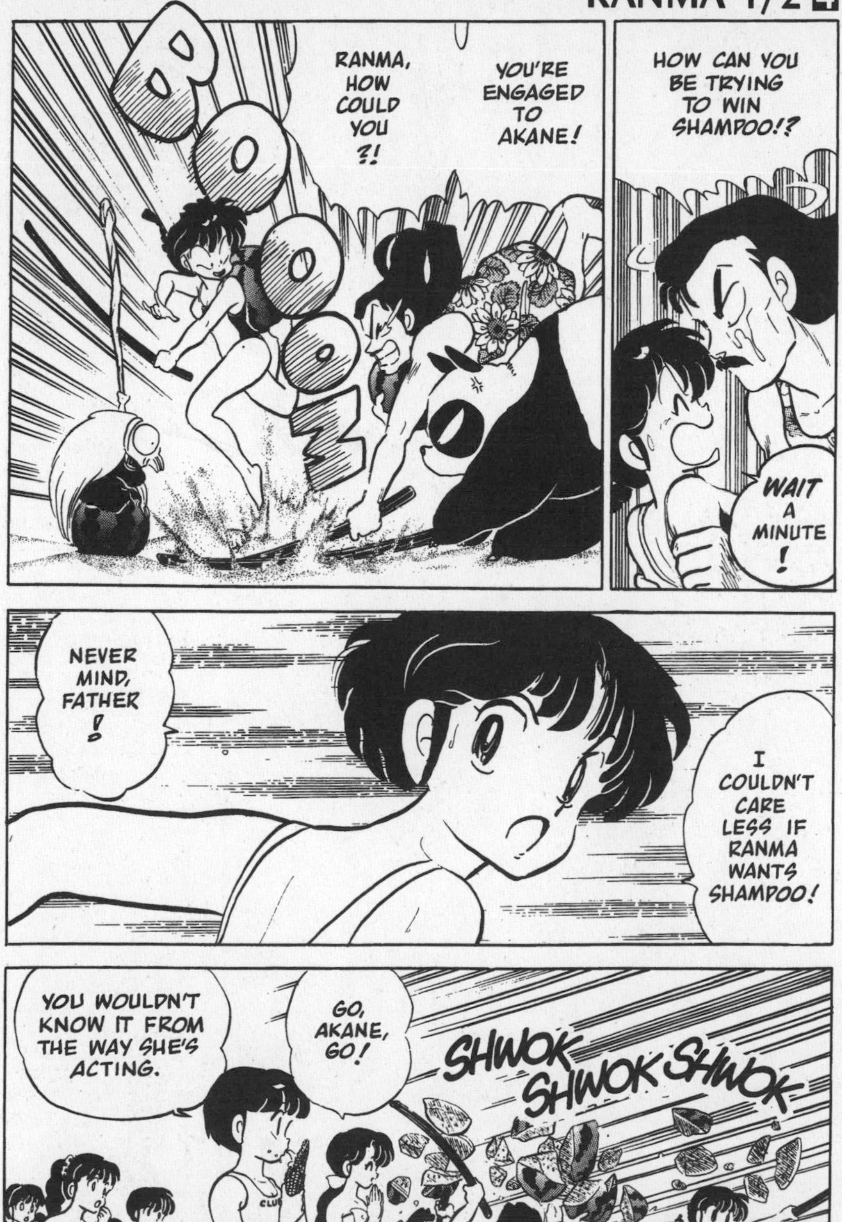
BOOOOM
RANMA, HOW COULD YOU ?!
YOU'RE ENGAGED TO AKANE!
HOW CAN YOU BE TRYING TO WIN SHAMPOO!?
WAIT A MINUTE !
NEVER MIND, FATHER !
I COULDN'T CARE LESS IF RANMA WANTS SHAMPOO!
YOU WOULDN'T KNOW IT FROM THE WAY SHE'S ACTING.
GO, AKANE, GO!
SHWOK SHWOK SHWOK

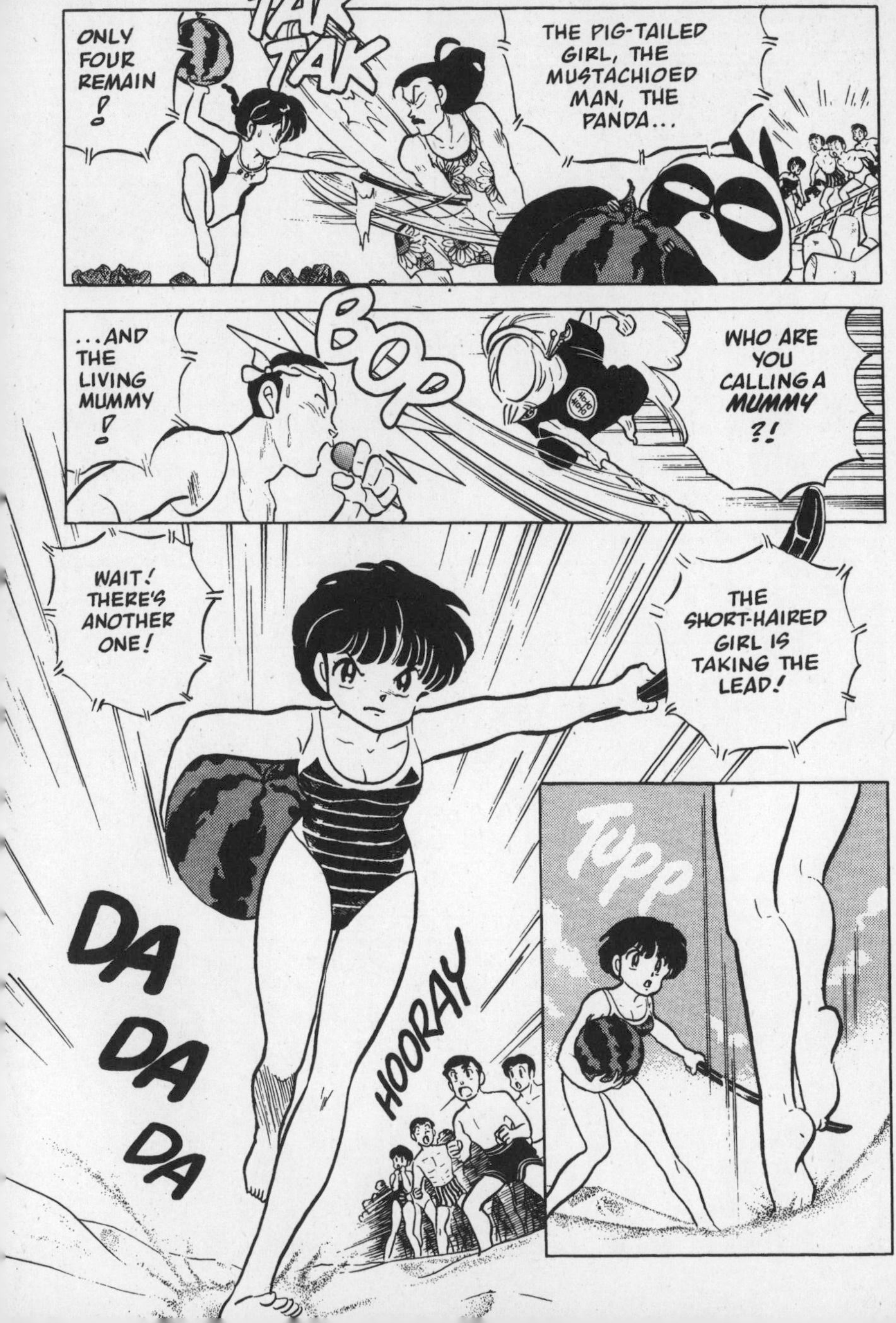
TAK TAK
ONLY FOUR REMAIN!
THE PIG-TAILED GIRL, THE MUSTACHIOED MAN, THE PANDA...
...AND THE LIVING MUMMY!
BOP
WHO ARE YOU CALLING A MUMMY?!
WAIT! THERE'S ANOTHER ONE!
THE SHORT-HAIRED GIRL IS TAKING THE LEAD!
DA DA DA DA
HOORAY
TUPP

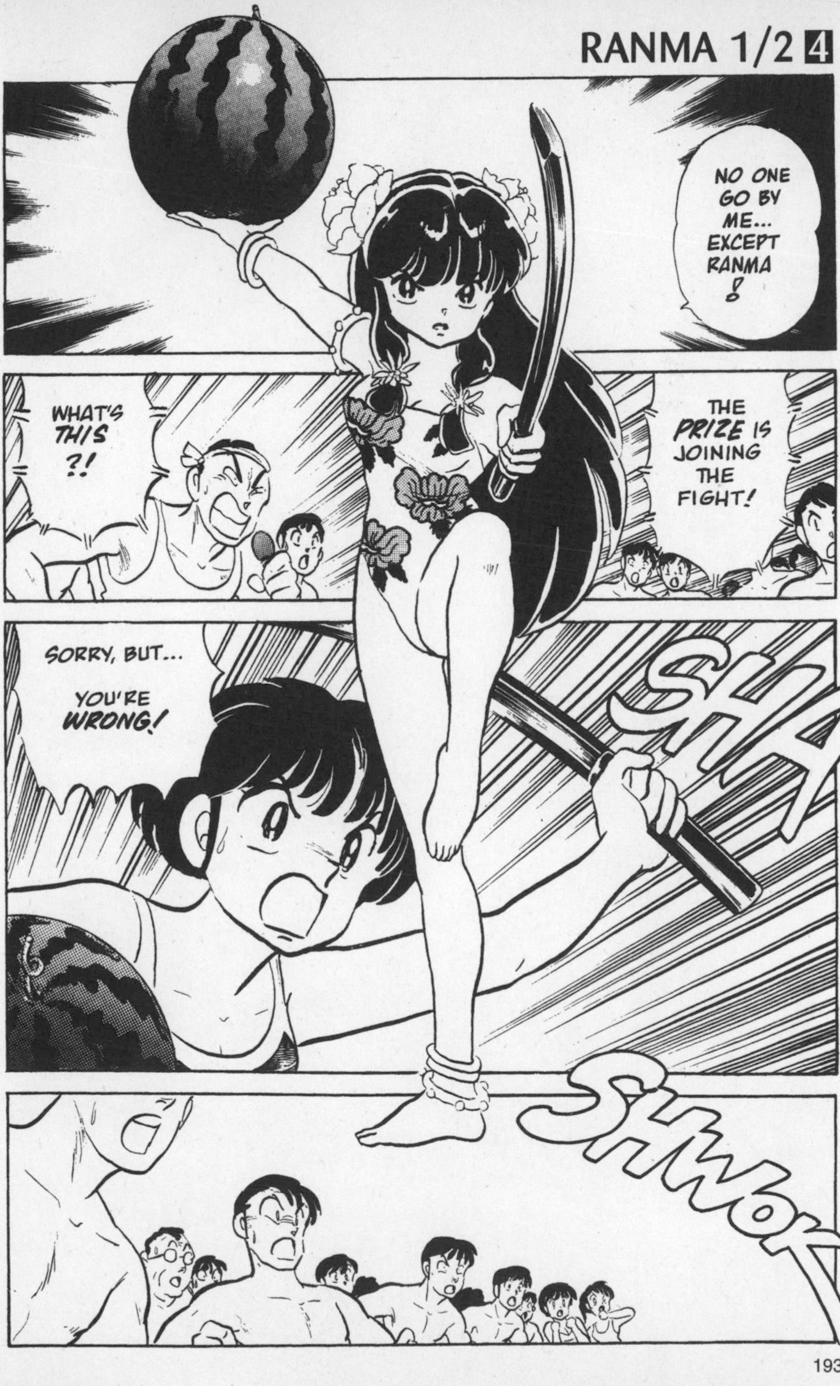
NO ONE GO BY ME... EXCEPT RANMA!
WHAT'S THIS ?!
THE PRIZE IS JOINING THE FIGHT!
SORRY, BUT...
YOU'RE WRONG!
SHA
SHWOK

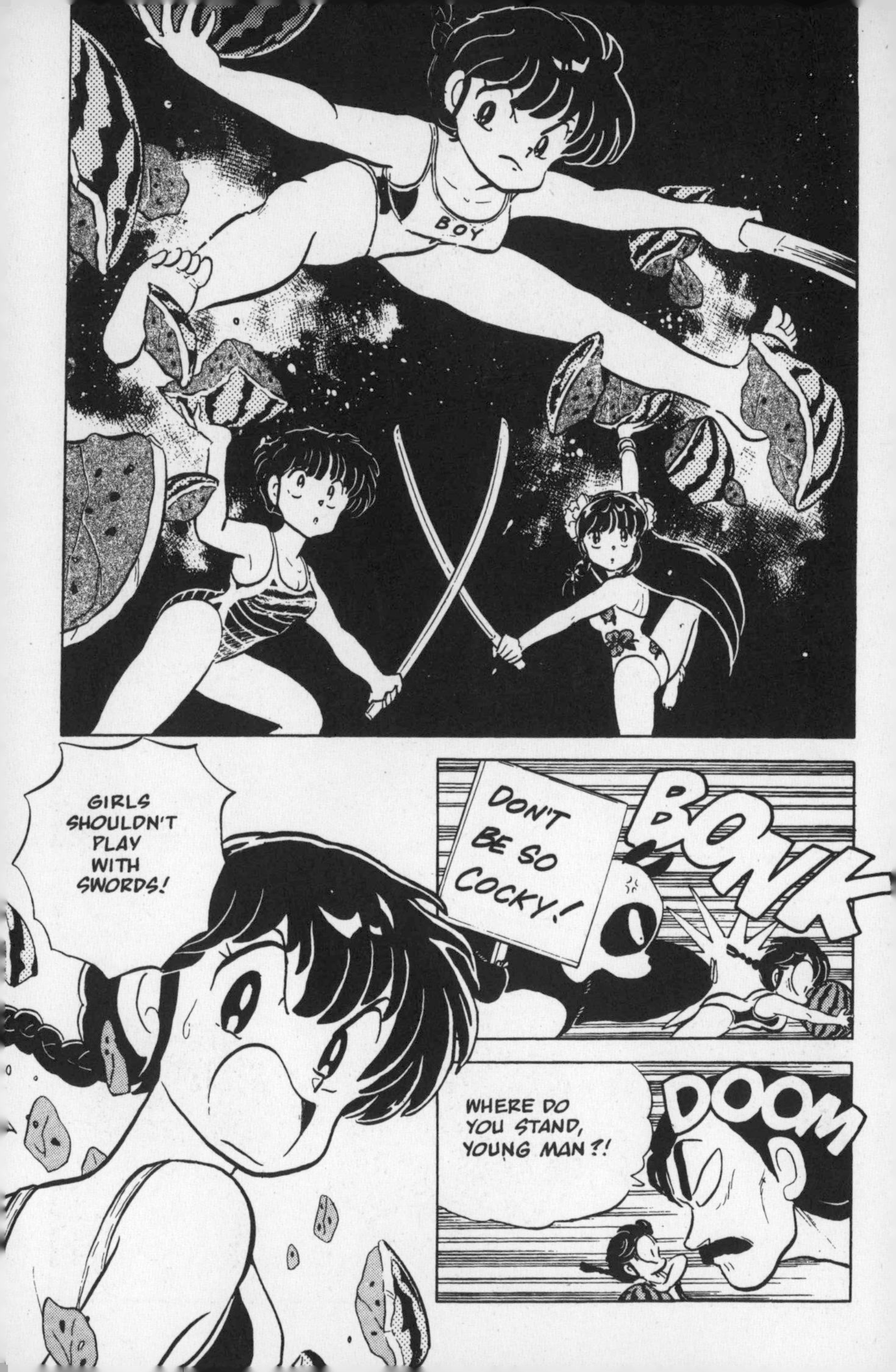
GIRLS SHOULDN'T PLAY WITH SWORDS!
DON'T BE SO COCKY!
BONK
WHERE DO YOU STAND, YOUNG MAN?!
DOOM

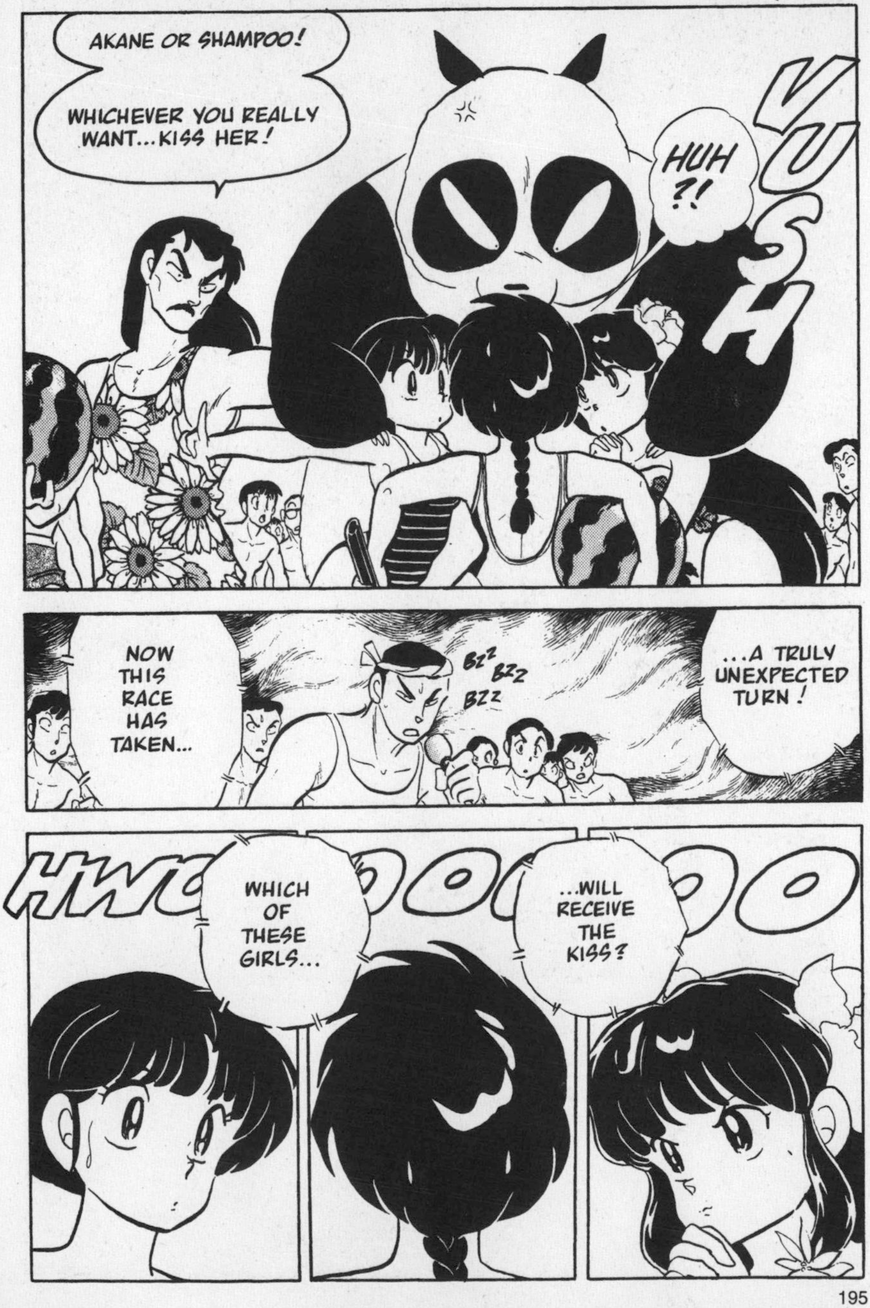
AKANE OR SHAMPOO!
WHICHEVER YOU REALLY WANT...KISS HER!
HUH ?!
VUUSH
NOW THIS RACE HAS TAKEN...
BZZ BZZ BZZ
...A TRULY UNEXPECTED TURN!
WHICH OF THESE GIRLS...
...WILL RECEIVE THE KISS?

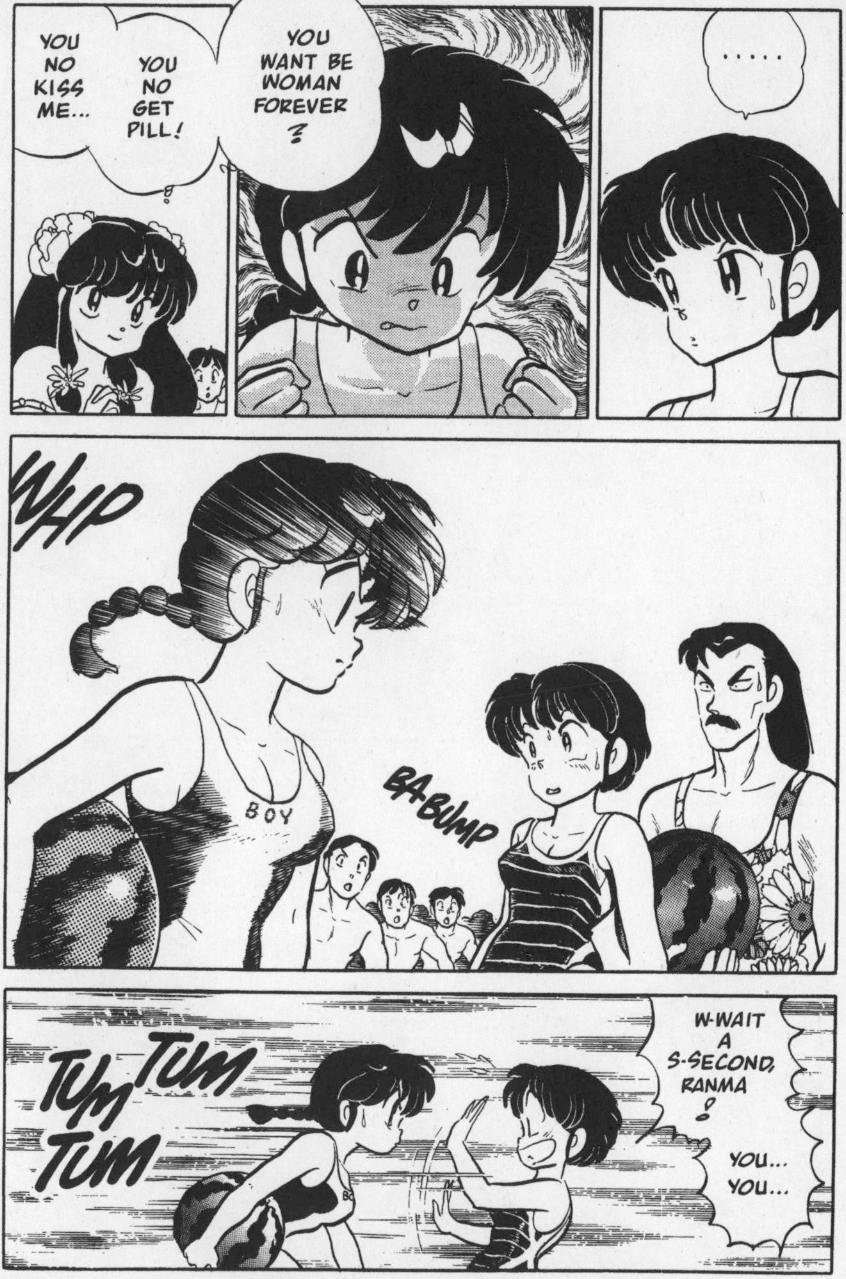

YOU NO KISS ME...
YOU NO GET PILL!
YOU WANT BE WOMAN FOREVER?
.....
WHIP
BA-BUMP
TUM TUM TUM TUM
W-WAIT A S-SECOND, RANMA!
YOU... YOU...

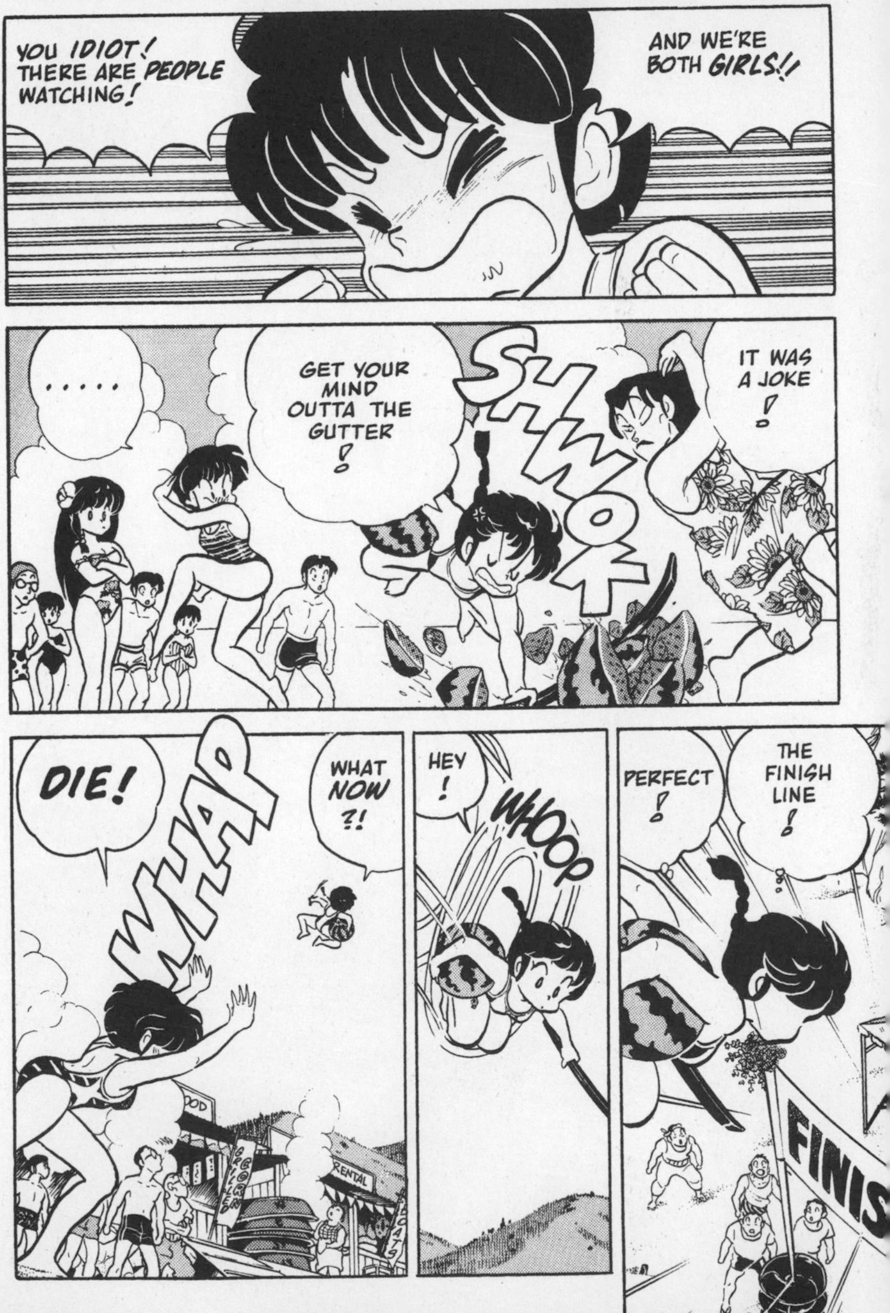
YOU IDIOT! THERE ARE PEOPLE WATCHING!
AND WE'RE BOTH GIRLS!!
......
GET YOUR MIND OUTTA THE GUTTER!
SHWOK
IT WAS A JOKE!
DIE!
WHAP
WHAT NOW?!
HEY!
WHOOP
PERFECT!
THE FINISH LINE!
RENTAL
BOATS
FINIS

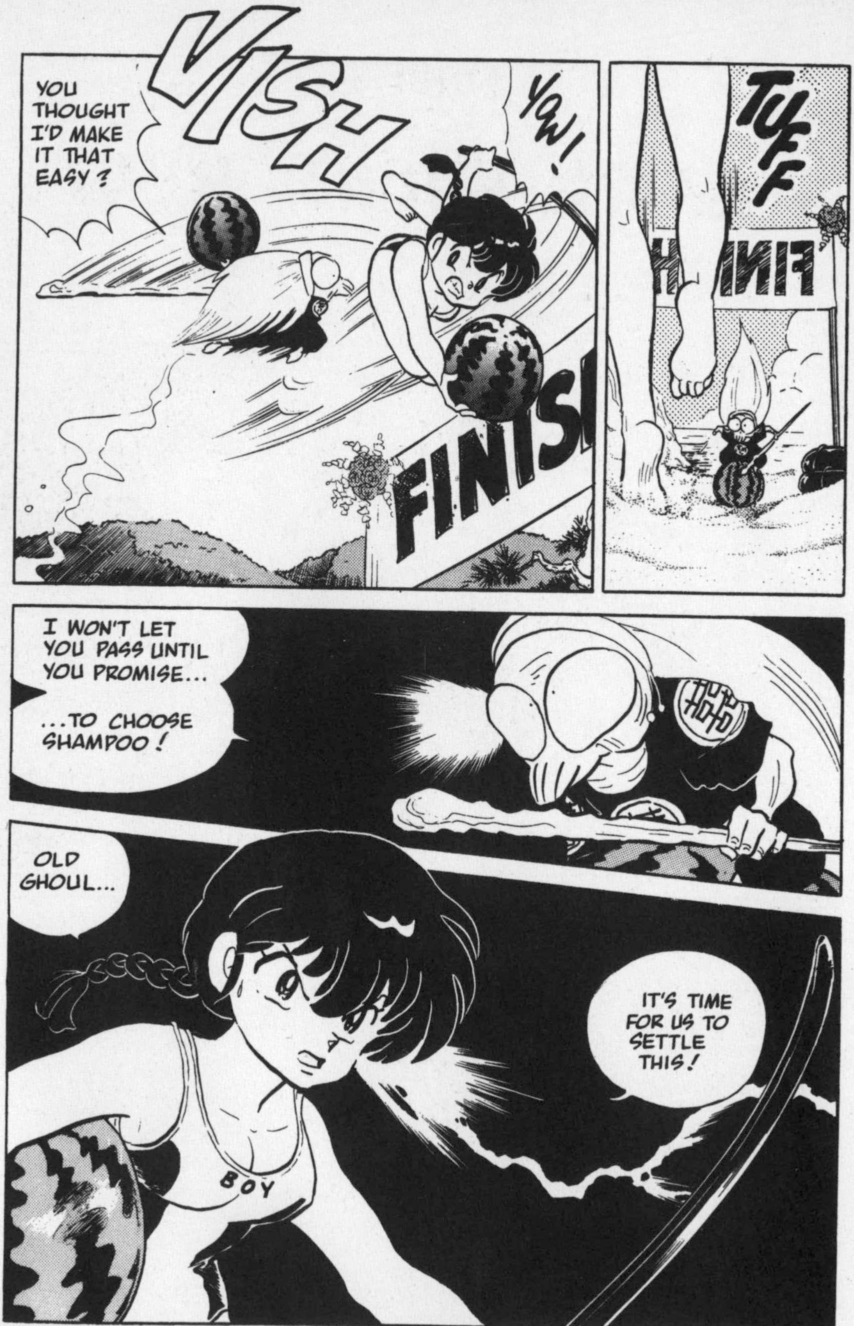
VISH
YOU THOUGHT I'D MAKE IT THAT EASY?
YAW!
FINISH
TUFF
FINI
I WON'T LET YOU PASS UNTIL YOU PROMISE...
...TO CHOOSE SHAMPOO!
OLD GHOUL...
IT'S TIME FOR US TO SETTLE THIS!
BOY

Part 13

NAVAL ENGAGEMENT

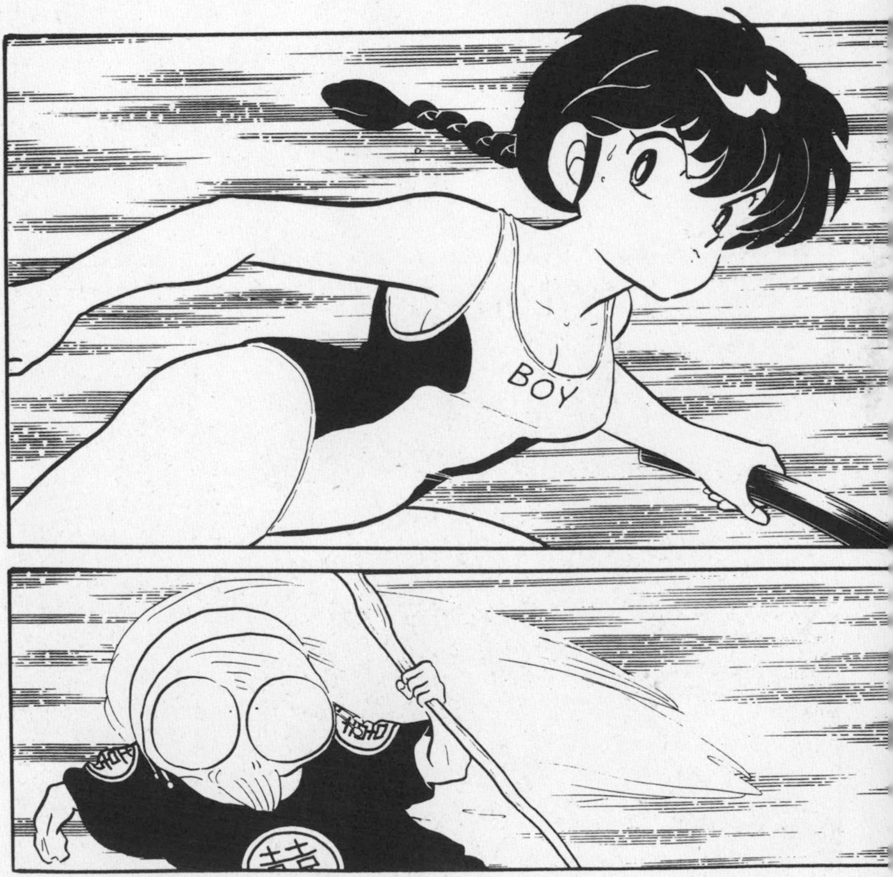
BOY

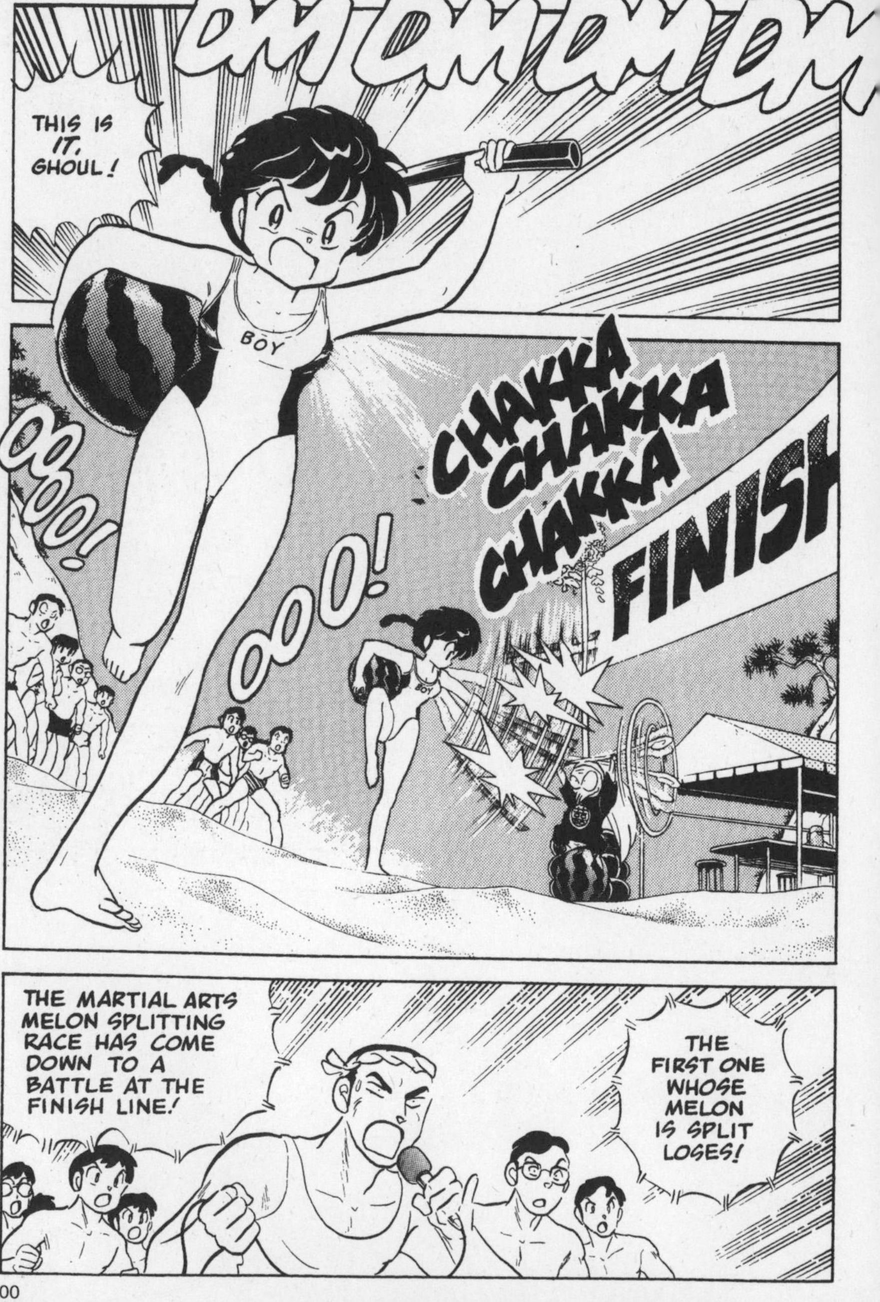
DMDMDMDM
THIS IS IT, GHOUL!
BOY
OOOO!
OOO!
CHAKKA CHAKKA CHAKKA
FINISH
BOY
THE MARTIAL ARTS MELON SPLITTING RACE HAS COME DOWN TO A BATTLE AT THE FINISH LINE!
THE FIRST ONE WHOSE MELON IS SPLIT LOSES!

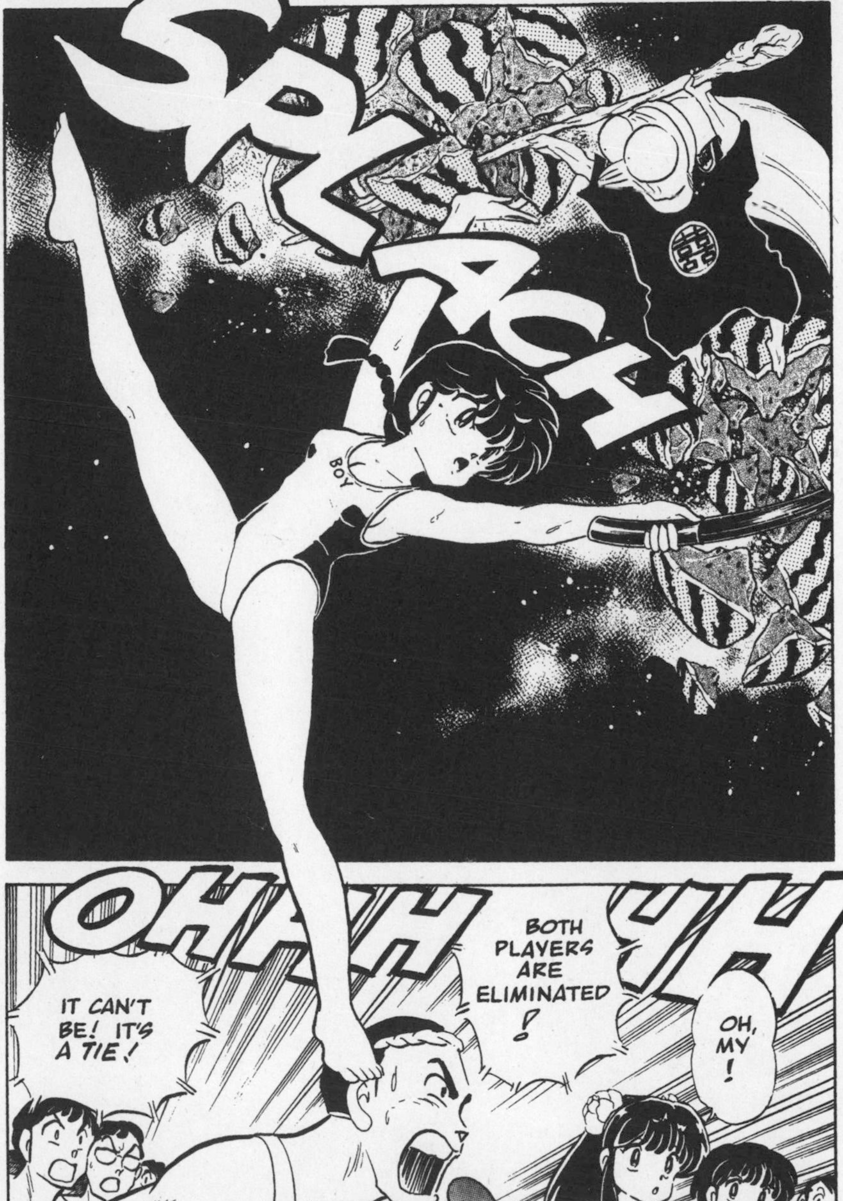
IT CAN'T BE! IT'S A TIE!
BOTH PLAYERS ARE ELIMINATED!
OH, MY!

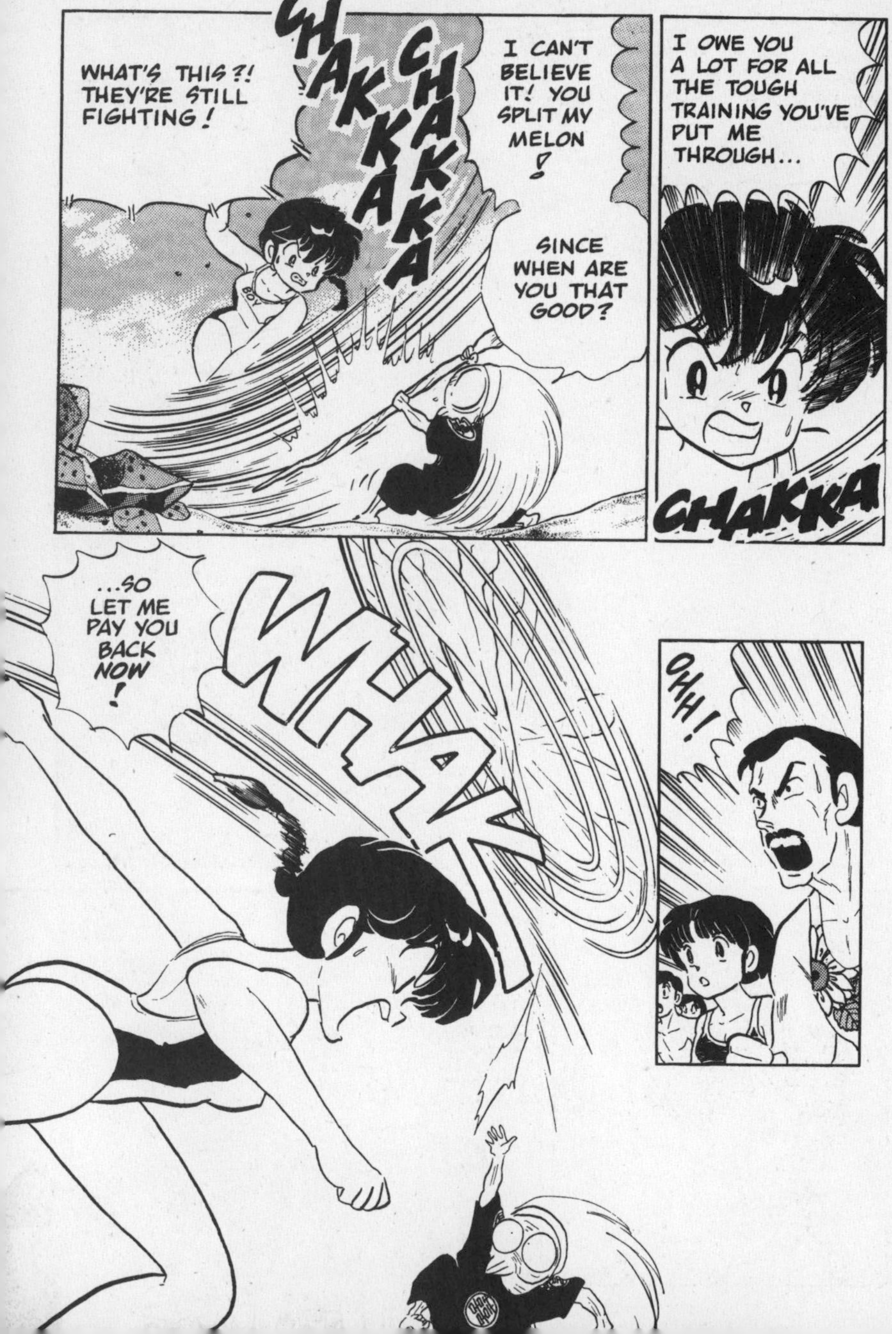
WHAT'S THIS?! THEY'RE STILL FIGHTING!
CHAKKA
CHAKKA
I CAN'T BELIEVE IT! YOU SPLIT MY MELON!
SINCE WHEN ARE YOU THAT GOOD?
I OWE YOU A LOT FOR ALL THE TOUGH TRAINING YOU'VE PUT ME THROUGH...
CHAKKA
...SO LET ME PAY YOU BACK NOW!
WHAK
OHH!

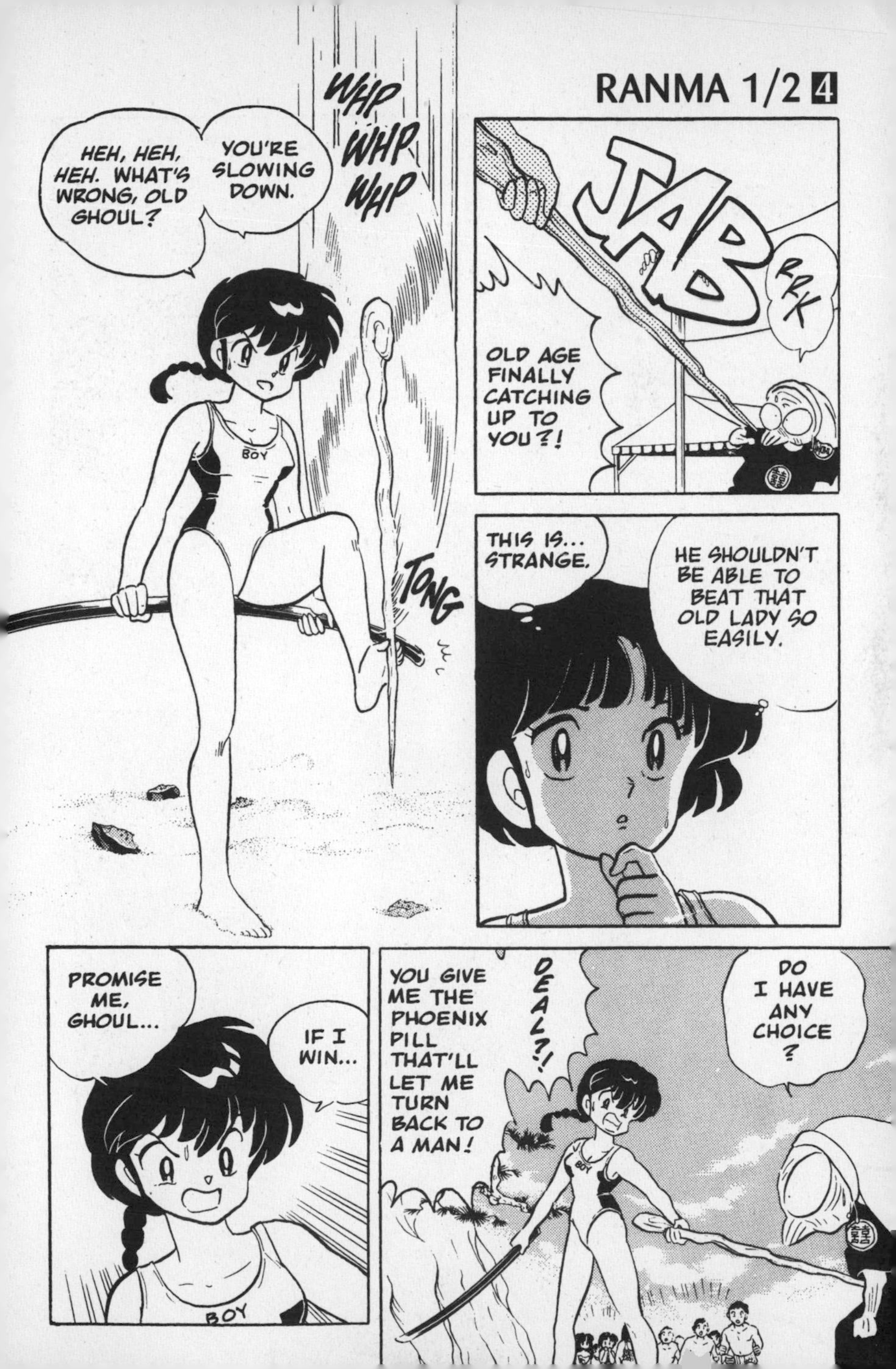
HEH, HEH, HEH. WHAT'S WRONG, OLD GHOUL?
YOU'RE SLOWING DOWN.
WHP WHP WHP
TONG
JAB
RRK
OLD AGE FINALLY CATCHING UP TO YOU?!
THIS IS... STRANGE.
HE SHOULDN'T BE ABLE TO BEAT THAT OLD LADY SO EASILY.
PROMISE ME, GHOUL...
IF I WIN...
YOU GIVE ME THE PHOENIX PILL THAT'LL LET ME TURN BACK TO A MAN!
DEAL?!
DO I HAVE ANY CHOICE?

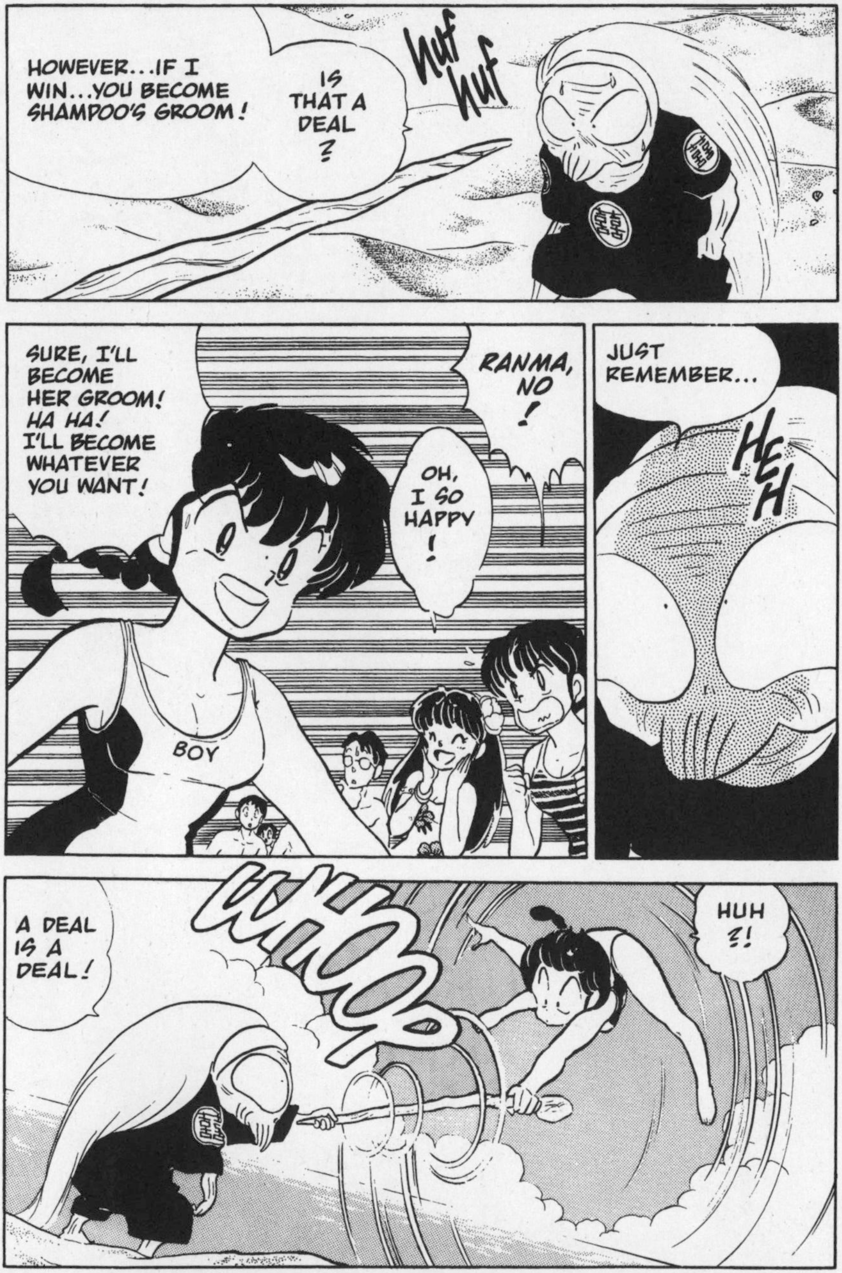
HOWEVER...IF I WIN...YOU BECOME SHAMPOO'S GROOM!
IS THAT A DEAL?
huf huf
SURE, I'LL BECOME HER GROOM! HA HA! I'LL BECOME WHATEVER YOU WANT!
RANMA, NO!
OH, I SO HAPPY!
BOY
JUST REMEMBER...
HEH
A DEAL IS A DEAL!
WHOP
HUH?!

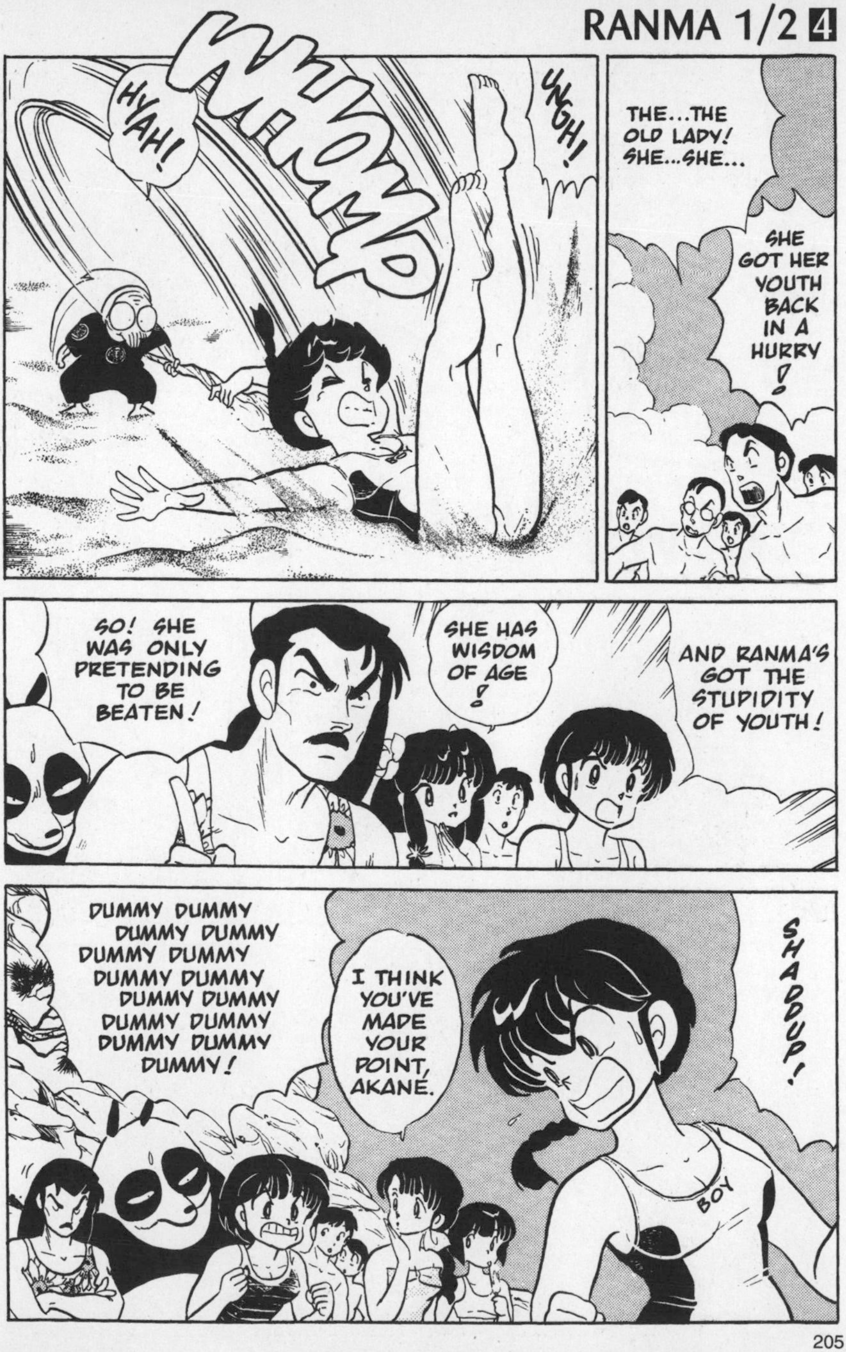
HYAH!
WHOMP
UNGH!
THE...THE OLD LADY! SHE...SHE...
SHE GOT HER YOUTH BACK IN A HURRY!
SO! SHE WAS ONLY PRETENDING TO BE BEATEN!
SHE HAS WISDOM OF AGE!
AND RANMA'S GOT THE STUPIDITY OF YOUTH!
DUMMY DUMMY DUMMY DUMMY DUMMY DUMMY DUMMY DUMMY DUMMY DUMMY DUMMY DUMMY DUMMY DUMMY DUMMY!
I THINK YOU'VE MADE YOUR POINT, AKANE.
SHADDUP!
BOY

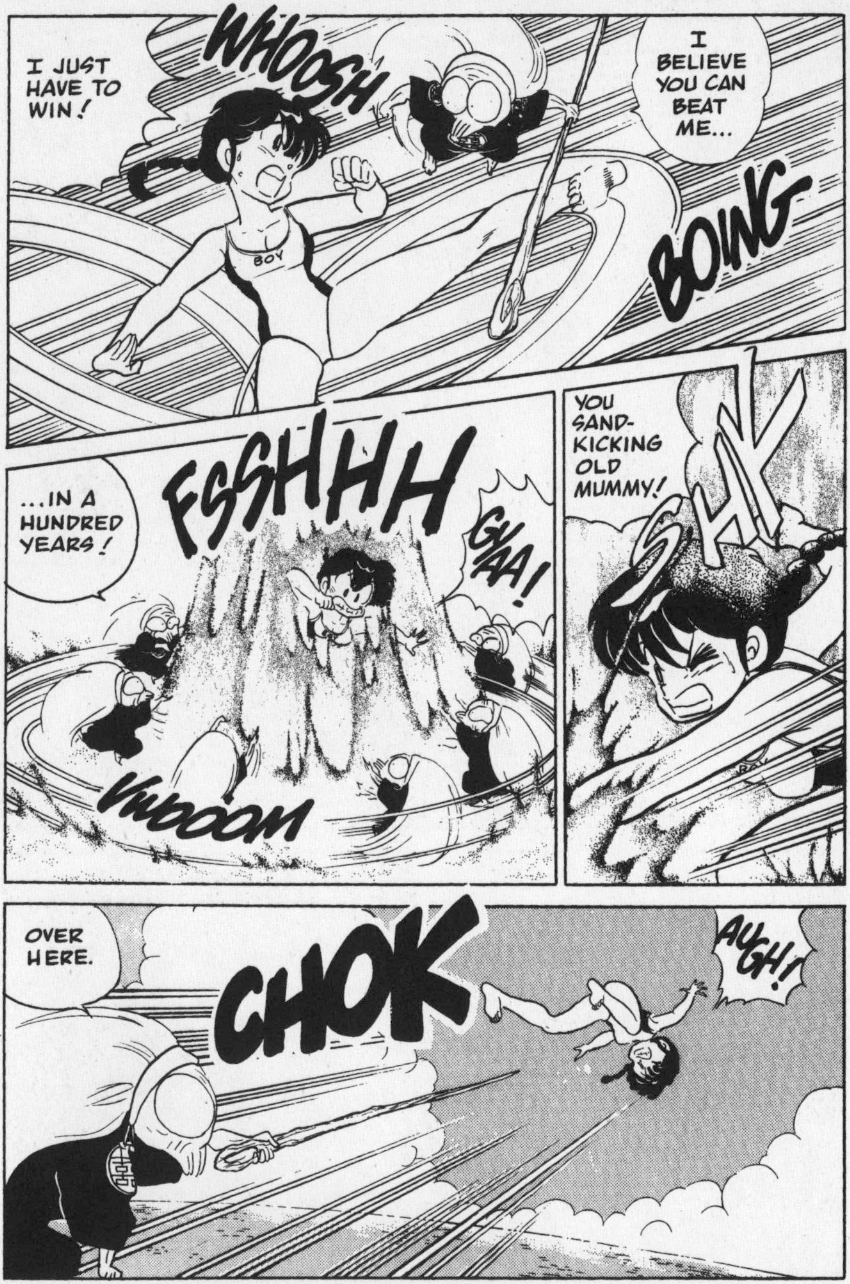
I JUST HAVE TO WIN!
WHOOSH
I BELIEVE YOU CAN BEAT ME...
BOY
BOING
...IN A HUNDRED YEARS!
FSSHHH
GYAA!
VWOOOM
YOU SAND-KICKING OLD MUMMY!
SHK
OVER HERE.
CHOK
AUGH!

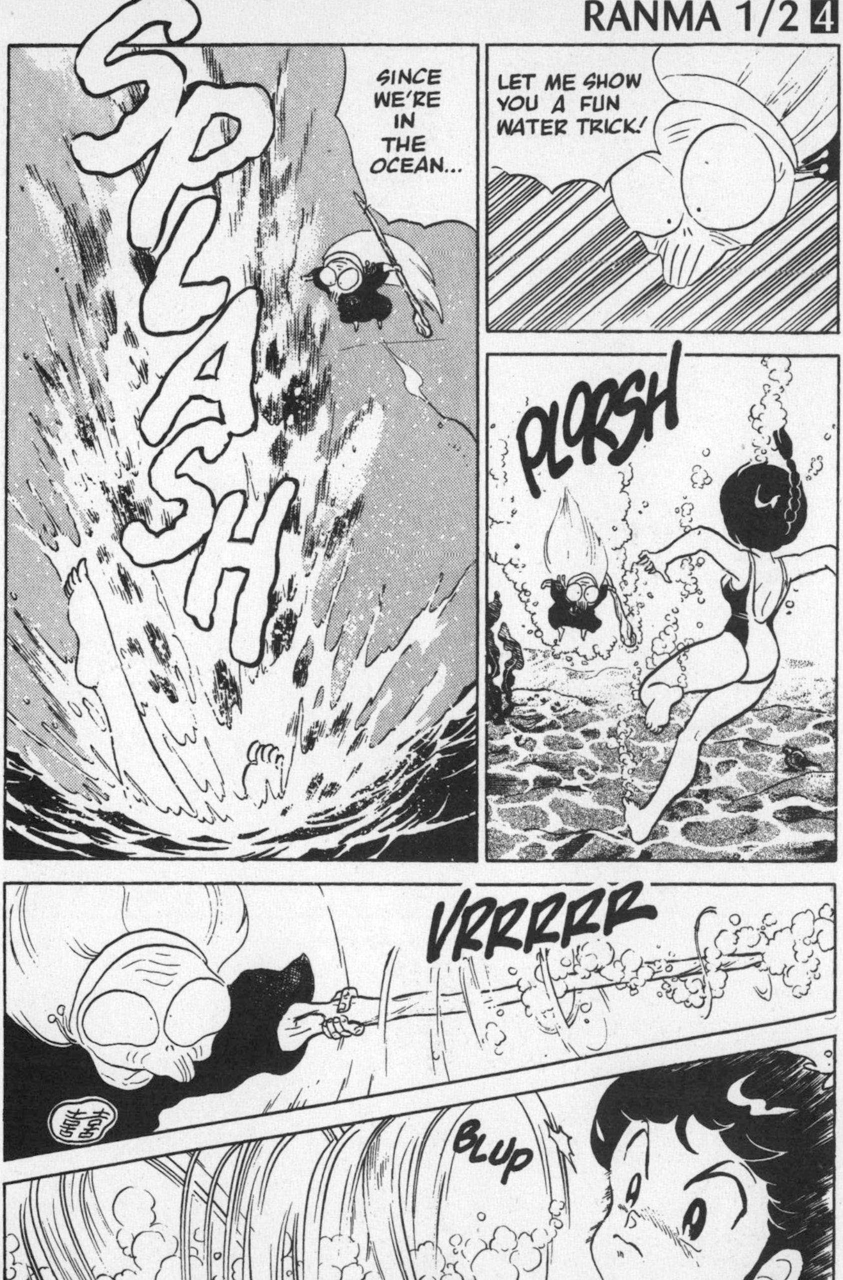
SPLASH
SINCE WE'RE IN THE OCEAN...
LET ME SHOW YOU A FUN WATER TRICK!
PLORSH
VRRRRR
BLUP

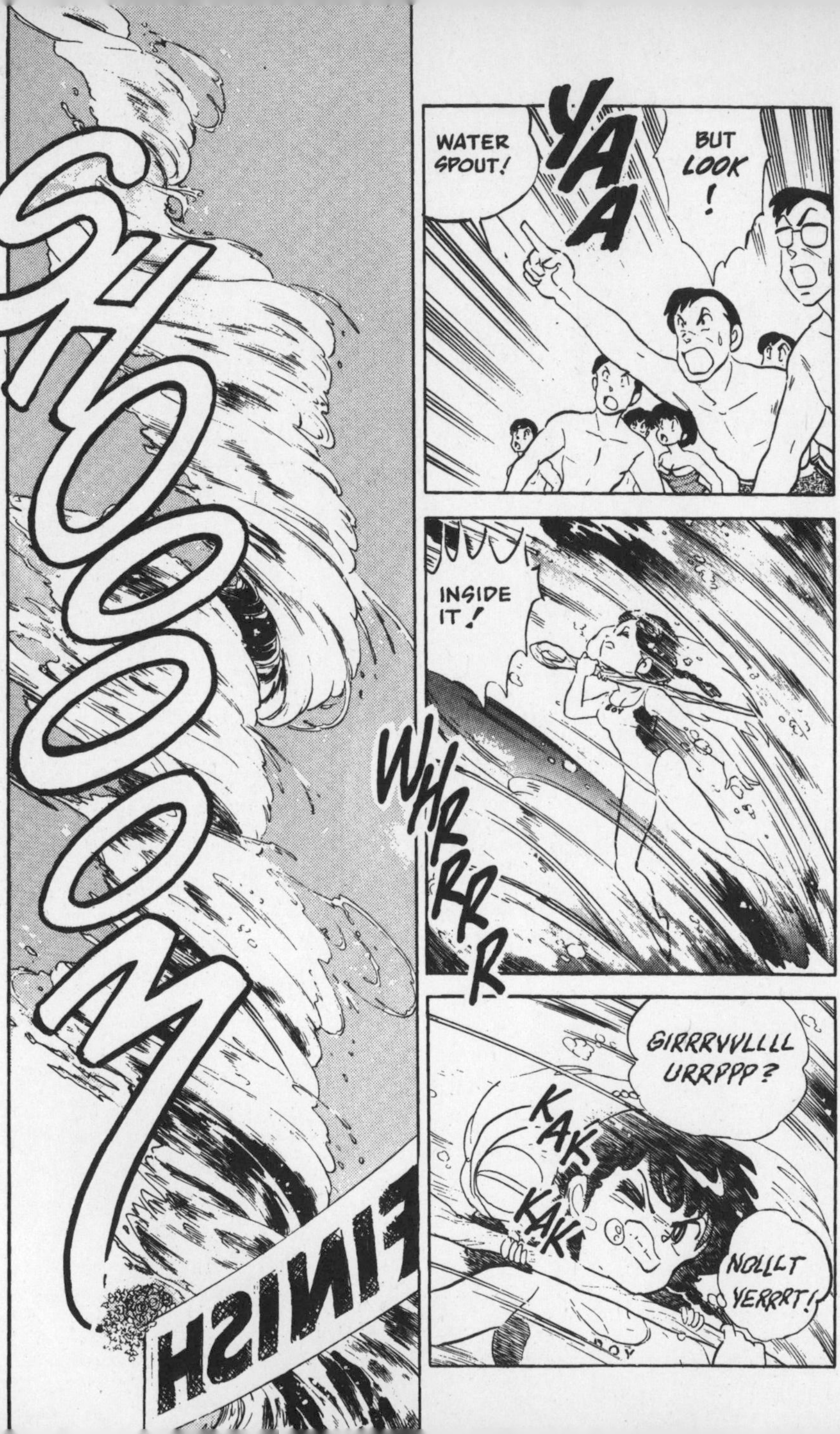
SHOOOOM
FINISH
WATER SPOUT!
YAA
BUT LOOK!
INSIDE IT!
WHRRRRR
GIRRRVVLLLL URRPPP?
KAK KAK KAK
NOLLLT YERRRT!

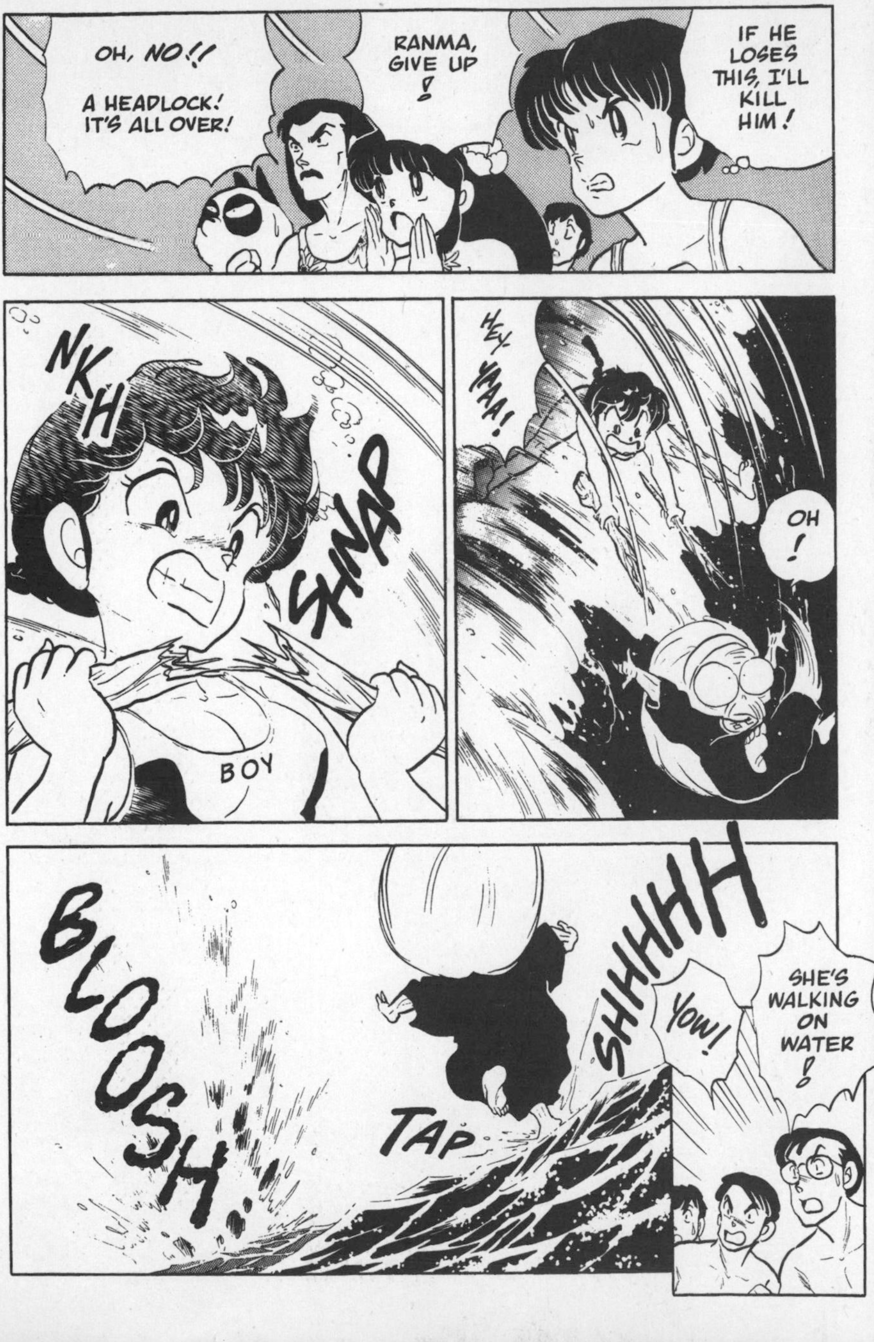
OH, NO!!
A HEADLOCK! IT'S ALL OVER!
RANMA, GIVE UP!
IF HE LOSES THIS, I'LL KILL HIM!
NKH
SHNAP
BOY
HEY-YAAA!
OH!
BLOOSH
TAP
SHHHHH
YOW!
SHE'S WALKING ON WATER!

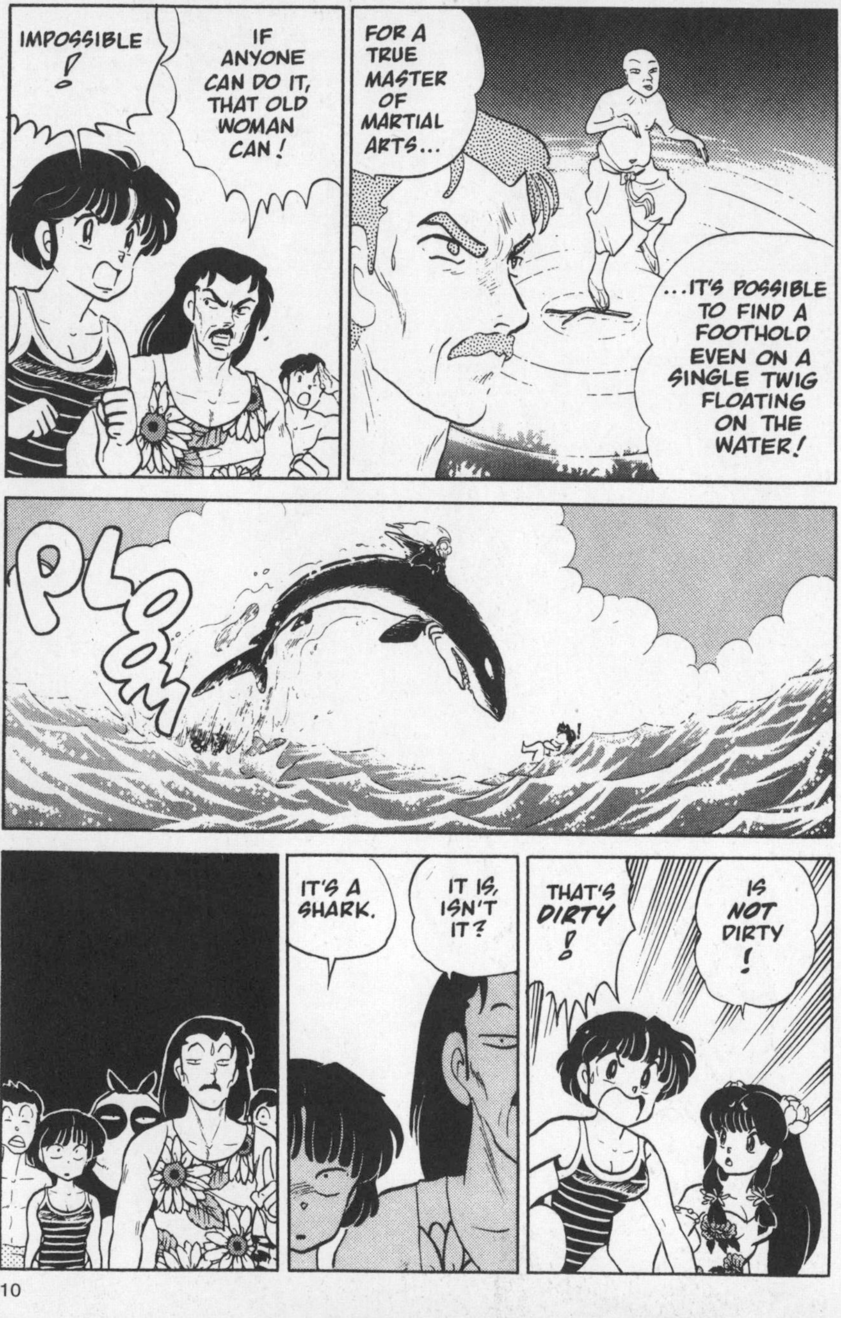
IMPOSSIBLE !
IF ANYONE CAN DO IT, THAT OLD WOMAN CAN !
FOR A TRUE MASTER OF MARTIAL ARTS...
...IT'S POSSIBLE TO FIND A FOOTHOLD EVEN ON A SINGLE TWIG FLOATING ON THE WATER !
PLOOM
IT'S A SHARK.
IT IS, ISN'T IT?
THAT'S DIRTY !
IS NOT DIRTY !

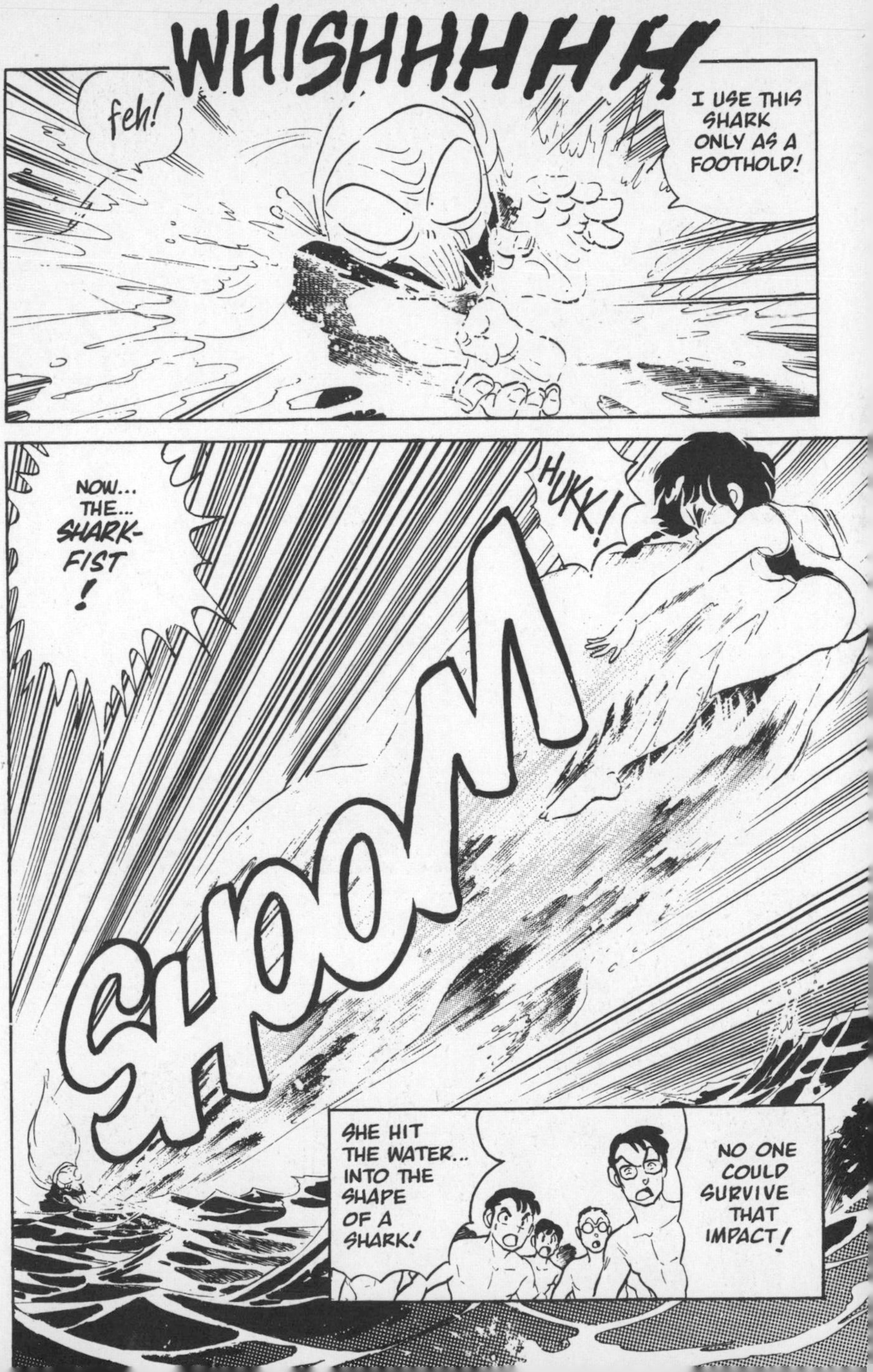
WHISHHHHH
feh!
I USE THIS SHARK ONLY AS A FOOTHOLD!
NOW... THE... SHARK-FIST!
HUKK!
SPOOM
SHE HIT THE WATER... INTO THE SHAPE OF A SHARK!
NO ONE COULD SURVIVE THAT IMPACT!

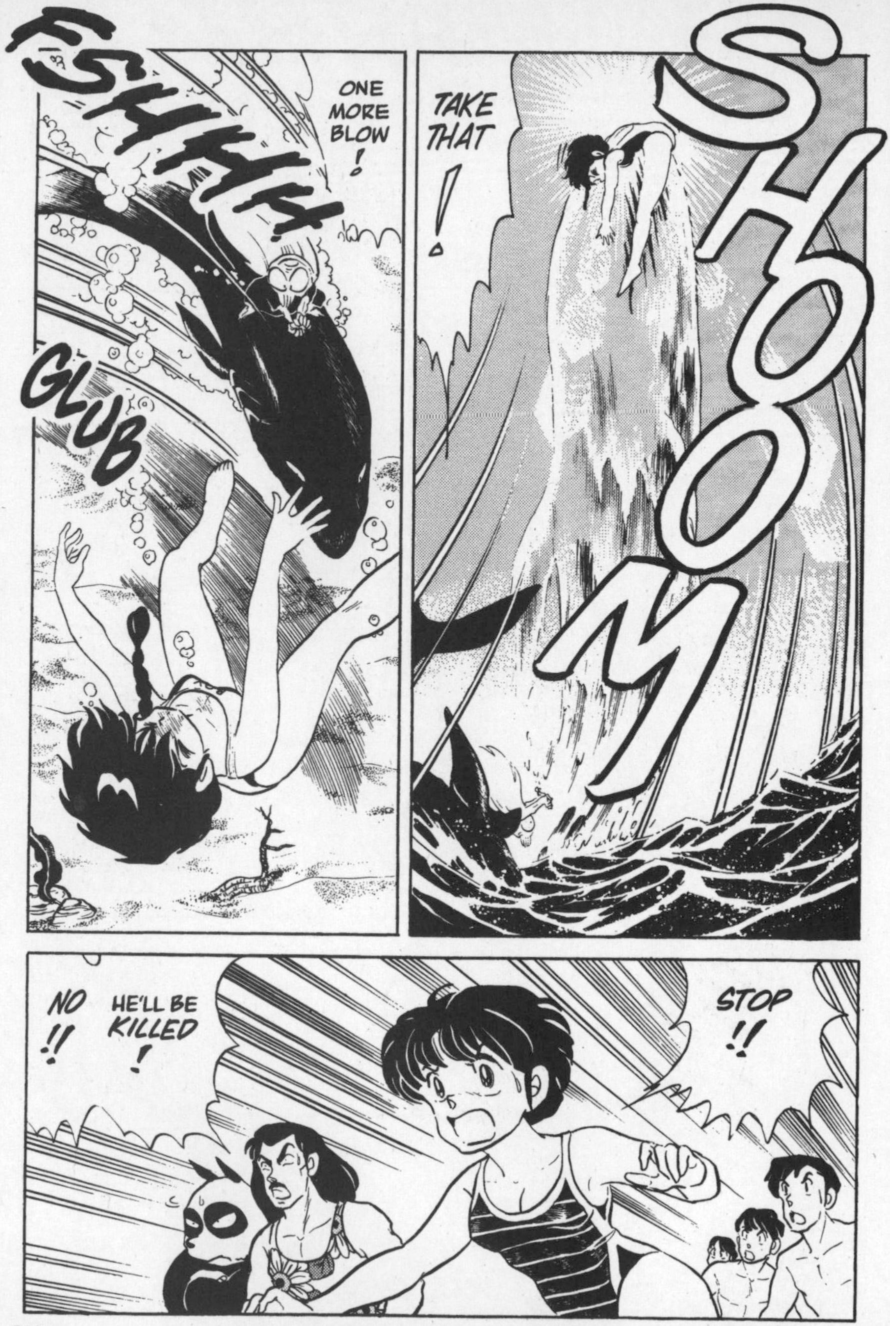
FSHHH
ONE MORE BLOW!
GLUB
TAKE THAT!!
SHOOM
NO!!
HE'LL BE KILLED!
STOP!!

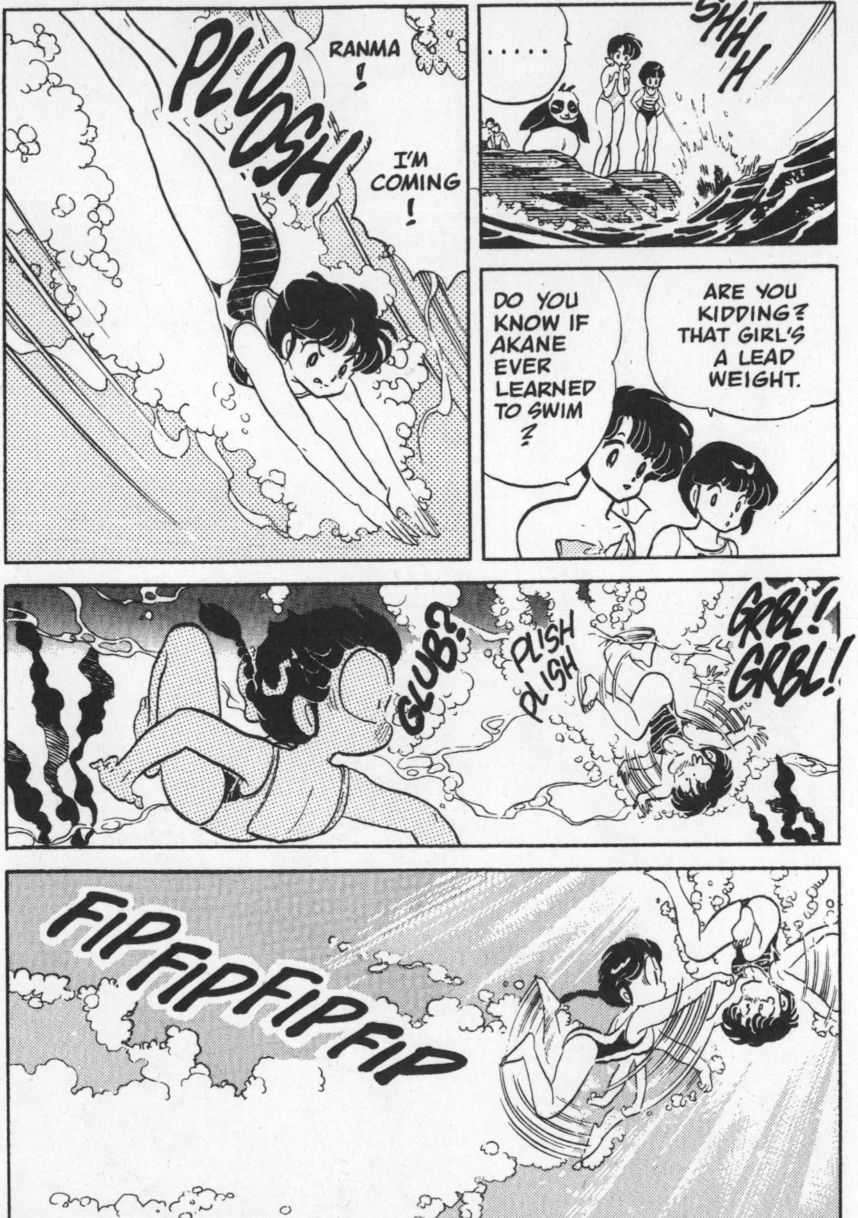
PLOOSH
RANMA!
I'M COMING!
.....
SHHH
DO YOU KNOW IF AKANE EVER LEARNED TO SWIM?
ARE YOU KIDDING? THAT GIRL'S A LEAD WEIGHT.
GLUB?
PLISH PLISH
GRBL! GRBL!
FIP FIPFIPFIPFIP

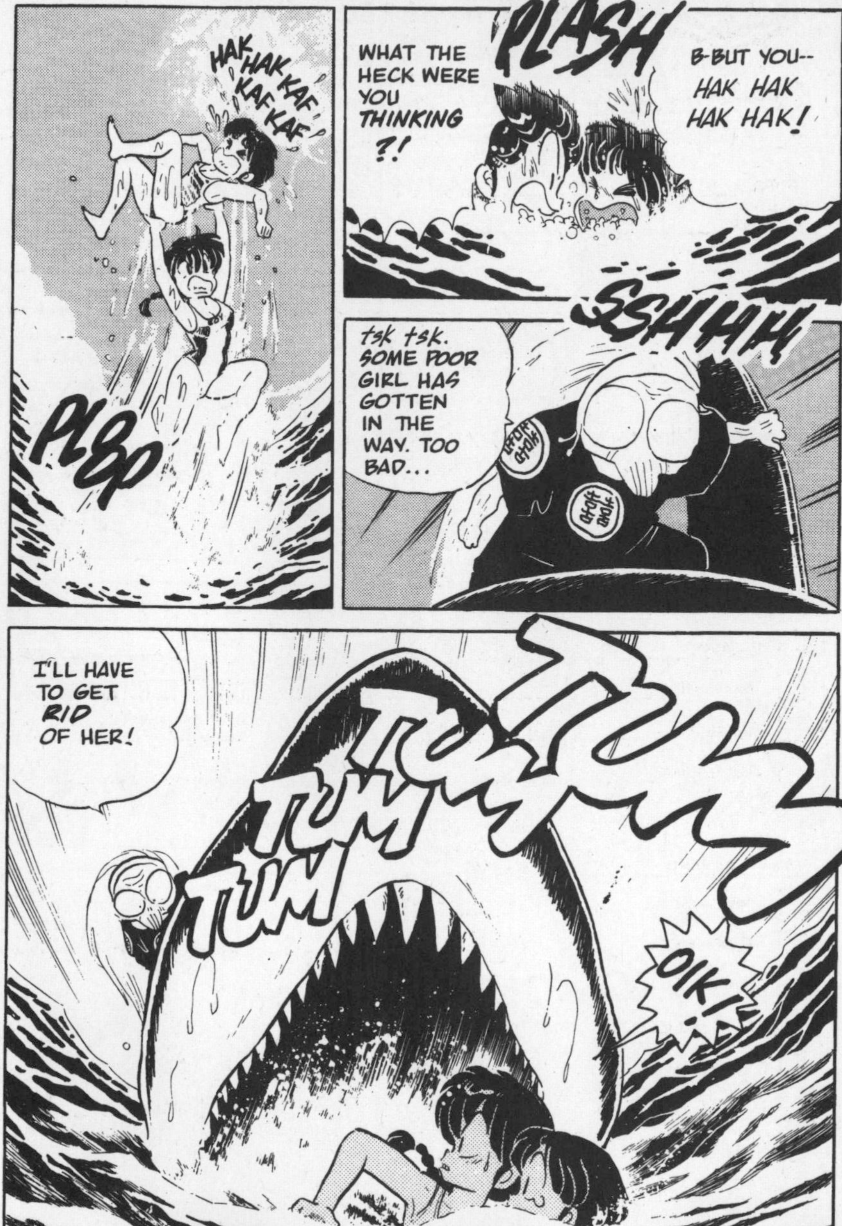
HAK HAK KAF KAF KAF
PLOP
PLASH
WHAT THE HECK WERE YOU THINKING ?!
B-BUT YOU-- HAK HAK HAK HAK!
SSHHHH
tsk tsk. SOME POOR GIRL HAS GOTTEN IN THE WAY. TOO BAD...
I'LL HAVE TO GET RID OF HER!
TUM TUM TUM TUM
OIK!

TO BE CONTINUED

COMPLETE OUR SURVEY AND LET US KNOW WHAT YOU THINK!

☐ Please do NOT send me information about VIZ products, news and events, special offers, or other information.

☐ Please do NOT send me information from VIZ's trusted business partners.

Name: _____

Address: _____

City: _____ **State:** _____ **Zip:** _____

E-mail: _____

☐ **Male** ☐ **Female** **Date of Birth** (mm/dd/yyyy): ____ / ____ / ____ (Under 13? Parental consent required)

What race/ethnicity do you consider yourself? (please check one)

☐ Asian/Pacific Islander ☐ Black/African American ☐ Hispanic/Latino

☐ Native American/Alaskan Native ☐ White/Caucasian ☐ Other: _____

What VIZ product did you purchase? (check all that apply and indicate title purchased)

☐ DVD/VHS _____

☐ Graphic Novel _____

☐ Magazines _____

☐ Merchandise _____

Reason for purchase: (check all that apply)

☐ Special offer ☐ Favorite title ☐ Gift

☐ Recommendation ☐ Other _____

Where did you make your purchase? (please check one)

☐ Comic store ☐ Bookstore ☐ Mass/Grocery Store

☐ Newsstand ☐ Video/Video Game Store ☐ Other: _____

☐ Online (site: _____)

What other VIZ properties have you purchased/own? _____

_____

How many anime and/or manga titles have you purchased in the last year? How many were VIZ titles? **(please check one from each column)**

ANIME	MANGA	VIZ
☐ None	☐ None	☐ None
☐ 1-4	☐ 1-4	☐ 1-4
☐ 5-10	☐ 5-10	☐ 5-10
☐ 11+	☐ 11+	☐ 11+

I find the pricing of VIZ products to be: **(please check one)**

☐ Cheap ☐ Reasonable ☐ Expensive

What genre of manga and anime would you like to see from VIZ? **(please check two)**

☐ Adventure ☐ Comic Strip ☐ Science Fiction ☐ Fighting

☐ Horror ☐ Romance ☐ Fantasy ☐ Sports

What do you think of VIZ's new look?

☐ Love It ☐ It's OK ☐ Hate It ☐ Didn't Notice ☐ No Opinion

Which do you prefer? **(please check one)**

☐ Reading right-to-left

☐ Reading left-to-right

Which do you prefer? **(please check one)**

☐ Sound effects in English

☐ Sound effects in Japanese with English captions

☐ Sound effects in Japanese only with a glossary at the back

THANK YOU! Please send the completed form to:

NJW Research
42 Catharine St.
Poughkeepsie, NY 12601

All information provided will be used for internal purposes only. We promise not to sell or otherwise divulge your information.